ENGIMAS AND RIDDLES IN LITERATURE

How do enigmas and riddles work in literature? This benchmark study investigates the literary trope of the riddle, and its relation to the broader term "enigma," including enigma as large masterplot. Cook argues for a revival of the old figure of speech known as "enigma" from Aristotle to the seventeenth century by demonstrating its usefulness. The opening chapter surveys "enigma personified" as sphinx and griffin, resuscitating a lost Graeco-Latin pun on "griffin" used by Lewis Carroll. The history and functions of enigma draw on classical and biblical through to modern writing. Wide-ranging examples concentrate on literature in English, especially modern poetry, with three detailed case studies on Dante, Lewis Carroll, and Wallace Stevens. An important contribution to studies of poetic thought and metaphor, this anatomy of the riddle will appeal particularly to readers and scholars of poetry, modern American and comparative literatures, rhetoric, and folk-riddles.

ELEANOR COOK is Professor Emerita, Department of English, University of Toronto. She writes mainly on poetry and poetics, especially modern, as well as on questions of allusion, the English Bible and literature, and the riddle. Her books include studies of Robert Browning and Wallace Stevens, as well as a collection of essays, *Against Coercion: Games Poets Play* (1998). Her essays have appeared in many books and journals, including *American Literature, Daedalus, ELH, Essays in Criticism*, and *Philosophy and Literature*. She has served as President of the Association of Literary Scholars and Critics, and is a Guggenheim Fellow, a Senior Killam Research Fellow (Canada Council), and a Fellow of the Royal Society of Canada.

ENIGMAS AND RIDDLES
IN LITERATURE

ELEANOR COOK

CAMBRIDGE
UNIVERSITY PRESS

CAMBRIDGE UNIVERSITY PRESS
Cambridge, New York, Melbourne, Madrid, Cape Town, Singapore, São Paulo

Cambridge University Press
The Edinburgh Building, Cambridge CB2 2RU, UK

Published in the United States of America by Cambridge University Press, New York

www.cambridge.org
Information on this title: www.cambridge.org/9780521855105

First published 2006

Printed in the United Kingdom at the University Press, Cambridge

A catalogue record for this book is available from the British Library

ISBN-13 978-0-521-85510-5 hardback
ISBN-10 0-521-85510-1 hardback

For Jay and Peggy
riddle-masters both
and for Graeme
who knows the mysteries of birds

Contents

Illustrations

Preface

This book grew out of general curiosity about the words "riddle" and "enigma." (The specific impetus is another story, to be found in the Introduction.) How do "riddle" and "enigma" function, especially in good writing? Sometimes they are used of a specific, circumscribed problem whose answer has clear implications. Sometimes they are used of a generally puzzling situation, with no clear implications for a possible answer, though this is unusual. Sometimes the word "enigma" (less often "riddle") is used of the mystery of great art or of religious mystery, which in turn evokes wonder. Enigma in St. Paul's famous text "For now we see through a glass, darkly" presents a special case. ("Darkly" translates Greek *en ainigmati*, "in an enigma.") Mostly, the words "riddle" and "enigma" pass by unexamined, as if we all knew quite well what they mean.

"Riddle" in the popular sense is simply a joke that turns on some incongruity, a throwaway gag. Riddles and enigmas in imaginative writing are much more interesting. Even a small conundrum can have a role to play. A large enigma may seem worlds away, and, in one sense, it is. Riddles do tend to be either very small in duration and apparent use or else very large – sometimes so large as to constitute everything, the enigma of the universe. When and how are little conundrums and large enigmas linked? One answer lies in the story of Oedipus and the Sphinx. There are countless examples of riddles and enigmas in many different contexts: Old English riddles and riddle poems, imitated to this day. Riddles that start off an adventure story, as in *Greenmantle*. Riddles that govern the structure of a work, as in *Pericles*. Riddling styles like James Joyce's, and so on. Yet literary scholars and critics seem oddly incurious about how the words "riddle" and "enigma" work.

Literary studies of the riddle are few and far between. There are studies of the remarkable Old English riddles. There are studies of riddles in specific authors: Virgil, Dante, Shakespeare, Donne, Joyce, Pynchon. It is possible to explicate small riddles within writers like Hopkins, and to connect such riddles with the over-arching enigma of all human life from Hopkins's perspective. This leads to studies of individual authors, but it does not advance our general knowledge of enigma and riddle, even if it is illuminating for specific instances. General and pertinent remarks about the workings of riddle, or about the words "riddle" and "enigma," remain scarce.

By contrast, folklorists have been studying riddles for well over a century, while anthropologists, linguists, sociologists, and psychologists also find them interesting. The lack of literary studies is all the more surprising because the riddle is an ancient literary form, whether generically as a riddle-poem or rhetorically as a figure of speech. There are fine entries on the riddle in learned studies by eminent Renaissance and seventeenth-century scholars like Joachim Camerarius and Gerardus Joannes Vossius. The collectors of riddles over the centuries have passed on accumulated knowledge about them. The Greeks delighted in them, whether as a focal point for tragedy (Sophocles, *Oedipus Rex*) or as dinner-party amusement (Athenaeus, *The Learned Banquet*). Today, we have excellent introductory books to riddles in general, such as Mark Bryant's *Dictionary of Riddles* (1990), or, casting a wider net, Tony Augarde's *Oxford Guide to Word-Games* (1984). But very few literary scholars and critics have taken up questions of riddle and enigma in general, though these do include writers of the stature of Northrop Frye, Dan Pagis, and Richard Wilbur. The theorists Gérard Genette and Tzvetan Todorov have also thought about these questions, though only in passing.

This book will try to remedy such a lack.

How might a literary scholar and critic as distinct from a folklorist or anthropologist speak about riddle and enigma, both generally and in specific works? How might we think of them chiefly in relation to an imaginative context rather than a social context? How might we account for riddles that go on generating meaning, even after they are solved? What light could a literary study shed on riddles that are embedded within a larger work, including familiar mimetic writing? What could it tell us about Jane Austen's riddles in *Emma* – say, the riddle that Mr. Woodhouse cannot fully remember? Are riddles themselves ever poetry? Not very often. Yet Frye found the kernel of one type of poetry in ancient riddles, and folklorists interest themselves in the affinities of poetry and riddles. Once we read by means of some literary focal points, it becomes clearer why some riddles remain fascinating, while others cause groans. Work on some key writers has suggested several such focal points, on which see the Introduction.

Throughout, I have treated the words "enigma" and "riddle" as virtual synonyms. So they are in English, on the whole – not quite identical twins, but close enough to be called fraternal twins. The Appendix briefly traces kinds and degrees of meaning in dictionaries over the years. Elsewhere, use of one word more than the other is governed by context. Thus the word "enigma" is prevalent in chapter 2 on enigma as figure of speech, while "riddle" dominates the discussion of genre in chapter 5.

I have not concentrated on any one historical period, though many examples come from modern and contemporary work, especially poetry. Most examples are in English. This book is meant to speak to readers at large, and also to teachers and students of all historical periods. My own interest is rhetorical, because I think rhetorical knowledge is the *sine qua non* for reading literature. But I have occasionally suggested some questions that historicist or cultural critics might find interesting. Teachers of rhetoric might find chapter 2 helpful for introducing students to a little rhetorical history. I have included some classical material, introduced with a little trepidation and much admiration. Classicists might at the least enjoy one Graeco-Roman pun I have re-discovered, a pun that Lewis Carroll made use of in *Alice in Wonderland.* The book is indebted to work done by folklorists, and I hope they too find some matters of interest here.

In one sense, this book opens a new area, offering a rhetorical basis for thinking about enigma and riddle in different contexts. It offers re-readings of specific uses of enigma and riddle in a number of writers. It could provide the basis for a course in riddle and enigma, variously shaped. Its widest objective is to encourage more thought about our use of the words "riddle and "enigma." How we resolve the riddles of our lives, our history, and our planet depends partly on how we conceive of "riddle" and "enigma" in the first place. We all look at ourselves and our world as an enigma, to some degree. The world presents itself as a riddle. "Here is what I am like," it says to us. "What am I?" Willy-nilly, we choose an answer to this riddle. Perhaps we wrestle with it, perhaps we divide it into manageable portions, perhaps we let others decide for us. Good writers help.

The book has also been a pleasure to write. It has drawn me into the largest and the smallest questions. It has lit up some of the best writing available. I hope others find some enjoyment in it too.

I am happy to acknowledge the invaluable gift of time provided by a Fellowship from the John Simon Guggenheim Memorial Foundation and a Killam Research Fellowship from the Killam Foundation (Canada Council). The Connaught Committee of the University of Toronto put at my disposal a research fund, given in connection with an honorary Connaught Fellowship.

This work could not have been done without the fine collections and staff of many libraries, especially the Beinecke and Sterling Libraries, Yale University; the Bodleian Library, University of Oxford; the British Library; the Houghton and Widener Libraries, Harvard University; the Huntington Library; the National Library of Scotland; and the Thomas Fisher Rare Book and Robarts Libraries, as well as the library of the Pontifical Institute of Mediaeval Studies, University of Toronto.

Parts of some chapters have appeared previously in earlier versions. I am grateful to editors and publications, as follows: "Enigma as Art," *Literary Imagination* 6 (2004), 132–47; "The Figure of Enigma: Rhetoric, History, Poetry," *Rhetorica* 19 (2001), 349–78; "The Flying Griphos: In Pursuit of Enigma from Aristophanes to Tournesol, with Stops in Carroll, Ariosto, and Dante," from my *Against Coercion: Games Poets Play* (Stanford: Stanford University Press, 1998), pp. 213–19; "The Function of Riddles at the Present Time," ibid., pp. 202–12, and in *The Legacy of Northrop Frye*, ed. Alvin Lee and Robert Denham (Toronto: University of Toronto Press, 1994), pp. 326–34; "Riddles of Procreation," *Connotations* 8.3 (1998/ 99), 269–82; "Scripture as Enigma: Biblical Allusion in Dante's Earthly Paradise," *Dante Studies* 97 (1999), 1–19. Occasions for exploring this subject, beyond those mentioned in my *Against Coercion: Games Poets Play* (1998), were provided by the Graduate Center of the City University of New York; the Department of English, Cornell University (Class of 1916 Lecture); and the University of Waterloo, at the conference, *Inventio: Rereading the Rhetorical Tradition*.

Finally, for rich conversation about enigma and riddle at large, and for questions and answers and suggestions that led to further thinking, I am indebted to Debra Fried, John Hollander (to whom special thanks), Robin and Heather Jackson, C. P. Jones, Herbert Marks, Carolyn Masel, Linda Munk, Lois Reimer, Emmet Robbins, Aubrey Rosenberg, Stephen Scully, Sam Solecki, and E. G. Stanley. More particular debts are acknowledged in the notes. I am grateful to Michael Dixon for reading the chapter on "Enigma as Figure of Speech," and to Carol Percy and Antoinette diPaoli Healey for reading an earlier version of the

Appendix. W. David Shaw read the entire manuscript and made very helpful comments, as did the anonymous readers for Cambridge University Press. I am especially grateful to Sarah Stanton and the able staff of Cambridge University Press, including my copyeditor, Lucy Carolan.

Over the years, the dedicatees have offered wit and wisdom, support and fun, with great generosity, as have my family, Ramsay, Maggie, Markham, and Vera.

Acknowledgments

A. R. Ammons, "Gravelly Run" from *Corsons Inlet* (1965), in his *Selected Poems, Expanded Edition.* © 1987, 1977, 1975, 1974, 1972, 1971, 1970, 1966, 1965 A. R. Ammons. Used by permission of W. W. Norton & Company, Inc.

John Ashbery, "Never Seek To Tell Thy Love" from *A Wave.* © 1981, 1982, 1983, 1984 John Ashbery. Reprinted by permission of Georges Borchardt, Inc., for the author. Reprinted in United Kingdom and Commonwealth by permission of Carcanet Press

Jorge Luis Borges, "Edipo y el Enigma" (and "Oedipus and the Enigma," trans. John Hollander), from *Selected Poems 1923–1967*, by Jorge Luis Borges, © 1968, 1969, 1970, 1971, 1972 Jorge Luis Borges, Emcee Editores, S. A. and Norman Thomas Di Giovanni. Used by permisssion of Dell Publishing, a division of Random House, Inc.

Amy Clampitt, "Balms" from *The Kingfisher,* © 1983 Amy Clampitt. Used by permission of Alfred A. Knopf, a division of Random House, Inc.; and by permission of Faber and Faber

Anne Hébert, "Vie de château" from *Œuvre poétique 1950–1990* (Éditions du Boréal/Seuil, Montréal, 1992). Quoted by permission, Les Éditions du Boréal

Anthony Hecht, "Riddles" from *The Transparent Man,* © by Anthony Hecht 1990. Used by permission of Alfred A. Knopf, a division of Random House, Inc.

John Hollander, "The Mad Potter" from *Harp Lake,* © 1988 John Hollander. Used by permission of Alfred A. Knopf, a division of Random House, Inc.

"Riddle and Answer" from *Movie-Going and Other Poems.* © 1962 John Hollander. Quoted by permission

"Isis" and "Egg" from *Poems Twice Told: The Boatman & Welcoming Disaster* by Jay Macpherson. © 1981 Oxford University Press. Reprinted by permission of the publisher

A note on the references

Works on riddle and enigma in the Select Bibiography are chosen for their general usefulness, whether large or small. In the text and footnotes, such works are referred to in short-title form. Works not generally pertinent for riddle and enigma appear in the footnotes in full and are indexed under the author's name. The Select Bibliography also includes editions of literary works cited. Collections simply listed by title are not included; most appear in chapter 10.

Abbreviations

AV
: Authorized (King James) Version of the English Bible (1611). Unless otherwise noted, all quotations from the English Bible are from this translation.

Lewis and Short
: *A Latin Dictionary*, comp. Charlton T. Lewis and Charles Short (Oxford: Clarendon, 1879).

Liddell and Scott
: *A Greek–English Lexicon*, comp. Henry George Liddell and Robert T. Scott, new edn., ed. Henry Stuart Jones, suppl. 1968 (Oxford: Clarendon, 1940).

NPEPP
: *The New Princeton Encyclopedia of Poetry and Poetics*, ed. Alex Preminger and T. V. F. Brogan (Princeton: Princeton University Press, 1993).

OCD
: *The Oxford Classical Dictionary*, 3rd edn., ed. Simon Hornblower and Antony Spawforth (Oxford: Oxford University Press, 1996).

OED
: *The Oxford English Dictionary*, 2nd edn. (Oxford: Clarendon, 1989).

Vulgate
: *Biblia Sacra iuxta Vulgatam Clementiam*, 6th edn. (Madrid: Biblioteca de Autores Cristianos, 1982). (Unless otherwise noted, all quotations from the Latin Bible are from this edition.)

Introduction

My own specific interest in riddles began some twenty years ago, thanks to Wallace Stevens, St. Augustine, and Northrop Frye in that order. Wallace Stevens because of his riddling language, his occasional riddle poem proper like "Solitaire under the Oaks," and his late work with the word "enigma." Once I began to unknot some of Stevens's riddling effects, I became absorbed in both his specific wit and wisdom, and the literary forms he worked with so expertly. Augustine, because I first learned from him that *aenigma* was known as a figure of speech, a trope. He works out the implications in a masterly discussion of St. Paul's text "For now we see through a glass, darkly; but then, face to face." Augustine also, because he made me think about enigma in its widest scope – the enigma of life, history, the earth, the universe, or what I have called "enigma as masterplot." Frye, because his essay "Charms and Riddles" helped at the start more than any other criticism. It traces traditions of both riddle poetry and charm poetry, outlining their ways of behavior. In Stevens, Augustine, and Frye, small riddles can also embody or point toward the largest enigmas of all. In the poets, whose business is with tropes, enigmas both small and large can be crucial. Thus from Sophocles down through Dante to Dickinson and Stevens.

In a 1983 essay on Stevens, I traced some of his riddling effects, linking them with an over-arching sense of riddle in his work. Only later did I find the word "masterplot" in Terence Cave's *Recognitions* and realize that this term described the area in which I was working. Stevens's wonderful sense of humor also began to come clearer, as I unearthed some of the buried puns and jokes and ripostes in his work. I began to ask myself what really qualified as a riddle poem or a riddle within a poem. This in turn led to questions of genre, for example, the difference between a riddle proper and riddling effects. Chapter 5 offers some suggestions about the practical application of this difference. As for a riddle within a poem,

I simply thought of it in those terms until I read Augustine. Chapter 2 is, in part, the story of Augustine the great teacher of rhetoric, and how useful he can be to this day.

This book suggests that we reinstate the figure of speech known for centuries as *aenigma*. It also suggests that literary critics and scholars and theorists stop being so sloppy in our use of the words "riddle" and "enigma." The word "riddling" would cover some effects, while more general terms should be found for other ones. One further suggestion stems from a nineteenth-century French writer: that we re-introduce the obsolete word "griph" to cover some comic riddle effects that take the form of schemes.

For those who are not literary specialists, some working definitions of "scheme" and "trope" follow. (For Renaissance and earlier specialists, I should note that I am using the term "figures of speech" in a modern sense, as including schemes and tropes.) Schemes are those figures of speech that devise surface patternings for words. This is the oldest meaning for "scheme" in the Oxford English Dictionary; it survives today in general use in the phrase, "rhyme scheme." Beyond rhymes, schemes include alliteration, chiasmus (an a–b–b–a pattern), and so on. Schemes do not overtly change the ordinary meaning of words. Rhyming "moon" and "June" does not change their meaning, at least in the first instance. (It might do so in context. And it does say other things. It says: this is a dim-witted writer or a satiric writer or possibly a courageous writer.) Tropes form a different class. They are figures of speech in which ordinary meaning is overtly changed or turned.[1] (Not that ordinary meaning is all that ordinary either, but the definitions hold nonetheless.) Metaphor was sometimes a synonym for the entire class of tropes, and it remains easily the best-known and most crucial trope, though we need to watch its definition. Synecdoche and metonymy also belong to this class. "All hands on deck" changes the ordinary meaning of the word "hands," unless some spooky or loony effect is wanted. We routinely accept that saying because the synecdoche is so familiar. Poems by definition work with schemes, but tropes are the *sine qua non* of poetry. Greeting-card verses use schemes too, but they are rarely poems. On the other hand, a good writer can turn even the slightest scheme into poetic gold.

This book might be thought of as one of those single-word studies like Terence Cave's 1990 study of the word "recognition" or Leo Spitzer's

---

1 The Greek etymon for "trope" means "turn."

earlier study of the word *Stimmung* (harmony).[2] As such, it belongs broadly in the history of ideas. More precisely, it belongs in what John T. Irwin calls that "branch of the history of ideas best designated as the history of the critique of figuration" (*The Mystery to a Solution*, p. xvii). Or, as I myself would call it, rhetorical criticism – rhetorical more in the Aristotelian analytical sense than the Ciceronian instrumental sense. "Rhetoric" once had a much wider meaning than our usual meaning nowadays. It was one of three basic subjects taught in advanced schooling, the other two being grammar (also with a wider meaning) and logic or dialectic. We cannot bring back the schools of Shakespeare's day, with their rigorous training in verbal use, a training that reads more like an undergraduate curriculum today. But of late, students have become increasingly interested again in what has always interested readers at large: how writing works, that is, rhetoric.[3] Rhetoric, as defined by Gerard Manley Hopkins, consists of "all the common and teachable element in literature." Just so. For him, rhetoric is to poetry (or imaginative literature) as grammar is to speech:

[The] rhetoric [about poetry] is inadequate – seldom firstrate, mostly only just sufficient, sometimes even below par. By rhetoric I mean all the common and teachable element in literature, what grammar is to speech, what thoroughbass is to music, what theatrical experience gives to playwrights.[4]

Wallace Stevens once wrote that "hypotheses relating to poetry, although they may appear to be very distant illuminations, could be the fires of fate, if rhetoric ever meant anything" (*The Necessary Angel*, p. 81). That ought to be enough to hearten rhetorical critics, even nowadays.

The first chapter provides an entryway by means of two legendary creatures, one obviously associated with riddle, the other much less obviously. The first is the Grecian Sphinx, and the second is the Griffin or Gryphon, best known from *Alice in Wonderland*. Both are familiar in

---

2 Leo Spitzer, *Classical and Christian Ideas of World Harmony: Prolegomena to an Interpretation of the Word "Stimmung"* (Baltimore: Johns Hopkins University Press, 1963); see also, e.g., William Empson's *The Structure of Complex Words* (London: Chatto & Windus, 1951).

3 This is, in fact, what Jonathan Culler has recently advanced as a new focus for English studies. In effect, he is reclaiming something of the age-old experience of teaching advanced rhetoric. See his "Imagining the Coherence of the English Major," *Profession* (Modern Language Association, 2003), 85–93.

4 Hopkins in 1886, quoted by Christopher Ricks, *Essays in Appreciation* (Oxford: Clarendon, 1996), p. 311.

sculpted forms, now chiefly decorative rather than symbolic. But their history in its riddling aspect is lively. This chapter offers a short survey of these riddling beasts, including a Graeco-Latin pun on "griffin" that Lewis Carroll introduced *sotto voce* into his great book.

The second chapter looks at the history of enigma as a figure of speech, and develops an argument for its reinstatement. Years ago, Augustine's passing remark that *aenigma* is a trope leapt off the page for me. He took for granted that this was common knowledge, and so it is for historians of rhetoric, but I had never heard of it. When I began to investigate, enigma as a trope proved to be a constant in the rhetoricians. It goes back to Aristotle and comes over into Latin with Cicero and Quintilian and others. Most important, it appears in Donatus, the great grammarian and rhetorician whom Dante places in the Circle of the Wise in heaven. Donatus wrote what would become the standard Latin school-text for centuries, in the days when Latin was the *lingua franca* of Europe and taught to all schoolboys and a few schoolgirls too. The trope of *aenigma* was part of their training. Chapter 2 traces the history and functions of this trope from its Greek beginnings through its Latin life into English and down to the seventeenth century, when this use of "enigma" died out.

Such a history helps provide a working definition of the trope of enigma. It also offers questions, cautions, and appreciation of this figure of speech. Many remain constant to this day. What is at stake when we use "enigma" – or indeed, use any figure of "similitude" – is laid out with exemplary clarity in Augustine's work. Why did this trope finally die out? The answer belongs to a larger history of the fortunes of figures of speech. The nub of this chapter's argument comes at the end, in a discussion of *similitudo* ("likeness" or simply "as") and why this matters so much in all uses of language.

The third chapter offers a proposed taxonomy of enigma as masterplot, a taxonomy expanded from my 1983 outline. There, I was working with three basic riddle plots; I now think that five masterplots make better sense. This is to work at the large end of the scale of enigma and riddle. Not riddle as a small puzzling conundrum or even a famous uncanny enigma, but as the riddle of everything. Stevens, Augustine, and Frye led very naturally to thinking about possible typic shapes of the enigma or riddle, and eventually of an anatomy. So it was that I became interested in mapping kinds of enigma, where it is considered as masterplot or an end-directed plot. I am mindful of the fact that all taxonomies are interpretive, that they are "theories of order, not simple records," to quote Stephen Jay Gould. I am also mindful of the hazards of synchronic argument.

Chapters 4, 7, and 9 offer case-studies on the work of Dante, Lewis Carroll, and Wallace Stevens respectively. These short studies necessarily focus on limited aspects of these writers: one passage (Dante) or one aspect (Carroll) or one time in a writer's work (Stevens). The case-studies are meant to show in practice how useful rhetorical criticism can be. Recognizing kinds of riddle and enigma can help to open out what a writer is doing, widening and deepening our sense of possible riches in a work.

We routinely classify writing in genres, sometimes quite unaware that we are doing so. Nobody (we hope) reads *Alice in Wonderland* as realistic fiction. What kind of genre is the riddle? Chapter 5 centers on this and related questions. Critics like André Jolles and Frye and Alastair Fowler argue that it is a genre, but they differ about how it behaves. What can we say of the single riddle as genre? How does the riddle behave within a larger work? In this chapter, I argue that riddles may usefully be thought about as generic and sub-generic types. It also helps a great deal to note when riddles are functioning as modes rather than genres. Otherwise, far too much is dubbed a "riddle," more for fancy effect than accuracy. Other matters are mentioned more briefly: relations with other genres, hierarchies of genre. Some suggestions for modern genre studies end the chapter.

Chapter 6 presents an argument about literary schemes, as distinct from tropes. It begins with the vexed and fascinating history of lesser forms of enigma and riddle like "charade" and "rebus" and "logograph." It then suggests that many of these forms now be classified as griph-type schematic riddles. Riddles that turn on living metaphors continue to absorb us, even after we have answered them. Thus the ongoing life of the Sphinx's riddle: "What walks on four feet in the morning, two feet at noon, and three feet in the evening?" A riddle shaped into the verbal artefact that we call art becomes an enigma, for the good reason that it uses the trope of enigma well. But literary works can also enjoy the fun and games of riddle-schemes. Readers appreciate them. So might literary critics, who are all too often solemn creatures, hardly knowing what to do with *jeux d'esprit*.

There are a number of standard figures for the riddle, such as knots or labyrinths, and they often indicate what kind of riddle is in play. Chapter 8 looks at common tropes for riddle and enigma. Not the workings of enigma as a trope, but specific figures of speech for riddles and enigmas themselves. Such figures can point toward the type of solution or the assumptions within a riddle. The words for solving riddles are just as interesting in their figurative implications, for, as Irwin puts it, there may be *The Mystery to a Solution*. The chapter includes an overview of an object and a trope closely associated with enigma, the mirror, especially in the phrase, "through a glass, darkly." It ends by looking at the crucial trope of inside and outside.

While this book concentrates on the literary workings of riddle and enigma, chapter 10 glances at some other functions of riddles. Ancient riddles like ancient charms were used as practical magic, and no doubt still are. Riddling was also once a diplomatic language, and political riddles are a constant. Riddles have been associated with dreams since the time of Joseph, and North American natives have an old and rich dream-lore that includes riddles. Riddles also flourish in social contexts. This chapter also looks briefly at collections and collectors: the best-known collections, who collected riddles, what aims the collectors had (or said they had), and so on. A full study could be made of riddle collections as popular art, and even so, the collections would have to be limited by language or country or date or more. Imaginative literature allows for representation of all these possible functions of the riddle.

This is a literary study, so that it concentrates on a literary reading of riddle and enigma, chiefly on figuration and on fictive constructs. But of course, writing speaks to actual life, as actual life speaks to writing. The Afterword looks at the behavior of riddle and enigma at large. It looks at riddle or enigma, the boundary figure, as embodied in enigma as trope and masterplot and elsewhere, and as hovering over the crucial crossing-places of our lives.

CHAPTER I

Enigma personified: the riddling beasts, sphinx and griffin

"What Do You Want To Be Inscrutable *For*, Marcia?"
(James Thurber[1])

Sphinxes and griffins are riddling in the general sense of mysterious and odd, perhaps menacing. They belong to a legendary world, and their hybrid forms, like those of sirens, chimaeras, harpies, centaurs, and other fabulous beasts, have intrigued humankind for centuries. (They intrigued Borges enough that he compiled an introductory dictionary of them, *The Book of Imaginary Beings*.) A primitive Egyptian griffin from about 3000 BCE is shown in Heinz Demisch's fine study, *Die Sphinx*.[2] The Egyptian sphinxes, those huge wonders of the ancient and modern world shaped with the body of a lion and the head of a man or god, date back to 2600 BCE. Various early forms of sphinxes (human head and animal body, usually a lion) and griffins (bird head, usually an eagle, and animal body) go back to the fifteenth to thirteenth centuries BCE. One elegant fourteenth-century sphinx comes from Megiddo in present-day Israel. Ancient sphinxes and griffins sometimes appear together, and sometimes appear flanking a tree of life – an unexpected conjunction. Yet it is logical enough, by way of contraries, for both beasts are sculpted on ancient Greek and Roman gravestones and sarcophagi.

In her classic Grecian form, the sphinx is tripartite, so that Ausonius claims her as one example in his *Griphus ternarii numeri* (Riddle of the Number Three, ll. 38–40). She possesses the head of a woman, the body of a lion, and the wings of a bird. Sometimes she is called double-natured, as in Nietzsche's *The Birth of Tragedy*, but this refers to her combination of human and animal natures. The griffin, as he evolved in Grecian art,

---

1 *Men, Women, and Dogs*, in Thurber, *The Thurber Carnival*, p. 351.
2 Demisch, *Die Sphinx*, plate 5, pp. 16–39 ("Die ägyptische Sphinx"), plates 107–12, plate 112, and plates 107, 110, 198–9, 204 (tree of life motif).

became defined as a creature with the foreparts of an eagle and the hindparts of a lion. The Grecian sphinx is virtually always a "she." Some examples of sphinxes with bearded male heads are known from the archaic period (OCD, "sphinx"), but they appear to have had no influence on the tradition. The griffin in literature is male. Both are fierce creatures, just what you want to guard the bones of your cherished dead. Both have other iconographic functions beyond tomb-guarding. Both have survived continuously for centuries in sculpted, carved, painted, and other forms, sometimes only as decorative motifs, sometimes as more. Both are associated with riddles, the Grecian sphinx famously and the griffin in its very name, though this piece of lore depends on a Graeco-Latin pun that was last heard in English by Lewis Carroll, as far as I know.

THE SPHINX

The sphinx as riddling beast is the Grecian sphinx and not the Egyptian, though possibly the Grecian sphinx began in Egypt. Or it may have been adapted from Mesopotamia, the other source of sphinxes dating back to the mid-third millennium BCE (OCD, "sphinx"). The Grecian sphinx, as it developed, came to differ markedly from the Egyptian sphinx in form and in function. Ancient sculpted Grecian sphinxes guarding tombs appear to be protective of the dead, and probably apotropaic in warding off evil. The Egyptian sphinx is also protective, but its scope is wider. It is known as "guardian of the gates of the Underworld on the eastern and western horizons" (Edwards, *The Pyramids of Egypt*, p. 140). As such, it points toward the mystery of death and presumably the hope of an afterlife. It is indeed enigmatic in a general way, especially to us who are so far from its original world.

But the great Egyptian sphinx does not enter into riddle stories. If riddles are associated with it, this is a later Greek addition. Plutarch knew the tradition: "They [Egyptian priests] place sphinxes appositely before the shrines, intimating that their teaching about the gods holds a mysterious wisdom. At Saïs the seated statue of Athena, whom they consider to be Isis also, bore the following inscription: 'I am all that has been and is and will be; and no mortal has ever lifted my mantle'" (*De Iside et Osiride* IX.354c). The editor of Plutarch, J. Gwyn Griffiths, observes that "no suggestion of mystery or enigma [is] attached to it [the Egyptian Sphinx]. Such a suggestion seems to have arisen first in the Theban

(Greek) legends of a king's riddle-contest with a sphinx."[3] Clement of Alexandria adapted it to his own purposes:

It is for this reason that the Egyptians place statues of sphinxes in front of their temples, in order to show that discussion about God is enigmatic and obscure; perhaps they also did it because one must love and fear God at the same time – love him as favoring and benevolent to the devout, fearing him as inexorably just to the impious. So also the sphinx enigmatically shows the image of a savage beast and of a human being at the same time.

(*Stromate* v.v.31; *Les Stromates*, pp. 76–7).

Clement also connected the enigmas of the Hebrew Bible to the hidden mystery of the Egyptian sphinxes (ibid., v.vi.32). He was a syncretist by temperament, and he rejoiced in the opportunity for melding that symbolism offered him. Mysteries he especially liked.

Riddle in general or in particular has been attached to the Egyptian tradition ever since. The American painting *The Questioner of the Sphinx* (1863), by the young Elihu Vedder, shows a man kneeling and pressing his ear to the stone lips of an Egyptian sphinx, buried in sand to the neck; a human skull lies nearby. Vedder, like many others, has transferred the Grecian sphinx's riddle into enigma as masterplot (unspecified), whose answer only the Egyptian sphinx knows. Jay Macpherson makes of the inscription of Isis a wickedly apt riddle-poem ("Isis"):

> I'm Isis of Saïs,
> If you'd know what my way is,
> Come riddle my riddle-mi-ree.
> It's perfectly easy
> For those who're not queasy –
> Say, am I a he or a she?
> There's no-one shall wed me
> And least of all bed me,
> In fact, no-one loves me but me:
> Aha, you don't know? you
> 'd prefer me to show you?
> The answer will slay you, you'll see!

Comparisons of the Greek and Egyptian sphinxes can be straight-forward and without preference. But the differences can be read in other ways. Guy de Tervarent, in his *Attributs et symboles dans l'art profane*

---

3 Plutarch, *De Iside et Osiride*, pp. 130–1, 283. Griffiths adds that "Rose, *Gk. Myth.* 188 thinks there may be Minoan-Mycenaean prototypes for the story."

Figure 1. "Oedipe et le sphinx" (Vatican, Museo Gregoriano), from *Dictionnaire des antiquités grecques et romaines*, ed. Charles Daremberg and Ed Saglio (Paris: Hachette, 1877), vol. IV.2, p. 1437

1450–1600, lists the attributes of the two sphinxes, which the Renaissance seems to have happily intermingled, at least in its iconography.[4] For him, these are distinguished as mysterious thought and voluptuousness. Mysterious thought is associated with the Egyptian sphinx, while voluptuousness is associated with the Grecian, at least in some later manifestations (cols. 363–4). On the other hand, Athanasius Kircher, in the frontispiece to his "Oedipus Aegyptiacus" (1652), places the Grecian sphinx high on a rock, her accustomed spot, but with an Egyptian background complete with pyramids, obelisks, temple and palm trees. For good measure, her hair is adorned with an Egyptian headband. Her features are placid and benign, and she is clearly a Wisdom figure, a female counterpart to the Egyptian sphinx.

4 Chastel calls the sphinx as used in the fifteenth century an ambivalent symbol. Sometimes it indicates hidden mysterious wisdom for initiates, sometimes bestial and culpable ignorance. He moves without distinction between Egyptian and Greek sphinx forms ("Note").

Figure 2. Frontispiece from Athanasius Kircher, *Oedipus Aegyptiacus* (Rome, 1652).

Sir Richard Burton was scathing about the notion that a mere riddle could be associated with the majestic Egyptian sphinx.

This series of puzzling questions and clever replies is still as favourite a mental exercise in the East as it was in middle-aged Europe. The riddle or conundrum began, as far as we know, with the Sphinx, through whose mouth the Greeks spoke: nothing less likely than that the grave and mysterious Scribes of Egypt should ascribe aught so puerile to the awful emblem of royal majesty – Abu Haul, the Father of Affright.[5]

The tone is worth comparing with Hegel's on Sophocles' *Oedipus Rex* as against his *Antigone*. Is the thought of wordplay for high art and serious matters quite unbearable? Is it the story of Oedipus and the matter of incest? Is it a famous riddler who is female? Burton is very much of his time and place, late-nineteenth-century England, in disdaining such low forms as the riddle.

Demisch lists ten aspects in which the Grecian sphinx figures in painted or sculpted forms. The first is as a death-daimon, for example, on gravestones and sarcophagi. The second is as riddle-poser and destroyer of Thebes, for example, on vase-paintings, sculpture, and gems. The third through sixth are chiefly paired sphinxes, sometimes beside a tree of life, sometimes flanking a god or demon or beast, sometimes with animals or other hybrid creatures. The seventh and eighth suggest an apotropaic function, for example, in places of worship or on votive-stones, altars, and throne-seats. The ninth and tenth are ornamental, as decoration on ceramics, weapons, vessels, jewels, and furniture. The second aspect, the sphinx as riddle figure, immediately concerns us here, rather than her full and fascinating history in sculpted and painted forms. Nonetheless, the sphinx's iconographical history hovers around her riddling function, and should not be ignored. Even decorative sphinxes can serve notice of some guardianship or give pause in other ways. The form of the sphinx herself is intrinsically riddle-like, a fact that writers from Sophocles to Borges have exploited to the full.

The famous riddle is attached to her from the early sixth century BCE, but she exists in literature before that without a riddle. Hesiod in the *Theogony* says that the Phyx or Sphinx "destroyed the Cadmaeans" (*Th.* 326–7), and in the incomplete *Oidipodeia*, she causes the death of the young and "noble Haimon" (Hesiod, p. 483, Loeb). The *Theogony* along with the *Oidipodeia* provide literary evidence for the sphinx's behavior

5 *The Book of the Thousand Nights and a Night*, vol. XII, p. 71n.

from the seventh and sixth centuries BCE. The art of the same period shows a monstrous being who preys on young males. For some time, the accepted view was that Oedipus originally killed the sphinx by force and not by intelligence. (The view built on the work of Erich Bethe in 1891 and on a 1911 discovery among the holdings of the Boston Museum of Fine Arts. Tests eventually showed that the crucial scene painted on the Boston vase is modern, not ancient.) Jean-Marc Moret argues persuasively that the sixth century BCE knew the motif of the enigma in both literature and painting or sculpture. The two motifs of enigma and combat, he writes, are not mutually exclusive, but rather a matter of emphasis. "When the enigma seemed too childish [trop puérile] to be taken seriously, it was necessary to stress violent action, in order to enhance the heroic character of Oedipus and give the myth a prestige that was threatening to grow dim."[6] The question of the place of enigma often turns on the difference between force and guile, an ancient contrast. In Western literature, it goes back to the heroic protagonists in Homer's two epics, Achilles the strong warrior and Odysseus the warrior of many wiles. Oedipus belongs to the Odysseus type, though less schooled in self-awareness.

The earliest connection of the sphinx and the riddle in literature is in a fragment from Pindar: "the riddle from the savage jaws of a maiden" (fr 177d). Only in Asklepiades, as quoted in Athenaeus, and not in *Oedipus Rex* do we learn the actual riddle. But the words *kai tri* ("and three–") appear on an entrancing cup in the Vatican (Vat. 16541), contemporaneous with Aeschylus, where Oedipus faces the Sphinx (Fig. 1). Euripides in *The Phoenician Women*, 409, says that she sang her riddles, a spooky thought. ("What Song the Syrens sang" was one of the ancient mysteries, and may suggest that the two fabulous beasts sometimes interchange their roles. Siren-song, however, can be beneficent; it does other things than lure sailors to their death. The riddling sphinx, singing or not, is deadly.) Jocasta refers to the sphinx early in Euripides' play (ll. 45–9) in an epithet variously translated as "witch-maiden" (Arthur S. Way, Loeb) and "clever girl" (Elizabeth Wyckoff), saying that Oedipus "read the Sphinx's song" (l. 50, *mousas*). Later in the play, the Sphinx is remembered as swooping down, "the maiden that sang us a chant of doom, / An untuneable cry" (l. 808, Arthur S. Way;

---

6 Moret, *Œdipe, la Sphinx et les Thébains*, vol. 1, p. 84. Moret observes that M. Delcourt even argued in 1944 in *Oidipous: la légende du conquérant* that enigma came first and combat later (ibid.).

apomousotataisi). Antigone, with her own song of grief, recalls the "singing Sphinx": "the ruin began / when he unriddled the riddling song [*melos*] / of the singing Sphinx and slew her dead" (ll. 1503–5, Wyckoff).

The Grecian sphinx is usually fierce and inimical in literature, unless she is the subject of parody, as she doubtless was in the satyr-play Aeschylus wrote to end his trilogy about the Oedipus story. ("The production record shows that *The Seven against Thebes* was the last unit in a tragic trilogy that covered the fate of a great royal house over three generations. It was preceded by *Laius* and *Oedipus* and was followed by a satyr-play entitled *Sphinx*, which must have relaxed the audience's tensions by guying one of Oedipus' still most famous heroic achievements."[7]) Fragments survive of the two lost tragedies, *Laius* and *Oedipus*, but alas, none of the satyr-play, though there have been attempts to imitate it. A recent example is Erika Simon's *Das Satyrspiel Sphinx der Aischylos* (1981).

James Thurber got it exactly right, as usual. His cartoon "What Do You Want To Be Inscrutable *For*, Marcia?" is *in nuce* a satyr-play titled *Sphinx*. There is something faintly ridiculous about wanting to get yourself up as an enigma, if only for the good reason that all human identity is enigmatic enough on its own. His cartoon is filled with heavy solid black lines: oval black mirror frame, oval black rug, huge black urn to the left, black urn-shaped lampshade to the right; seated black cat seen from the back, black baseboard. The hapless Thurber male asks Marcia his question, while she sits to the right, body facing right and head turned back in profile. Her hair hangs loose, her hands are folded, she occupies a stool, and her features are indeed inscrutable. The male plays dog to her cat, lying crouched on the sofa and facing her, profile to profile. He is hairless, his hands hanging paw-like over the sofa arms, as if obedient or supplicatory. She is not crouching like a sphinx, being sibylline as well as sphinxine. If the positions were reversed, and the male in charge, with Marcia crouching sphinx-like but subdued, we would have Thurber's cartoon "That's My First Wife Up There, and This Is the *Present* Mrs. Harris" (*The Thurber Carnival*, p. 343). In this second cartoon, Oedipus has conquered the inscrutable, enigmatic female.

Riddles regularly take the trope of braiding and enfolding, to say nothing of tangling. Sculptors evidently think about the choice of hair

---

7 Hetherington, *Aeschylus*, p. 79.

arrangement for their sphinxes, so that braided or curled or tangled hair may well enter into the troping of the sphinx. Then too, hair completely loose on the head of an adult woman was a sight once seen only in intimate circles. Milton, clearly susceptible, imagined this as a condition of paradise and dwelt lovingly on Eve's hair. The analogy with answering riddles lies in the openness of hair hanging loose. Conventions of hair arrangement also enter into the possible sexual resonances of a sphinx figure.

A smiling sixth-century-BCE Etruscan stone sphinx in the Sackler Museum at Harvard has her long locks braided or tightly curled to the scalp, as do other very early sphinxes. Thus also the contemporaneous Sphinx of the Naxians at the Delphi Museum, except that the few braids or tightly rolled curls fall separately. The braids or ringlets appear to follow a well-established convention. The smiling, handsome, breasted sphinx of the Belvedere Palace in Vienna (c. 1710–20) has one braid down each side in front, with other hair arranged in swathes at the top of the head. At Blenheim Palace, seat of the Duke of Marlborough, the pensive sphinx has its head modeled on the then Duchess of Marlborough, wondrous to relate. The Blenheim Palace sphinx realistically follows contemporary fashion, and presumably the Duchess of Marlborough when her hair was not elaborately arranged, by pinning the hair informally at the nape of the neck. At Versailles, the hair appears to combine Egyptian convention (side hair braided or contained in a vertically marked, straight-edged arrangement, hanging down the front) and contemporary fashion (hair gathered at the crown and falling in curls plus curled locks at the hairline in front and back). But the Egyptian effect may simply imitate the sculpting of "ringlets" in some early Greek sphinxes, as for example in the Sphinx in the Corinth Museum. Botero's contemporary creature is cheering, voluptuous, earthy, and formidable all at once. Her hair is arranged simply in a single braid down her back.

In painting and some sculpture, one way of lessening the dread of the sphinx is to emphasize her female qualities. Thus with the seductress in Ingres and Moreau, and the earth-mother in Botero. But as with the sphinx's riddle itself, this does not work, as Ingres and Moreau and Botero also know. Moreau, much influenced by Ingres's *Oedipus and the Sphinx* (1808, Louvre), exploited the possibility of a female who is riddling, alluring, deeply menacing, and part animal to boot (*Oedipus and the Sphinx*, 1846, Metropolitan Museum, New York). The power of legend colors the fabric of human femaleness in this art, which plays back and forth between legend and human female. It is like our twofold response to the famous riddle.

Like the term "enigma," the sphinx in literature can typify any puzzling and mysterious creature. French decadent literature of the mid- to late nineteenth century especially liked the sphinx personified as demonic female, with her riddle sometimes transferred into perverse sexual capacities. "C'était, je vous l'ai dit un sphinx . . . un sphinx qui dévorait le plaisir silencieusement et gardait son secret" (It was, as I told you, a sphinx . . . a sphinx who silently devoured pleasure and kept her secret). "Sphinx aux yeux d'émeraude, angélique vampire / Elle rêve sous l'or cruel de ses frissons" (Sphinx with emerald eyes, angelic vampire, / She dreams beneath the cruel gold of her shudders).[8] She became for Jung "the formal personification of the 'terrible' or 'devouring' mother."[9]

D. H. Lawrence's female sphinx is possessed of his own bête noire, self-consciousness:

> But why do I feel so strangely about you?
> said the lovely young lady, half wistful, half menacing.
>
> I took to my heels and ran
> before she could set the claws of her self-conscious questioning in me
> or tear me with the fangs of disappointment
> because I could not answer the riddle of her own self-importance.
>
> > ("Sphinx")

This helps us map the possibilities of the sphinx, especially as a trope for some aspect of a female. But it leads us away from the verbal form of the riddle, for Lawrence like others does not treat the riddle of the feet. William Empson does so, changing the classic riddle into a sympathetic allegory of a female Egyptian sphinx in "Four Legs, Three Legs, Two Legs."

The riddle gave Matthew Prior a fine satiric weapon in his 1710 lampoon, "The Riddle," supposedly sent by "a Sage, studious of *Egyptian* knowledge."[10] Oedipus duly answers the sphinx's riddle, then puts one to her in turn:

> Now in your turn, 'tis just, methinks,
> You shou'd resolve me, Madam *Sphinx*,
> What stranger Creature yet is he,

---

8 J. Barbey d'Aureville, *Les Diaboliques*, Albert Samain, "Une," cited in Ramacciotti, *La chimera e la sfinge*, pp. 70, 71.

9 "la personification formelle de la mère 'terrible' ou 'dévorante,'" C. G. Jung, *Les Métamorphoses de l'âme et ses symboles*, trans. Yves le Lay (Geneva: Georg, 1953; orig. pub. 1912), pp. 306–11.

10 *Literary Works*, vol. 1, pp. 393–4.

> Who has four Legs, then two, then three;
> Then loses one; then gets two more;
> And runs away, at last, on four.

The answer is Sidney Godolphin, the British statesman who was Lord Treasurer, and hence held the staff of office. He lost it, then crawled away, when Queen Anne dismissed him in 1710.

The sphinx can even be tamed for home amusement, though she still sounds a little dangerous. In London in 1664, a certain W. B., Gent. (William Bagwell) published *Sphynx Thebanus, with his Oedipus: or, Ingenious* RIDDLES, *with their Observations, Explications, and Morals. Excellently suiting with the Fancies of Old or young, and exceeding useful to advance a Chearful Society, and to continue and preserve Mirth.* An anonymous Oxford collection of 1812 allowed the sphinx no dignity whatever in its title, *The Frolics of the Sphynx.* A Victorian periodical was more respectful: *The Sphinx: A Journal of Humour and Criticism* (Manchester, 1868–).

In folk riddles attached to narratives, there is a continuing tradition of some spirit waiting on the road to ask riddles, then killing those who cannot answer. David Fitzgerald quotes an Irish *leath-rann* or half quatrain for which the riddling creature requires the second half. In one version, the demon sits astride the roof of an Abbey, smoking tobacco, and challenging the would-be passerby in Gaelic: "Tobacco and pipe for the rider of the church: / Put thou an answering rhyme to that" ("Of Riddles," 190). Similar stories go back centuries, and there are numerous analogies, including ones from the Middle East. Here the riddle has changed, while the sphinx-as-roadside-challenger stays, at least in the form of some unearthly creature.

Ben Jonson, who disliked mystification, declawed the sphinx by making her mother of "the Follies, which were twelve she-fools" in his masque, *Love Freed from Ignorance and Folly.* She challenges Love with riddles based on the paradoxes of Nicholas of Cusa. Love is rescued, not by his own wits, but by the twelve priests of the muses (ll. 257–60, p. 183):

> Vanish, Follies, with your mother;
> The riddle is resolved.
> Sphinx must fly when Phoebus shines,
> And to aid of Love inclines.

Solving the riddle-paradoxes requires no Oedipus, but simply transferring Nicholas's questions and answers from God Almighty and his domain to King James and Britain.

A sphinx is also a kind of moth, a hawk-moth. Few take advantage of this fact for troping, but the possibility of it enters into Gjertrud Schnackenberg's lines from the Oedipus story, as retold through three human generations and the eyes of the gods in her *The Throne of Labdacus*.

> The tablets showed only an expanse of illegible waves
>
> Like a depiction of Zeus's rain in undulating sheets
> Whipping a storm through Thebes
>
> With the rustling of a pair of suddenly folded,
> Wet Sphinx-wings; but then,
>
> Beneath the freshly written law of Zeus,
> The old story began showing through –
> (Three: "What-Is and What-Is Not")

It is the word "wet" along with "suddenly folded" that uncannily evokes the sphinx-moth of today, even as the hovering flying monster of ancient legend also folds its rain-wet wings and settles into the wet clay tablets. To be sure, the Sphinx's wings are wet because of a storm that arises from the wet clay tablets. Yet she comes alive in a kind of metamorphosis as the sphinx-moth evolves from the caterpillar in sphinx pose that gives it its name. So also the old story begins to show through on the "fresh, still-wet tablets, with the Oedipus tale."

As Roberto Calasso says, "Oedipus was drawn to the Sphinx, and he resolved the Sphinx's enigma, but only to become an enigma himself. Thus anthropologists were drawn to Oedipus, and are still there measuring themselves against him, wondering about him." So are many of us, wondering perhaps how much of us is Oedipus and how much is monster. Especially if we have read Borges' extraordinary sonnet, "Oedipus and the Enigma."

THE GRIFFIN-RIDDLE

Personified figures of enigma are quite rare, and the Grecian sphinx is better known than the griffin. But the griffin qualifies nicely. It's also a hybrid creature.[11] So is enigma, for all that – hybrid in a manner of speaking, as it momentarily combines seemingly incongruous parts.

---

11 E. G. Stanley has drawn my attention to the fact that the bird *grifo(n* is in Spanish a term of abuse: "also the son of a black woman, and a mulatto" (Delpino's *Dictionary*). For another prejudicial use of the griffin's nature, see OED, "griff" (also "griffin") as a mulatto in US usage (giving the origin, from Littré, as Buffon). Webster adds a second definition of "a person of mixed Negro and American Indian blood."

Like the sphinx, the griffin is of ancient vintage, with depicted examples from Babylonia, Persia, Assyria, Palestine, Anatolia, Cyprus, Crete and Mycenae surviving from as early as 3000 BCE.[12] Griffins are found on ceramics and clay tiles, on silver and gold and gems and ivory, on coins, and sculpted in stone. They range in size from huge friezes on a temple to small sculptures that fit in the palm. They come over into Greek art, with the classic design established as a hybrid creature with the foreparts of an eagle (head, wings) and the hindparts of a lion (body and tail); from early representations on, the tail sometimes curled into a decorative vegetative form. The Romans continued to recreate the creature. Christiane Delplace has thoroughly surveyed and analysed examples of the griffin in archaic and classical art.[13]

Griffins are frequently shown as fierce creatures, thus bearing out their legendary nature as recounted in Herodotus, Pliny, and elsewhere. A number of representations depict them battling men or seizing creatures like horses or deer. They are the iconographic creatures of Nemesis, especially the wheels of Nemesis, as she distributes justice, herself fierce and implacable.[14] The griffin's strength and ferocity must also account for its presence on Roman armor, particularly breastplates, though even here the depiction is not uniform. (See below on the statue of Augustus; another breastplate shows two griffins being offered water by two Arimaspians, or so they are identified [Delplace, *Le Griffon de l'archaïsme*, fig. 269]; the motif is repeated elsewhere.) But this motif of the fierce griffin is far from being the only motif in classical and later art. One unusual example, for instance, even shows a female griffin guarding a young griffin. Griffins are also associated with Apollo, as well as drawing the chariot of Alexander upward into the heavens.

Ancient sculpted griffins, like sphinxes, often functioned as tomb-guardians. They also turn up as guardians for more than tombs. High on the outer wall of the Great Altar to Zeus at Pergamum (c. 170 BCE), there originally stood four griffins, shown in the scale reproduction that

---

12 Bartscht, "The Griffin," p. 92. See also Dürrbach, "Gryps ou Gryphus," Ziegler, "Gryps," Bisi, *Il grifone*, Delplace, *Le Griffon de l'archaïsme*, and Nigg, *Book of Fabulous Beasts*.
13 Ruskin draws a distinction between depictions of "true" and "false" griffins in *Modern Painters*, vol. III, chap. 8. "False" griffins are the familiar stylized classical sort, while "true" griffins are naturalistic, as illustrated. Ruskin's adjectives are, of course, *parti pris*. See also John Drury, *Times Literary Supplement*, 7 Jan. 2000.
14 Armour, "Griffins," pp. 76–7. See also the illustrations in Bernard de Montfaucon, *L'antiquité expliquée et représentée en figures* (Paris, 1719), e.g., vol. I, part II, pp. 307–8.

accompanies surviving sculptures in Berlin. A first-century "carved relief of emerging griffin" from the Department of Antiquities in Amman, Jordan, was shown at the Metropolitan Museum, New York, in 2003, with the observation that "Throughout the ancient Near East, griffins were usually paired with sphinxes to guard palace and tomb entrances." Among the engaging architectural features of Philip Carter's new Toronto Public Library building, which houses children's literature, is its front door, flanked by a sculpted lion and griffin. Presumably they are guardians of both books and children, and descend most immediately from Lewis Carroll. For modern sculpture and architecture, griffins are largely decorative, but occasionally they come with other possibilities.

In the bestiaries, which draw on Herodotus and later Pliny, griffins are said to dwell in the Hyperborean Mountains and to guard hoards of gold from the one-eyed Arimaspians. A recent exhibit at the Royal Ontario Museum titled "Scythian Gold" included many griffins among its prodigious golden pieces; all the golden griffins that I saw were fierce and some were attacking horses, their traditional enemies. The artefacts came from the area around ancient Scythia (modern Ukraine).[15] Herodotus records lore about Scythian warriors, known as great horsemen, and the lavish gold about their persons and their horses. Perhaps the gold came from the hordes that the legendary griffins guarded. It is tempting to speculate that the Scythians, who liked depicting griffins and had access to a lot of gold, placed griffin figures by the entrance to their gold mines and stores, and thereby started a legend.

In fact, they may have placed actual "griffin" bones there, if the origin of the creature itself grew out of fossil remains in ancient Scythia and surrounding territory. That is, the huge fossil bones of the area may well have suggested to the Scythians that similar huge live creatures lived nearby. What better guard for their gold? This is Adrienne Mayor's intriguing argument in *The First Fossil Hunters*. The suggestion is not new, but it has recently been revived. It dates from the founder of modern paleontology, Georges Cuvier (1769–1832), who, as Mayor points out, was a scientist with an eighteenth-century classical education.[16]

Perhaps the architects of a 1928–30 Art-Nouveau bank building in Toronto's financial district also had a classical education. They used

---

15 Bartscht cites Georges Charrière, *Scythian Art: Crafts of the Early Eurasian Nomads* (New York: Alpine Fine Arts Collection, 1979).
16 Mayor, *The First Fossil Hunters*, p. 5; see chap. 1, "The Gold-Guarding Griffin," pp. 15–53.

Figure 3. Gold-guarding golden griffins, Toronto heritage building, 320 Bay Street, originally built for the Canada Permanent Trust, 1928–30. Photograph by Markham Cook.

griffins as a motif, and guarded the entry to the Canada Permanent Trust's main hall with a handsome screen, including two golden griffins flanking a central tower (see Fig. 3). Did the tower serve as an emblem for the main vaults of the Trust?[17] Much earlier, the trade cards of two eighteenth-century gilders and carvers use a griffin as a motif, so that the creature may have retained this iconographic meaning for some time.[18]

Nothing in all this artistic tradition suggests the griffin as a riddler in the manner of a sphinx, nor does the literary tradition. Rather, the griffin

17 The building is at 320 Bay St. Two architectural firms are listed by Toronto's Preservation Board (F. H. Wilkes, Mathers, & Haldenby; as well as Sproatt and Rolph), and two more in the architectural index of Ontario (archindont.ca, a reference I owe to Christopher Armstrong).
18 "John Johnson, Carver and Gilder in General" and "Geo. Hennekin, Carver and Gilder in General" (Bodleian Library, John Johnson Co., Trade Cards, Box 24: 38, Box 24: 49). I am indebted to Jay Macpherson for these examples.

is a riddle, mostly a comic riddle, though not invariably. Perhaps the best way to explain this is anecdotally, as it came to me.

You do not burst out laughing in rare-book libraries. Not that a reader necessarily feels

> Hemmed in by the prim
> deodorizing stare
> of the rare-book room.
> (Amy Clampitt, "Balms")

Not at all. Still, my explosion in the Houghton reading-room at Harvard was muted. It was precipitated by one Gerardus Joannes Vossius, the learned Calvinist scholar who lived from 1577 to 1649, and wrote about all knowledge, as you still could then. He was very well known in the seventeenth century; some of his works were reprinted frequently, and a folio edition of his complete writings (*Opera Omnia*) was published in Amsterdam some fifty years after his death. Bishop Berkeley owned the six-volume set, which he presented to Yale College as part of his library.

Vossius compiled an etymological dictionary, the *Etymologicon Linguae Latinae*, and I was duly checking the entry under *aenigma*. I went on to check for an entry under *griphus*, a somewhat specialized term I'd first encountered in Nicholas Reusner's 1602 riddle collection and then intermittently elsewhere. There the word was, in the 1695 Amsterdam edition:

Griphus Latinis quod Graecis αἴνιγμα, quemadmodum scribit Agellius [Gellius] . . . & Apuleius, II Florid. Poëmati quoque Ausoniano nomen *griphus.*

(Griphus in Latin writers is what the Greeks call *ainigma*, of which Gellius writes . . . and Apuleius in ii Florida. A poem by Ausonius is called by the name *griphus.*)

A paragraph of synonyms and other sources followed.

Just why I then decided to check the Latin word for "griffin," I cannot clearly remember. But Dante must have been the reason, of which more in a moment. Latin "griffin" is *gryps*, and there it was on the facing page of this edition, transliterated from the Greek, γρύψ, along with something more:

Gryps . . . Dicitur & *gryphus* . . . Avis est fabulosa . . . De bello eorum cum Arimaspis ob auri custodiam, vide Herodotum; lib. III, & IV . . .

(Gryps . . . is also called *gryphus* . . . A fabulous bird . . . On their war with the Arimaspians over the custody of gold, see Herodotus, books III and IV . . .)

Lewis and Short confirmed what I had noticed: "griphus . . . an intricate or puzzling question, a riddle, enigma (post-class. and very rare)." And in the next column: "gryps . . . (gryphus) . . . a fabulous four-footed bird, a griffin." The OED also offered both "griph" and "gryph": "griph *Obs*. . . also in L. form griphus . . . A puzzling question; a riddle, enigma"; "gryph (e *Obs*. Also . . . griph(e. [A perversion of GRIPE, after L. gryphus . . . .] I. A griffin . . . .."

That was when I nearly laughed out loud, because the possibilities of a pun on *griphus/gryphus* (riddle/griffin) suddenly flashed – the verb is just right – on my inward eye.

The possibilities of this pun are not likely to flash on everyone's inward eye, so a word of explanation is due. Over a decade and more, I had become increasingly intrigued with Dante's treatment of enigma in his earthly paradise. I meant "enigma" in the largest possible sense, all the way from small riddles through to large, as well as enigma as figure of speech, and enigma mindful of a long history of famous riddles. Of course I was aware of Dante's well-known griffin in the great vision that overwhelms him shortly after his entry into Eden. (Blake's version of the creature, drawing the chariot of the Church, was the one in my mind's eye, though there are many other illustrations.) But before this Graeco-Latin pun arrived on the scene, I had no thought of a griffin as possible personification of enigma.

Shortly afterwards, Carroll and his Gryphon came to mind, and behold, there was my pun, flourishing in 1865, in chapter 9 of *Alice's Adventures in Wonderland*, "The Mock Turtle's Story." For anyone with Carroll's enchanting Gryphon in mind, the pun on *griphos* as both a riddle and a griffin (a *griphus* and a *gryphus*, so to speak) is irresistible. All the more so because he is a pun that Alice Liddell's father, the lexicographer of Liddell and Scott's *Greek–English Lexicon*, would have recognized. This becomes very evident in the word-play on "Laughing and Grief" and "Latin and Greek," word-play we should now complete as "grief, Greek, *griphos/gryphus*." (See further in chapter 7.)

Ariosto and his hippogryph and this pun in *Orlando Furioso* preceded Carroll by over three hundred years. The name "hippogryph" is itself a contradiction in terms, as commentators note. Griffins are the traditional enemies of horses, so much so that Virgil's Damon can describe a detested love-match as impossible, as heralding a time when *iungentur iam grypes equis* ("griffins soon will mate with horses," *Eclogue* VIII.27). The quotation is regularly cited in connection with Ariosto's creature. It's as if some beast were called a wol-amb, half wolf and half lamb. Either we are in some paradise where wolf and lamb dwell together, or we are faced with a riddle. Surely Ariosto's hippogryph is playing with the *griphus/gryphus* pun. For, as I discovered eventually, the word *griphus* had just re-entered Latin at about this time.

The word γρῖφος (*griphos*) is not rare in Greek, as *griphus* is in Latin. It goes back to Aristophanes, the earliest citation in Liddell and Scott being from line 20 of *The Wasps*, produced in 422 BCE. Douglas M. MacDowell's 1971 edition notes that "This is the earliest instance of the word, and the earliest mention of the custom of posing riddles at drinking-parties. Neither is heard of again until the middle of the fourth century, in Antiphanes 74, 124, 194; these fragments of Middle Comedy are preserved in Ath. [Athenaeus] 448b–459b, where riddles are discussed and quoted at length" (p. 130). Here is the passage from Aristophanes, translated by Moses Hadas (p. 145):

SOSIAS: I dreamt, too, an extraordinary dream. But tell me yours first.
XANTHIAS: A big eagle, I thought, flew down into the market place,
    Grabbed a bronze shield in his talons, carried it to the sky – Then I saw it was
    Cleonymus who'd thrown it away.
SOSIAS: Cleonymus is a perfect riddle [γρῖφον].
XANTHIAS: How?
SOSIAS: A man asks at table, What beast is it throws its shield away
    Alike on earth, in heaven, on sea?
XANTHIAS: Something terrible will happen to me – such a dream!
SOSIAS: Don't worry, nothing terrible, I swear it.
XANTHIAS: A man throwing his shield away *is* terrible. Tell your dream.
SOSIAS: Mine's big, about the whole ship of state.

The Loeb edition says of lines 15–19 (lines 2–5 above) that "The big eagle changes into bulky Cleonymus." (Cleonymus is the Sir John Falstaff of Aristophanes' comedies.) It also notes "a play on ἀσπίς [aspis] = (1) a shield, (2) a snake," and refers the reader to *The Acharnians*, line 88, where there is a play on the words for "gull" and "phoenix." Could not the Cleonymus-eagle of *The Wasps* be (or be also) a Cleonymus-griffin? Or a griffin manqué, having discarded his lion parts? MacDowell notes in his Introduction (p. 14) that Aristophanes was "happy to use [as puns] words which are only similar," here *griphos* and *gryps*. That is, could this pun be some 2,400 years old rather than 130 or 480 or nearly 700 years old?[19]

---

19 Note the remarks by Georg Curtius, *Principles of Greek Etymology* (London: Murray, 1886), trans. Augustus S. Wilson and Edwin B. England from *Grundzüge der Griechischen Etymologie*, 4th edn.: "γρῖφος has no quite certain etymology. The most probable comparison . . . seems to me . . . that with ῥίφ (gen. ῥῖπ–ος) and Lat. *scirp-us*, OHG. *sciluf*" (vol. 1, p. 127).

The word *griphus* disappeared from general use in Western Europe some time after Ausonius (d. 390) and his *Griphus on the Number Three*. In the early sixteenth century, as far as I can make out, it re-entered Latin where it led a vigorous life. Exactly where and through whom this happened, I am not altogether sure, though northern Italy is the most likely place and Ambrogio Calepino of Bergamo (1435–1511) the most likely person. The first edition of his influential *Dictionarium* (Reggio nel Emilia, 1502) includes the word at the end of the entry for *grypes* (griffin): "Gryphi uero ut Gellius inqt aenigmata sunt" (Griffins in a different meaning, as Gellius says, are enigmas).[20] An entry under *gryppos* gives a further definition as *sermo implicitus* (puzzling diction), again citing Gellius. So there it was in one paragraph, the griffin-riddle pun, for anyone wanting it, including Ariosto.

Ariosto, who lived from 1474 to 1533, published an early forty-canto version of *Orlando Furioso* in 1516; the hippogryph was there from the start. (He began working on the poem about 1503 to 1505.[21]) In the same year, 1516, a commentary on the *Griphus* of Ausonius by François Dubois was published in Paris. Then there was Lilius Gregorius Giraldus of Ferrara (1479–1552), who like Calepino studied Greek, and who put together a collection of riddles in which he discussed both *aenigmata* and *griphi* (1551). In 1514, also in northern Italy (Venice), the first printing of Athenaeus' *Learned Banquet* appeared, with definitions and examples of the *griphos*-type riddle. (Other sixteenth-century editions followed, including a bilingual one by the great scholar, Isaac Casaubon, in 1597.) Calepino was reading and annotating Gellius late in the fifteenth or early in the sixteenth century. Someone was reading Athenaeus early in the sixteenth century. Someone also saw the pleasures of this pun. Was it Calepino himself or was it the younger Ariosto? I'd like to have been present when someone else burst out laughing at the thought.

And Dante's great, mysterious griffin, drawing the chariot in that extraordinary procession, beheld by Beatrice in rapt contemplation? A fine Graeco-Latin pun is all very well, but what if the word was not even available to Dante? In fact, it was, though very rare. It was available

---

20 Later editors would list the word separately, first as *gryphus* and by 1559 as *griphus*. For editions of Calepino, see Albert Labarre, *Bibliographie du Dictionarium d'Ambrogio Calepino* (Baden-Baden: Valentin Koerner, 1975).

21 Reggio Emilia, where Calepino's *Dictionarium* was published in 1502, was very much in Ariosto's bailiwick. I am indebted to Teodolinda Barolini for this information.

in Gellius, a strange term from the Greek (as the pagan author Gellius said), but also a type of enigma that could contain the world. To me, the strongest reason for a personified riddle figure just here in Dante's poem is that his entry into the Earthly Paradise is the most extraordinary poetic treatment of Pauline enigma that I know. But all that is another story.

If this Graeco-Latin pun was current up to Lewis Carroll's time, why did nobody mention it explicitly? The answer is that they did. It could hardly be otherwise. Though I found the references long after my muted explosion in the Houghton reading-room, Claude-François Ménestrier was explicit in 1694, as was Angelo de Gubernatis in 1872. Doubtless, there are more examples. In his chapter on "Des Griphes," Ménestrier comments on the familiar device of the printer Gryphius. "The mark of Gryphius was enigmatic [énigmatique]; it was a Griffin with extended wing attached by one foot to a squared stone or to a closed book, from which hung a ball between the two wings" (p. 62). The device is often reproduced; it appears, for example, on the cover of a recent biography of Camerarius by Stephan Kunkler.[22] Ménestrier refers to the device as a rebus. In 1872, an Italian professor of Sanskrit, Angelo de Gubernatis, included an entry on griffins in his *Zoological Mythology*. At the end, he notes that griffins are sacred to Apollo, then concludes: "And as Apollo is the prophetical and divining deity, whose oracle, when consulted, delivers itself in enigmas, the word *griffin*, too, meant enigma, logogriph being an enigmatical speech, and griffonnage an entangled, confused, and embarrassing handwriting."[23]

Now that senior high school and university graduates no longer read Latin, the griffin-riddle pun has lapsed into oblivion. Unlike the enduring Grecian sphinx and her riddling, the griffin-riddle has gone. Still, his sculpted forms keep appearing, and, if Carroll is right about his temperament, this must amuse him very much. The sphinx does not usually go in for amusement.

---

22 Stephan Kunkler, *Zwischen Humanismus und Reformation: der Humanist Joachim Camerarius (1500–1574)* (New York: Olms, 2000).
23 Gubernatis, *Zoological Mythology*, vol. II, p. 205.

CHAPTER 2

Enigma as trope: history,
function, fortunes

> It is sometimes said that a man's philosophy is a matter of
> temperament, and there is something in this. A preference for
> certain similes could be called a matter of temperament and it
> underlies far more disagreements than you might think.
>
> (Ludwig Wittgenstein[1])

The great mid-twentieth-century folklorist, Archer Taylor, reflected over
the years on folk riddles, literary riddles, and occasionally poetry. Poetry
was a peripheral subject for him, but as usual his intelligence shone when
he wrote about it. "I . . . suggest," he says in a 1947 note, "that the essence
of riddles is closely allied to the essence of poetry and by offering this
suggestion [I intend] to lead you to read riddles more attentively and
more appreciatively." To be sure, "The subjects of most riddles prevent
any poetic emotions from arising." Taylor has in mind "such prosaic
objects as eggs, cows, vegetables, or household objects."

Such a limited view of the objects fit for poetry and "poetic emotions"
may sound squishy for so an excellent scholar. In fact, Taylor's instincts
are sure, if his poetic vocabulary is not, as witness the following remarks.

The example that has perhaps impressed me most strongly is a Uraon [Oraon]
riddle for birth and death:

> Clenched fists coming, open hands going.

. . . The inventor . . . has chosen a form that is entirely adequate even in a
translation that can preserve only the parallel structure of the original and must
sacrifice the rhythm of the verse. Like many pieces of great poetry, he states a
simple fact truthfully and at the same time is richly suggestive. We may see in the
scene an angry man appeased by his opponent. We may see a symbol of the fact
that a newborn child has the world in its grasp and a dead man's relaxed fingers
take nothing with him. ("Riddles and Poetry," 247)

---

1 *Culture and Value*, ed. G. H. von Wright, trans. Peter Winch (Chicago: University of Chicago
Press, 1980), p. 31c (1937).

Taylor's riddle depends less on any symbol than on close observation, like many remarkable tropes. An infant possesses an astonishingly strong grasp (try loosening your hair from a tiny fist). The language of hands is a longstanding literary and artistic language, which this riddle employs with great economy. (See Milton's language of hands in *Paradise Lost* or Keats's in "This living hand, now warm and capable." The language of infant hands is not common, though in the visual arts Käthe Kollwitz uses infant hands with fine effect, while her language of hands and death is unforgettable.)

In this example, Taylor senses what the late Israeli poet, Dan Pagis, would pinpoint more exactly. In 1986, Pagis published a study of some three hundred Hebrew literary riddles and their attached explication-poems, *Al sod hatum* or *A Secret Sealed*.[2] He later expanded one chapter in an article, "Toward a Theory of the Literary Riddle," where he develops an important argument:

While a riddle that has been solved ceases to be a riddle for the solver, it does continue to exist for him as another kind of poem. In fact, many riddles, especially those founded on paradoxical metaphors, become impressive poems when solved for the very reason that their metaphoric texture is now revealed. (p. 98)

It is this troping ability of a riddle that can transform it into poetry. In good troping, we are left with a vital figure of speech that stays with us and illuminates our days. The Sphinx's riddle remains alive for this very reason. To expand the remarks by Roberto Calasso already quoted:

The Greeks were drawn to enigmas. But what is an enigma? A mysterious formulation, you could say. Yet that wouldn't be enough to define an enigma. The other thing you would have to say is that the answer to an enigma is likewise mysterious. . . Resolving an enigma means shifting it to a higher level, as the first drops away. Oedipus was drawn to the Sphinx, and he resolved the Sphinx's enigma, but only to become an enigma himself. Thus anthropologists were drawn to Oedipus, and are still there measuring themselves against him, wondering about him. (*The Marriage of Cadmus and Harmony*, pp. 343–4)

---

2 The riddles were written from before 1650 to after 1850. A short summary in English precedes the Hebrew text; I am surprised that no one has yet translated *Al sod hatum*. Robert Alter kindly translated the chapter titles for me, as follows: 1. The Area and the Research. 2. The Origins of the "Shape" Riddle and the Bilingual Riddle. 3. The Riddle as a Social Genre. 4. The Social Function of the Shape Riddle. 5. The Entity of the Riddle-Shape and Its Appendices. 6. The Device of Bilingualism. 7. The Aramean, the Hebrew, and the Integration of the Solution-Word Incidentally. 8. The Body of the Shape Riddle. 9. The Entity of the False "Solution." 10. Patterns.

We might go one step further. We might substitute another figure of speech in place of Pagis's "paradoxical metaphors" and Calasso's "higher level," a figure related to metaphor in Aristotle, then co-opted as a species of allegory. It is, in fact, the trope of enigma itself: αἴνιγμα (*ainigma*) in Aristotle and the Greek grammarians and rhetoricians, *aenigma* in the Latin, and "enigma" or "riddle" in the English. It was commonly known as such for centuries to those who could read. When a riddle has a "metaphoric texture," we might say it is using the trope of enigma.

There is a surprising sentence about enigma in St. Augustine's treatise, *De trinitate*. Nobody, says Augustine, can really understand the word "darkly" (for him, *in aenigmate*) in Paul's text, "For now we see through a glass, darkly," unless they have learned about tropes. For, Augustine adds, *aenigma* is a trope, a species of the genus allegory (*De trin.* XV.9.15). He says this as a matter of course, not as some specialized or esoteric knowledge. We sometimes forget that professionally Augustine was a teacher of rhetoric, first in Carthage, then, in a breakthrough for him, as professor of rhetoric for Milan. He would have been interested professionally in the rhetoric of the sermons of Bishop Ambrose, the man who would later influence him so profoundly.[3] Following his conversion, Augustine's own preaching demonstrated his mastery of rhetoric in practice. He knew the literature in the field, and he knew what was at stake in disputes about tropes.

To start with Augustine is to approach the trope of enigma backwards, so to speak. It means that enigma is not solely defined rhetorically as a small puzzle, perhaps trivial, having nothing to do with large concerns. On the contrary. It is true that enigma may well be "of the piecemeal, eclectic type . . . dealing not with the global meaning of the work, but more often with specific elements within that work," as Robert Lamberton says of allegory (*Homer the Theologian*, p. 270). But enigma can also trope on "the global meaning" of a work, including the meanings of Scripture. So says Augustine. Paul himself used the names of rhetorical tropes – deliberately, Augustine assumed. Thus the use of a form of the word *aenigma* in Paul's text. (In fact, Paul's home, Tarsus, was known as a center for rhetorical study, and scholars have recently become increasingly interested in Paul's epistolary and other rhetoric.[4]) It is also true that

---

3 See Peter Brown, *Augustine of Hippo*, pp. 65–72, 83–4.
4 On Tarsus as a center for rhetoric, see Roberts, Introduction to Demetrius, *On Style*, pp. 278–80. Roberts mentions the rhetoricians Archedemus of Tarsus (130 BC) and Hermogenes of Tarsus (AD70). On Paul's rhetoric, see, e.g., Betz, *Plutarch's Theological Writings*.

virtually all classical rhetoricians ignore the broader implications of enigma as a rhetorical trope, though there is one exception. The large enigmas of Aeschylus and Sophocles belong properly to poetics, while classical rhetoricians bend their attention chiefly to political and forensic eloquence, and not drama, epic, lyric, or history. From time to time, classical rhetoricians offer examples of threatening enigmas, but they do not connect them with the great mysterious enigmas. Except for one. Demetrius links allegory and enigma with the Mystery religions and their "shuddering and awe" (*On Style*, II.101, see below).[5] In Christendom, it was Augustine who crucially connected small tropes of enigma with large enigmas, notably biblical ones. Not so much in his brief listing in the *De doctrina christiana* III, a locus classicus on literal and figurative reading where Augustine advises lettered men to study tropes in order to interpret scripture. Rather, in the extraordinary discussion in the *De trinitate* of Paul's "per speculum in aenigmate" ("through a glass, darkly"). In late antiquity, and down through the Latin Middle Ages and later,[6] the broader meaning is there for the taking in that master rhetorician, Augustine.

Biblical scholars, both Jewish and Christian, have touched on the Greek term *ainigma*. Hans Dieter Betz, for example, connects Paul's *ainigma* with Plutarch's use in his writing on the *mythos* of Apollo.[7] Guy G. Stroumsa has considered the term in the hermeneutics of early Christian writers on the scriptures, and how myth "turned into an *ainigma*, a riddle" ("Moses' Riddles," p. 230). More recently, he has argued for a "much broader meaning of *ainigma*" than that of "a literary trope," a meaning showing the "identification of myth as enigma" in Plutarch, Strabo, Porphyry and others (p. 272). Both Betz and Stroumsa are helpful for the larger sense of enigma in connection with myth and belief. But I want to argue as a literary scholar and critic for the rhetorical force of enigma as trope, following the lead of Augustine.

---

5 If Demetrius (whose dates are disputed, see below) was a contemporary of Plutarch, and also attached to the temple at Delphi, this remark would link Plutarch's use of the term *ainigma* with contemporary rhetorical analysis.

6 Writers of the twelfth and thirteenth centuries were interested in the term. See Dronke on Richard of St.-Victor, Guillaume de Conches and Abelard, cited in Lamberton, *Homer the Theologian*, p. 287n.

7 Notably in "The E at Delphi" (*Moralia*), on which see chap. 3 below; see also Betz, *Plutarch's Theological Writings and Early Christian Literature*, pp. 89, 161, and *Hellenismus und Urchristentum*, pp. 200–2. For an overview, see Classen, "St. Paul's Epistles."

When Augustine mentions enigma as a trope, he refers to "books that contain the doctrine of those modes of speech which the Greeks call Tropes." What books on "the doctrine" of tropes does Augustine have in mind? ("Doctrine" is how the doctrinally minded English translators rendered his *doctrina* in 1887, better translated as "teaching" or "instruction.") What books on tropes followed Augustine (354–430), and what do they say about the trope of enigma? Are they helpful for writers and readers? This chapter will follow the fortunes of enigma as trope from its beginning in Aristotle to its waning and virtual demise in the seventeenth century.

FROM ARISTOTLE TO DONATUS: TOWARD ENIGMA
AS CLOSED SIMILE

Ainigma as a rhetorical term was there from the start in Aristotle's *Rhetoric*, the first complete classical rhetorical treatise that we possess. The term moved into Latin rhetoric as *aenigma* with Cicero's *De oratore*, then Quintilian's *Institutio oratoria*, and continued through late classical and patristic into medieval, then Renaissance and seventeenth-century rhetorical writing.[8] Donatus, the fourth-century rhetorician and grammarian,[9] classified the trope of *aenigma* as one of the seven species of allegory in his *Ars maior*, thereby guaranteeing it longevity for centuries.[10] Enigma is variously defined nowadays, but it is not defined as a figure of speech.

"Allegoriae species sunt septem," Donatus says. "There are seven species of allegory." The seven are surprising, for our own rhetoric, however inchoate, does not classify irony and sarcasm this way: *ironia, antiphrasis, aenigma, charientismos, paroemia, sarcasmos, asteismos* (loosely: "irony, antiphrase, enigma, euphemism, proverb, sarcasm, and urbanity").[11] Donatus then proceeds to define the species, including *aenigma*:

---

8   The full texts of the *De oratore* and the *Institutio oratoria* were unavailable to medieval writers (Murphy, *Rhetoric in the Middle Ages*, "Epilogue: Rediscovery and Implications," pp. 357–63).

9   I have used the term "rhetorician" more often than "grammarian," because it is clearer to a modern reader. But *grammaticus* had the wider meaning for the ancients ("scholar" or "man of letters"). Demetrius, says Roberts, would rather have been called a *grammaticus* than a *rhetor* (Introduction to Demetrius, *On Style*, p. 277).

10 His *Ars minor*, the Latin grammar for beginners, "became so popular that the term 'Donat' or 'Donet' became a medieval synonym for 'primer' or elementary textbook" (Murphy, *Rhetoric in the Middle Ages*, p. 32).

11 For early senses of the term "irony," see Knox, *Ironia*. For a modern example of *asteismos* (urbanity), see Genette's analysis of "what classical rhetoric called *asteism*" in Proust (*Figures of Literary Discourse*, pp. 252–65).

Aenigma est obscura sententia per occultam similitudinem rerum, ut

> *mater me genuit, eadem mox gignitur ex me*

cum significet aquam in glaciem concrescere et ex eadem rursus effluere.[12]

(Enigma is a statement that is obscure because of some hidden likeness of things, for example, "My mother bore me, and soon was born of me," which means that water solidifies into ice, and then flows back out of it.)

This is neat and to the point. Donatus goes to the rhetorical heart of the matter in his word *similitudinem*: a likeness, even a simile, though one that is concealed (*occultam*). This is quite simply how a riddle works as a trope. A simile asserts openly that X is like Y. The trope of enigma makes simile into a question: *What* is X like? We might call the figure of enigma a closed or hidden simile.

The teaching treatises of Donatus may be for students, but they are the work of a master teacher, "the greatest teacher of that age" (OCD, "Jerome"). Donatus was the teacher of Augustine's contemporary, Jerome (c. 348–420), and Augustine would have known his work. When he began to think about St. Paul's enigma as trope, he paused over that word *similitudo*, "likeness."

But first, we need to look at what lay behind Donatus, starting with Aristotle. It is to Aristotle we turn for the first systematic study of rhetoric, while not forgetting Plato's philosophical and parodic treatments of rhetoric and style. The term *ainigma* as a figure of speech turns up three times in Aristotle's *Rhetoric* and once in the *Poetics*.[13] Aristotle's remarks present some of the standard questions about enigma to this day, at least *in nuce*. The *Poetics* commends writing that is clear but not mean, because it includes "strange words, metaphors, lengthened forms, and everything that deviates from the ordinary modes of speech." "But," warns Aristotle, "a whole statement in such terms will be either a riddle [ainigma] or a barbarism [barbarismos], a riddle, if made up of metaphors, a barbarism, if made up of strange words." He then describes how a riddle functions: "The very nature indeed of a riddle is this [ainigmatos te gar idea], to describe a fact in an impossible combination of words (which . . . can be done with a combination of metaphors); e.g. 'I saw a man glue brass on another with fire' (*Poetics* xxii [1458a], Barnes). An "impossible combination of words" is accurate, but not as helpful as the close linking of enigma and metaphor in the *Rhetoric*. (The answer to Aristotle's closing

12 *Donat,* ed. Holtz, p. 214; text, p. 672.
13 Liddell and Scott also list a verbal form of *ainigma* ("form guesses about it") used in *Meteorologica* 347a.6.

riddle, by the way, is the medical procedure of cupping, which was still practiced in the eighteenth century and may be seen in the film *The Madness of King George*.)

In *Rhetoric* III, Aristotle stresses the importance of metaphor in both poetry and the orator's prose. Metaphor above all "gives perspicuity, pleasure and a foreign air, and it cannot be learnt from anyone else. . . And, generally speaking, clever enigmas furnish good metaphors; for metaphor is a kind of enigma, so that it is clear that the transference is clever" (*Rhet.* III.ii.9, 12, Loeb). A riddle may mislead the listener at first, but only for the sake of good metaphor and wider knowledge: "For . . . the mind seems to say, 'How true it is! but I missed it.' . . . And clever riddles are agreeable for the same reason; for something is learnt, and the expression is also metaphorical" (*Rhet.* III.xi.6, Loeb). Some of Aristotle's reasons for liking good enigmas are germane simply because enigma is part of the large class of metaphor. Metaphors and perforce enigmas give perspicuity, pleasure, and the stimulation of fresh, unusual language.

Perspicuity or learning something is not a function much emphasized by later rhetoricians, partly because they commonly deal with small, joking riddles. Yet even the little flash of amusement at the answer to such riddles can be enlightenment, if only about the fun of language. But to this day, we seldom think of figures of speech as providing insight – a marked weakness of our own training in both logic and rhetoric. Pleasure remains a constant when effects of enigma are considered, though it is under-developed in many discussions. Among effects of enigma in Aristotle, the "shuddering and awe" of Demetrius do not appear, for he does not include this type of enigma. The example from Stesichorus on cicadas being forced to chirp from the ground (*Rhet.* II.xxi.8 and III.xi.6, and see below) is obviously a threat and meant to induce dread. But this is a particular example rather than a class of enigma.

Later rhetoricians will discuss all these effects in varying kinds and degrees. Christian rhetoricians, for instance, use the teaching function of riddles for instruction in Christian scripture and doctrine. This often results in riddle collections that are not riddles at all, but simply catechisms, as scholars have noted. The 460 "holy riddles" in Part II of Thomas Wilson's 1615 *Theologicall Rules* ("Aenigmata sacra, holy riddles") are 460 catechism questions. Similarly with certain questions in the Talmud and in midrashim that have been classified as riddles. As Pagis says, "The questions 'Who is strong, wise, rich?' are simply rhetorical, drawing the listener's attention to the direct continuation of the moral teaching. They really imply declarative sentences: 'This is a strong man – he who subdues his evil inclination.'"[14] Similarly in parts of Africa "from the Ivory Coast (Baulé) to Namibia (Ovambo)," as recorded by Grigorij Permjakov ("Logical Structure," p. 107). Similarly in Hindu teaching through "ethical riddles" (Sternbach, *Indian Riddles*, pp. 25–6). Riddles in catechism form become overtly didactic, but a strain of instruction exists in many a riddle apart from those used by pastors or rabbis or elders or priests teaching their flocks.

Another standard question raised by Aristotle is appropriateness, which looms large in most discussions of enigma as figure of speech. He includes it in a caution about metaphor, which must not be far-fetched, especially in an orator's speech (*Rhet.* III.ii.9). Riddles that mislead are justified only if they produce good metaphor. Parody riddles or what some call "catch riddles"[15] also mislead the listener into assuming some logical or language-game answer, only to find all expectations confounded by a ridiculous solution. These would be "far-fetched" riddles for Aristotle, not in themselves very interesting, even as quips. Amusement from them is short-lived, and their literary function minimal.

For the Latin world, down to the middle ages and beyond, Cicero (106–43 BC) was the dominant master rhetorician. Ciceronian rhetoric had political goals chiefly in mind, being markedly instrumental. The Ciceronian tradition, which viewed rhetoric as "a part of political science" and made "efficiency – that is, the procuring of results – the main criterion of good speech," was "practical rather than philosophical," with "rather mechanistic theories of style," and thereby differed from the tradition of Aristotelian rhetoric (Murphy, *Rhetoric in the Middle Ages*, pp. 8, 9).

Cicero's *De oratore* is an exception, being quite Aristotelian. Book III treats metaphor: its definition, its pleasure, what to avoid when using it. Cicero follows Aristotle in connecting enigma with metaphor, though his remarks on the effects of metaphor do not add substantially to Aristotle's, and his warnings about misuse are sterner ("avoid obscurity [obscuritas fugienda est]," III.xlii.167). In one way, Cicero set the later conditions for enigma when he noted a development of metaphor "in a chain of words linked together" (III.xli.166). This is the type of writing that he would

---

14 Pagis, "Toward a Theory of the Literary Riddle," p. 103. He is arguing against Georg Nador, *Jüdische Rätsel aus Talmud und Midrasch* (Cologne: J. Hegner, 1967).
15 E.g., "Why did the chicken cross the road?" Opie and Opie, "Catch Riddles," *The Lore and Language of Children*, pp. 82–4.

elsewhere call by the Greek term "allegory" ("hoc Graeci appellant
ἀλληγορία" [*Orator* 27.94]). Greek lexicons themselves cite Cicero as
among the earliest sources for the noun *allegoria*, that umbrella word
under which the much older term *aenigma* would later find shelter.[16] If
Demetrius belongs in the first century AD,[17] he, like Quintilian, is using a
term retrieved by Cicero and/or Philodemus from unknown sources, a
term that catches on.[18] Allegory's interest for enigma is that, by the third
century, enigma was classified as one species of allegory, and there it
stayed for centuries.

Quintilian, the great first-century rhetorician (35–95), is also of crucial
importance, though his work was lost for many centuries during the
Middle Ages. He follows the lead of Cicero and thereby Aristotle: "when
an allegory is more obscure [obscurior], it is called a riddle" (*Inst. or.* VIII.
vi.52). Like Cicero, he regards riddles as generally a blemish (he has
orators in mind). But he does note that poets use riddles, citing the
example from Virgil's *Eclogue* III.104–5:

> Dic, quibus in terris (et eris mihi magnus Apollo)
> tris pateat Caeli spatium non amplius ulnas.

(You'll be Apollo if you can tell me where / The land is, where the sky is five feet
wide. [Ferry])

The solution is uncertain to this day.[19] "Even orators sometimes use them
[riddles]," Quintilian adds. For riddles "are, after all, intelligible if you
can get someone to explain them" (VIII.vi.53) – a memorable defense.[20]

The merits of metaphor and enigma, as Aristotle discerned them (perspicuity, pleasure, and a change from common prosaic diction) are not

---

16 Liddell and Scott give Cicero, *Letter to Atticus* 2.20.3, for allegory as "veiled language," and his
    Orator 27.94 for allegory as "figurative, metaphorical language." For two other uses, see Lewis and
    Short.

17 The *OCD* ("Demetrius" 17) places him as late Hellenistic or early Roman, not born c. 350 BC, as
    traditionally dated; Roberts says AD 50–100, and that he is Demetrius of Tarsus, who takes part
    in Plutarch's "On the Cessation of Oracles" (Introduction to Demetrius, *On Style*, pp. 268–81).
    He notes affinities between the styles of St. Paul and Demetrius. *On Style* is the selfsame treatise
    whose opening sentence opens Marianne Moore's poem "To a Snail": "If 'compression is the first
    grace of style,' / you have it. Contractility is a virtue. . ."

18 Jon Whitman, who has traced the history of the term *allegoria*, notes the possibility that
    Cleanthes, a third-century BC Stoic, used the word earlier (*Allegory*, Appendix 1).

19 The riddle is not found in Virgil's model, Theocritus. See Clausen, *A Commentary on Virgil's
    Eclogues*, pp. 116–18. The favored solution is a reference "to one looking up at the sky from the
    bottom of a well or cavern" (Virgil, *Eclogues*, Loeb). See also Putnam, "The Riddle of Damoetas,"
    and Hardie, "Virgil: A Paradoxical Poet?"

20 Butler (Loeb) says "too obscure" for *obscurior*, but I think "more obscure" works better in
    context, as Quintilian is not forbidding enigmas, simply advising caution.

developed by Cicero or Quintilian, though both praise allegory. It is the hazard of riddling that is highlighted. A passing reference in Quintilian associates *aenigma* with *ambages* or ambiguity (VI.iii.51), and ambiguity continued intermittently to be associated with enigma, though it was not prominent.[21] Chaucer describes the term well: "ambages, / That is to seyn [say], with double wordes slye, / Swiche [Such] as men clepen [call] a word with two visages" (*Troilus and Criseyde* v.897–9).[22] Double words or two-faced words: this is how some riddles work – obscene ones for example.

Quintilian, by the way, distinguishes "figure" and "trope," as do others, but I am using the term "figure of speech" in the modern sense that includes "trope." Tzvetan Todorov has clarified this older usage, observing that figures (e.g., oxymoron, paradox) are different in kind from tropes (e.g., metaphor, synecdoche). He thus disagrees with the division of riddles (*devinettes*) into figures based on metaphor and figures based on paradox, because metaphor and paradox function on different planes ("Analyse du discours," 140). He is right. Literary paradox is a large term that includes a variety of effects and functions.[23] (Logical paradox is something other. For me, a so-called riddle working with logical paradox is not a riddle at all.) Todorov observes acutely that there is always a dissociation between figure and trope in the riddle, figure having to do with the thought-processes of riddle ("Recherches," 228n). It would be interesting to hear more of this, with examples. For instance, is figure-as-thought-process part of the wider implications of the trope of enigma, in contrast to its immediate answer? Is there more than one possible figure for some riddles, e.g., the Sphinx's riddle?

Tryphon (or Trypho), an important Greek grammarian at Rome who lived a little later than Cicero, appears to have been influenced by both Rome and Cicero, for he is somewhat stern about this trope. *Ainigma* is an artful frivolous expression, hiding its thought by obscurity or as something impossible. Nonetheless, he pays attention to this trope, distinguishing six types. The first two are defined by similitude, and Latin *similitudo* is a key term in Donatus later: (1) similarity (similitude using resemblances), and (2) opposition (similitude affirmed and then denied, as in the eunuch riddle of "a man and not a man").[24] The others work by

---

21 See Sonnino, *A Hand-Book to Sixteenth-Century Rhetoric*, pp. 13–14.
22 Chaucer took the term from Boccaccio, who in turn took *ambiguitas* from Isidore (*Etym.* 2.20) for his *Filostrato* (6.17.3). I am indebted to a reader for the journal *Rhetorica* for noting this.
23 See NPEPP ("paradox") and Colie, *Paradoxia Epidemica*, as well as chap. 5 on the question of true riddles.
24 The riddle (*griphos*) is ascribed to Panarces in Athenaeus X.452c; Plato refers to it (as an *ainigma*) in *Republic* v.479c. "'Tis fabled that a man and not a man / Saw and saw not a bird and not a bird /

(3) correspondence (a riddle on dice), (4) research (a learned or esoteric riddle), (5) homonymy (a punning riddle), and (6) what we would now call kennings or stock epithets.[25]

The major treatise of Demetrius, *On Style*, is of special interest, for he connects allegory and *ainigma* with the Mysteries. No earlier surviving rhetorician appears to have connected enigma with religious mystery in general or the practice of the Mystery religions in particular.[26] Or, for that matter, with the general ambience of the word "mystery" in Greek (*mysterion*).[27]

> There is a kind of impressiveness also in allegorical language. This is particularly true of such menaces as that of Dionysius: "their cicadas shall chirp from the ground" . . . Any darkly-hinting expression is more terror-striking, and its import is variously conjectured by different hearers. On the other hand, things that are clear and plain are apt to be despised, just like men when stripped of their garments. Hence the Mysteries are revealed in an allegorical form in order to inspire such shuddering and awe as are associated with darkness and night. Allegory also is not unlike darkness and night. (*On Style* 11.99–101, Loeb)

Enigmatic allegory like the cicada riddle[28] not only reveals the Mysteries appropriately, but also compliments the listener or reader. There are limits, to be sure: enigmatic allegory is fine, but an enigma like the cupping-riddle is judged too recondite.

The next notable step in the rhetorical history of enigma as figure of speech was schematization. Someone, somewhere, decided by the third century that there were seven types of allegory, one of them being enigma. But types of allegory had evidently been studied for a long time before that, at least among Greek grammarians. Philodemus, a contemporary of Cicero, "appears to know a distinction [of allegory]" into *ainigma, paroimia, eironeia, griphos,* and *asteismos* (Schenkeveld, *Studies,* p. 105). Lamberton notes that "Ps.-Plutarch (*De vit. Hom.* 70) offers

---

Upon a tree and no tree, and struck at it / and struck not with a stone and not a stone.'" The solution: a eunuch, a bat, a fennel plant, a bit of pumice (Panarces, in *Elegy and Iambus, with the Anacreontea,* trans. J. M. Edmonds [Cambridge, Mass.: Harvard University Press, Loeb, 1931], vol. II, pp. 78–9).

25 I am indebted to Wallace McLeod for kindly translating the Greek for me.

26 This is confirmed by Schenkeveld: "Demetrius is the only author who stresses the menacing element in the use of ἀλληγορία [allegoria]" (*Studies in Demetrius* On Style, p. 106n.).

27 See Burkert, *Ancient Mystery Cults,* Greek index, *mysteria;* Jaeger, *Early Christianity and Greek Paideia,* pp. 55, 132n; R. E. Brown, "Mystery (in the Bible),"and Prümm, "Mystery Religions, Graeco-Oriental"; Kittel, *Theologisches Wörterbuch,* "*mysterion.*"

28 For a reading of the cicada riddle, see chap. 10.

a definition linking it [allegory] to irony and sarcasm" (*Homer the Theologian*, p. 20n). Tryphon sketches the grouping that Donatus would later use, uniting allegory (along with enigma) and irony and antiphrasis (*Donat*, ed. Holtz, p. 214). Pollux (2nd cent.) also briefly mentions *ainigma*, distinguishing it from *griphos* (*Pollucis Onomasticon* 6.108). Among Latin rhetoricians, the earliest record of seven species appears to be in the *Artes grammaticae* of Marius Plotius Sacerdos, a third-century grammarian.[29] There he lists the seven species of allegory as *ironia, antiphrasis, aenigma* or *griphus, cacophemia, paroemia, sarcasmos,* and *asteismos.* He offers what will become the standard example, the "mater me genuit" riddle, as well as the next favorite example, Quintilian's choice, from Virgil (Sacerdos, *Artes*, p. 462). By the time of Donatus, *cacophemia* had given way to *charientismos,* and *griphus* as a partner for *aenigma* had disappeared. Otherwise the seven species would hold for centuries, and for this, Donatus must have been largely responsible.

Rhetoricians who are roughly contemporary with Augustine continue the classification of Donatus. Charisius and Diomedes repeat the seven types of allegory. (Diomedes illustrates *aenigma*'s use of the impossible with a riddle on Jocasta and her children-cum-grandchildren by Oedipus, an *aenigma* cited down through the Renaissance.[30]) An engaging fifth-century commentator on Donatus, Pompeius, deserves a star among Latin rhetoricians for mentioning the amusement of riddles, even if it is "amusement for children."[31]

Defining enigma as a closed simile may appear contrary to Aristotle's classification of enigma as a kind of metaphor. But the sharp contrast of simile and metaphor, and the idealizing of metaphor, is post-Romantic. Simile is better read as simply one type of metaphor, not as an inferior trope, different in kind. Nor does defining enigma as a closed simile run counter to Dan Pagis's sense of a metaphor that remains after a good riddle has been solved. On the contrary. Pagis has, in fact, rediscovered the old rhetorical trope of enigma.

---

29 The *Artes grammaticae* of Sacerdos is "the first large-scale Latin *ars* to survive in (roughly) its original form" (*OCD*, "Sacerdos"). Sacerdos is not commonly mentioned in rhetorical overviews, though Tomasek has recently quoted his work in *Das deutsche Rätsel im Mittelalter*, p. 75.

30 The Jocasta riddle is in Keil, *Grammatici latini*, vol. 1, p. 450. For more on Charisius, Diomedes, and Pompeius, as well as Julius Victor, see my "The Figure of Enigma."

31 See Dronke on the popularity of the "mater me genuit" riddle in both colloquial and hexameter form, as given in Pompeius (*Fabula*, pp. 20–1n); he cites Tupper, *The Riddles of the Exeter Book*, and others.

AUGUSTINE ON ENIGMA: THE FIGURATIVE AND THE FIGURAL

It is Augustine, the "prime figure in the . . . rhetorical history of this period [c. 400 to c. 1050],"[32] who develops the trope of enigma most remarkably in his *De trinitate*, during a discussion of the word, both divine and human (Book xv).[33] Here is the passage on Paul's *in aenigmate* in relation to tropes.

> The meaning of this addition, *in aenigmate*, is unknown to any who are unacquainted with the books that contain the doctrine of those modes of speech which the Greeks call Tropes [doctrina quaedam de locutionum modis quos graeci "tropos" uocant], which Greek word we also use in Latin. But there are several species of this kind of trope that is called allegory, and one of them is that which is called enigma. . .as every horse is an animal, but not every animal is a horse, so every enigma is an allegory, but not every allegory is an enigma. . .An enigma is, to explain it briefly, an obscure allegory, as, e.g., "The horseleech hath three daughters" [Prov. 30: 15].[34] (xv.9.15)

But then, after offering so small a conundrum, Augustine moves to the largest of enigmas: "as far as my judgment goes, as by the word glass [i.e., mirror] he [Paul] meant to signify an image [nomine speculi imaginem], so by that of enigma any likeness you will, but yet one obscure, and difficult to see through. . .nothing is better adapted to this purpose than that which is not vainly called His image [imago eius]" (xv.9.16). Augustine's "obscure allegory" follows Quintilian's phrasing, but his chief interest lies in the word *similitudo*, "likeness," Donatus's word for the trope of *aenigma*.

There follows an extraordinary meditation on Paul's text. It centers on what it might mean to say that mankind is made in the image of God, and also on human words, "that word of man, by the likeness of which. . .the Word of God may be somehow seen as in an enigma" (ibid.). Augustine emphasizes unlikeness as well as likeness: "But now, who can explain how great is the unlikeness also [dissimilitudo], in this glass, in this enigma, in this likeness [similitudine] such as it is?" (xv.11.21). "Wherefore, since we have found now in this enigma so great an unlikeness to God [dissimilitudo

---

32 Murphy, *Medieval Rhetoric*, p. 31.

33 *De trinitate* is a mature work, "begun by 399 and very probably completed after 422" (Stock, *Augustine the Reader*, p. 243, on which see also the problem of dating this work).

34 The AV and modern Vulgate give two daughters in Proverbs 30: 15. *Corpus Christianorum* (hereaser *CC* in the text) 50A, pp. 480–2.

dei] and the Word of God, wherein yet there was found before some likeness [similitudo] . . ." (xv.16.26).

Rhetorically, Augustine is putting pressure on the word "like" in a simile, and implicitly in an enigma. We tend to concentrate our attention on the A and B and X of a metaphor, and of a simile too. (A is like B in that both show X.) But the word "like" in this formulation, that is, the process of likening, we tend to slide over. (So also, we tend to slide over the "is" of metaphor, as both Northrop Frye and Paul Ricoeur have reminded us.[35]) Sometimes sliding over the word "like" is not important, though it's always useful to be reminded of our assumptions. Achilles is like a lion in that both show courage. In another culture where the lion was known for its tawny skin, for example, the simile would work quite differently. Still, lions can be observed, and likenesses can be drawn or inferred. But to say that man is made in the image of God, and therefore is somehow, in some kind or degree, like God – however faint or small or fallen the likeness – to say this introduces just that pressure I mentioned on the word "like" and the whole matter of "likeness." Similarly with the likeness – and unlikeness – of human words to the divine Word.

Imago dei: this is how humans were created in the biblical story. "Let us make man in our image, after our likeness," says the Deity at the birth of creation, in the first account in Genesis. "Faciamus hominem ad imaginem et similitudinem nostram," reads Augustine's Bible. "So God created man in his own image [ad imaginem suam], in the image of God [ad imaginem dei] created he him; male and female created he them" (1: 26–7, AV, Vulgate). How can humans be said to be like God or the human word like the Word of God? Augustine is not content to leave the phrase vague, or the words "like" and "likeness" as a catch-all. The result is a discussion of "likeness," hence of something like simile, where it gradually becomes clearer why the figure of enigma is so valuable for Augustine. Simile is explicable in logical terms. Even metaphor, for all its surprise and delight and cognitive power, does not include a hidden mystery to be solved later, as with this *similitudo*. Augustine is unwilling to move toward a mystical position, and unwilling to move too soon toward something like an *O altitudo*, an outburst of praise or hymn.

---

35 Frye, *Anatomy of Criticism*, pp. 123–5; Ricoeur, *La Métaphore vive* (1975), trans. Robert Czerny as *The Rule of Metaphor: Multi-Disciplinary Studies of the Creation of Meaning in Language* (Toronto: University of Toronto Press, 1977).

Not simile but enigma, then. If we define enigma as a closed simile, where the likeness is concealed until an answer is provided, that works very well in the light of Paul's text. For some things, to be sure, especially in the matter of *imago Dei*, we must wait for a final answer, accepting that here we know only in part (1 Cor. 13: 12). "This perfection of the image," Augustine goes on, "is to be at some time hereafter," and here he takes the step that links the smallest of riddles in the Bible to the enigma of everything:

> The good master [Paul] teaches us . . . that "with face unveiled" from the veil of the law, which is the shadow of things to come, "beholding as in a glass the glory of the Lord," i.e., gazing at it through a glass, "we may be transformed into the same image from glory to glory, as by the Spirit of the Lord" [2 Cor. 3: 18] . . . we shall see Him, not through a glass, but "as He is"; [1 John 3: 2] which the Apostle Paul expresses by "face to face" [1 Cor. 13: 12]. (*De trin.* xv.11.20–1)[36]

For the transition from now to then, Augustine draws together the three texts above, progressing from law (veiled) to grace (unveiled) to seeing fully. He moves to a wide sense of trope, as when we say A's work is troping on B's. So also, we may say that the New Testament is troping on the Hebrew Scriptures, using the trope of enigma. The Hebrew Scriptures are read as if they were "under the veil," to repeat Paul's expression. In typological terms, the Hebrew Scriptures become the Old Testament by this reading, wherein they shadow forth what stands clear in the New Testament. This is the first stage of seeing by means of a clearer *speculum* or mirror and in a less obscure enigma. The second stage will come at the end of time, to follow Augustine's text from John's Epistle, when all the Scriptures will be fulfilled in the sudden unveiling which is apocalypse.[37] Dante draws on the selfsame passage for his important invocation in *Purgatorio* 29. The end of enigma comes when it dissolves into the mystery of God, and is no more.

Augustine emphasizes, however, that human perfection is not the same as divine perfection, even at the end of time, in a fully redeemed state in the afterlife. He draws a strict line between Creator and creature, and maintains a sense of unlikeness between even perfected humankind and

---

36 Augustine is quoting the Vetus Latina (old Latin Vulgate) for 2 Cor. 3: 18 ("de gloria in gloriam"), which is more literal, rather than Jerome's and the Modern Vulgate, which retains "gloriam Domini" but changes to "a claritate in claritatem" (Marks, "Hollowed Names," 171n).

37 Pascal, writing on typology, follows Augustine's threefold progression, law, grace, and glory (*Pensées* nos. 642–91, esp. 643, p. 238), drawing on 2 Cor. Auerbach also notes this three-stage pattern in "Figura," p. 41. Apocalypse means "sudden unveiling" etymologically.

God. This may help to account for his attraction to the trope of enigma and rhetorical reading. If, like Clement of Alexandria, you wish to emphasize the likeness of human beings to their Maker or the merging of the redeemed with the divine, then you will prefer the mirror of Paul's text. Clement did just that: "Clement often omits the words ἐν αἰνίγματι [*en ainigmati*], although it is clear that he knew them to be part of the text; in this way the idea of the obscurity of the vision 'in a mirror' is mitigated."[38] But Augustine is emphatic that *aenigma* is a trope having to do with unlikeness as well as likeness. Rhetorical reading trains us to read how X is like *and unlike* Y.

Such readings as Clement's pull toward mystery rather than enigma. The relation of the two words, "mystery" and "enigma" bears watching, for their significations overlap but by no means entirely. In English-language lexicography, and no doubt elsewhere, distinguishing the two is a lexical test. "Enigma" virtually always implies an answer of some sort, whereas some mysteries elicit only wonder, even ecstasy. This is true of both transcendental and human mystery. "Mystery" in turn often shades over into "mystical." The distinction is worth keeping in mind because the Apostle Paul also uses the word "mystery" (*mysterion*) a number of times. Mystery is not a trope. Rather it lends itself to a process of symbol and symbolism.[39]

Frye observes that "Typology is a form of rhetoric, and can be studied critically like any other form of rhetoric." He argues that the rhetorical form of typology is metaphor, of the kind that identifies an individual with its class. Frye's rhetorical overview is synchronic. Theologically it is Messianic and teleological, and appropriately so. But I am interested in the unfolding of typology over time, for which the figure of speech known to the ancients as enigma is more appropriate. Frye separates "typology as a mode of thought and as a figure of speech." As a mode of thought, typology (he argues) leads to a theory of history.[40] But I prefer not to separate rhetoric from history in this way.

38 Mortley, "The Mirror and 1 Cor. 13,12 in the Epistemology of Clement of Alexandria," 120.
39 See M.-D. Chenu, *Nature, Man, and Society in the Twelfth Century*, ed. and trans. Jerome Taylor and Lester K. Little (Chicago: University of Chicago Press, 1968) from selections from *La Théologie au douzième siècle* (1957), for a detailed working out of the Augustinian use of sign and allegory (with allegory's later decline into rationalistic allegorizing), and also for the use of symbol by Ps.-Dionysius with its tendency to mysticism.
40 Frye, *The Great Code*, pp. 80, 87, 80–1.

FROM AUGUSTINE TO AQUINAS: PATRISTIC RHETORIC
AND BIBLICAL ENIGMA

Several of the early Fathers besides Augustine also knew about rhetoric, notably Jerome and Basil.[41] A number of patristic writers would continue work in the rhetorical tradition, usually in the exegesis of scripture, sometimes in enyclopedic works. Encyclopedias, those outlines of all knowledge, included the seven liberal arts, which began with the trivium of grammar, dialectic, and rhetoric, which last included the study of figures and tropes, which tropes often included that minor one, enigma.

Minor it may be in some ways, yet it was invaluable to some patristic exegetes of scripture. Here we need to distinguish exegetes who simply note the trope of enigma in passing, and those few for whom the trope is interesting in itself. The remarkable encyclopedists Cassiodorus (c. 480–575) and the even more influential Isidore of Seville (c. 560–636) followed Augustine's lead in providing biblical examples of tropes. Cassiodorus especially liked the trope of allegory, including its species, enigma. In his long commentary on the Psalms, enigma helps with obscure passages such as Psalm 96: 3–6 (AV 97) on fire, lightnings, hills, and heavens. "Quod schema," Cassiodorus concludes (though enigma is regularly a trope and not a scheme) – "This scheme is called enigma, that is, an obscure saying [obscura sententia] which says one thing and means another" (*CC* 98 [1958], p. 873). The examples do not strike a modern reader as riddles in the least. Like most patristic writers, Cassiodorus was uninterested in the workings of trope, that is, in the processes of imaginative, figurative thinking in the Bible. Enigma simply offered the possibility of allegorical reading for puzzling bits of scripture. We are beginning to see the double function of allegory in action: allegory as rhetorical figure and allegory as interpretive method. In Augustine the two functions are intertwined, but not in Cassiodorus or most patristic commentators.

In his great encyclopedia, Isidore of Seville includes a definition of enigma under allegory ("De tropis," 1.xxxvii), which comes with its usual seven parts. He succinctly rewords the definition of enigma, emphasizing its before-and-after metamorphosis:

---

41 A propos of Basil, it is worth remembering that Augustine lived only one generation after the Cappadocian fathers, and is said to share many characteristic features with a Greek patristic tradition. See Jaeger, *Early Christianity and Greek Paideia*, p. 101. Jerome, like Tertullian before him, observed that scripture itself mentions three tropes, *allegoria, parabola,* and *aenigma* (e.g., Jerome, Epistola 62.2, Migne, ed., *PL* XXII, col. 665).

Enigma is an obscure question that is hard to understand, unless it is explained [Aenigma est quaestio obscura quae difficile intelligitur, nisi aperiatur], for example this one (Judges 14: 14): "Out of the eater came forth meat, and out of the strong came forth sweetness," meaning that out of the mouth of a lion, a honeycomb was extracted. The difference between allegory and enigma is this: the force of allegory is double, as it shows something figuratively [figuraliter] under other things; enigma is a dark meaning, adumbrated through certain images [obscurus est, et per quasdam imagines adumbratus]. (1.xxxvii.26)

Isidore's introduction of the word *adumbratus* (adumbrated or fore-shadowed) is especially interesting because *adumbratus* is a standard typological term. (Old Testament types adumbrate or shadow forth the clear, revealed antitypes of the New Testament.) Enigmas work in a similar way, with their before-and-after, obscured-then-clear way of being. Whether Isidore has Augustine's connection of enigma and typ-ology in mind, or whether *adumbratus* is simply part of enigma's obscure ambiance, I do not know.

In any case, Isidore had found a neat little riddle, one like "Mater me genuit . . ." in that it sounds proverbial, though mysterious, and has a clear engaging solution. (But it is unlike in that no logic or wit will provide the answer.) For good measure, the riddle is part of a memorable story that includes a riddle contest and Delilah's betrayal. The riddle itself became famous, commonly acting in a proverbial sense.

The Authorized Version repeats the word "riddle" eight times in all in Judges 14. As it happens, the Vulgate does not use the word *aenigma* at all, but rather *problema* (following the Septuagint, on which see the Appendix) and *propositio*. Readers would not be reminded of their Augustine and the trope of enigma just here. At least, not because of the specific word. (Possibly, some version of the older Latin Vulgate I have not seen includes the word *aenigma* in Samson's story.) But Isidore is right; this is a classic example of the trope of enigma.

When Augustine chose a neat circumscribed example of enigma from the Bible, he chose a puzzling one on the horseleech and his daughters in Proverbs 30: 15. No solution is offered in Proverbs, so that the riddle challenged Augustine's wits as Samson's riddle did not. Augustine liked being his own riddle-master.

The Venerable Bede (c. 673–735) in his *De schematibus et tropis*, the first rhetorical handbook in England, drew his definitions chiefly from Donatus and his examples entirely from the Bible. The definition of *aenigma* repeats Donatus, word for word, but after the *ut*, Bede does not insert Isidore's engaging example of Samson's riddle. Instead, he cites a text from the Psalms, "Yet shall ye be as the wings of a dove . . ." (Ps. 68: 13). "Which means that," Bede goes on, "cum significet" (*CC* 123A [1971] pp. 162–3) – and once again the great usefulness of the seven species of allegory becomes apparent. As with Cassiodorus, so with Bede. The general method offered carte blanche for exegesis, and the figure of enigma for just those knotty, puzzling passages of Holy Writ that might vex a Sunday preacher. Bede's example is interesting because it is *not* especially perplexing. It demonstrates the allegorical method of reading scripture, including a fourfold reading – in Bede's hands, rather wooden.

Types of biblical examples in rhetorical handbooks and treatises: this is an interesting question in itself. Why did so few follow Augustine's example and offer Paul's enigma in 1 Corinthians 13: 12 as an example of the rhetorical trope of enigma? Not for teaching at an early stage, of course. And it would need guarding, as a sacred example not to be readily imitated. Nonetheless, as a master trope, why not?

Was it that many *aenigmata* in the Bible appeared out of bounds, perhaps too large and sacred? Consider, for example, God concerning Moses (Numbers 12: 8) and God or his messengers to Ezekiel or to Job or to John of Patmos. Or was it that some enigmas are unspecified (what Sheba and Solomon talked about) or else very general (how to acquire true wisdom)? For a long time, it appears, nobody was so bold as to include Paul's enigma as an example of the rhetorical trope of enigma. Very few even mentioned the text in connection with this trope.[42] Even in preaching manuals, where interest in the figure of enigma is practical (what do we do with Daniel and Ezekiel and the Apocalypse?) – even here, Paul's enigma does not enter into the discussions I have seen. It appears to be too large, too sacred, despite what Augustine specifically said. Not until the eighth century, and the work of the learned Rabanus Maurus, does Augustine's full argument about enigma reappear.

When, after four centuries, he took up Augustine's argument about enigma in the *De trinitate* xv, Rabanus repeated and expanded it, examining a number of texts with the word *aenigma* or its synonyms, as well as the words *parabola* and *allegoria*. He discusses Numbers 12: 8, where God says he does not speak to Moses in enigmas, and also Numbers 21: 27: "Wherefore they that speak in proverbs say, Come into Heshbon . . . " (AV). So also with Psalm 49: 4: "I will incline mine

---

42 This may readily be checked through the electronic Concordance to Migne, ed., *PL* (Chadwyck), using forms of *aenigma* and of *tropus.*

ear to a parable: I will open my dark saying upon the harp" (AV).[43] In the exegesis of 1 Corinthians 13: 12, Rabanus quotes Augustine word for word on the need to know about tropes. He thus passes on large swatches of the *De trinitate* on the trope of enigma, as seen in St. Paul.[44]

Three centuries later, Peter Lombard also quoted the *De trinitate* on Paul's famous text, and the *De doctrina christiana* as well (Migne, ed., *PL* CXCI, cols. 1662–3). Like Rabanus, he himself does not add any reflections on enigma as a figure. Still, some knowledge had been retrieved, knowledge of how a reader advanced beyond elementary-school rhetoric might meditate on a certain trope. Other rhetoricians around the watershed of 1200 (as Murphy calls it) sometimes include the trope of *aenigma*, even with lively examples, but do not further the work of Rabanus and Peter Lombard. Matthew of Vendôme mentions enigma (c. 1175), though others like Geoffrey of Vinsauf do not. To the usual examples of Virgil's riddle in *Eclogues* III.104–5 and "mater me genuit," Matthew adds a riddle of Narcissus. Alexander of Villedieu, in his well-known textbook, *Doctrinale* (1199), gives as his first example a riddle playing on *pater* and *mater*. The answer is Thomas à Becket, martyred in 1170 – especially striking as a contemporary and post-canonical example.

Augustine simply proved too difficult for many, I think. You have to know something about tropes (as he said) in order to comprehend what he might be getting at. Paul's famous chapter and text generated much commentary in both the Greek and Latin Fathers. But very few among the Latin Fathers take up Augustine's argument that we cannot read Paul's *in aenigmate* well unless we know something about rhetorical writing on tropes. Of those few, most simply mention the fact that enigma is a trope, sometimes giving a brief standard definition out of Donatus or Isidore. It is also true that the Carolingian reform of education stressed a knowledge of figures. "Since Holy Scripture is strewn with figures of speech [schemata, tropi et cetera], no one can doubt that every reader will the more quickly understand it spiritually the earlier and the more fully he has been instructed in the art of letters." This does sound like Augustine. It is from an edict composed about the time when Rabanus Maurus was born (780).[45]

---

43 The modern Vulgate gives as title to this psalm [48], "Aenigma prosperitatis iniquorum," and the corresponding verse reads: "Inclinabo in parabolam aurem meum; Aperiam in psalterio propositionem meam."

44 Migne, ed., *PL* CVIII, cols. 664, 723; CX, cols. 693–4; CXII, cols. 125–7.

45 Quoted in Curtius, *European Literature and the Latin Middle Ages*, p. 48. Curtius cites J. de Ghellinck's view that such educational reforms in the teaching of grammar and rhetoric led to the enriched Latin poetry from the later eleventh century onward.

Interestingly enough, Thomas Aquinas himself incorporates the rhetorical language of enigma into his discussion of 1 Corinthians 13: 12. He also provides the standard example.

the likeness . . . is double [similitudo . . . est duplex]; on the one hand, it is clear and open [clara et aperta], if it is in a mirror [in speculo]; on the other hand, dark and hidden [obscura et occulta], and then this way of seeing is called enigmatic [aenigmatica], for example, when I say: My mother bore me, and then was born of me. This is through a hidden simile [per simile occultum], and it is said of ice, which is born of frozen water, while water is born of dissolved ice. But [seeing] through a clear and open simile [per simile clarum et apertum] produces a different species of allegorical seeing.

(*Super I ad Cor. XI–XVI*, cp 13, lc4, *Omnia Opera*, vol. VI, p. 386)

But though Thomas gives the standard example of enigma in the rhetoricians and adapts the language of rhetorical definitions, he differs markedly from Augustine in saying nothing about tropes. One would like to hear more rhetorical discussion about hidden simile (*occultum*) in relation to clear and open simile (*clarum et apertum*). As Armand Strubel observes, Thomas shifts the discussion from Augustine's and Bede's rhetorical bases to the "allégorie des théologiens" – a move toward logical and comprehensive scholastic theory at the expense of reducing the space for literary creation ("'Allegoria in factis,'" p. 356).

RENAISSANCE ENIGMA, 1416–1605: RECOVERING GREEK AND RE-ORDERING TROPES

The explosion of knowledge and thought that defines the Renaissance included new knowledge and thought about rhetoric. So impressive is this rhetorical work that E. H. Gombrich judges the analysis of figures and tropes by Renaissance rhetoricians to be "perhaps the most careful analysis of any expressive medium ever undertaken."[46] European grammar schools, first in Italy and later in England, reflected such work. Grammar, dialectic (or logic), and rhetoric still marked the areas of verbal training, but a reformed curriculum taught new analytical techniques for reading and using rhetorical effects. "It is no mere coincidence that the early leaders of the Renaissance in various countries were schoolmasters and authors of school texts that were used internationally: Erasmus, Agricola, Vives, Melancthon, Sturm" (Joseph, *Shakespeare's Use of the Arts*

46 Quoted in Vickers, ed., *English Renaissance Literary Criticism*, p. 22n.

of *Language*, p. 8).[47] In the grammar schools of Tudor England, John Colet first introduced this rigorous curriculum in 1516, with the help of Erasmus. It trained students for long hours in Latin grammar, logic, and rhetoric, with reading and imitation of prose and poetry, both classical and biblical. (Upper-form students "must first be grounded in the topics of logic through Cicero's *Topica* before [they] could properly understand the one hundred and thirty-two figures of speech defined and illustrated in Susenbrotus' *Epitome*" [ibid., p. 9].) A little Greek was added for good measure. It is very probable that Shakespeare attended such a school.

Classical manuscripts lost to the Middle Ages were re-discovered, among them a complete text of Quintilian's *Institutio oratoria* in 1416, found "in a most miserable dungeon [in teterrimo . . fundo]" of the monastery of St. Gall in Switzerland. Quintilian provided a rationale for the use of rhetoric and a coherent educational program, and the *Institutio* was rapidly integrated into rhetorical method and practice. The discovery "made it possible, for the first time since the collapse of Roman schools in the fifth century, for a reader to view rhetoric as part of an integrated social system built around a respect for civic life." It marked "the beginning of a new European outlook on rhetoric" (Murphy, *Rhetoric in the Middle Ages*, pp. 358–61).

For the fortunes of enigma as trope, two aspects of this rhetorical revolution are important beyond the lively and far-reaching educational reform: the use of Greek language and literature, and the changing taxonomy of tropes.

If 1416 is a significant date, 1453 is a crucial one. "With the Greeks who emigrated after the fall of Constantinople (1453) there came to Italy the whole literary tradition of the Byzantine East." Werner Jaeger adds that "the works of the Greek fathers were its choicest part . . . the number of manuscripts of their works in the library collections of that period surpasses by far those of the classical authors" (*Early Christianity and Greek Paideia*, pp. 100–1). To move from the exclusively Latin medieval rhetoricians in the West to Renaissance rhetoricians who also read Greek is to enter another world. While Latin remained the *lingua franca* of literate Europeans, some Renaissance scholars read Greek literature widely, and quoted it extensively. The eminent classical scholar and Reformation humanist Joachim Camerarius (1500–74) included among

---

47 Joseph draws on Baldwin, *William Shakspere's Small Latine and Lesse Greeke*. The name of Vossius can be added to the list, thereby extending it into the seventeenth century (see Rademaker, *Vossius*, pp. 188–206). See also Joseph, ibid., p. 3 and *passim*.

his 150 works translations into Latin of Herodotus, Sophocles, Lucian, and other Greek classics. The recovery of Greek meant that the word αἴνιγμα (*ainigma*) itself now began to appear, often with its etymology from *ainos*. But Renaissance rhetoricians were not much exercised over etymology. It is the scope of illustrative examples, including many from Greek literature, that is so remarkable. With this literature, including patristic writing, comes a fuller sense of wit and humor, paradox and play, the *ludus* of experience. This rich imaginative fare provided suggestive patterns for reading and practicing the trope of enigma.

One Greek riddle from Hesiod's *Works and Days* (1.40) now begins to appear regularly. Mosellanus (Schade), in his short 1529 *Tabulae de schematibus et tropis*, includes it, citing it as a very apt example (*aptissimum*) of enigma. He gives it as quoted by Plato. Hesiod's saying seems as much a proverb as a riddle, but a proverb that Plato decides to explain: "Was not their error that they forgot the solid truth of Hesiod's saying that 'the half is often more than the whole'? He meant that when it is useful to get the whole, but the half is sufficient, then the modestly sufficient, the better, is more than the disproportionate, the worse."[48] Melancthon refers to the same enigma in his *Elementorum rhetoricae* (1531), Cassander cites it without mentioning Plato (1553), and it turns up in 1550 in Sherry without derivation or explanation,[49] so that it must have been familiar by mid-century. Whoever recovered Hesiod's riddle-cum-proverb provided a neat, appealing example, no doubt a welcome variation on the standard "mater me genuit . . ." Not that this long-familiar riddle of ice and water disappeared, any more than Virgil's riddle from *Eclogue* III did. Or any more than Isidore's choice, Samson's riddle, did. Pagninus, for example, cites Samson's riddle in "De figuris" (1526) and is brisk. Again, the brevity implies that this example too must have been very familiar.[50]

Camerarius's discussion of the trope of enigma in his 1540 *Elementa rhetoricae* is one of the best during this period. "De aenigmatis" is one of only twenty-two chapters, most of which concern larger rhetorical matters, as we now judge them (verisimilitude in narrative, different ways of treating stories, etc.). Was it his wide acquaintance with Greek writing that stimulated this interest in the rhetorical functions of

---

48 Plato, *Laws* III.690.d–e, trans. A. E. Taylor, *The Collected Dialogues of Plato*, p. 1285.
49 "Aenigma. Sermo obscurus, a riddle or darke allegorie, as: The halfe is more then the hole."
50 Incidentally, the edition of Pagninus's *Institutiones Hebraicae* that I saw at the Houghton Library at Harvard was printed backwards, something of an enigma in itself. Was Pagninus following Hebrew practice?

enigma? Perhaps. In his first chapter, on Aesop's fables, he classifies some of them as enigmas, thereby widening enigma's scope to include narrative plotting and proverbial conclusions: "Sometimes these [fables] are set out more obscurely, and are what are called enigmas: the compiling and interpreting of which the ancients favored greatly, yet always as a kind of practice where play is woven into teaching by means of clever things [ludus quidam ingenii in doctrina retextus est]." As with Aristotle's perspicuity or Augustine's learning, the teaching function of enigma is valued; the ludic is a possible teaching tool, not a frivolity. Camerarius's definition of *aenigma* does not echo standard Latin authorities, though it does use the important word "similitude." Rather, he emphasizes what is implicit and ambiguous in this trope: "often as enfolded. . . in ambiguity in the form of a similitude [frequenter veluti implicantur. . . ambiguitate in forma similitudinis]."

Oracular riddles and prophecy interest Camerarius greatly: how Croesus consulted the oracles at Delphi and elsewhere, how the Pythia prophesied to him in hexameters and in riddles, what riddle was given to Philip of Macedon by the oracle, how others consulted the oracles too (Herodotus 1.47–57, 63–8, 84–5). He also mentions oracular dreams, and refers his reader to Cicero on the gods. This citation of oracles is an extension of *aenigma's* meaning not emphasized since Demetrius' *On Style*, itself newly prominent in the Renaissance. What Camerarius omits is as interesting as what he includes, for his examples are solely classical. His readers would easily move to the parallel of Christian prophecy, dreams, and riddling sayings in scripture, but Camerarius himself retains the separation of silence.

The new knowledge of Greek language and literature wonderfully enlarged the sense of enigma's workings, especially in the hands of someone like Camerarius. But it did not challenge the fortunes of enigma as trope in principle. The re-ordering of tropes did. The longstanding seven species of *allegoria* began to break their boundaries early in this period. Irony, for example, had never been neatly contained under allegory. (See Dilwyn Knox's *Ironia*.) Allegory itself had begun to develop its two distinct functions centuries earlier, the rhetorical function and the interpretive function. Melancthon, for one, mentions both functions, distinguishing them by calling interpretive allegories "sacred" and listing the fourfold categories (literal, tropological, allegorical, anagogical). The trope of enigma remained linked to allegory, but now more often as a lesser type than as one of seven species. In earlier rhetoricians, such as Melancthon (1531), Rivius (1552), and Cassander (1553), *aenigma* remained a species of allegory, or it was associated with allegory (Richard Sherry [1550, 1555], Minturno [1559]).[51] More often, *aenigma* was simply an *obscura allegoria*. The routine seven species of allegory had ceased to be routine.

The species themselves began to vary in kind and number, as Renaissance rhetoricians considered new taxonomies. Donatus had taught fourteen major tropes in his *Ars maior*, twenty-eight in all if the species are included. But during the sixteenth century, new tropes multiplied, and various rearrangements of tropes and schemes began to take hold. As the number of rhetorical types grew by leaps and bounds in the enthusiasm of Renaissance invention, less attention was paid to enigma as trope. Some rhetoricians still saw its importance, but others were perfunctory.

The influential traditional Ciceronians from the earlier sixteenth century, Erasmus, Melancthon, and Mosellanus, all treat the trope of enigma. The latter two, however, discourage its use in oratory without paying much attention to its strengths. Erasmus's 1514 discussion in his influential *De copia* (cap. xviii), though brief and general, is much to the point. He follows Aristotle and Cicero in saying that allegory is "a continuous metaphor," and hence has some of the force of any metaphor. He follows both Aristotle (on perspicuity) and Augustine (on exercising the mind), when he asserts that writing should make readers "investigate certain things and learn." He is short and sensible on the use of enigmas by orators. (They should restrict enigmas to an audience of learned men, though enigmas are appropriate for a general audience when in writing.[52]) Too bad that Melancthon and Mosellanus did not heed him more. Their contemporary, Despauterius, adapts Donatus, also citing Quintilian and Diomedes. He is defensive: Donatus does not count *aenigma* as a blemish (*vitium*) but lists it among the tropes. An ongoing minor dispute about the trope of enigma – blemish or not? – is evident.

Susenbrotus, whose 132 figures of speech were part of upper-level work in grammar schools, includes the trope of enigma in his 1540 *Epitome troporium ac schematum*. It is defined as "an obscure allegory, concealed in wrappers of words, as well as hidden sense [*obscura Allegoria, &*

---

51 The first rhetorical work published in English, Leonard Cox's *The Arte or Crafte of Rhetoryke* (c. 1524), did not include the trope of enigma.
52 See also Edgar Wind on Erasmus and Politian concerning *aenigmata* in his *Pagan Mysteries in the Renaissance*, rev. edn. (New York: Norton, 1968), p. 164.

verborum involucris tecta, atque velata sententia].” The usual “mater me genuit” example follows. Allegory itself is “evidens, clara, & manifesta” while enigma is “somewhat obscure and latent [subobscura ac latens].” Once again, the trope of enigma is part of the language of biblical typology. (The contrast of “latent” with “manifest” is standard language for latent Old Testament types and their fulfilling patent New Testament antitypes.) Susenbrotus mentions the many enigmas in the Prophets and the Apocalypse, then adds that enigmas are “also in pagan writings [Ethnicos scriptores] about the gods and in the Sibyls’ oracles.” His mind is running on the great riddles and on enigmas associated with prophecy. He does not choose amusing or historical riddles. The schoolbook example of “mater me genuit” is useful as an introduction, but there may be larger matters at stake in this figure, notably in the interpretation of scripture. Susenbrotus moves to them at once. Was that why English grammar schools liked his *Epitome troporium ac schematum*?

An irreverent senior grammar-school student, stuffed with Susenbrotus’s 132 figures of speech, might have relished a thought of Rabelais. The closing chapter of Book 1 of *Gargantua and Pantagruel* (1532) is titled “A Prophetic Riddle” and contains a long verse enigma. Gargantua deciphers it as a well-trained Susenbrotus student would: “‘This is not the first time that men called to the Gospel faith are persecuted. . . [The meaning is] the continuance and steadfastness of Divine Truth.’” And so forth. The accompanying monk will have none of it. “‘By St. Goderan! That is not my explanation. The style is like Merlin the Prophet. You can read all the allegorical and serious meanings into it that you like. . . For my part, I don’t think there is any other sense concealed in it than the description of a game of tennis wrapped up in strange language.’” And he proceeds to unravel all 108 lines (“‘The waters are the sweat,’” and so on) (1, pp. 160–3).

In mid-century, Petrus Ramus (Pierre de la Ramée, 1515–72)[53] challenged the hold of traditional grammar, logic, and rhetoric, pressing for re-ordering and simplifying the categories, as well as the relations between the three disciplines. Battles between Ramists and more traditional rhetoricians, such as the Ciceronians listed above, were vigorous. (“As for Erasmus and those who clove to his views. . .” said the Ramist Gabriel Harvey, “I not only scorned them as perfectly infantile, but even pursued them with hate as utter enemies.”[54]) In his 1544 *Rhetorica*,

53 He died in the Massacre of St. Bartholomew, where “odium academicum and odium theologicum combined to ensure his death” (Seaton, Introduction to Fraunce, *Arcadian Rhetorike*, p. xn).
54 Quoted in Howell, *Eighteenth-Century British Logic and Rhetoric*, p. 251.

Audemarus Talaeus (Omer Talon, d. 1562) proposed simplifying things by classifying tropes under the four major tropes of metonymy, irony, metaphor, and synecdoche (the same four tropes that Kenneth Burke designates as "master tropes" in *A Grammar of Motives*). *Rhetorica* was closely based on the rhetorical views of Talaeus's friend and colleague Ramus, and was widely reprinted and translated.[55] Under *Metaphora*, the headings in Talaeus include *Allegoria*, followed by *Aenigma*, which is given equal billing: "If allegory is a little more obscure, it is called enigma." An astute distinction is made between enigmas that are genuine tropes, and so have affinities with metaphor, and those that are not. Genuine tropes have a "transferred or figurative meaning" (pp. 33–4). Talaeus is intelligently drawing *aenigma* back into the fold of metaphor.

Unfortunately for the fortunes of enigma, later editions were often shortened and omitted this trope. It is not to be found in two influential English translations, Dudley Fenner's *The Artes of Logike and Rhetoricke* (1584) and Abraham Fraunce's *Arcadian Rhetorike* (1588), though the full entry is adapted and expanded in the French version by Antoine Foquelin (1557). In any case, the discussion of this trope in the *Rhetorica* of Talaeus is brief. It is discussed more often and more fully by the traditionalists than by the Ramists. Those that Sister Miriam Joseph calls figuralists take the greatest interest.

The influential, mysterious J. C. Scaliger (the first chapter of a recent study is called "Lives and Works") focuses on terms, distinctions, and categories in *Poetices Libri Septem* (1561). He takes no interest in oracles or, for all that, biblical examples. There is nothing innovative here, though Scaliger's learning is impressive, and his gathering of inter-related terms is valuable. Book III (cap. 84, under allegory) expands on Book 1.57, mentioning myth, enigma, griphus, and the eunuch riddle, as well as Pollux on the humor of enigma. The association of enigmatic speech with the whole process of story-telling is emphasized by including myth.

About the time of Shakespeare's first plays, two important rhetorical treatises appeared in England, George Puttenham's *Art of English Poesie* (1589) and the enlarged edition of Henry Peacham's 1577 *Garden of Eloquence* (1593). Both take an interest in enigma.

Puttenham, like Peacham, gives the essentials for the trope of enigma, but with flamboyant flourishes: "allegorie [is] but a duplicitie of meaning

---

55 For the tangled publishing history of the *Rhetorica*, see Seaton's excellent Introduction to Abraham Fraunce's *Arcadian Rhetorike*, p. xiiin, drawing on Charles Waddington.

or dissimulation under covert and darke intendments. . . [even in the] common proverbe or Adage called Paremia," and so on through all the species, in similar dramatic fashion (chap. 7). The "dissimulation" of figurative language continues in chapter 18, "Of sensable figures altering and affecting the mynde. . ." Allegory begins to sound like a character out of Spenser ("Allegoria, or the Figure of false semblant"), while "Enigma, or the Riddle" is even worse:

We dissemble again under covert and darke speaches, when we speake by way of riddle (Enigma) of which the sense can hardly be picked out, but by the parties owne assoile, as he that said:

> It is my mother well I wot,
> And yet the daughter that I begot.

Meaning by it the ise which is made of frozen water, the same being molten by the sunne or fire, makes water againe.

Readers of Puttenham would certainly know how to take "covert and dark intendments" or "covert and darke speaches," things that take place, so to speak, under the covers. (The joke is familiar from the sparring of Beatrice and Benedick in *Much Ado about Nothing*.) All the more so when Puttenham goes on to offer a riddle with a double sense, the more obvious answer being indecent.

My mother had an old woman in her nurserie, who in the winter nights would put us forth many prety ridles, whereof this is one:

> I have a thing and rough it is
> And in the midst a hole Iwis:
> There came a yong man with his ginne,
> And he put it a handfull in.

The good old Gentlewoman would tell us that were children how it was meant by a furd gloove.

"Some other naughtie body," says Puttenham with a straight face, "would peradventure have construed it not halfe so mannerly. The riddle is pretie but that it holdes too much of the Cachemphaton or foule speach and may be drawen to a reprobate sence." As Alan Bennett says (of tennis, not riddles), this is an example of "the English at their usual game of trying to have it both ways" (*New Yorker*, 22 May 1995, p. 74).

On the topic of rude or indecent riddles, Peacham is straightforward in *The Garden of Eloquence* (1593), unlike Puttenham's nudge-nudge wink-wink:

The Caution.

In this figure, regard ought to be had, that the similitudes be not unfit, strange, or unchaste. If they be. . . unchaste or uncleane, they make it odious, by leading of the minde to undecent things, of which sort there be many of our English riddles.

No high and heavenly visions, no precious metals and stars, appear in Puttenham's examples of *aenigma* as they do in Peacham's (see below). One wonders if the Reverend Mr. Peacham and Mr. Puttenham ever met.

Rhetoricians largely ignore rude riddles, though not entirely. Presumably readers of rhetorical handbooks know that a sense of decorum comes with the territory. Cicero does advise against gross metaphors: "one must avoid all unseemliness [omnis turpitudo]. . . [or] an ugly idea [deformis]" (*De or.* III.xli.164, Loeb). Demetrius mentions low riddles; his judgment is short and crisp: "Jests of this kind are ugly and suited only to the lower varieties of drama" (*On Style* III.151, Loeb). Quintilian dismisses coarse riddles, "certain metaphors which fail from meanness [humiles]. . . or they may even be coarse [sordidae]" (*Inst. or.* VIII.vi.14, Loeb). Rude riddles mostly have to do with sexual activity. Folklorists are familiar with this favorite type, whose focus and function are different from the transformations of the ice-water riddle. Rude riddles aim to make the riddlee blush or hoot or smirk. Some Elizabethan riddle collections cheerfully included obscene riddles. They could claim that the French began it all (see chapter 10).

Peacham knew what was at stake for his purposes in the trope of enigma. In the 1593 *Garden of Eloquence,* he gives a standard definition and four examples (a candle, fire, a tree, a book), then moves at once to biblical examples.

Ænigma: a kind of Allegorie, differing onely in obscuritie, for Ænigma is a sentence or forme of speech, which for the darknesse, the sense may hardly be gathered.

> Examples: I consume my mother that bare me. . .

This figure although it be full of obscuritie, and darknesse yet it is found in the sacred Scriptures both in speech and in visions, the dreames of Pharaos chiefe Butler, and chiefe Baker, and also Pharaos owne dreames were Ænigmatical, whose significations Joseph expounded.

Also the vision of Nebuchodonozor was Ænigmatical, & most aptly proportioned in the similitudes . . . The meaning whereof Daniel by divine grace expounded.

Peacham follows the line of Susenbrotus in continuing to list biblical examples of enigma. It is an implicit defence of the trope. The use of this figure, he says in standard fashion, "is more convenient to Poets than to Orators," then adds, in contrast to Puttenham, that enigma is "more agreeable to high and heavenly visions." More than that, the very darkness of enigma can give "delectation." It is this point that marks the dividing-line between rhetoricians who appreciate enigma and those who do not.

Sometimes notwithstanding darknesse of speech causeth delectation, as that which is wittily invented, and aptly applyed, and so proportioned as that it may be understood of prompt wits and apt capacities, who are best able to find out the sense of a similitude, and to uncover the darke vaile of Ænigmatical speech. For indeede this figure is like a deepe mine, the obtaining of whose metall requireth deepe digging, or to a darke night, whose stars be hid with thicke cloudes.[56]

John Smith was a follower of Peacham in his 1657 *The Mysterie of Rhetorique unvail'd*. He adopts Peacham's definition of the trope of enigma, and ends with a series of scriptural examples: Joseph's dreams, Nebuchadnezzar's vision in Daniel, Samson's riddle, the rod of Jesse (Isaiah 11: 1, 2), and various biblical references (Ezek. 17: 2, Prov. 26, etc.), where "you shall find divers riddles and dark sayings, and the same opened and explained in the demonstration of the same Spirit of wisdom they were proposed" (p. 89). Smith was explicit on the connection of enigmas and wisdom literature. But he came too late. By mid-century, the tide of rhetorical debate had turned against enigma.

Gerardus Joannes Vossius (1577–1649) was another Camerarius, learned, widely read, articulate, and thoughtful. His numerous Greek quotations are printed in the original, then translated into Latin. He expanded his 1606 *Institutions oratoriae* in later editions,[57] and is especially valuable for his literary judiciousness. Enigma is for him a species of allegory, though not one of the longstanding seven. Proverb (*paroemia*) is the only other species remaining from the old taxonomy; apologue and myth are added. (Scaliger also works with these terms, differently ordered.) The etymologies and definitions are clear, and the terms are inclusive. (Vossius lists *griphos* and *scirpus* as well; his *Etymologicon linguae latinae* includes long and useful entries on them.) His examples cast a wide net.

---

56 Howell oddly regards this kind of analysis as more "husks" than kernel, a "mechanical routine" (*Eighteenth-Century British Logic and Rhetoric*, p. 134). He evidently had no acquaintance with the workbench of a good poet.
57 *Institutiones oratoriae* (1609), etc. See Rademaker, *Vossius*.

One citation is from Augustine's *De civitate dei* III.xvii, a scornful attack on ambiguous oracular answers that can be true either way.[58] The closing quotation from Heliodorus notes how dreams as well as oracles can help us decide about events.

But it is his discrimination about tropes that marks Vossius as a remarkable rhetorician. Samson's riddle is not a true riddle, he judges, because the Philistines did not know about Samson's dead lion. He then adds that Samson's riddle actually signifies the resurrection of Christ. This bit of typology works well enough (honey from a dead body, life out of death), though Vossius does not go on to claim it as a class of Pauline enigma. Plato's eunuch riddle also does not qualify as a riddle proper. A true riddle must be rhetorically a trope, and no trope is present in some riddles. Homonyms for example are not tropes. He is quite right. Homonymns are schemes in the first instance, though schemes are capable of suggesting tropes. Vossius does not mention schemes or go on to develop a distinction between tropes and schemes. Nonetheless his insistence on the metaphoric power of a true riddle places him in the line of the major rhetoricians of enigma, from Aristotle and Augustine down to Dan Pagis in our own day.

ENIGMA EMBATTLED: SIMILITUDE VERSUS OBSCURITY

The principle of the trope of enigma, derived from Donatus and prevailing down through Thomas Aquinas and later, did not at first materially change in the Renaissance. Enigma may still be defined as a closed simile, as in Donatus. ("Aenigma est obscura sententia per occultam similitudinem rerum.") But the definition began to shift, and the crucial word *similitudo* is seen less often. Where Donatus is quoted or paraphrased, a form of *similitudo* does appear: thus in Despauterius (1537), for example. Camerarius, while not quoting Donatus, knows the importance of the word: "ambiguitate in forma similitudinis" (1540). Peacham's first edition of *The Garden of Eloquence* in 1577 does not use the word at all, but his much-enlarged 1593 edition repeats it three times in the entry on enigma. Nicholas Reusner's remarkable collection, *Aenigmatographia* (2nd edn., 1602), opens with Donatus and Diomedes almost verbatim: enigma is an "obscuram sententiam, per occultam rerum similitudinem"

---

58 Augustine takes this from Cicero's *De divinatione*; for an analysis, see Augustine, *Concerning the City of God against the Pagans*, ed. David Knowles, trans. Henry Bettenson (Harmondsworth: Penguin, 1972), p. 144n.

(L. G. Gyraldus, "Praefatio," pp. 3–4). Henri Estienne, in his later *Art of Making Devises*, speaks of an "occult similitude of things" in enigma, again citing Donatus and Diomedes. Though not a rhetorician, he provides a rhetorical base for enigmas, following the method of Tryphon: "These are commonly derived from Similitude, Dissimilitude, Contrariety, Accidents, History, Equivocall termes, and other figures of Rhetorick" (p. 6).

But when the idea of a similitude is downplayed, and this trope's obscurity or concealing or veiling becomes its major or even sole characteristic, trouble may be brewing for enigma.

Attacks by plain-style advocates against a highly ornamented, baroque, perhaps overdone style sometimes developed into attacks on all tropes. Aristotle's warnings about commonplace diction were ignored. The story is familiar enough. In the second half of the seventeenth century, all this would metamorphose in England into a prolonged struggle between plain speech and rhetorical speech, often defined as ornamental. The struggle is not new in principle, but the force of historical events, notably the emergence of science in the modern sense, deepened the old tension: there were attacks by the Royal Society (notably by Thomas Sprat). Our current view of rhetoric is still marked by this dispute.[59]

Disputes over enigma are, of course, related to the whole matter of reading the mysteries of the Bible, including Protestant reading of the Bible in the vernacular. Peacham, for one, includes a warning about enigma: "Lastly, that this figure be not used to seduce by obscure pro-phecie, as oft it hath bene to many a mans destruction, nor amongst simple and silly persons, which are unapt and unable to conceive the meaning of darke speech, and therefore a vanitie." Biblical enigma had its dangers. On a broader front, a number of seventeenth-century clerics defended tropes, including the trope of enigma. The Jesuit Cyprianus Soarez gives a very brief definition along with Virgil's riddle in his *De arte rhetorica* (1609). Baltasar Gracián treats it in his *Agudeza y Arte de Ingenio* (1648). Abbé Cotin compiled a collection of riddles, *Recueil des Enigmes de ce temps* (1655, 1661). The Jesuit Claude-François Ménestrier collected and analyzed riddles, enigmas, and related phenomena in his *La Philosophie des images énigmatiques* (1694), though fully half the book warns against dangers to the faithful. It is easy to see why the clergy might have been apprehensive about attacks on tropes. Their own sacred scriptures work

59 See Shuger, *Sacred Rhetoric*, pp. 56–7 and *passim*.

with tropes, and, as Augustine said centuries before, distinguishing literal and figurative is a *sine qua non* in reading the Bible. Empirical knowledge at any given time and place is not a helpful yardstick for reading parts of the Bible, or, for that matter, for reading *Don Quixote* or *Alice in Wonderland*. Useful as one kind of test, it fails with the wrong kind of evidence.

The homiletic demands of a pastoral vocation, from the early *ars praedicandi* to the present, present a special case. The case is not as easy as we might at first suppose, as witness St. Augustine's congregations, who delighted in intricate word-play. Disputes in the early Church about preaching center on the same question, as do rabbinical discussions about the Hebrew Scriptures and their true congregation. Still, there is one crucial difference from the Royal Society polemic. Jewish and Christian exegetes commonly insist that the Hebrew Scriptures or the gospel are available to all, according to their capacity. They are open and not hidden. No special inner light is guaranteed to the learned or the adept or the insider. Christian enigma cannot be esoteric in any essential way. Taking up Erich Auerbach's argument about the plain style of preaching, the *sermo humilis*, Stroumsa notes the difference between Christian enigma and Hellenic or Alexandrian religious enigma. While some matters of Christian doctrine are difficult, and understood only by a few, "it is only the level of teaching (and not of the doctrines themselves) which should differ in accordance with the level of understanding of the listeners" ("Moses' Riddles," p. 242, citing Augustine). The same is true of Judaic doctrine, as Meir Sternberg argues: "The Bible has many secrets but no Secret, many levels of interpretation but all equally accessible" (p. 49).[60]

While the gospel is available to all, Augustine, for one, stresses the responsibility of literate and learned people to pursue subtler points. In the English Renaissance, however, "sacred rhetoric is a polemical issue, possibly even a heresy," to follow Debora Shuger. She quotes a 1610 English version of Augustine's *The City of God*: "'*Augustine* makes *Paul* a Rhetorician. Well it is tolerable, *Augustine* saith it: Had one of us said so, our eares should ring of heresie presently, heresies are so ready at some mens tongue ends'" (p. 3). The downfall of rhetoric from Augustine's or Rabanus's or Camerarius's day is amazing.

---

60 For apparent esoteric riddles in the Bible, e.g., in Numbers 12: 8 or corresponding examples from Mark and John, see chap. 10, citing Ashton, "Intimations of Apocalypse," pp. 383–406.

If the plain-speech advocates mistrusted tropes, how especially they must have mistrusted the trope of enigma. Far from being a trope of revelation, it now appeared as a trope of obfuscation, doubly damned. At the same time, posing or writing riddles gradually became a popular pastime in England and in France. When written, they often appeared in verse, mostly overlong and tedious verse, a diversion for a leisure class. Molière attacked them in the person of Trissotin (that is, *trois fois sot*, thrice a fool [Pléiade edn.]) in *Les Femmes Savantes*. Trissotin was based on Abbé Cotin, the riddle-compiler, and, *pace* Molière, author of an intelligent introduction to the collection. Still, battle-lines were drawn, and feelings ran high. They were still present some 120 years later during the fad for charades in France and England, and no doubt elsewhere.

Enigma also became prominent in another area, mystic, alchemical, symbolic, cabbalistic. We are no longer in the world of the rhetoricians when we look for definitions of enigma in Michaelus Maierus (*Septimana Philosophica, qua Aenigmata Aureola*, 1620),[61] Athanasius Kircher (*Oedipus Aegyptiacus*, 1652–4), or Jacob Masen (*Speculum imaginum veritatis occultae*, 3rd edn., 1681). They belong in a different world to a greater or lesser degree. To be sure, enigma has always appeared regularly in writing on the occult, where its rhetorical function is not emphasized, though rhetoric could be useful. In 1517, for example, the occult philosopher Johann Reuchlin suggested in his *De arte cabalistica* "that Pythagoras' doctrine on the transmigration of souls was an ironia which had often been misinterpreted literally rather than as an enigma through which Pythagoras had intimated to initiates a secret unknown to his age" (Knox, *Ironia*, p. 44). He had been trained in rhetoric.

The teaching of rhetoric would decline after the seventeenth century, and the knowledge of tropes and figures would all too often dissolve into vague belles lettres. In part, the rhetoricians brought this on themselves by over-elaborate, ever-dividing categories. Shakespeare mocked such pedantry, notably in the figure of Holofernes in *Love's Labour's Lost*. Yet Shakespeare himself was trained in a rigorous school of rhetoric. Later rhetorical commentary would flail or meander helplessly among unordered figures of speech. Though rhetoric is unavoidable when we use words, good training in its benefits and hazards virtually disappeared. Figures of speech became "mere words."

---

61 On Jung's use of Maier, see Willard, "The Enigma of Nicolas Barnaud," p. 203.

AGAINST ENIGMA: "MERE WORDS"

I began with Augustine, and that is where I shall end, even though many of his presuppositions about reading are very different from ours, to say nothing of those who preceded him.[62] But he remains a crucial rhetorical thinker to this day. In the *De trinitate* xv, Augustine moves from a small trope right over into reading Old and New Testament typologically. He moves, that is, from figuration in the sense of tropes and schemes to the figural or historical, which is also read by means of trope. What interests me is that for Augustine, there is no break between the figurative and the figural, when both are rightly read. As moderns, we read figural interpretation (i.e., interpretation of sacred history) as a question of belief, past or present. The realm of figuration, tropes and schemes, we instinctively assign to the imagination. Even if writers conceive of the imagination (or its historical equivalent) as in the hands of God (thus Dante or Herbert or Milton, for example) – even then, we tend to read their tropes as if they were apart from the story of belief constructed by these writers.[63] It takes an effort of the historical imagination to take seriously all the tropes of a poem, tiny to immense, figurative and figural both. It takes an effort "to cut the Gordian knot of a true fiction," to quote Teodolinda Barolini.[64] Yet by following Augustine's lead, we can hear how one of the great rhetorical minds is telling us to read. For Augustine, to repeat, there is no break between figurative *aenigma* and figural *aenigma* when both are rightly read, and the figural is for him historical.

Rhetorically, this suggests we pay attention to such recent arguments as Jeanne Fahnestock's on figures of speech as epitomes of action in her *Rhetorical Figures in Science*. "While most people have a practical lexicon of the emotions that can be expressed by certain figures, they do not have a corresponding lexicon for lines of argument . . . The figure, then, is a verbal summary that epitomizes a line of reasoning. It is a condensed . . . rendering of . . . a relationship that constitutes the argument and that could be expressed at greater length" (pp. 23–4). For Augustine, the trope of enigma in the horseleech's-daughters riddle can epitomize in little the same condition epitomized in St. Paul's all-encompassing enigma. For a

---

62 See Peter Brown, *The Making of Late Antiquity, passim.*
63 Compare, on this question, Veyne, *Did the Greeks Believe in Their Myths*, especially the concept of the "constitutive imagination."
64 Teodolinda Barolini, *The Undivine Comedy: Detheologizing Dante* (Princeton: Princeton University Press, 1992), p. 13.

modern example of the trope of enigma functioning in a similar way, we might look at Wallace Stevens' phrase "the obscurer selvages" (see chapter 9).

Augustine's move also cautions us against our near-automatic use of "mere" in the phrase "mere words." Someone like Tertullian, who insisted bluntly on the historical actuality of key events in scripture, as against their figurative sense, might encourage us to follow an either-or way of reading,[65] history versus figuration. Tertullian argues forcefully in the *De resurrectione carnis* (On the Resurrection of the Flesh) that the biblical account of the resurrection cannot be read as figurative. To quote the chapter heading (21) in a standard English translation: "No mere metaphor in the phrase Resurrection of the Dead." The trouble is that I find nothing whatever in Tertullian's text to justify that word "mere." How easily we slide over it, with our modern assumptions about figuration – "modern" here including the 1869 editors of the Tertullian texts in the English-language *Ante-Nicene Christian Library*. To be sure, Tertullian does not seem much interested in rhetorical thinking. Scripture offers both literal and figurative language. The crucial passages, says Tertullian, are clear, straightforward, and historically true.

But the figures, the *figurae verborum*, are no less true in their way. *Verborum* does not imply "mere" words. How could Tertullian or Augustine think such a thing of scripture, any more than the great rabbinical commentators on the Hebrew Bible could think such a thing? We are the ones who have demoted figurative language, not they. We are the ones who casually add "mere" to this day, hardly noticing what we are saying. In the distinction between *figurae sententiarum* and *figurae verborum* (figures of sayings or content, and figures of words), the *figurae sententiarum* refer to something historically true. But the *figurae verborum* are not "mere" words.[66] *Figurae verborum* are figures that are just as true in their own way. The principle is essential for reading all literature. Todorov made the point in the seventies, but it bears repeating, so strong is the inertia of stereotyped language. "Tropes (i.e. verbal allegory) are all just as 'factual' as factual allegories themselves."[67]

---

65 See Zeeman, "The Schools Give a License to Poets," arguing against an either-or way of thinking in a related context.

66 For modern examples of the habit of saying "mere words," even when unjustified, see pp. 374–6 in my "The Figure of Enigma." The habit infests translations.

67 Todorov, "On Linguistic Symbolism," 111–32.

If all words are in the hands of God, as Augustine assumed, and the human word is enigmatically a likeness (and unlikeness) of the divine Word, this includes both figurative and figural language. Figurative and figural both turn on *like* – how something is like and unlike something other – so that Augustine's mind leaps to the greatest question of the word "like" for him: the likeness of mankind and its words to God (and the unlikeness), in that mankind is made in the image of God. That great enigmatic pattern of likeness, the *imago Dei*, governs all the smaller likenesses. The story of like and unlike, we might say, is the story of the Bible.

The smaller likenesses of this earth include tropes like similes and enigmas. If we could figure out, and figure forth, the main likeness, the main "as," then the rest would follow. Augustine's main likeness or "as" is far from the thinking and imagination of Wallace Stevens. Yet for Augustine, it is also true that

> . . . the theory
> Of poetry is the theory of life,
> As it is, in the intricate evasions of as,
> In things seen and unseen, created from nothingness,
> The heavens, the hells, the worlds, the longed-for lands.
> ("An Ordinary Evening in New Haven" xxviii)

It is true, that is, in scriptural writing. (Not that Augustine would likely use that word "evasions," even if "evasions" has a benign as well as a pejorative sense for Stevens.) Post-canonical writing is another matter, to be sure, and modern readers read with a difference. But the principle of likeness or similitude remains. Some sense of what is at stake in the reading of tropes matters to this day in everything that we read and think.[68]

---

68 Brian Vickers observes that "rhetoric has had a great revival in critical esteem over the last fifty years." He adds that "those who have only studied it superficially still tend to dismiss the figures and tropes as mere itemizations of linguistic effects" (*English Renaissance Literary Criticism*, p. 19).

CHAPTER 3

What is the shape of the riddle?
enigma as masterplot

What is the shape of the sibyl? Not,
For a change, the englistered woman. . .
(Wallace Stevens, "The Sail of Ulysses," VIII)

Of course, not all masterplots turn out the way St. Paul's does. I have taken the word "masterplot" from Terence Cave's discussion of the place of *anagnorisis* or recognition in plotting, he in turn adapting it from Peter Brooks: "what Peter Brooks will call the 'sacred masterplot', the plot whose outcome is guaranteed by a providential order." Brooks has in mind the Christian masterplot, the dominant masterplot in the West over much of the last two millennia. Cave identifies the "masterplot for all these [types of recognition plots] . . . [as] constituted by the typological and anagogical interpretation of the Bible, which retains its power as a paradigm at least until the late seventeenth century" (pp. 145, 230). Enigma, in the Pauline sense, holds as in a nutshell the Christian history of the world and time; its resolution points toward eternity. Here, as Augustine argues, the trope of enigma shows the entire shape of Scripture.

But there were other masterplots earlier, of some authority, and yet others compete nowadays. The riddler Humpty Dumpty puts the case very succinctly: "'The question is,' said Humpty Dumpty, 'which is to be master – that's all'" (*Through the Looking-Glass*, chap. 6). Other masterplots use other kinds of emplotment, take other kinds of shape, yet still have some claim as masterplots. These various shapes may be plotted as if on a graph: upward toward a felicitous ending, downward toward a dark ending, with or without a definite ending, and so on. There are at least five distinct shapes I can ascertain, and I want to suggest thereby a taxonomy or anatomy of enigma as masterplot. In central examples for all five, the word "enigma" figures prominently in the large, commodious sense outlined above. In all five, however, enigma comes with different assumptions, notably about the kind and degree of resolution to its implicit questions. What sense of an ending prevails in these various masterplots? What kind of answer does each enigma assume? Here are the five:

1 Pauline, as in the enigma in St. Paul's first Epistle to the Corinthians, 1 Cor. 13: 12.
2 Oedipal or more precisely Sphinxine, as in the riddle of the Grecian Sphinx.
3 Cyclic, as in one reply to the enigma of E at Apollo's temple in Delphi, as given in Plutarch.
4 Random, as in Epicurus, or in some deconstructionist enigma.
5 Sibylline or long-term, as in Wallace Stevens's use of "enigma" in his late work.

There may be more types or fewer, depending on ways of distinguishing. For example, a cyclic pattern (type 3) in certain ways combines types 1 and 2, Pauline and Sphinxine, and some taxonomists might make it an auxiliary to them. Or a sixth possible type might be mystic and sporadic, as in Walter Benjamin's Messianic moments in time, though this is to move the word "enigma" toward the domain of "mystery." Then too, Paul is drawing on the antecedent *hida* (riddle) in the Hebrew Bible. What would be the shape of *hida* as masterplot based on Jewish tradition, if such a masterplot could be ascertained? There are also later developments over the centuries, as in more secular versions of a Pauline masterplot, for example, in some Enlightenment thinkers.

I am taking a strongly synchronic approach, and so I want to sound a preliminary note of caution. The focus of this book is on enigma in its literary context and thus on the realm of imaginative literature, but the realm of individual lived experience and the realm of history (history as writing, not history as event) also offer stories with plots. All three realms interact with each other, while also retaining their own distinctions.[1] In many ways, the largest challenge of any masterplot is how to translate it into the here and now, the specific temporal story or specific trope. This is true of individual experience, and of writing, whether sacred

---

1 The word "fiction" may be used of both imaginative and historical writing. Paul Ricoeur prefers to use it only in connection with imaginative writing. Otherwise two different meanings of the word "fiction" become blurred: (1) "a synonym for narrative configurations"; (2) "an antonym to historical narrative's claim to constitute a 'true' narrative" (*Time and Narrative*, vol. 1, p. 64).

or secular writing, whether history or imaginative literature or other. For one thing, as Paul Ricoeur rightly points out, no "universal superplot" (*Temps et récit,* vol. III, p. 332, n. 15) can account for all narrative variations, a useful reminder for the term "masterplot." The "plot whose outcome is guaranteed by a providential order" (Brooks's phrase) may be sufficiently enigmatic to individuals uncertain of exactly what providence is guaranteeing for them. One recalls Samuel Johnson, so remarkably sure of himself on most grounds, and so remarkably unsure on the question of his own salvation, devout as he was. Yet while multiple plots exist within human time, Pauline-type enigma nonetheless posits one sure end. How all these various patterns of enigma translate into day-to-day life or specific narrative and trope is a matter that will concern us later.

FIVE MASTERPLOTS

The first two types of enigma are two master riddles that are contraries: Pauline riddling and Oedipal or Sphinxine riddling. Pauline riddling appears in the text already quoted, "For now we see through a glass, darkly; but then face to face." Thus the Authorized Version, drawing on the Geneva Bible. Tyndale's 1534 translation reads: "Now we see in a glass even in a dark speaking," "a dark speaking" being another common translation of the Latin word *aenigma* at the time. It is close to Luther's 1522 translation: "Wir sehen jetzt durch einen Spiegel in einem dunkeln Wort." As noted, the original Greek uses a form of "enigma" (*en ainigmati*) and the Vulgate repeats the word in its Latinate form: "Videmus nunc per speculum in aenigmate, tunc autem facie ad faciem." The text is so familiar that I need hardly observe that this kind of enigma will end in revelation, in light, in the dispersal of cloud, in the clarifying of the obscure, in the answering of the inexplicable, in the straightening of the labyrinthine, and so on through many a well-known trope for enigma. Light comes with our death, in God. Such lexis or troping of the riddle is standard, though not always noted as such. Donne offers a compendium: "Poore intricated soule! Riddling, perplexed, labyrinthicall soule!" (Sermon XLVIII, 1628/9, here describing an atheist). This is Edward Young's type of riddle:

> Nothing this world unriddles but the next. . .
> 'Tis Immortality decyphers Man,
> And opens all the myst'ries of his make.

Without it, half his instincts are a riddle;
Without it, all his virtues are a dream.
     (*Night Thoughts* VII.466, 507–10)

As with Donne, the lexis of riddle is used against the opponent of
Christianity: "Retract, blasphemer! And unriddle this" (ibid., 974). Such
language is common in homiletic or didactic or hortatory writing.

So dominant is Pauline enigma as masterplot that we still tend to think
in its terms, especially its tropes, even as we alter their context. Yet it is
important to exercise our historical imaginations and attempt to recreate
Paul's own context. Paul himself was building on a tradition of Jewish
hida. His famous text echoes Numbers 12: 8: "With him [Moses] will I
speak mouth to mouth, even apparently, and not in dark speeches; and
the similitude of the Lord shall he behold." But the books of the Hebrew
Bible do not end with a vision of Apocalypse. What happens to thinking
about enigma as masterplot when we return to the Hebrew Bible, setting
aside Paul's type of enigma? We move away from the Book of Revelation,
the Apocalypse, as the moment of closure for the scriptures, and hence to
a different sense of how an end-directed plot might work. Judaism, in
adhering to Scripture, retains the sense of enigma resolved by God,
together with the troping of light, full knowledge, and so on, existing in
the mind of God. Does this come closer to type-1 (Pauline) enigma or to
type-4 (Sibylline or long-term) enigma? Would it constitute another type?
Or does the question depend on how acute an eschatological or messianic
sense is at work in any given Jewish tradition? Of course, Jewish apoca-
lypticism was (and is) one strain only within Judaism. A sense of the end
of time does not press in the same way on Jewish theology and rabbinical
teaching. Does a prevailing sense of God as ultimately good offer a
common answer to Pauline and Hebrew enigma? Paul himself would
insist on differentiating, of course.

In Christendom, a sense of the end of time was a given, and occasionally acute. This is true not simply for primitive Christianity, but intermittently for centuries. In 1746, for example, Newton's successor at
Cambridge, William Whiston, expected the Millennium in twenty years
time, though such active millenarianism became less and less usual
through the eighteenth century.[2] Eugen Weber has recently shown in

---

2 At the same time, as Keith Thomas also observes, intellectual curiosity and a desire to put things
   in order motivated astrological work of the time. Some astrologers' observations about patterns of
   behavior stand to this day, though the notion of astrological causation now remains only a
   popular superstition (*Religion and the Decline of Magic*, pp. 387–8).

his *Apocalypses: Prophecies, Cults, and Millennial Beliefs through the Ages*
how the sense of an apocalyptic ending to an age or to all human
history appears to be a constant in human apprehensions of time in the
West. For a literary context, one good starting-point is Frank Kermode's
The Sense of an Ending. The Apocalypse, as Ricoeur puts it in his analysis of Kermode, "offers the model of a prediction that is continually
invalidated without ever being discredited." In more recent times, he
adds, this "has given rise to a truly qualitative transformation of the
apocalyptic model . . . from the last days . . . to become a myth of crisis"
(*Temps et récit*, vol. II, p. 23).

Pauline-type riddling provided an authoritative masterplot in Christendom for centuries, and not only for the verbal disciplines. Newton's
prolonged work on the enigmas of the Book of Revelation was not inimical
to his work in physics but consistent with it. Both were part of the same
master enigma. John Maynard Keynes saw this very clearly:

Why do I call him a magician? Because he looked on the whole universe and all
that is in it as a *riddle*, as a secret which could be read by applying pure thought
to certain evidence, certain mystic clues which God laid about the world. . . He
regarded the universe as a cryptogram set by the Almighty – just as he himself
wrapt the discovery of the calculus in a cryptogram when he communicated with
Leibnitz . . . He *did* read the riddles of the heavens. And he believed that by the
same powers of his introspective imagination he would read the riddle of the
Godhead, the riddle of past and future events divinely fore-ordained, the riddle
of the elements . . . (Keynes, "Newton, the Man," p. 366)

Nor was Newton atypical.

It is still difficult for some of us to appreciate the continued fascination of great
European intellects of the seventeenth and eighteenth centuries with the
interpretation of Daniel and the Apocalypse. . . Many of the scientists and
apologists of science in Newton's circle . . . tried their hands at the exposition of a
prophecy, and the number of such works composed in England during Newton's
adult life is staggering. (Manuel, *The Religion of Isaac Newton*, pp. 88–9)

Riddles remain today but that once-authoritative biblical masterplot
has radically altered, if not largely vanished. When scientists think about
the riddle of the universe (and they still do), what masterplots do they
choose? How do the plots differ one from another? How far do they
influence the practice of science, if at all, for example, the choice of
specific experiments? The shape of a masterplot certainly bears on bioeth-
ics, on arguments about artificial human reproduction or cloning or
human genetic manipulation. The problems of a masterplot also pressed

on Newton and other scientists of the seventeenth and eighteenth centuries. Newton's work on the riddles of the Book of Revelation and the riddles of the Book of Nature was indeed entirely consistent, but what happened when there was a conflict in the evidence? In Newton's day, another plot was slowly forming around the enigmas of the natural world.[3] How, and how far, is the masterplot of Christendom an influence, when Christian doctrines are altered, thinned, or abandoned over the years, and challenged from within and without?

There is also a question whether a masterplot exists in viewpoints such as Enlightenment thinking or Marxism. It is a commonplace to say that both envision earthly versions of the Christian apocalypse without the accompanying upheavals (or with their own kinds of upheaval), a move to a new heaven and a new earth in one. The "enlightenment project," as described by the French *philosophes* and Kant, envisages following the Ariadne thread through our present labyrinth (the trope is D'Alembert's) and out into full daylight. This future realization may grow out of the end of things as envisaged by Paul and prophesied by John of Patmos. The vision of enlightenment remains, along with the sense we live in an enigma. But salvation (to call it that) is through the right use of reason, and revelation will come on this earth in a gradual process of learning. The end result is also different: perfecting mankind and living in the highest human community. Enlightenment does not come in a sudden uncovering. It does not entail a different order of existence, and the end of time as we know it. These things may lie in the future for some Enlightenment thinkers, but meanwhile, "Know then thyself, presume not God to scan; / The proper study of Mankind is Man." Pascal's *Pensées* lie behind the sixteen lines that follow this well-known couplet from Pope's *Essay on Man* (ii.1–18). The sixteen lines end: "Sole judge of Truth, in endless Error hurl'd; / The glory, jest, and riddle of the world!" But Pascal ends with mankind as the "gloire et rebut de l'univers" (the glory and the refuse [or scum] of the universe). No language of riddles enter Pascal's powerful sentences on mankind. It is in the study of Scripture, not in the study of man, that *l'énigme* appears in Pascal.[4]

---

3 Newton's secret alchemical experiments remind us that "the change [from an animistic to a mechanical conception of the universe] was not accomplished overnight" (Thomas, *Religion and the Decline of Magic*, pp. 171–2, and see pp. 151–73 on prophecy).

4 The OED cites Pope as the earliest example of "riddle" used of mankind as a whole. Pascal, *Pensées*, no. 434, "Quelle chimère est-ce donc que l'homme? . . . Juge de toutes choses. . .. de l'univers" (p. 173).

Marxist desire for an earthly paradise without a celestial one is a materialist reversal of Hegelian spiritual progress toward the absolute. Stéphane Mosès outlines how three men who grew up in Germany in the twenties variously repudiated a Hegelian and teleological type of masterplot. Instead, each conceived a view of history as discontinuous or broken. One was Benjamin, and the other two were Franz Rosenzweig and Gershom Scholem.

> This vision of history cannot be reduced to the teleological model that is typical of Western historical thinking, at least under the religious form of a Christian theodicy, which permeates history [immanente à l'histoire] in the secularized form of a dialectic of Reason. (Mosès, *L'Ange de l'histoire*, p. 24)

What about Benjamin's end-directed Messianic thinking? Benjamin separates it from secular regimes. If he desires revolution, he is also clear that "the Kingdom of God is not the *telos* of the historical dynamic," as he defines it. Rather than the goal, it is the finish of things from the standpoint of history. Insofar as individuals work in the Messianic tradition, it means suffering rather than happiness. A non-sacred order, Benjamin wrote, should base itself on a goal of earthly happiness.[5]

Oedipal or Sphinxine riddling moves downward to darkness. It is Pauline riddling turned upside down. Not the Epistle to the Corinthians, but the man from Corinth, Oedipus. Paul's enigma reverses Oedipal / Sphinxine riddling. Oedipus begins by answering the famous riddle of the Sphinx. If you don't answer her riddle, she kills or eats you, a graphic rendering of the inside-outside logic of the trope of enigma. (See chapter 8.) But Oedipus has more than one riddle to answer, and the story of *Oedipus Rex* ends in darkness and blinding. Paul reverses the inside-outside logic. We already see as *in aenigmate*, within an enigma, but then we shall see face to face. Sight, not blindness; the riddle solved by God, not by us; light eventually though not in this life. Greeks innately disliked what was obscure and riddling, to follow W. B. Stanford. Such "distrust and uneasiness . . . were relics of the dark days when the utterances of Sphinx or Oracle or Seer were too often things to be dreaded" (p. 24). Paul, I assume, is designing a Christian enigma that moves out from Mosaic *hida* or riddle, and moves against a Sphinxine-type enigma as well as the dark oracular enigmas of the Mystery religions. It also moves against the Apollonian Delphic oracles, at a different angle of opposition.

---

5 "Theologico-Political Fragment," pp. 312–13. He also praises Bloch's *Spirit of Utopia* for repudiating "with utmost vehemence the political significance of theocracy" (ibid.).

Is it possible, incidentally, that Paul had in mind the connection of Corinth with famous riddles, when he used a form of the word *ainigma* in his letter to the church at Corinth? He did have in mind a text in Numbers (Num. 12: 8), but why echo it just here, to this congregation? This is the only use of the word *ainigma* in his epistles, and in fact in the entire New Testament. (It appears in the Septuagint nine times, translating the Hebrew word *hida*.) The congregation at Corinth was largely Greek, so that an allusion to the Oedipus story would rouse their interest and make a valuable point. On the other hand, Paul might be echoing Plutarch's use of the word *ainigma* at the temple at Delphi, without any thought of the famous Oedipus riddle or other Corinthian associations with riddling.[6]

It is, I think, precisely because the Sphinx's riddle and biblical riddling constitute two contrary types that Dante juxtaposes them in the closing canto of the *Purgatorio*. In her apocalyptic warnings to Dante, Beatrice sets him a riddle of her own, modeled on those in the Book of Revelation. "And perhaps my dark tale, like Themis and the Sphinx . . . this hard enigma" (*Purg.* 33.46–50, Sinclair). So also Milton contrasts the Sphinx's riddle and biblical enigma at the end of *Paradise Regained*. Satan, having vainly tempted Christ, falls in a prolepsis of his final fall:

> And as that *Theban* monster that propos'd
> Her riddle, and him who solv'd it not, devour'd,
> That once found out and solv'd, for grief and spite
> Cast herself headlong from th'*Ismenian* steep,
> So struck with dread and anguish fell the Fiend.
>
> (IV.572–6)

Northrop Frye describes "the opening colloquy between Satan and Christ in the first book [as] already a clash of oracular powers. Satan's dialectical instrument is the evasive or quibbling oracle . . . Christ . . . as the Word of God . . . has solved the verbal riddle of human life, putting all the words which are properly attributes of God into their rightful context."[7] This is the Miltonic assertion. Here we might simply note the contrast between Pauline and Sphinxine riddle, and also observe that the Sphinx's riddle is not radically evasive or quibbling. It is potentially terrifying, as Borges knew ("Edipo y el Enigma").

Type-2 enigma is essentially Sphinxine rather than Oedipal in the work of Dante and Milton. I make the distinction because of the full story of

---

6 See Betz, *Plutarch's Theological Writings and Early Christian Literature.*
7 Frye, "The Typology of 'Paradise Regained,'" *Modern Philology* 53 (1956), 232.

Oedipus in Sophocles. I am indebted to Anthony Hecht for pointing this out, and for putting it so well:

Only [*Oedipus Rex*] ends that way [in blinding and darkness]. . . At the very eloquent and moving end of the Colonus, Oedipus, who has never failed to assert his perfect innocence, since he was forced by fate to commit his crimes *unwittingly*, is quite miraculously, enigmatically, received into the bosom of the gods. . . The story of Oedipus ends in divine enlightenment, though without solving the enigma of the irreconcilable differences between human and divine wisdom. . . The wisdom of the gods is justified and celebrated by Oedipus himself at the end of his life and the end of his story. In this the story is not only like Paul's enigma, but like Job's; and it is the enigma of Theodicy – the incommensurability of human and divine wisdom and justice.[8]

To this admirable statement, I would only add that Jocasta is equally innocent but not so favored by the gods. Is this because she abandons them, in her appeal to Chance and her saying, "Best to live randomly (*eike kratiston zen*, 979)"? Dramatically, to be sure, it is better to have her hang herself than to keep existing as a fellow-sufferer, demanding our sympathies along with Oedipus. And the two Oedipus plays are centered on him and not on her, as, say, the *Antigone* centers on the destiny of a daughter of Oedipus.

We might also ask what the effect would be if we had the satyr-play to add to the trilogy. Aeschylus wrote a satyr-play called *Sphinx* to follow his trilogy about the Oedipus story, of which only one play survives, *The Seven against Thebes*. What was Sophocles' satyr-play like? What effect did it have on his masterful trilogy? Perhaps simply the practical effect of preparing the audience for everyday life again, after the exhaustion of the Oedipus story. Like some satyr-play, small riddles can also turn our minds back to everyday life and manageable puzzles after the overwhelming enigma of death and justice.

Hegel reads Oedipus in his full story as well, though he moves rather hastily away from the dark demands of what I have called Sphinxine enigma. He casts the *Antigone*, as the highest example of tragic action, a collision of wills. Cave observes how Hegel finds the story of Antigone's father "alien to our sensibility," and how he tames it by reading it as a spiritual and psychological inner drama. "Oedipus' 'dreadful realization' of what he has done, his 'solution of the riddle in his own person,' becomes an episode in an inner drama which culminates in spiritual vision and purification . . . [in a] 'reconciliation within his own self and

---

8 Letter to the author, 5 July 1995. Quoted by permission.

personality'" (pp. 154–62). Hegel was not the man for satyr-plays, let alone the messiness of the great Oedipus enigma.

It is also worth repeating the question whether Pauline masterplot is essentially the enigma of theodicy. If the theodicy of a benign God or gods is accepted, then the answer to the enigma of theodicy is also ultimately good. This kind of overview governs both the great Greek tragedies and Shakespearean tragedy. In a larger perspective, the terrible enigmas of tragedy are seen as nonetheless part of a benign scheme. Perhaps Pauline enigma as masterplot should be a genus with several species: the enigma of 1 Corinthians and its Christian masterplot, the *hida* of the Hebrew Bible with its masterplot, and Greek tragic *ainigma* with yet another related masterplot. All posit a benign theodicy. Sphinxine enigma as masterplot has no benign answer. "Whereas the oracles point upward to a divine, albeit mysterious order, the Sphinx points downward to what is dark, monstrous, subhuman" (Segal, *Tragedy and Civilization*, p. 238).

There is another reason for distinguishing between Oedipal and Sphinxine riddling, and that is Freud's masterplot. I do not have in mind the so-called Oedipus complex, for it has little to do with classical accounts of Oedipus. Rather, it is the mythic dimension of Freud's thinking and its sense of enigma. Wittgenstein thought that Freud had made a new myth of the old one:

He has not given a scientific explanation of the ancient myth. What he has done is to propound a new myth. The attractiveness of the suggestion, for instance, that all anxiety is a repetition of the anxiety of the birth trauma, is just the attractiveness of a mythology. . . Much the same could be said of the notion of an "Urszene". This often has the attractiveness of giving a sort of tragic pattern to one's life. . . Many people have, at some period, serious trouble in their lives. . . And it may then be an immense relief if it can be shown that one's life has the pattern rather of a tragedy . . . a pattern which was determined by the primal scene.[9]

Bernard Knox, arguing against Freud's description of *Oedipus Rex* as a "tragedy of fate," also affirms that "he is concerned not so much with Sophocles' play as with the basic mythic material."[10] If Freud's new myth also follows the pattern of a fall, of light versus darkness, of outside versus inside, the context is very different from that of Sphinxine riddle as conceived by Milton, Dante, and perhaps St. Paul. For Oedipus is partly a wisdom figure, a master interpreter of riddles, and was so known for

9 Ludwig Wittgenstein, *Lectures and Conversations on Aesthetics, Psychology and Religious Belief* (Berkeley: University of California Press, 1967), p. 51.
10 Bernard Knox, *Oedipus at Thebes*, p. 197. Harold Bloom calls Freud's term "Oedipus complex" an "unfortunate formulation" (*Sophocles' Oedipus Plays*, p. 1).

centuries, as for example in Athanasius Kircher's *Oedipus Aegyptiacus* (1652). Oedipus as master interpreter makes a figure for psychoanalysis itself insofar as it reads enigmas rather than being read by them.

For a recent poetic example of a dark Sphinxine enigma, consider the ending of John Ashbery's "Never Seek To Tell Thy Love" (ll. 17–23) from *A Wave*:

> They don't make rocks like us any more.
>
> And holding on to the thread, fine as a cobweb, but incredibly strong,
> Each of us advances into his own labyrinth.
> The gift of invisibility
> Has been granted to all but the gods, so we say such things,
> Filling the road up with colors, faces,
> Tender speeches, until they feed us to the truth.

What causes the shock of the last line is the conjunction of mountain-top, walking and rock-climbing, advancing upward and onward, especially when holding on to that fine, strong thread. Climbing up a mountain should issue in a vison of truth, as in Dante's *Purgatorio*. Or as in Donne's quest for truth: "On a huge hill / Cragged and steep, Truth stands, and hee that will / Reach her, about must, and about must goe; / And what the hills suddennes resists, winne so" (Satire III). Surely, having that thread and being such rocks, even when we advance into our own labyrinth – surely we are to expect an Ariadne rescue at the end of the journey. But no, apparently the gods have decided to feed us to a modern Minotaur. Ah, but even the ancient monster would be better. This Minotaur, it seems, *is* the truth, at least if it governs our masterplot of enigma. Perhaps, however, the gods simply feed our bodies back to earth, fire, water or to other creatures, in a truth we cannot know. This last possibility moves away from a monstrous, Sphinxine masterplot.

For the third pattern of enigma as masterplot, a dualistic pattern, we might take the example of Plutarch's "The E at Delphi." Plutarch's speakers are considering the mystery of the letter E, the fifth letter of the Greek alphabet, which was inscribed on the temple of Apollo at the famous shrine at Delphi. The Greek name for this letter (later epsilon) was EI, a diphthong, which also meant "if" and the second person singular of "to be." It seems only right that a riddle should be part of the worship of Apollo, to follow one speaker: " 'Since . . . inquiry is the beginning of philosophy, and wonder and uncertainty the beginning of inquiry, it seems only natural that the greater part of what concerns the god should be concealed in riddles (αἰνίγμασι, *ainigmasi*) and should call for some account of the wherefore and an explanation of its cause' "

(385c). Clearchus, the acknowledged authority on riddles quoted by Athenaeus, also connects them with philosophy: " 'The solution to riddles is not alien to philosophy' " (Ath. x.457c). Even *griphoi* (the word for "riddles" here) are not alien to philosophy.

Plutarch's group offers six possible solutions to this well-known enigma, of which the last two have the dimensions of a masterplot. The preceding four are as follows:

1 E is a dedication by the five renowned Wise Men, meant to show there were only five of them, and to reject imposters (EI is E, or five, *pente*).
2 E stands for the sun, since it is the second vowel and the sun is the second planet, closely identified with Apollo – an argument dismissed as "idle talk" even in the telling.
3 E as EI indicates "if," and so is part of the regular questions to the oracle by petitioners wishing to know *if* they should do A or B. They may also petition the god, using the formula "if only."
4 E as EI indicates "if," and so is a necessary word in a logical syllogism. Apollo himself is fond of logical reasoning, which is one way of demonstrating truth, the aim of philosophy.

These four answers neatly map types of responses to the very shortest of riddles, a letter. EI is

1 the signature and cypher of a group of people, or
2 a cosmic correspondence, or
3 a grammatical key for inquiring or praying, or
4 a logical key.

The fifth and sixth answers propose

5 a numerical key, and
6 the formula for universal affirmation of the gods.

The fifth solution, E as the number five, works from philosophical arguments about the essence of numbers out to numbers in a pattern of nature, a masterplot in which we mortals necessarily partake. This is a cyclical ongoing pattern of life and regeneration followed by death and destruction; it is based on the annual round of the seasons. The transformations of nature give rise to rituals in the worship of Apollo: "They give him the names of Dionysus, Zagreus, Nyctelius, and Isodates; they construct destructions and disappearances, followed by returns to life and regenerations – riddles (*ainigmata*) and fabulous tales quite in keeping with the aforesaid transformations" (389a). The transformations of nature are indeed enigmatic, both the destruction of winter and the regeneration of spring. This third type of enigma remains partly dark and destructive, and partly light- and life-bringing, as befits Apollo in his different aspects. Plutarch's speaker suggests a ratio of three to one, based on a seasonal analogy in a temperate zone, where winter takes up one quarter of an annual cycle: three parts Apollonian and regenerative, and one part Dionysian and breaking down. Such a cycle combines the riddle that ends in light and order (Apollonian) and the riddle that ends in breaking and destruction (Dionysian). This is the enigma of a natural order of things. Someone like T. S. Eliot, yearning for the certainty of a Pauline masterplot, will read seasonal cycles as ironic; thus in *The Waste Land*. In Plutarch's symposium, it is mitigated by the sixth solution, the supernatural or the forces represented by the gods, especially Apollo.

The sixth solution to the enigma of the E is "Thou art": "For the god addresses each one of us as we approach him here with the words 'Know Thyself' . . . and we in turn reply to him 'Thou art' " (392a). This simple affirmation points to an eternal world of the gods beyond mortal vicissitudes. The best human wisdom, according to this speaker (who sounds congenial for Plutarch), consists in knowing and praising this eternal world by uttering a reverential "Thou art," while also acknowledging human limitations by studying the maxim "Know thyself." In Plato's dialogue, *Charmides*, Critias calls this Delphic maxim "Know thyself" a sort of riddle: "*ainigma-todesteron*" (164e). Such a masterplot posits eternal light, though it offers no promise that humankind may finally be enlightened. The two types of enigma at work in the seasonal round resemble somewhat the Pauline and the Sphinxine, the light-bringing and the destructive. But in their combining of light and dark (rather than a radical enmity) and in the regular recurrence of their yearly cycle (rather than a transcendent or mythic plotting), they differ from types 1 and 2. No final and necessary ending of time resolves this type of enigma, as it does Pauline Christian enigma.

In Gjertrud Schnackenberg's sequence on the house of Oedipus, *The Throne of Labdacus*, the seventh section, "The Riddle in Reverse," opens thus:

> In Delphi, the Sphinx reverses her riddle:
> *What is man?*
>
> *What is* – visible to all, but uninterpretable,
> Like a Mycenaean beast engraved on a gem,
>
> *Animal, mortal, footed, biped, wingless. . .*

The riddle at Apollo's temple in Delphi moves one step onward (or one step back), distancing itself from the Oedipus riddle. Or does it? "What is man?" sounds more like an enigma out of wisdom literature, more like the question that the Delphic maxim, "Know thyself," answers. But when the Sphinx utters it, it does not lose the shadow of a monstrous beast, whether the Sphinx herself or the four-, two-, and three-footed creature of her riddle. Schnackenberg is juxtaposing dark, Sphinxine riddle with the Delphic over-arching masterplot, the power of Apollo the light-bringer that governs the cyclic round. The unbearable tension of such juxtaposition informs all her sequence. It arises from "the incommensurability of human and divine wisdom and justice," to repeat Hecht's words.

By contrast, A. R. Ammons in "Gravelly Run" echoes and revises both Plutarch's over-arching masterplot and St. Paul's:

> for it is not so much to know the self
> as to know it as it is known
>   by galaxy and cedar cone,
> as if birth had never found it
> and death could never end it.

The first allusion is to the inscription at Delphi, "Know thyself," which Ammons slightly shifts and modernizes as "to know the self." The Pauline allusion is to the full text of 1 Cor. 13: 12, "For now we see through a glass, darkly; but then face to face: now I know in part; but then shall I know even as also I am known." Ammons's double allusion moves through historical time, evoking an entire system of knowing with each allusion, and two different masterplots for enigma. The sharp enjambment that follows moves us forward to an entirely naturalistic kind of knowing, submitting to the unknown masterplot – or, as it may be, non-plot – of the universe.

Such twofold patternings as the seasonal rounds in Plutarch may be found elsewhere in plots of mythic dimension, though it is Plutarch who associates enigma with them. An early classical form similar to type 3 can be seen in Empedocles' cosmology, where the elements join or clash as governed by Love (*Philia*) or its contrary, Strife (*Neikos*). Dualistic masterplots appear more widely in early Christendom, where it is usual for light to prevail over darkness. The radical dualism of Manichaean thought is one exception, for here the struggle is between equal forces. Two opposing masterplots of equal strength battle one another, a sense of the world that prevails in Melville's *Moby Dick*. Melville ends his extraordinary chapter "The Whiteness of the Whale" (chap. 42) thus: "Though in many of its aspects this visible world seems formed in love, the invisible spheres were formed in fright." The battle between love and terror rages throughout his book. In early Gnostic thought, a dualist mythology resulting from what Stroumsa calls the "hermeneutical revolt of the gnostics" combines two masterplots, one subservient to the other but very powerful (*Hidden Wisdom*, p. 54). The Archons, or evil powers governing this world, must ultimately give way to the eternal powers of the Aeons, but meanwhile go on causing untold human misery.

For the five types of enigma as masterplot, only the first and possibly the second require a certain chronology, directed toward a final end. Pauline Christian enigma is rooted in history and a story, and so very readily provides a chronological plot. By contrast, Plutarch's fifth and sixth solutions both sound a good deal more static. The plots of individual lives have shapes, and in the end the shapes reflect the will of the gods or fate. But how far individuals see anything of divine will or fate is another matter. No prophecy promises to all the faithful that eventually they will see "face to face" at the end of time.

There is another shape that enigma takes as masterplot, different from the three dominant ones outlined above, and so classified as type 4. I began to consider it when I asked myself what type of enigma some deconstructionists assumed when they used the word "enigma." Deconstructionists are highly aware of most rhetorical figures, and usually wary of them. Paul de Man, for example, casts such figures as a gallery of dubious females: "As for metaphor, the mischief wreaked by this wiliest of Pandora's boxes . . . The dangerously seductive powers of paranomasis . . . euphony is probably the most insidious of all sources of error" (*Blindness and Insight*, p. 285). But there is one rhetorical figure they do not mistrust, seductive as she is. On the contrary: they adore her, they remain faithful to her. She is their blue flower, always pursued though never possessed. She alone is not deconstructed. Her name is enigma. Enigma does not possess the status of metaphor as a rhetorical figure, but she is just as ancient in rhetorical treatises, starting with Aristotle. It intrigued me then to read of lyric poetry as "an enigma which never stops asking for the unreachable answer to its own riddle" (ibid., p. 186). "Deconstruction," to follow Geoffrey Galt Harpham, "seems to have sprung from a passage in Nietzsche's *Beyond Good and Evil* which describes a 'new species of philosopher' who wants 'to remain a riddle.' "[11] We might say that enigma is to deconstruction what metaphor is to so-called logocentrism.

In *La Dissémination*, Jacques Derrida knows very well what masterplot Claudel has in mind in the following quotation, especially as Claudel goes on to quote a second verse from St. Paul. "We see everything," writes Claudel, "in an enigma and as if in a mirror [en énigme, et comme dans un miroir]." Derrida comments: "Thenceforth all finite books [les livres finis] would become opuscules modeled after the great divine opus, so many arrested speculations, so many tiny mirrors catching a single grand image." He goes on to speak of "this return of the theological seed to itself," and later of Mallarmé's book ("the world is made to end up as a beautiful book") as "without any doubt . . . a descendant of the Bible."[12] The great enigma (though Derrida does not put it this way) has one assumed answer, an essentially Pauline answer. Needless to say, deconstructionist enigma attempts to break this dominance. In Paul de Man's work, the word "enigma" functions so as to indicate that no answer is forthcoming.[13]

Such a riddle-type would be the unanswerable riddle, the riddle whose answer we do not know or whose answer we shall never know, the self-enclosed riddle, the self-mirroring riddle. The radical form would be the riddle that has no answer. Its classical antecedents would include the view of Epicurus that the cosmos is the result of accident, and the more negative thinking of Pyrrhonian scepticism. As noted, Jocasta in Sophocles' *Oedipus Rex* turns to such a pattern in her fear. "Beyond the questions of time, change, and the multiplicity and fluidity of identity, Oedipus' tragedy also asks whether human life is trapped in a pattern of its own or others' making or is all random, as Jocasta says" (Segal, *Tragedy and Civilization*, p. 248). Sphinxine enigma may be horrible, but it has some meaning, unlike the radical form of this type. Faced with Sphinxine enigma, we can reflect, with Michael Wood: "There is a plot, but it may be against you; it may be against you, but there is a plot" ("Consulting the Oracle," 110). Random, plotless enigma constitutes my type-4 enigma.

In literary practice, such an enigma as masterplot presents an obvious problem: boredom. Infinite wanderings and mazes, all self-mirroring,

11 *The Ascetic Imperative in Culture and Criticism* (Chicago: University of Chicago Press, 1987), p. 264.
12 Derrida, *Dissemination*, pp. 46, 48, 55, 54.
13 See the quotation above, also "the enigma of language" (ibid., p. 185) and "an undecidable enigma" from the title essay of *The Resistance to Theory* (Minneapolis: University of Minnesota Press, 1986), p. 18.

become tiresome eventually. The promising television series *Twin Peaks* simply petered out, unwilling and then apparently unable to find a satisfying conclusion. It tried to be a detective story, but wandered unwittingly into a romance and became lost in its own structureless structure – the perennial hazard of the romance genre.[14] For a brilliant, modern literary treatment of type-4 enigma, we would turn to the work of Borges. Its special brilliance lies in the way Borges plays this type of enigma against the possibility of other types of enigma as masterplot.

In the latter part of the nineteenth century through much of the twentieth century, the alternative to Pauline enigma was often seen as a radical type-4 enigma: random, unanswerable, and hence threatening. We are still, I think, working through the sense of such a threat, as witness our occasional fears or bafflement or nostalgia. Even Kermode allows the word "disappointment" in the last sentence of *The Genesis of Secrecy*:

World and book, it may be, are hopelessly plural, endlessly disappointing; we stand alone before them, aware of their arbitrariness and impenetrability, knowing that they may be narratives only because of our impudent intervention and susceptible of interpretation only by our hermetic tricks. Hot for secrets, our only conversation may be with guardians who know less and see less than we can; and our sole hope and pleasure is in the perception of a momentary radiance, before the door of disappointment is finally shut on us. (p. 145)

When there is no fear or bafflement or nostalgia, nonetheless the dissolution of an end-directed masterplot raises questions. Ricoeur, for example, broods over the question of what happens when the concept of divine eternity vanishes. He wonders whether "the eternity [of] . . . works of art . . . guards against the forgetfulness of death and the dead, and remains a recollection of death and a remembrance of the dead." And he identifies the most serious question his *Temps et Récit* may ask as: "to what degree a philosophical reflection on narrativity and time may aid us in thinking about eternity and death at the same time" (vol. 1, pp. 86–7). Jürgen Habermas writes in another context of "this new situation, [where] moral philosophy depends on a 'post-metaphysical level of justification.' "[15]

---

14 On this hazard, see Patricia Parker, *Inescapable Romance: The Poetics of a Mode* (Princeton: Princeton University Press, 1979); for an able modern handling of the genre, see David Lodge's *Small World*. The older masters are, of course, Ariosto, Spenser, Cervantes, etc.

15 *The Inclusion of the Other: Studies in Political Theory* (Cambridge, Mass.: MIT Press, 1998), p. 11.

So far then, we have four masterplots for enigma. The question "Is there a fifth kind?" was originally stirred by Stevens's late work on the word "enigma." For some years, I read Stevens's kind of enigma as a variation on type 4, the unanswerable riddle. But I now think it constitutes a fifth type, a type I want to call Sibylline.

Consider this italicized speech from Stevens's 1943 essay, "The Figure of the Youth as Virile Poet":

No longer do I believe that there is a mystic muse, sister of the Minotaur. This is another of the monsters I had for nurse, whom I have wasted. I am myself a part of what is real, and it is my own speech and the strength of it, this only, that I hear or ever shall.

Stevens's imagined youthful poet is making a declaration of independence from a certain kind of muse: this much is clear. He is turning against any muse suggesting inspiration from the outside, such as Milton's Urania, who works with Milton's greater muse, the Holy Spirit. Stevens's last sentence sounds like a deconstructionist formulation, and has been so read. Yet when Stevens goes on to end the entire essay with a revised version of this speech, he does not follow such a line of thought. We might suppose he would sweep away Minotaurs and labyrinths and muses, together with the whole *le-pli* family of riddling, folded, implicated, inextricable, labyrinthine words. Not so. Here is the revision, now spoken by the young poet himself:

Inexplicable sister of the Minotaur, enigma and mask, although I am part of what is real, hear me and recognize me as part of the unreal. I am the truth but the truth of that imagination of life in which with unfamiliar motion and manner you guide me in those exchanges of speech in which your words are mine, mine yours.[16]

Stevens has re-invented, even invoked, this mysterious female. She is no longer mystic, no longer a monster, but still sister of the Minotaur, and now "inexplicable," now an "enigma," now a "mask." The familiar sister of the Minotaur is Ariadne, *la tua sorella*, as Dante calls her (*Inferno* 12.20). She is the rescuer from labyrinthine riddles with a devouring monster at the center. She holds the thread, the clue. Stevens at first sounds as if he has laid waste both the Minotaur and some Ariadne, and so he has, in the form of both the labyrinthine riddle and the standard rescue plot.

16 Stevens, *The Necessary Angel*, pp. 60, 67.

But his alternative is not the unanswerable enigma, type 4. Nor does he turn his back on end-directed plots. A sister of the Minotaur has returned as mask and enigma, and explicitly as guide. "Mask" as persona is easy enough. But "enigma"? That's also easy enough in one sense: the mystery of creation, and so on. Yet Stevens's own figurings of enigma are so intelligent and precise that I doubt he wanted to end his essay on so ready and general a thought. To trace Stevens's work on the figure of enigma is a task for chapter 9. For now, we might simply turn to his poem "The Sail of Ulysses," published in 1954, the year before his death. The poem ends thus:

> *The great sail of Ulysses seemed,*
> *In the breathings of this soliloquy,*
> *Alive with an enigma's flittering. . .*
> *As if another sail went on*
> *Straight forwardly through another night*
> *And clumped stars dangled all the way.*[17]

I want to call this type of enigma Sibylline, because of Stevens's Sibyl figure in the poem. The ancient Sibyls were riddlers, of course, first classical riddlers, then Christian prophetesses. Stevens's late Sibyl is descended from these, but different in kind. She descends more immediately from his 1943 inexplicable enigma and mask in his essay, "The Figure of the Youth as Virile Poet." She is an everyday Sibyl. She is like the ordinary or commonplace or plain sublime of Stevens's 1949 poem, "An Ordinary Evening in New Haven."

"Alive with an enigma's flittering": what masterplot would this enigma exemplify? The enigma of that flittering sail, the sail of Ulysses, voyaging, in a poem written by a man of seventy-four. Not sailing toward the Mount of Purgatory in an angel-winged boat, eventually to come to the stars of the heavenly paradise as in Dante's *Paradiso*. For Stevens says at the start that Ulysses is sailing under the "middle stars." Not sailing past the Pillars of Hercules on a thanatos death-voyage, nor (it appears) on a perpetually curving dualistic course, whether seasonal or Love-versus-Strife or Manichaean. Not sailing randomly or round and round: "straight forwardly," says Stevens.

The male figure for this type-5 enigma is Ulysses, many-wiled Ulysses, a favorite figure for Stevens himself from his youth to his old age.[18] The

---

17 Stevens, *Opus Posthumous*, p. 131. The ellipsis is Stevens's own.
18 See my *Poetry, Word-Play and Word-War in Wallace Stevens*, p. 301.

female figure for this type-5 enigma would be a Wisdom figure, but of this earth, and so neither Athena (patron of Ulysses) nor the eternal Sophia. She would be the woman who corresponds to Ulysses, a many-wiled woman – perhaps, as in Stevens, a Penelope or the ordinary Sibyl of the epigraph to this chapter. Old men ought to be explorers, Eliot had written some ten years before, but he did not have in mind Ulysses. (The troping changes its tone somewhat again, when we say: old women ought to be explorers.)

In a 1992 review, Denis Donoghue argued that "when readers lost interest in 'first and last things' and set about a political program of one kind or another," interest in work like Frye's went into eclipse (p. 28). Does it help to say, with Stevens, "long-term things" rather than "first and last things"? Only to a degree, for the contrast Donoghue lays out is not a necessary one, as Paul Celan and Vladimir Nabokov remind us. "But where in great poetry is it *not* a question of last things?" Celan asked a correspondent. ("Aber wo ist, in grossen Gedichten, *nicht* von letzten Dingen die Rede?"[19]) As for Nabokov, he considered the fashionable disdain for first and last things, and sardonically rejected it:

First and last things often tend to have an adolescent note – unless, possibly, they are directed by some venerable and rigid religion. Nature expects a full-grown man to accept the two black voids, fore and aft, as stolidly as he accepts the extraordinary visions in between. Imagination, the supreme delight of the immortal and the immature, should be limited. In order to enjoy life, we should not enjoy it too much. I rebel against this state of affairs.(p. 9)

Stevens was wary of first and last things in a Pauline masterplot. Yet he centered his later work on the possibility of a supreme fiction,[20] which would assuredly be a supreme achievement of the imagination. The supreme fiction is the type of mythic story that seems most appropriate for a type-5 masterplot. It is not an eternal masterplot, for Stevens specifies "It Must Change," the title of Part II of "Notes toward a Supreme Fiction." But neither is it short-lived.

---

19 Cited in Felstiner, *Paul Celan: Poet, Survivor, Jew*, p. 134, from a letter of 29 January 1959; I am grateful to him for helping me locate the original German, in Victor Terras and Karl S. Weimar, "Mandelstam and Celan: A Postscript," *Germano-Slavica* 2 (1978), 361–2.
20 "The author's work suggests the possibility of a supreme fiction, recognized as a fiction, in which men could propose to themselves a fulfilment" (Stevens in 1954 on his work, *Letters*, p. 820).

NECESSITY, TRICKSTERS

I have been working with a synchronic overview, as noted at the start. But synchronic overviews are also historical in the sense that they have some starting-point, some *terminus ab quo*, that is necessarily a historical point in time. Paul's famous text from Corinthians grows out of the Hebrew Bible. Long before Plutarch there existed different perceptions of the gods.

From that time comes another pattern that does not fit the contrast between light and dark or the motion of up and down. Perhaps it should not even be called a pattern. It is primordial. In Greek writing, it is the world that precedes the Olympians, the world of those elemental gods known as the Giants or Titans. These gods are more animistic or abstract than the Olympians, who take on human form and act out understandable passions. Behind the Olympians lie the gods they conquered, Kronos and Gaia and the rest, those personified natural forces thrust back into the roles of forerunners. Their moment of passing caught the imagination of Keats in *Hyperion* and *The Fall of Hyperion*. Roberto Calasso speaks of the ancient rule of the goddess Necessity, sometimes called Ananke, with her three daughters, the Fates.

Can enigma as masterplot exist in the world of Necessity? If primitive humans knew only or chiefly of this rule, then the main riddle would likely be one's own personal fate or the fate of one's community. A masterplot moving up or down, toward light or dark: this type of enigma implies a curiosity or questioning less likely in the world of all-powerful Necessity. Endurance and practical ingenuity would surely matter most.[21] Classical scholars debate over when and how a sense of the rule of law, or of the justice of Zeus, became established.[22] Riddle and enigma seem especially verbal: they are interwoven inextricably with words. What evidence can we have for them before written records or known oral traditions?

Ancient Jewish tradition moved early to monotheism, and set itself against animistic or abstract gods. The ways of God himself, Yahweh, whose true name was not to be spoken: these are enigmatic in the way of a

---

21 Segal observes that, in other fifth-century authors, Jocasta's phrase " 'to live randomly' describes the disordered, 'beast-like' life of precivilized man" (*Tragedy and Civilization*, p. 211). He cites Aeschylus and Hippocrates. The perspective sounds like Hobbes' view of savage life as mean, solitary, nasty, brutish and short.

22 See Bernard Knox, *Oedipus at Thebes*, Segal, *Tragedy and Civilization*, and Lloyd-Jones, *The Justice of Zeus*.

masterplot. This is a world that seems to have been verbal from the start, or was conceived to have been. The Hebrew Scriptures record in their creation narrative that God spoke. He *said*, "Let there be light, and there was light. Let there be a firmament . . . and it was so. Let us make man in our image, after our likeness . . . male and female created he them." He did not create wordlessly, in a lightning bolt and thunder crash. Even in the ancient Book of Job, with its debate over undeserved human suffering, and the old conflict between God and a powerful Satan – even here, words argue out, describe, say how things are. The sense of riddle and enigma, and especially of enigma as masterplot, runs very deep and far in Jewish tradition. It has remained alive continuously to this day.

Where do such figures as the trickster god belong? Tomson Highway says that the native Amerindian trickster god "straddles the consciousness of man and that of God, the Great Spirit," and is "as pivotal and important a figure as Christ," teaching us about nature and the meaning of existence.[23] Does a trickster god resemble Necessity, also requiring endurance and practical ingenuity? Or can a trickster be sublimated into the Holy Spirit, a thought that Frye recorded in a late notebook: "The trickster is sublimated in some religions (Hinduism) into a benevolent providence. Xy [Christianity] too . . . the Holy Spirit, blowing where it listeth, is a trickster."[24] Later, he notes "a trickster element in God, which is there to prevent the idea of God from becoming predictable, always behaving according to human notions of what he ought to be doing, as in Bohr's remark to Einstein." "That's why, of course, there's so much about a whimsical, irritable, unpredictable, tricky and downright mean God in the O. T."[25] The classical trickster god is, of course, Hermes. In W. H. Auden's 1946 Phi Beta Kappa poem, "Under Which Lyre: A Reactionary Tract for the Times," Hermes is the patron of writers, and not Apollo.

MASTERPLOTS IN LITERARY CRITICISM

Literary criticism itself follows these types of masterplot. To turn to criticism is to move from story to interpretation, that is, from Paul's or

---

23 Highway, "A Note on Nanabush," *Dry Lips Oughta Move to Kapuskasing*, pp. 12–13. Highway adds that there is no gender in North American Indian languages, so that the trickster is male in an earlier play and female here.

24 Frye, *Late Notebooks*, vol. v, pp. 72–3, item 397.

25 Ibid., vol. vi, p. 623, item 54, and pp. 636–7, item 129. To Einstein's remark, "Do you really believe God resorts to dice-playing?", Bohr replied, "Don't you think caution is needed in ascribing attributes to Providence in ordinary language?" (ibid., p. 872n).

Sophocles' writing to the writing of Aristotle or Augustine. Yet interpretations also follow narrative patterns, and so do interpretive methods like
biblical typology. For all that, Paul himself is writing interpretation of the
Hebrew Scriptures, laying the foundation of typological reading. To
quote Cave, the distinction between narrative and interpretive method
may be overcome, "in theory at least, by positing that interpretation
is indeed a narrative (a meta-narrative)."[26] What kinds of contemporary
criticism follow the five types of masterplot outlined above?

This is a literary study of riddle and enigma, so that the famous
example from the Apostle Paul may give pause in one way. Paul's epistles
are sacred literature, part of the Christian Bible. Does this make a difference in a literary reading? For some readers, there is an important
difference between the act of reading sacred texts and the act of reading
secular ones. Other readers do not divide writing in that way. For Stevens,
the biblical books were the work of poets. Far from drastically diminish-
ing their authority, Stevens offered this view of the biblical books as a
tribute to the power of the human imagination. He had great faith that
the power of the human imagination would continue, though someone
like Harold Bloom is more melancholy and elegiac on this question. In
Frye's *Anatomy of Criticism*, sacred writing, notably the Christian Bible, is
read as literature because Frye is offering a taxonomy of literary criticism.[27] Literature may be "driven by the same desire as is religion," but it
is not identical.[28] Ricoeur notes Kermode's difficulties in *The Sense of an
Ending* when he intermingles literary models with eschatological myths of
belief. Frye avoids this difficulty by "according the apocalyptic myth only
a literary status, without passing judgment about the religious significance
it may bear from the eschatological perspective of a history of salvation...
he does not allow literature and religion to become mixed or confused
with each other" (*Time and Narrative*, vol. II, p. 27). It is a useful caution.

---

26 Cave, *Recognition*. He goes on to say that "allegory is simply the form in which narrative most
    openly declares its diegetic [narrative] hand. Allegory then becomes the narrative of narrative"
    (p. 230n).
27 In later work, Frye allows the concept of *kerygma* or message to enter his studies of the Bible and
    literature (not the Bible as literature), thus acknowledging the function of scripture as a sacred
    text. See *The Great Code*, pp. 29–30, and *Words with Power: Being a Second Study of the Bible and
    Literature* (Toronto: Viking Penguin, 1990), pp. 100–1, 116–18.
28 Ricoeur, "*Anatomy of Criticism* or the Order of Paradigms," in *Centre and Labyrinth: Essays in
    Honour of Northrop Frye*, ed. Eleanor Cook et al. (Toronto: University of Toronto Press, 1983),
    pp. 11–12.

James Kugel observes that patristic exegesis of Scripture could study it in literary terms because its sanctity lay elsewhere:

To say that it [scripture] is composed in meter, or follows the laws of Greek rhetoric; to see tropes and figures in it, or to read it in a way not essentially different from the way one reads other books – these do not touch the sanctity of the text, *because that is not where the sanctity lies.* And that is why Christian exegesis of the Hebrew Bible, though often hampered by incomplete mastery (if not total ignorance) of the Hebrew text, is far more attentive to real and imaginary nuances of style as such than the Rabbis.

(*The Idea of Biblical Poetry*, p. 140)

Augustine himself is the authority for using – more than this, the duty to use – literary and rhetorical knowledge when reading scripture. He is the one who offers an ancient answer to the question about a literary approach to sacred writing, as we have seen.

Contemporary literary criticism following a Pauline-type riddle would be preeminently that of Frye. Other like-minded critics include, for example, Piero Boitani in his *The Tragic and the Sublime in Medieval Literature*. Frye's criticism is sometimes said, and justly so, to follow a romance or quest pattern. He even wrote early in his career: "It is part of the critic's business to show how all literary genres are derived from the quest-myth."[29] But the masterplot it follows is that of the Pauline riddle.

For criticism following the pattern of Oedipal or rather Sphinxine riddling, we would turn to Freudian critics: to the work of Brooks, for example, in *Reading for the Plot: Design and Intention in Narrative*. In his chapter "Freud's Masterplot: A Model for Narrative," Brooks suggests that "the work of Freud . . . still offers the most probing inquiry into the dynamics of the psychic life, and hence, by possible extension, of texts" (p. 90). (Here, Brooks's terms define the boundaries of his masterplot; the "psychic life" is not the same as the spiritual life, nor is there mention of a communal or civic life.) As an end-directed plot, Freud's masterplot takes the shape of a "necessary dualism" (p. 105), that is, of eros and thanatos. "The drive toward the end" is the death instinct, yet a death instinct still desiring knowledge. "As Sartre and Benjamin compellingly argued," Brooks writes, "the narrative must tend toward its end, seek illumination in its own death. Yet this must be the right death, the correct end" (p. 103). In the type-2 Sphinxine-Oedipal riddle that I have outlined, the sphinxine

---

29 "The Archetypes of Literature," in his *Fables of Identity: Studies in Poetic Mythology* (New York: Harcourt, Brace & World, 1963), p. 17.

portion corresponds to the simple death drive, and the Oedipal portion (wise interpreter) to the persistent desire for knowledge, even in the face of death. Both Sartre and Benjamin stress this persistent desire for knowledge.

In a turn on Freud, Stevens called the desire for understanding "the last nostalgia" ("Esthétique du Mal" x), so that this desire too may be part of the death drive. All depends on what and where home is. For home or *nostos* is what nostalgia desires, and Stevens's speaker "had studied the nostalgias." "It was the last nostalgia: that he / Should understand." Such understanding disentangles Stevens's speaker "from sleek ensolacings" and enables him to live to the end. Stevens's word "last" is both conceptual and chronological.

The work of Bloom is also strongly influenced by Freud, at least in its middle stage, his work being dialectically related to Frye's work.[30] In his *Ruin the Sacred Truths: Poetry and Belief from the Bible to the Present*, Bloom concludes with a chapter on Freud (pp. 145–204), but he denies being a Freudian literary critic: "I think there is no such thing as a Freudian literary critic . . . Freudian literary criticism is like the Holy Roman Empire: not holy, not Roman, not an empire; not Freudian, not literary, not criticism" (Salusinszky, *Criticism and Society*, p. 55). Freud for him codifies and abstracts Shakespeare, who is the true inventor, says Bloom, of Freudian psychology. Bloom is essentially a Gnostic, and his Freud a Gnostic Freud. The temporal masterplot ends darkly and shadows our lives. Yet there is mitigation in gnosis, the deep secret knowledge that can link us, however sporadically, with the knowledge of the eternal powers. (Stevens' phrase, "the last nostalgia," also glosses this kind of knowledge.)

Wolfgang Schultz was not a literary critic, but a very learned folklorist flourishing around the turn of the last century and responsible for the long entry on "Rätsel" in the 1914 edition of *Paulys Realencyclopädie*. When he wished to solve the riddle of riddles – to offer an Ur-riddle, so to speak, or a meta-riddle as we might say nowadays – he favored a mythical answer. All riddles, for him, live within the over-arching myths of Sun and Moon. His masterplot resembles Plutarch's in being related to the natural cycle; it is type 3. Schultz was very much of his time, as we all are. Archer Taylor spoke gratefully in 1951 of the last generation of folklorists and their "new endeavor to use riddles in mythological studies" in a systematic way (*English Riddles in Oral Tradition*, p. 2). With Taylor, however, the perspective of folklorists changed, and it has shifted again nowadays.

30 As he says in Salusinszky, *Criticism and Society*, pp. 62, 71.

The desire of deconstruction is to evade the circle implied by their very term, logocentrism, including criticism along what might be called the Frye–Bloom axis. Ricoeur argues that deconstruction poses a problem diametrically opposed to that of Frye in *Anatomy of Criticism*. Deconstructionists "ferociously attack the very idea of a 'still center of the order of words.'"[31] As noted above, criticism corresponding to a type-4 enigma, the riddle with the "unreachable answer" (De Man) is deconstruction. Derrida and others have moved away from such "ferocious" attacks to concentrate on other questions. But the focus of the early attacks is what I have called Pauline enigma, and the alternative is the unanswerable enigma.

Where might we find criticism following a Sibylline or type-5 enigma? In post-modern thinking, there is likewise no sense of a masterplot or no meta-narrative, to call it that. The question then becomes what form of telos, if any, is at work in post-modern thinking and writing. What kind of large enigma or riddle intrigues post-modern thinkers and writers? What kinds of answer are supposed possible? Are they chiefly type-4 enigmas where a random or non-answer is assumed? Or could Stevens's sense of a long-term end be called post-modern? Even post-modernists must make decisions to some end. To what end, and how far ahead do they look? Does recent deconstructionist work move away from type-4 enigma and toward Sibylline enigma? Jean-François Lyotard is commonly cited for his statement that there are no more meta-narratives or master-narratives ("grands récits"). Linda Hutcheon argues that this is itself a theory of meta-narrative.[32] Perhaps some re-thinking of the prefix "meta-" is in order, together with Stevens's long-term rather than final end-plot.

As for feminist criticism, it is worth noting how readily these riddle-types can be mapped in familiar female types. As Amos Elon once remarked, "When men are mystified, they often turn to the feminine gender."[33]

Type 1: Enigma as resolved in or by a Beatrice or a Madonna (old-style).
Type 2: Enigma as propounded by the Grecian Sphinx, the female who eats you if you can't answer her question.

---

31 Ricoeur, "*Anatomy of Criticism* or the Order of Paradigms," p. 13, referring to Frye's phrase in *Anatomy*, p. 117.
32 Jean-François Lyotard, *The Postmodern Condition: A Report on Knowledge* (Minneapolis: University of Minnesota Press, 1984, orig. pub. 1979). Linda Hutcheon, *A Poetics of Postmodernism: History, Theory, Fiction* (New York and London: Routledge, 1988), p. 198. Both cited in McHale, *Constructing Postmodernism*, pp. 5–6.
33 Amos Elon, *Jerusalem: City of Mirrors* (Boston: Little, Brown, 1989), p. 51.

Type 3: The enigma of a Mother Nature.
Type 4: The unanswerable enigma that all women are, as we know.
Type 5: A Wisdom figure, e.g., the Sibyl.

In mapping female riddlers, incidentally, I was struck by the fact that there appeared to be no figure corresponding to Oedipus or Solomon, no female arch-interpreter of riddles or riddle-master. I was not quite right: there are a few such as the engaging and gifted Cleobulina, called by her patronymic as daughter of one of the Seven Wise Men (Plutarch, "The Dinner of the Seven Wise Men," *Moralia* 148D, and see further in chapter 5). But only one has gained anything like the prominence of Oedipus. This is a figure out of the Hebrew Scriptures, though not herself Jewish, the Queen of Sheba. In Kings and Chronicles, she asks riddles (unspecified), but in legend and in allegorical uses she sometimes also answers them. She exists in different legendary traditions,[34] and she can turn up in any one of three types above.

The question for those interested in enigma as masterplot is whether and how far and why the riddle aspect enters into her remarkable attraction. Does it intrigue an audience no matter whether she is benign or malign? The account in the Hebrew Scriptures is entirely benign, like many another. She comes as a foreign head of state to visit Solomon, and she comes bearing appropriate gifts from a prosperous kingdom. That this head of a wealthy state is female makes her of interest in history and legend both. It adds to her interest that she comes from the south, and is sometimes identified as "black, but comely" (Song of Songs 1: 5) – thus in the Ethiopian tradition, including its enchanting pictorial representations. She also comes prepared to engage in a riddle-challenge, those forms of diplomatic manoeuvering known in ancient times. What riddles she asked, the Hebrew Scriptures do not say, though other writings have happily supplied them.[35] They tend toward the esoteric and ingenious, of the kind that just might require divine grace or telepathy. Solomon, as the story requires, answers them all. As the legend variously developed, the Queen of Sheba was both elevated and demonized.[36] As a type-1 riddler in one Christian tradition, she is likened to the Sibyls. As a type-2 riddler

34 See, e.g., Pritchard, ed., *Solomon and Sheba*, which includes essays on the Queen of Sheba in Judaic, Islamic, Christian, and Ethiopian traditions.
35 See Silberman, "The Queen of Sheba in Judaic Tradition"; also Schechter, "The Riddles of Solomon in Rabbinic Literature."
36 Her riddle-solving capacities are "not widely developed in later Jewish thought" (Silberman, "The Queen of Sheba in Judaic Tradition," p. 79). Two recent books, among others, have treated the radical division, Beyer's *Die Königin von Saba* and Lasner's *Demonizing the Queen of Sheba*.

in one Jewish tradition, she is demonic and related to Lilith. As a type-3 riddler, she is the mysterious female, herself a riddle. When she holds power, a corresponding masterplot also holds sway.

As already observed, the relation of a masterplot to various temporal plots is crucial. This is the area in which historicist literary critics take special interest. While there is no single historicist viewpoint, all ask literary criticism to move toward the outside historical context of a given piece of writing. Or at the least, to take it into greater account in the overall picture. In a given masterplot, all riddle-solving may have one consistent final end in view, but what happens in the translation to a specific plot in time? What order of resolution takes precedence if there is a contradiction in evidence or hard practical choices to be made? How does this affect our sense of a masterplot?

Stevens thought a good deal about end-directed plots:

> But that's the difference: in the end and the way
> To the end. Alpha continues to begin.
> Omega is refreshed at every end.
> ("An Ordinary Evening in New Haven," VI)

Stevens's Alpha and Omega come straight out of the Book of Revelation, and straight out of the Greek alphabet that makes up the Book of Revelation. Stevens is also fully aware that Christ says in Revelation, "I am Alpha and Omega, the first and the last" (Rev. 1: 11). Both Alpha and Omega, Stevens writes, "alike appoint themselves the choice / Custodians of the glory of the scene" (ibid.).

All the varieties of type-1 enigma may envision one final end, with essentially the same full revelation, light, and enlightenment for the individual soul. Similarly with the other masterplots, though the end envisaged differs radically among them. But the ways to the end, the historical and particular choice of ways, together with their embodiment in imaginative writing, can differ greatly too. We must all find a way to move from an Alpha to an Omega, a way to arrange all the letters between.

CHAPTER 4

Case study 1
Enigma in Dante's Eden (Purgatorio 27–33)

> E forse che la mia narrazion buia,
> qual Temi e Sfinge . . .
> . . . .'ntelletto attuia;
> . . . questo enigma forte . . .

(33.46–50, And perhaps my dark tale, like Themis and the Sphinx . . . clouds thy mind . . . this hard enigma . . .[1])

The word *enigma* appears only once in all of Dante's *Divine Comedy*, in the last canto of the *Purgatorio*, where Beatrice devises an "enigma forte" for Dante the pilgrim to ponder (see below). To this day, it has not been solved conclusively. Dante the poet modeled it on the riddles of the Apocalypse, notably the number of the Beast, 666 (Rev. 13: 18). He set it in a prophetic speech where Beatrice borrows language from that most enigmatic biblical book.

In the last seven cantos of the *Purgatorio*, Dante the pilgrim has climbed nearly to the top of the Mountain of Purgatory. The Earthly Paradise or Eden lies just above him. Purged of his sins, he prepares to enter Eden with the blessing of Virgil, his beloved master and leader thus far. Dante is now sinless and should take his will as his guide – or so says Virgil. That sounds pleasant, and more than pleasant. But Dante the poet will not allow his pilgrim-self directly or easily into Eden and beyond. Who would have thought to slow down the transition so far? A lesser writer would have given his pilgrim-self the full enjoyment of an unfallen Garden of Eden, earth at its most blessed and beautiful. Then would come the transition to the heavenly Paradise and its inhabitants, perhaps by chariot. Dante does no such thing. For one canto only, canto 28, Dante wanders blissfully through Eden, with its birdsong, its stream, its fragrant winds, its dappled trees. Joyce summed it all up in *Finnegans*

---

1 *The Divine Comedy*, trans. Sinclair. Unless otherwise indicated, the English translation is his.

Wake (147.6–7): "Aves Selvae Acquae Valles!" (Birds, Woods, Waters, Vales!). He hears the exquisite song of the genius loci of Eden, Matelda. This, we readily agree, is the way Eden should be. What next?

Something quite unexpected. A dazzling light, a visonary procession, Beatrice, judgment, enigma.

How was Dante to work out this transition, the most difficult in all of the *Commedia*? No classical author could help, not even the revered Virgil, "that excellent master of speech [who] knew well the force of words, and had looked into the nature of thought" (Augustine, *De trinitate* xv.16). At most, as Matelda says, classical writers might dream of a Golden Age or the like. The transition to hell is easy to portray, alas. But the transition into Eden is different. It demands a shift from ordinary human life to perfected life. It moves from what Blake calls the world of experience to the world of innocence, to be followed by the world of absolute goodness in the *Paradiso*. (For a comparable dream-vision transition in movies, I am told that the standard convention is to use blurred images. If you add harp music, you are risking cliché or else working with parody.) The reader, along with Dante the pilgrim, is also slowed down and undergoes difficulty in translation. For this is a translation from one mode of existence to another, "translation" in the biblical sense, as when Enoch was "translated so he should not see death" (Heb. 11: 5, *translatus est*). *Translatio* is literally a carrying over from one place to another. *Translatio* is also a trope or metaphor. In Dante's context, the various transferences of rhetorical figures themselves serve as tropes for this radical translation from earthly to heavenly life. They include the *translatio* of the trope of enigma.

Dante suffuses this passage with the Apostle Paul's text, a favorite of his own: "Videmus nunc per speculum in aenigmate, tunc autem facie ad faciem." So often does Paul's text hover about commentary on these cantos that this observation may sound superfluous. But I want to concentrate on specific troping rather than general hovering, and especially on the phrase *in aenigmate*. How might a great poet trope on seeing by means of a mirror[2] and in an enigma, and then face to face? How might he be mindful of enigma itself as trope? For Dante was certainly aware of enigma as a figure of speech. The circles of the wise in Dante's *Paradiso* include Donatus and Rabanus Maurus (canto 12), as well as Peter

---

2 I do not have in mind simply a theme-and-image treatment or an exercise in analogy like, say, Allen Tate's spiritual variety in "The Symbolic Imagination: The Mirrors of Dante," in his *Collected Essays* (Denver: Alan Swallow, 1959), pp. 408–31.

Lombard, Isidore, and Bede (canto 10). In *Paradiso* 12.138, Donatus is described as "he who deigned to set his hand to the first art," i.e., grammar, including tropes.

I am not arguing that Dante the poet simply converted Paul's text into a morality play. That would give us personified Mirror and Enigma, with the pilgrim peering into Mirror, then approaching dark Enigma and finding it turn inside out in a blaze of light. Nor do I suppose that this one biblical text alone informs these cantos of the *Purgatorio.* Yet more than any other biblical passage, it permeates this gradual entry into the full earthly paradise. Dante goes from the world of *nunc,* the "now," of earthly existence to the world of *tunc,* "then," which in this visionary space becomes the pilgrim's *nunc* for as long as his vision lasts. St. Paul's rhetoric is precipitate, his contrast sharp, in his move from now to then. Dante, as great a master of literary pacing as Paul or Proust, slows things down. For all that, Paul's entire chapter on love or *caritas* (Greek *agape*) informs this transitional passage, not exclusively but centrally.[3]

These seven cantos are permeated with enigma in multiple ways. Mirror reflections prepare us for mirror's fellow in Paul's text, enigma. Scripture is read as enigma. The enigmatic language of Ezekiel and the Apocalypse is echoed. Dante sets his own cryptic, coded riddle, the *enigma forte* of the "cinquecento diece e cinque" (five hundred, ten, and five) within the riddling apocalyptic prophecy by Beatrice. Dante treats enigma in his earthly paradise in the widest possible sense, all the way from small riddles through to large, as well as enigma personified, enigma as figure of speech, enigma with its own kind of lexis and troping accumulated over the centuries, enigma mindful of a long history of famous riddles. In these cantos, Dante offers an entire spectrum for the figure of enigma in a Pauline masterplot, from tiny conundrums through to the largest of enigmas. At the largest end of the scale, enigma shades over into mystery and eventually vanishes in Dante's mystery of the Godhead at the end of the *Paradiso.* So also, all rhetoric and grammar and dialectic become subsumed in the Word that is God.

---

3 Dante the poet, who speaks with the tongue of men and of angels, also learns that without love, all this is nothing. Dante does not give his body to be burned (1 Cor. 13: 3) but he readily could do so by breaking the terms of his exile, and he remembers the sight of human bodies burned to death as he faces the wall of fire (*Purg.* 27.17–18). Dante the pilgrim is even now in some ways like a child, as Virgil says (ibid., 43–4). Is he recalling Paul? "When I was a child, I spake as a child, I understood as a child, I thought as a child: but when I became a man I put away childish things" (1 Cor. 13: 11; Tyndale translates "I spake as a child, understood as a child, *imagined* as a child").

MIRROR AND ENIGMA

What Paul offers in 1 Corinthians 13: 12 is a series of figures, than which nothing is more important for a writer qua writer. Seeing in this life is troped first as seeing by means of a mirror, and then as seeing in an enigma. Seeing in the afterlife is troped as seeing face to face. Dante knows full well how mirrors belong with enigma in the Pauline text. As a prelude to the earthly paradise, Dante's dream in canto 27 of Leah and Rachel provides the only reflecting surfaces in all of cantos 27 and 28. In contrast, cantos 29 through 31 offer many such surfaces, inescapable and extraordinary.

Leah and Rachel prefigure the appearance of Matelda and Beatrice, and show forth the active and the contemplative life. The active spirit as much as the contemplative sees herself in a mirror, one being satisfied with doing, the other with seeing. Dante invites us to imagine these perfected beings seeing themselves in perfected mirrors face to face, without re-proach. More than without reproach: self-delighting, to use Yeats's word from "A Prayer for My Daughter" (though not his concept). Rachel's mirroring is higher in kind, as Beatrice's domain is higher than Matelda's. What is worth noting, for the dream is well read by critics, is the difference between the two mirrors, Leah's *specchio* (the usual term for our familiar mirror) and Rachel's *miraglio*. Rachel's *miraglio* offers the only example of this unusual word in the *Commedia*, a word somewhat strange and of foreign origin, apparently from Provençal. The Bosco–Reggio commentary addresses the difference (many do not), pointing out that *miraglio* means "mirror" but is used in "a transferred [traslato] or metaphoric sense, signifying contemplation."[4]

After Dante's dream, there is little reflection until canto 29. There, as the procession begins, "The water shone on my left [sinistro] and, even like a mirror [specchio], gave back to me my left side [sinistra costa] when I gazed in it" (29.67–9). This is the same little stream that suddenly blocked Dante's progress in canto 28. "And lo [ed ecco], my going farther was prevented by a stream" (28.25). These little streams we may recognize from later types, say, Browning's in "Childe Roland to the Dark Tower Came" and its contrary in "Thamuris marching . . ." in his *Aristophanes' Apology*. Browning knew paradisal landscapes and their demonic mirror-images, and, for that matter, had "all of him [Dante] in

---

4 *La Divina Commedia*, ed. and comm. Umberto Bosco and Giovanni Reggio (Florence: Le Monnier, 1979), note on 27.105.

my head and heart."[5] Again, in that classic and enigmatic mirror-image book, Carroll's *Through the Looking-Glass*, the chess boundaries are marked by streams that are more than ordinary streams.

Dante gives a good deal of attention to his stream, emphasizing how it hides nothing – surprisingly for a stream that is called Lethe, river of forgetfulness. However this Lethe manages to expunge the memory of past sins, it is not by hiding them. Dante is too good a psychologist for that. The stream that conceals nothing ("che nulla nasconde") is unlike the hiddenness of enigma, to say nothing of human deception – the blessed, as Auden said, having nothing to hide ("In Praise of Limestone"). A stream concealing nothing will reflect an image of ourselves that also conceals nothing. Dante the pilgrim does not reflect on this possibility, but Dante the poet has it well in mind and will make use of it. Dante's walk now matches Matelda's, step for step, so that he makes a mirror image of her. If a repeated *sinistra* sounds a little strange, given the standard iconography for *sinister* (the left side is unfavored, the side of the damned), it reminds us that Dante has not yet crossed this strange stream. It also reminds us that mirrors reverse images. (The theologian Karl Barth used this point to make an allegorical reading of Paul's text.[6])

Literal reflection is part of Dante's confession in canto 30. "My eyes fell down to the clear fount, but, seeing myself in it, I drew them back to the grass, so great shame weighed on my brow" (30.76–8). We commonly think of seeing someone face to face in one direction only. I see you. But seeing face to face for Dante requires seeing his own face, face to face. Earthly mirrors and glass are far from perfect, of course, beginning with Paul's *speculum* through to the modern type. (They show our image at half size and reversed, they can squeeze it or expand it, and so on.) We usually assume that we would like to see in a true and perfect seeing, just as we would like to have enigmas answered. But when it happens, Dante cannot bear it. The imperfect *speculum* of earth shelters us from ourselves, as does its *aenigma*.

---

5 Letter to Elizabeth Barrett, 3 May 1845, *Letters of Robert Browning and Elizabeth Barrett Barrett, 1845–1846*, 2 vols., ed. Elvan Kintnor (Cambridge, Mass: Harvard University Press, 1969), vol. I, p. 54.
6 For Barth, creatureliness is like a mirror. "The original, God's primary working, is the divinely ruled history of the covenant. The mirror has nothing to add to this. . . . It cannot repeat it, or imitate its occurrence. It can only reflect it. And as it does so it reverses it, the right being shown as the left and vice versa. Yet the fact remains that it gives us a correspondence and likeness." (*Church Dogmatics*, trans. G. T. Thomson from *Die Kirchliche Dogmatik*, 4 vols. in 13 [Edinburgh: T. & T. Clark, 1936–70], vol. III, *The Doctrine of Creation*, Book III, p. 49.)

It is only when Dante has gone into and across the river, and drunk of it, that he will see Beatrice face to face. But not at first. Beatrice is first discovered gazing in contemplation at the Griffin, and Dante gives us his brightest image of reflection thus far in 31.121–3: "Even like the sun in a mirror [Come in lo specchio il sol], the twofold beast shone within them [Beatrice's eyes], now with the one, now with the other nature." Dante the pilgrim has gone through his mirroring stream and come out the other side. Now he sees in another glass, different in kind, finding not his own image but the image of the Griffin.

The doubleness of all the reflecting surfaces thus far now moves toward a threefold seeing. Not just Beatrice's eyes but what her eyes see. Dante's own eyes see both at once. Not his own face being transformed, but the Griffin continually transmuting itself. The Griffin gleams, not just as in a mirror, but as the sun in a mirror. Dante can apparently now look upon a reflected light so intense that we on earth cannot look without hurting our eyes, as he reminded us at the start of canto 30. It is true that he is seeing at one remove. Beatrice can gaze directly at the changing Griffin, presumably as one of the fully redeemed.

The move from *nunc* to *tunc*, from Paul's earthly to heavenly, here reaches its specular fulfillment. The quest of the eyes has come to its Edenic completion. From now on, we hear chiefly of Dante's eyes. (One exception is in canto 33.18.) Nor are there more mirrors or face-to-face meetings or reflections, whether in mirrors or in water or in eyes. These must wait for the *Paradiso*.

Without such barriers in Dante's Earthly Paradise, it would have been as if there were a mirror of sorts but no enigma, no *in aenigmate*. It would have been as if Eden were simply a mirror projection, a heightened image of our known world that we could enter at will if only we could find it. This is the way we often read earthly paradises now, but it is not the way Dante imagined it. Something in him said that we must earn our right to go back to such a world. Otherwise we will repeat what mankind usually does with earthly paradises. Although we tend to read Edens nowadays as projections of this earth, we still understand this part of the old story: that we need to do something about ourselves before we can inhabit a perfect place. Whether we are transformed through religious rite or through psychological or ethical action, the need for transformation seems a constant. It is a standard plot-line to this day to have some outsider find an earthly paradise only to ruin it, wittingly or unwittingly. Dante lived before the main European discovery of America, but that form of the pattern (insofar as it applies) is all too familiar. Discoveries in space are still writing their own stories.

SCRIPTURE AS ENIGMA

When Dante the pilgrim approaches and then enters the Earthly Paradise, biblical allusions multiply. There is, I believe, a pattern to these allusions in the last seven cantos of the *Purgatorio*, a pattern especially clear in cantos 27 and 28. Again and again in these closing cantos, the biblical allusions turn out to be twofold or threefold. When threefold, they draw on the Old Testament, the New Testament (usually the Gospels), and the Apocalypse. That is, Dante's allusions act out the threefold pattern of a Pauline and Augustinian reading of Scripture outlined in chapter 2. Verses from Genesis, Psalms, especially the Song of Songs, Ezekiel, and elsewhere are read in the light of the Gospel narratives, the point of these biblical allusions. In turn, the Gospel narratives point toward the end of time. Scripture itself is enigma here, in the following sense. In the first change, we come out from under the veil (to follow this Pauline trope) though we still see *in aenigmate*. In the second change, this enigma too will dissolve. Such a patterning may be seen in the full range of Dante's biblical allusions, whether they consist of quotation, allusion proper, or echo ranging from strong to clear to faint.[7]

This is part of a larger process wherein Dante gives the effect of gathering up language itself through his references as well as his allusions.[8] These references and allusions often work out from one word, sometimes implicitly, sometimes explicitly, a word that signifies a physical object or a place in the examples I have noticed. Such glancing or focused uses of the word build a story, a fictive construct, of that word. It is as if the possible stories of a given word were ingathered and put in order, or rather seen in

---

7 The three terms are used as follows. (1) Quotation is marked as such, e.g. by italics. (2) "Allusion" is the intermediate stage between quotation and echo, what a likely reader would likely recognize at a given time and place. ("Allusion" in a general sense refers to the over-all process.) (3) Echo works on a scale of probability, as indicated. See "Questions of Allusion," in my *Against Coercion*, pp. 99–106. The scale is adapted from John Hollander, *The Figure of Echo: A Mode of Allusion in Milton and After* (Berkeley: University of California Press, 1981).

8 By "reference," I mean a remark referring to a biblical event or person or text, without using the actual words of the Bible. Allusion involves verbal repetition. The difference sounds small until we reflect on what poets do with words, and how good allusive work can bring a weight of context to bear. Sources work differently. Alas that Dante's allusions are so often read as dead sources. For the difference, see my "Questions of Allusion." On different types of sources, see Michael Whitworth, " 'Sweet Thames' and *The Waste Land*'s Allusions," *Essays in Criticism* 48 (1998), 35–58.

their right ordering. As this goes on through the closing cantos of the *Purgatorio*, the end of such ordering gradually appears to be the Edenic form of the word and its referent, *verbum* and *res*. We seem to come outside riddling words, words seen *in aenigmate*, and instead begin to see them face to face in their unfallen form, so to speak. Dante is preparing us for a face-to-face seeing of language in the *Paradiso*, at least as far as human words can shadow forth such a thing.[9]

Canto 27.27 offers an extraordinary example of ingathering biblical allusion. Here Dante comes to the wall of fire he must traverse in order to enter Eden. Virgil reassures him that purgatorial fire is not earthly; "it could not touch a hair of thy head [non ti potrebbe far d'un capel calvo]." Commentators regularly mention Luke 21: 18, where Jesus also reassures his disciples that persecution cannot finally harm them: "But there shall not an hair of your head perish." But this seems to me less persuasive than an earlier text from Daniel: "nor was a hair of their head [capillus capitis] singed" (Dan. 3: 94; AV: 3: 27; different numbering because the AV follows the Hebrew Bible). Jesus does not mention fire; the verse from Daniel does. And as a companion for passing through a wall of fire, I would certainly choose the angel that went into Nebuchadnezzar's fiery furnace with the three Jews and walked around with them, all four unharmed inside the flames. The Book of Daniel, like Ezekiel and Revelation, is appropriately apocalyptic for this passage.[10]

In the Book of Daniel (Vulgate version, not the Hebrew or Protestant Bible), there is a hymn sung in the fiery furnace, "The Canticle of the Three Children" (Dan. 3: 52–90). The hymn was "also used in some Masses of the Roman and other Latin rites during the Middle Ages."[11] It repeats anaphorically, in a schematic echoing, forms of the word "Benedictus." Consider the effect of a triple echoing, as Dante's trio passes through the flames. First (27.8), "*Beati*,"[12] from a beatitude in Matthew,

9 Changing the metaphor from visual to acoustic, from sight to echo, we might say that Dante is also preparing us for a face-to-face hearing of language, "mouth to mouth," as God speaks to Moses in the text echoing behind Paul's "face to face" (Num. 12: 6–8). Or rather, the paradisal form of a face-to-face hearing. In both, the enigmas of this life have dissolved.

10 C. H. Grandgent mentions this text in addition to Luke 21: 18, the only commentator in the Dante Dartmouth database to do so; he adds no comment. Note to Canto 27. 27, in *La Divina Commedia*, ed. C. H. Grandgent, rev. edn. (Boston: Heath, 1933).

11 *The New Harvard Dictionary of Music*, ed. Don Michael Randel (Cambridge, Mass.: Harvard University Press, 1986), "canticle."

12 "Beatus" (from *beo*), to follow Lewis and Short, was widely used, and included the meaning of "happy." "Benedictus" (also "blessed") is ecclesiastical Latin (the example in Lewis and Short is from Matthew).

"Blessed are the pure in heart"; second, "Benedictus," from the story of the fiery furnace in Daniel (27.27); third, *"Benedicti,"* again from Matthew, this time with a prophecy of the Last Judgment (27.58). Or rather, not a triple echoing but two quotations framing the memory of a very possible multiple echo. As always, the literary distinctions matter, here for Dante's command of allusive technique. The first "Blessed" (*Beati*) sounds out, then a memory of Daniel recalls (if this is allusion) or may well recall (if this is echo) a series of "Benedictus" words. But these are not voiced in the text; they are just there as potential. The triumphant final *"Benedicti"* is heard at the moment when all three, like the three in Daniel, emerge from the fire. For those with Scripture in their heads, the mind's ear repeats "Benedictus," fainter or louder, throughout the ordeal by fire, until the word itself emerges from the flame and into the text, and we hear it spoken aloud in the form in which Jesus used it. It is as if we hear that move through the wall of flame taking the time it takes to sing those thirty-nine verses and thirty-nine instances of "Benedictus" or "Benedictum" or "Benedicite" or "Benedicat." It is also as if the echo comes from the Old Testament into the New, where it changes from echo to quotation. Hence also, as if echo is to Old Testament type as quotation is to New Testament antitype.

Once again, we are hearing a pattern of multiple allusion, following the sequence of Old Testament, Gospel, and Apocalypse. And our faintest hearing, an echo, is from "under the veil," while the two quotations draw on louder, clearer, and less enigmatic New Testament verses.

Similarly, the opening quotation from Canto 27.8: *"Beati mundo corde!"* As commentators regularly note, Dante implicitly reminds the reader of what the blessed see, through the portion of the text he does not quote. "Blessed are the pure in heart [Beati mundo corde], for they shall see God" (Matt. 5: 8). If readers hear the Psalm behind this beatitude, Psalm 23 (AV 24), they will hear of another holy mountain and another "Benedictus": "Who shall ascend the hill of the Lord, and who shall stand in his holy place? He that hath clean hands and a pure heart [mundo corde]" (3–4). And then: "He shall receive the blessing [benedictionem] from the Lord" (5). Once again, we have the pattern of an Old Testament echo (Psalms) emerging in a quotation from the Gospels (the beatitude), itself pointing toward the end of time ("for they shall see God"). Allusion itself can act out the process of "Videmus nunc per speculum in aenigmate, tunc autem facie ad faciem," unveiling the Hebrew Scriptures, while still anticipating a completely unveiled reading at the end of time.

THE LEXIS AND TROPING OF ENIGMA

One small example that wonderfully shows the process of redeeming language, of moving it from *in aenigmate* to its Edenic form, is what happens to the word *capra* (goat). It appears first in the six-tercet epic simile of Canto 27 (76–93). Having passed through the wall of fire that guards Eden, Dante and his two companions, Virgil and Statius, are overtaken by nightfall and must sleep on the mountain-steps leading up to the Earthly Paradise. "As goats that have been quick and wanton . . .lie mildly chewing the cud . . . I like a goat and they like shepherds . . . So ruminating and so gazing at them, sleep seized me" (27.76–91). Commentators rightly note both Virgilian and biblical pastoral traditions here. This is all very well, but why does Dante call himself a goat, first figuratively and then pointedly ("Quali . . . le capre . . . io come capra"), and a ruminator, first figuratively and then pointedly (*ruminando . . . .. ruminando* frame the whole eighteen-line epic simile). It is not just that biblical goats do not often lead a happy life, even if classical ones do. It is especially and inescapably that, only six tercets earlier, an angelic voice guiding Dante through the flames has quoted the Gospel of Matthew (27.58): "*Venite, benedicti Patris mei*" (Come, blessed of my Father . . . Matt. 25: 34). Jesus is foretelling what will happen in the Last Judgment when the blessed will be welcomed into heaven. What just precedes Dante's quotation is: "and he shall separate them one from another, as a shepherd divideth his sheep from the goats [oves ab haedis]: and he shall set the sheep on his right hand, but the goats on the left [a dextris suis, haedos autem a sinistris]" (Matt. 25: 32–3). These goats do not get into heaven.

And is it an accidental felicity that when dawn comes following Dante's prophetic dream, "le tenebre fuggian" (27.112), "the shadows were fleeing," in the English of Binyon and Sinclair, who surely (and rarely among the best-known translators) had the 1611 English Bible in their ears.[13] For the Song of Songs repeats the clause, "the shadows flee away" ("Until the day break and the shadows flee away, turn my beloved"; 2: 17 and see 4: 6). It is a verse I have not seen cited, yet consider the context of daybreak, the use of the verb "turn" (*revertere* in the modern Vulgate) along with Dante's many other words for "turn" throughout these cantos, the use of

---

13 Laurence Binyon, Dante's *Purgatorio with a Translation into English Triple Rhyme* (London: Macmillan, 1938).

the Song of Songs yet once more in the entry into paradise.[14] In Canticles 2:
17, the verse continues: "turn, my beloved, and be thou like a roe or a young
hart upon the mountains [revertere; similis esto, dilecte mi, capreae]," for
indeed a *caprea* as against a *caper* is a roe, to follow the 1611 Authorized
Version. (The term *caprea* is also used in Virgil's *Georgics* II.374, just as
haedis is, IV.10; a *caper* appears in *Eclogues* VII.7. All three terms and more
appear in the Vulgate, which is to say that Dante was familiar with them.) Is
Dante quietly acknowledging the blessedness that has brought him here, in
spite of everything, *caper* though he has been?[15] The blessedness that will let
him know something of what a *caprea* might know on the mountains of the
Song of Songs, themselves one type for the Earthly Paradise? I think so.
Gian Roberto Sarolli has inferred something similar, not from Dante's art
of allusion, but from the double tradition concerning goats in Isidore, who
conflates *caprea* with *caper*, *capra* and so on.[16]

The idyllic forest of Eden in canto 28 is much as we expect, not least
because Dante's earthly paradise has informed so many later ones. Canto
29 and its most enigmatic vision are something other. Dante writes
enigmatic narrative after the manner of the Apocalypse, yet he also
embeds in it quotations from the Psalms (29.3), Song of Songs (30.11),
the Gospels (29.51), the Epistles (29.38), and even Virgil (30.21). In
comparison, all these latter quotations are simple, sensuous and passion-
ate, to quote Milton's words on poetry as compared with prose. The effect
is to suggest the possibility of a simpler, clearer apprehension of apocalypse. It also reminds us that some passages in the enigmatic Ezekiel and

This is an extraordinary if quiet exercise in lexis. The field of association for the word "goat" changes, and Dante thereby shows a world
changing.[17] The very word "goat" can be shown now redeemed and no
longer damned. If these allusive echoes are resounding here, this too
shows Dante's threefold patterning of Old Testament (Song of Songs),
New Testament Gospel (Matthew), and Apocalypse (anticipated in the
parable in Matthew).

---

14 See also Lino Pertile, *La puttana e il giganto. Dal Cantico dei Cantici al Paradiso terrestre di Dante*
    (Ravenna: A. Longo, 1998).
15 Goats are traditionally known as lascivious, as witness Shakespeare's Touchstone (*As You Like It*
    III.iii.7–9).
16 Sarolli, *Prolegomena alla "Divina Commedia"* (Florence: Leo S. Olschki, 1971), pp. 404–5,
    especially p. 405n.
17 Milton does something similar with words, showing them in an unfallen then a fallen sense. I
    wonder if he learned it from Dante. See "The Senses of Eliot's Salvages" in my *Against Coercion*,
    pp. 120–7.

Daniel and John of Patmos are themselves simple, sensuous, and passion-ate. For all the strangeness of Dante's vision in canto 29 and later, his rhetorical effects and his argument are peculiarly lucid and peculiarly enigmatic all at once. Dante's mastery of the language of enigma and the language of transparence and reflection is everywhere evident. If we think of mirrors and glass as offering clarity to some degree, then this peculiar combining of lucidity and enigma will again evoke Paul's text. All the more so when the climax of these cantos is the face-to-face sight of the redeemed Beatrice herself.

In the penultimate line of canto 31, two words about Beatrice unveiled sound as if they form an oxymoron, "harmonies" and "o'ershadowed": "Heaven with its harmonies overhanging thee [armonizzando il ciel t'adombra], when in the free air thou didst disclose thyself [quando nell'aere aperto ti solvesti]." Surely, we might think, we have now come past shadow. Yet the word is exactly right. The *ombra* of heaven is obviously different from the *ombra* of hell, but also, Dante quietly implies, even from the *ombra* of the earthly paradise at its most glorious. In comparison with the light of heaven, even the light of this revelation is overshadowed. The language of enigma concentrates itself here with logic and economy.

Something else is at work in the veiling of Beatrice herself (30.28). All through this passage, the *oscura* of everyday seeing *in aenigmate* is grad-ually dissolving. *Nebbia, velo, (ombrata), vapori, nuvola,* and then *vel.* Beatrice is not yet *manifesta*, the word "manifest" being part of the standard lexis of enigma and a biblical term for revelation (in the AV, sometimes "shewing forth," sometimes the latinate "manifest"). Beatrice's power is mysterious enough to be called *occulta*. Though she cannot be seen distinctly, Dante knows in whose presence he stands, and he trembles because of the "hidden virtue [occulta virtù] that came from her" (30.38). Again, this is a word that belongs to the lexis of enigma, whether *occulta* is for good or for ill. Gradually, through this passage, enigma shades over into what we might call "mystery."

We are also watching the continuing purgation of words themselves. Just as the word "goat" was purged of its fallen meanings, so also the lexis of enigma, and markedly the word *oscura*. Dante's famous "selva oscura" at the very start of the *Commedia* introduces so powerful an *oscura* that it will resonate throughout.[18] Here in Eden, the *oscura* gradually becomes entirely that of creatureliness, so that before Dante leaves Eden, he will

18 See Hein's introductory pages in his *Enigmaticité et Messianisme dans la "Divine Comédie."*

know only the *oscura* that the unfallen Adam and Eve knew. Similarly the living stream with a will of its own is quite dark, "mova bruna bruna" (28.31), the word *bruna* itself being purged from its infernal uses (as in "l'onda bruna," the dark water, *Inferno* 3.112). So also "sotto l'ombra perpetüa" purges the words "perpetual shade."

A knot, like a cloud, may also be troped so as to indicate sin. In *Purgatorio* 9.126, "'l nodo digroppa" means "disentangles or unloosens the knot of sin," to follow the commentary of Porena cited in Singleton's edition. The closing *nodo* in the *Commedia* in Paradiso 33.91 is utterly different in kind. Like the Mountain of Transfiguration, it gathers in, even as it governs, every *nodo*. The trope of nets and traps works similarly. Beatrice reproaches Dante for his folly: "in vain is the net [rete] spread or arrow shot in the sight of the full-fledged bird" (31.62–3). The reader may also smile when Beatrice's holy smile draws like the old net, "così lo santo riso / a sé traéli con l'antica rete" (32.5–6). Singleton recalls the old love ("d'antico amor," 30.39) and the old flame ("l'antica fiamma," 30.48), and stresses the connection of *antica* with the *vita nuova*. But in the sequence that *antica* marks, *amor*, *fiamma*, *rete*, all these words are read in a newly redeemed erotic and enigmatic context. *Amor* itself, like enigma, will metamorphose as in Paul's chapter in Corinthians.

THE GRIFFIN-ENIGMA AGAIN

Dante's famous Griffin in the great vision that overwhelms him in *Purgatorio* 29 comes to our mind's eye from illustrations or from its separate existence in bestiaries and sculpture. When the Graeco-Latin pun on *griphos-griphus* and *gryps-gryphus* arrives on the scene, things change. The Griffin becomes a possible personification of enigma.

As noted earlier, the Latin word *griphus* was not generally known in the Latin of the Middle Ages. It does not turn up in standard lexicons such as the *Catholicon* (1286) of Balbus[19] and the *Glossarium mediae et infimae Latinitatis* of Du Cange. Nor is it listed in the *Summa Britonis* of William Brito (d. 1356), or the *Promptorium Parvulorum* (c. 1440); the 1483 *Catholicon Anglicum* lists only enigma under "Rydellynge."

But the word was available to Dante in Aulus Gellius, who mentions it in its Greek form, *griphos*, in the *Noctes Atticae* (1.ii.3–4). The term simply signifies a "riddle." Two medieval dictionaries also list one example each

---

19 For information about Latin, Latin–English and English–Latin dictionaries, from Balbus on, see Starnes, *Renaissance Dictionaries*.

of the word *griphus*. The first is a single and anomalous listing.[20] The second, more interesting for Dante, is a twelfth-century quotation from Peter of Blois: "neither the invisible riddles [griphos] of Plato nor the ingenuities of Aristotle" (*Serm.* 649c).[21] The interest lies in the source and also in the fact that a *griphos* comes with no comic associations whatever. On the contrary, it refers to large and significant enigmas. Some mid-sixteenth-century English lexicographers also included the word *griphus* without distinguishing it from *aenigma*. In 1629, visions in the Book of Daniel are called *griphes* in one of the numerous collections of sermons by Pierre de Besse, sometime "predicateur ordinaire du Roy."[22] Similarly with the Abbé Cotin (see chapter 6).

Where the word *griphus* is well known, a pun on "griffin" comes with strong comic connotations and would hardly seem appropriate in Dante's great vision in *Purgatorio* 29. But for him, it was a very rare word, and Dante did not know Greek literature except for what was available to him in translation. Nor should our sense of generic fitness be imposed on him, for both historical and aesthetic reasons. In the *Cambridge Companion to Dante*, Joan Ferrante notes his punning,[23] while Giuseppe Mazzotta's *Dante's Vision and the Circle of Knowledge* (1993) includes a section on "Theologia Ludens."[24]

With this punning possibility in mind, I want to venture briefly on to the hazardous ground of the allegoresis of Dante's great mysterious Griffin at the end of the *Purgatorio*. The general lines of argument are well known. Is the Griffin allegorically Christ (the usual identification) or is it not (a minor but quite well-founded dissident movement)? On the majority side, the creature has two natures in one, and its colors are readily seen as those of Christ. (The eagle portion is gold, and the leonine is white mixed with "vermiglio" [29.114], the colors of the lover in the Song of Songs 5: 11, allegorically Christ.) Beatrice gazes at it in rapt contemplation, and Dante in wonder, seeing it reflected in her eyes. The Griffin later binds the chariot's pole to the tree of Eden (32.49–51),

20 R. E. Latham, ed., *Revised Medieval Latin Word-List from British and Irish Sources* (London: Oxford University Press, 1965): *gliphus (griphus)*, meaning "enigma" and dated c. AD 1000.

21 D. R. Howlett, ed., *Dictionary of Medieval Latin from British Sources*, Fasc. IV (London: Oxford University Press for the British Academy, 1989), "griphus." I am grateful to E. G. Stanley for drawing this to my attention.

22 Pierre de Besse, *Conceptions Theologiques sur Toutes les Festes des Saincts et Autres Solemnelles de l'Année* (Douay: Laurent Kellam, 1629), p. 546.

23 "A Poetics of Chaos and Harmony," in *The Cambridge Companion to Dante*, ed. Rachel Jacoff (Cambridge: Cambridge University Press, 1993), pp. 153–71.

24 *Dante's Vision and the Circle of Knowledge* (Princeton: Princeton University Press, 1993).

allegorically re-attaching the cross to its original tree, a Christ-like act. On the contrary side, the strongest reason against is the blessing offered to the Griffin (quoted below). In tone it is tactless at the least, and in poetic resonance oddly dead for Dante. Colin Hardie put the case strongly some years ago, and Peter Dronke and Peter Armour have done so more recently.[25] No consensus about an alternative has been reached.

I want to work out from a logical surmise. Apart from Griffin and chariot and Beatrice with her handmaidens, the procession shows the books of the Bible as living creatures, the living word. If we ask: what sustains the Christian Church along with the Word, the answer is simple. Word and sacrament, as the common pairing goes. If the chariot is in some way the Church, is the Griffin in some way the sacrament, in particular, the sacrament of the Eucharist? Not in an either-or sense, which may be the chief problem with the question about the Griffin, as put above. More precisely put, is the Griffin Christ after all, but not Christ pure and simple? Rather Christ as embodied in the Eucharist, that is, as the sacramental way of crossing from earth to heaven? Is Dante portraying Christ through threefold biblical reference, Old Testament (Song of Songs), Gospels (earthly life and death), and Apocalypse (his gold or eternal nature) – all offered in one as a means by which humans may also be changed, that is, the Eucharist?

If Dante the poet is punning on *griphus* and *gryphus*, then the mostly hidden, double meaning of the Griffin-Enigma would be one reason among several for choosing this particular legendary creature. Not just because Alexander's flight aloft was powered by griffins. But also because a griffin-enigma comes from the edge of the world; comes from the mountains in these mountain-cantos; attacks those that would steal its gold and thus knows how to defend its own golden part, especially against the one-eyed. Its traditional enemies, the Arimaspians, are one-eyed – in legend, thieves and brigands, and in a trope, perhaps those who see with single vision, as Blake put it. Rabelais identified those inhabitants of northern Europe who accepted the Reformation as one-eyed Arimaspians, having lost the eye of faith (*Gargantua*, IV.16 and V.29). As for Dante reading *griphus* as "enigma," certainly the nature of Jesus as the Christ is a mystery. The OED lists Wyclif's use of the word "riddle" (1380) for the

---

25 Colin Hardie, "The Symbol of the Gryphon in *Purgatorio* XXIX 108 and following Cantos," in *Centenary Essays on Dante* (Oxford: Clarendon, 1965), pp. 103–31; Peter Dronke, "The Procession in Dante's *Purgatorio*," *Deutsches-Dante-Jahrbuch* 53–4 (1978–79), 18–45; Peter Armour, *Dante's Griffin and the History of the World: A Study of the Earthly Paradise* (Oxford: Clarendon, 1989).

two natures of Christ, and also Jeremy Taylor's use of the word "enigma" (1678). Just as certainly, the Eucharist is also a mystery – *aenigma et parabola*, as Thomas Aquinas called it.[26] Lampe's *Patristic Greek Lexicon* offers three meanings for *ainigma*, the third being "symbol, sign," of which the last instance is "sacramental." The illustrative quotations in Lampe all come from Dante's much-favored Dionysius the Areopagite, and two refer to the Eucharist.

So read, Beatrice's rapt gaze is of the Eucharist in its own being and mystery (31.119–20). "As in a glass," Dante goes on, "Come in lo specchio" (31.121), that is, *per speculum*. "Think, Reader, if within myself I marveled, / When I beheld the thing itself stand still, / And in its image it transformed itself" (31.121–6; Longfellow, chosen because he uses the prefix, "trans-" in "transformed" for Dante's "transmutava")[27]. So read, the double creature shines first with its gold or heavenly aspect and then with its white and red or earthly aspect – the white and red of flesh and blood, and also of wafer and wine, transmuted, to follow the doctrine of transubstantiation (defined in 1215), into the flesh and blood of Christ. It is as if Dante sees the Eucharist itself come alive, and so perforce an earthly form of Christ, continually transmuting itself into a heavenly form. The Eucharist effects a change of substance even as earthly bodies will themselves be changed.

Dante, overcome by a hymn he hears and cannot endure, falls into a death-like sleep, then wakes as to a revelation and as if he had been on the Mount of Transfiguration with Jesus, Moses, and Elias, and as in heaven. He experiences in sleep a passage as if from death to life; it is embodied in two epic similes. An enigma, I have argued, is rhetorically a closed simile, where one term of the "like" in a simile is hidden. Suppose you experience the passage from death-like sleep to life, as if living out the mystery of the Eucharist, as if dying Jesus' death on the cross, then awaking to resurrection and eventually ascension. How are you to translate this into words, how to trope it? It is untranslatable, and still mysterious and partly unremembered, so you say so. But it is like other stories, so you say that too: it is like a pagan story of death and a Gospel story of experiencing a taste of heaven while on earth. It is like ingesting, first the bitter fruit, the *discindere*, of the tree, and then the sweet fruit. Dante can only endure this

---

26 *Super Evangelium Johannis*, cp 6 (lc 7 [241]), on Matt. 26: 26 and body, blood, and the sacraments. In the *Summa Theologiae tertia pars*, he quotes 1 Cor. 13: 12 in a discussion of the necessity of the sacraments: "per speculum in aenigmate *cognoscimus*" (qu 61, ar 4, my itals).

27 Other translations are: "varying" (Cary), "changing" (Carlyle-Wickstead, Sinclair, Singleton), "change" (Sayers), "working change on change" (Ciardi).

miraculous crossing-over while unconscious, nor can he understand the hymning of it or recall any dream. But he knows what the experience is like. This is how the great enigmas may be apprehended: indirectly by their effects and by the indirections of troping.

This is not the place for a fuller exploration of this reading, but it is worth mentioning that one iconographical tradition of the griffin goes some way toward supporting it.

A number of commentators have thought that the Eucharist should find a place at the end of the *Purgatorio*. Dante's excellent translator John Sinclair speaks for them:

The total absence of the Eucharist from the *Purgatorio* would be strange in itself and it would be especially so in the conditions of the time, when the subject was prominently before the mind of the Church . . . The culminating scene . . . seems singularly fitted to express . . . the beatific vision under the limiting symbolic conditions of the earthly life, the eucharistic presence of Christ . . . It is a fair question whether it is credible that Dante – a "transubstantially-minded man" as he has been well called – should have totally ignored the Eucharist in such a work as the *Purgatorio*; and if the Eucharist is not here it is nowhere in the *Divine Comedy*.[28]

Perhaps the Eucharist has been enigmatically and mysteriously hidden in too evident a place, rather like Poe's purloined letter. If the Griffin is verbally a synonym for enigma and iconographically a partaker of the Eucharist, and if Dante's Griffin has been read over the centuries as Christ, then we might consider a full reading of the creature as Christ-as-Eucharist.

In the Sphinx's riddle, she kills or eats you (one of humankind) if you can't answer her riddle (the answer being you yourself, humankind). Her leonine portion, unlike the Griffin's, menaces human creatures. In the Griffin-Enigma of Christ-as-sacrament, you eat the riddle itself, and thereby move from seeing inside an enigma to containing the mystery of the enigma inside you. You do not eat it in the way the Sphinx eats, that is, destroying it in the eating. Rather, it gives you life, yet retains its own life, thereby doubly conquering death.

There are other monsters throughout the *Commedia*, but only the Sphinx offers herself as an embodied, personified form of enigma. Or rather, of inimical enigma, as against Dante's Griffin if we read him as a

---

28 Singleton, quoting Grandgent, also notes "that 'benedictus qui venit' are the last words sung by the assistants before the Canon of the Mass, expressing the expectation of the bodily coming of Christ" (note to 30.19).

personified enigma. The Sirens (*le serene*), who turn up in canto 31 in Beatrice's lesson on how to avoid them, are deceptive but not particularly enigmatic. Sirens appear along with sphinxes on various friezes and pottery, and also on lists of classical monsters. The two types make a nice pair. Both use traps. (Old birds, says Beatrice, know how to avoid the trap of a net [*rete*].) Both are hybrid creatures. The sphinx traps through riddle and the siren through song – or through riddle and charm (etymologically *carmen* or "song").

There is another personified figure of enigma, well known through Virgil and others. That figure is the Sibyl, especially the Sibyl of Cumae, Virgil's expounder of enigmas. At the end of the *Purgatorio*, Dante offers us the personified enigma figure of the Griffin, together with a reminder of the personified figure of inimical enigma, the Theban Sphinx. At the end of the *Paradiso*, he offers us "la sentenza di Sibilla" (33.66, the Sibyl's oracle) as part of his great vision of the eternal heavens.

When Beatrice ends her dark utterance, the tone of the canto relaxes. Dante naturally enough asks why her words are so far beyond his comprehension, to which she answers in words like God's to Job or to the Psalmist. She then promises, like Jesus in John's Gospel, to speak plainly in the future. The enigma lesson is over.

The rhetoricians' standard example of enigma was the mother-child or ice-water riddle. In the closing canto of Dante's great work (*Paradiso* 33), St. Bernard begins his hymn to the Virgin Mary with the paradoxical line "Figlia del tuo figlio" (daughter of your son). We might call this the sacred and unique form of the mother-child ice-water enigma. The tragic or perverted form of such a generational paradox would be found in Jocasta and Oedipus. We might go on to consider an aesthetic form of this standard enigma as well. It would involve a Dante who creates Beatrice in the *Commedia*, a Beatrice who in turn becomes an agent, a muse figure, and a guiding spirit of Dante's creation itself – for him a *figlia del tuo figlio*.

CHAPTER 5

Questions of riddle and genre

Game-forms have always been in literature.
(Northrop Frye, *Late Notebooks*, vol. II, p. 604)

Is the riddle a simple preliterary form, as André Jolles calls it? Or is it a generic seed or kernel, starting off new trees in the field of genre, as Northrop Frye implies? Or is it already a complex genre itself rather than a seed, as Alastair Fowler suggests? And how helpful are such questions?

In his 1976 essay, "Charms and Riddles," Frye sets out a biological analogy in order to draw boundary lines for the study of genres—a somewhat odd analogy apart from the final trope. Genres of imagery are the roots of literature, genres of narrative the stems and branches, and genres of structure the leaf–flower–fruit cycles. "And finally, there are generic seeds or kernels, possibilities of expression sprouting and exfoliating into new literary phenomena." Both charms and riddles are such generic seeds or kernels (p. 123). Six years later, Alastair Fowler quietly revised this in the course of arguing with André Jolles's *Einfache Formen*. Jolles like Frye, but more systematically and widely, posited "nine pre-literary genres as the building blocks for more complex genres." They include riddle and proverb. But, Fowler objects, these "simple forms turn out themselves to be complex genres, many of them, in their own right, with their own developmental and in part literary history" (*Kind of Literature*, p. 151). Is the riddle a complex genre or a generic seed? It is not, in any case, a simple form, at least considered in its own right. Neck-riddles (see p. 119 below), folk riddles and more suggest that the genre is far from simple.

Perhaps it is both a complex genre and a generic seed. The separate or free-standing riddle does qualify as a genre, to follow the fifteen typical characteristics ascertained by Fowler. So does an expanded form of riddle such as the well-known Old English riddles. But the riddle also appears as part of numerous other works: sacred writing (epistolary, etc.), tragedy, comedy, romance, lyric kinds, even the novel. Here its function varies widely. Sometimes it does act like a generic seed. Structurally, for example, the detective story or apocalyptic writing can be seen as sprouting from the riddle. One riddle like one proverb can make a fable in little. Some riddles and enigmas are very condensed forms of a masterplot, Ur-forms so to speak, that may be expanded into various narratives. Like the dramatic monologue, which encapsulates the action of a potential play in one speech, so also enigma as masterplot. The Sphinx's enigma can encapsulate Sophocles' great play. St. Paul's rhetoric moves quickly from now to then, *nunc* to *tunc*, in his encapsulated vision of present enigma and eventual light. Such condensation tempts us toward originary and small tropes like seeds and kernels.

Similarly with the "root" metaphor, when the riddle is defined as one of the roots of lyric poetry, as in Andrew Welsh's trope.[1] Welsh illustrates his case by quoting small riddle-like passages or metaphors from such poets as Hopkins, and then linking them with enigma in a large sense related to mystery. That is, he follows Frye in ascertaining a line of riddle poetry and charm poetry. What Frye and Welsh are mainly talking about, however, are riddling effects rather than riddles proper. I make the distinction because the adjective "riddling" describes certain styles and a certain line of inheritance in English poetry, as sketched by Frye and outlined below. I make the distinction also because, as Fowler notes, an adjective ordinarily defines a mode rather than a genre. It helps a good deal to identify this last function of riddle as a mode. Just as comedy can be one capacious and complex genre, while comic X or Y can function as a mode within other genres, so also with riddle and riddling effects.

The question is more than a matter for specialists. Just as it helps to think of enigma as a figure of speech, both a trope and a scheme, so also it helps to think of enigma as both genre and mode. Above all, the distinction between riddle as genre and riddling as mode acts so as to set some reasonable limits to the terms "riddle" and "enigma." Otherwise, just about anything can be classified as riddle or as rooted in riddle.

Beyond riddle as mode, we can also find ourselves all too easily en route to calling every question or puzzle or mystery in writing, whether large or small, a plant of the species "riddle." Critics intrigued by odd diction or unexpected tropes can make riddles of them where none exists. We need

---

1 Welsh expands Frye's essay in his *Roots of Lyric* (1978).

to ask whether unfamiliar or odd or imaginative wording is really in a riddling mode, even if the distinction sometimes blurs. If such wording retains its enigma after we know the answer, then we do have a riddle or a riddling mode. Otherwise, the terms are in danger of becoming mere hype.

If we enlarge the term "riddle," moving it toward "mystery," its functions widen accordingly. John Bayley observes that "the novel and story depend a good deal on mystery"; he quotes Tzvetan Todorov's observation "that Henry James's stories mostly depend on a query and a riddle, which their endings formulate with complete artistry but without solving: the puzzle is itself the solution."[2] A concrete symbol may function in a riddling way, central to a given plot. "Henry James' golden bowl is an object which is also a focus of consciousness: it seems to contain the whole secret of the story; it's a riddle to be read."[3] This does sound like Jolles's sense of the riddle form. Not so much his mistaken description of the riddle as a simple form, as his sense of the riddle as an originating force in the development of literature.[4]

In what follows, I want to expand a little on the argument about riddle as mode compared with riddle as genre, as well as suggesting some lines of thought about other generic matters. I have disregarded genre studies that try to dispense with genre altogether, an impossible notion. For me, as for Adena Rosmarin in 1985, genre makes sense as "a tool of critical explanation" ("Defining a Theory of Genre," pp. 48–9).[5] Modern anti-genre wars go back to at least 1971, and Todorov's essay "The Origin of Genres." There he quotes Maurice Blanchot's comment that many writers of the time were "'subject to that impetuous pressure of literature that no longer recognizes the distinction between genres and seeks to destroy their limits.'"[6] But, Todorov observes, "'genre' as such has not disppeared; the genres-of-the-past have simply been replaced by others" (p. 14). *Plus ça change, plus c'est la même chose.*

---

2 John Bayley, *London Review of Books*, 8 October 1992.
3 Frye, *Late Notebooks, 1982–1990*, vol. II, p. 426.
4 Ducrot and Todorov call Jolles's description of simple forms and their function "inadequate." But they do find his work on such forms suggestive for the typological study of literature. As against the longstanding traditional pattern of genres (lyric, epic, dramatic), Jolles does take into account "certain verbal forms, such as the proverb, the enigma, and so on" (*Encyclopaedic Dictionary*, p. 155). Genette's *The Architext* demonstrates in detail that this "traditional pattern of . . . lyric, epic, dramatic" does not appear as such in classical writing, as widely assumed. It is in effect an eighteenth-century formulation.
5 See also her astute analysis of genre wars in "Theoretical Introduction."
6 Blanchot, *Le Livre à venir* (Paris: Gallimard, 1959), p. 136, quoted in Todorov, "The Origin of Genres," in his *Genres in Discourse*, p. 13.

THE FREE-STANDING RIDDLE: GENRE AND SUB-GENRE

Genres commonly display certain traits, and Fowler suggests that we can test a specific case by asking how far it shows these characteristics. This method is flexible and practical, while the last of Fowler's traits provides a place for the reader's interpretive role, a matter of interest for genre studies following his book. The traits include form, theme, and situation, and thereby a wide spectrum of evidence. Of fifteen features commonly observed in a genre, the single riddle or riddle-poem regularly shows the following nine. (I have retained Fowler's numbering for clarity; the categories not applicable are listed in the notes.[7])

(2) "Every kind is characterized by an *external structure*." The riddle is characterized by the structure of question and answer.

(4) "As every kind has a formal structure, so it must have a *size*." The riddle has by definition a small size, being remarkably condensed. Even when expanded, riddles are short. Ausonius managed to write ninety lines on the enigma of the number three in his *Griphus ternarii numeri*, but this is really a series of riddles and pseudo-riddles all clustered around one answer.

(6) "*Subject*" is limited generically, according to ancient and neoclassical decorum. Riddles seem remarkably unrestrained in subject matter, though Fowler observes that "proverbs are about common shared experiences" (p. 65). We might say that riddles are about common shared experience that is seen in an uncommon way.

(7) "Closely related are the *values* inherent in all kinds." Here is a strong characteristic of riddle and enigma, as witness the heated disputes over their usefulness. The range of value attributed to them runs from Aristotle's and Augustine's esteem to disdain.

(8) "Each kind has an emotional coloration, which may be called *mood*." For riddle and enigma, this can be complicated, though mostly it is straightforward. The initial mood is curiosity, followed by satisfaction that should provide amusement or enlightenment or both. The kind and degree of curiosity and satisfaction can vary a great deal. If further moods are engendered, this indicates that a given riddle may be an enigma with troping power.

(9) "Many kinds used to have a characteristic *occasion*." Riddles indeed used to have, and sometimes still do, a characteristic occasion: social gatherings, playground amusement, neck-riddle contests.

7 See *Kinds of Literature*, pp. 60–74.

(10) "Occasion . . . coalesces with the stylistic feature *attitude.*" Riddle and enigma involve a riddler and a riddlee. The attitude of both is ordinarily good-humored, but even good humor can vary. Beyond good humor, the attitude ranges widely, all the way to sinister.

(14) "Every kind has its range of appropriate *style.*" Here is a strong characteristic of riddle and enigma, a characteristic that could raise hackles and cause controversy.

(15) Some constituents have been more recently suggested, such as "the reader's *task.*" Fowler remarks that "one of the pleasures of reading is that hermeneutic activity differs with kind." With riddle and enigma, as with the detective story, the reader is invited to join in solving the question.

Such tabulated characteristics may reinforce the notion that genre is prescriptive and that genre studies consist of pigeon-holing various works. Not at all. In his 1991 *Genres and Readers*, Gian Biagio Conte devotes a chapter to showing yet once more how a sense of genre helps us to read ("Genre between Empiricism and Theory"). Similarly with Claudio Guillén's earlier argument that "genres operate as problem-solving models."[8] Writers rely on their readers' ability to ascertain a given genre, especially when they wish to vary it or expand it or mix it with another genre.[9]

If it helps to think of the riddle as a genre (and I think it does), how are types of riddle such as the literary riddle and the neck-riddle related, to take only two well-known examples?

The literary riddle is a neatly circumscribed example, or so it seems at first. What we commonly call the "literary riddle," as defined by Archer Taylor, appears to constitute a minor genre or sub-genre. Literary riddles are "riddles composed by conscious literary artists" as against riddles of unknown origin, that is, folk riddles (The Riddle," 143). Though the distinction between folk riddles and literary riddles is important to folklorists, there is little reason to separate them structurally as forms of

(1) A "distinctive *representational aspect*" does not apply to riddle, as it is too short.

(3) Ancient criticism associated certain genres with a certain "*metrical structure*"; this does not apply.

(5) "*Scale*": the riddle is too short for this to be in play.

(11) "Narrative kinds may have a distinctive *mise-en-scène.*" The riddle is not a narrative kind, and does not.

(12) "*Character* is the focus of much existing genre theory." This does not generally apply to riddle and enigma, though the character of a given riddler sometimes matters greatly, as in Shakespeare's *Pericles.*

(13) Action of a certain kind may be related to genre. Here again, the riddle is too short for this to apply, unless the action of applying one's wit is pertinent.

8 Cited Fowler (p. 31), who observes that the idea is at least as old as Dante.

9 See Colie on *genera mixta* in her *The Resources of Kind.*

the riddle. But historically, one commonly follows the other, and a diachronic theory of genre rather than a synchronic one will try to distinguish. Of course, a folk riddle may have been originally invented by an author who was once known, before it began to spread as a popular riddle. (How did the Sphinx's riddle come to be so widespread? Do all the examples from Africa and Asia come from the riddle that Sophocles already knew and used? Or does his extraordinary treatment of the Sphinx's riddle help to explain its appearance around the world? See Taylor, p. 260 below.) Fowler suggests the importance of distinguishing primary and secondary kinds, for example, folk ballad and art ballad, or traditional proverb and Blakeian proverb. In this patterning, the folk riddle would be a primary kind and the literary riddle a secondary kind. "Primary" and "secondary" have to do with the continuous historical de-velopment of a genre, with no implication of superiority in either kind.[10] The point is important because of former, and lingering, associations with the word "folk," including folk riddles.

The word "folk riddle," like "folk song," "folklore," etc., is formed after the German *Volk-* pattern. The word "folk" in this sense goes back only to the nineteenth century in English. An archaic use of "folk" refers to an aggregation of people, sometimes distinguished from a leader or from God. (Langland's field full of folk in *Piers Plowman* is such a use.) A colloquial use nowadays refers to family, often in the plural (my "folks") or to ordinary people ("just plain folks"). But "folk art," folklore," and so on are rooted in a nineteenth-century interest in the history of *das Volk*, especially the German study of the subject. This word-history is of special interest for two reasons: (1) the way in which assumed stories about primitive peoples can become attached to the study of literary and linguistic questions; and (2) the way in which such stories are extended from regional to national (even nationalist) or cultural or religious matters.

An older view of the "folk" is evident in James A. Kelso's generally excellent 1918 article on riddles. "Origin and Development" (Part 3) opens by asserting that "The riddle originated in the infancy of the human race." At once we are placed in a story of human development, where there is only one place for adulthood, maturity, full flowering, and that is the present or the steadily-approaching full-flowering future. Kelso quotes Herder's *Vom Geist der hebräischen Poesie*, the origin of much mischief:

---

10 See Fowler's entire discussion, including a discussion of primitive versus artificial (*Kinds of Literature*, pp. 160–4).

"all peoples in the first stages of culture are lovers of riddles" (*The Spirit of Hebrew Poetry*, p. 208). As with the metaphor of infancy, so with the word "first." "The same spirit," Kelso continues, paraphrasing Herder, "which gave birth to the folk-song and folk-proverb likewise produced the riddle" ("Riddle," p. 767). Certainly, proverbs are also an ancient genre, and many folk songs have an ancient history. Certainly one may infer a certain spirit in which these literary forms were devised and repeated. But this is a fictive construct.

"A genuine folk-riddle," Kelso continues, "is a spontaneous expression, coming from the depths of the soul of a people or race, not from the mind of an individual, and consequently is anonymous." How does one demonstrate such a thing? Suddenly the ancient history of folk riddles and their anonymity has begun to spin a fiction suspiciously like other fictions about literary creation. Shakespeare, for instance, warbling his native wood-notes wild. All those primitive poets living in the late eighteenth and the nineteenth centuries, spontaneous as birds, every one of them. (Not that all birds are always spontaneous either.) Whitman, for one, was wise enough to take advantage of such nonsense.

By contrast, Kelso continues, Greek writers discussed the difference between *ainigma* and *griphos*, while their the two terms, *mythos* and *logos*, indicate "that Greek enigmas touched the domain of mythology." We have jumped from "the depths of the soul of a people" to some of the most sophisticated writing on this subject, and by individuals. For Kelso, "a sharp distinction ought to be made between the original folk-riddle and those more or less artificial ones which have come down to us through the channels of literature." The adulation of what is "primitive" is striking. So is the assumption that literary skill, that is, the ability to shape a verbal artefact, has no place in folk riddles. So pervasive is this general assumption that Derek Attridge recently found it necessary to affirm that artistic inventiveness is not limited to high culture.[11] Herbert Marks has made a similar point in a related context.[12] Writers like Herder included the ancient Jewish people under such "folk," and treated their work accordingly. The "folk," like the child or contemporary native, was being shaped for a purpose: idealized, distanced, simplified,

---

11 Derek Attridge, "Innovation, Literature, Ethics: Relating to the Other," *Publications of the Modern Language Association* 114 (1999), 30n.

12 "What is puzzling, however, is that they [Buber and Rosenzweig] should have considered the use of 'leading words' in poetic etymology [in the Hebrew Bible] as manifestations of oral comparison, rather than as signs of a sophisticated literary genesis" ("Writing as Calling," 23). See ibid. on Herder.

and – especially interesting for literary scholars and critics – kept "sharply distinguished" from the literary abilities that have produced the great classics of one's own civilization. Folk riddles seem at once too significant and not significant enough in this approach.

Folklorists today do not conceive of the "folk" as their forebears did a century ago. The difference is evident in Taylor's work, as seen in chapter 2. Or more recently, in Christine Goldberg's matter-of-fact reference to one folk-tale as "itself a work of art" with many variations where "it keeps its artistic integrity."[13] Folk riddles may sound as if they are by definition somehow purer, less artificial, less tampered with by literary artifice. But artifice runs deep, whether in high or popular art, and literary terms talk about something embedded in language, not detachable from it.

Literary riddles can range from the most tedious to the most gripping. They include the multitude of French versified *énigmes* so popular in seventeenth-century salons, most of which are excruciatingly boring and a fine target for Molière. As Nicholas Cronk says, there may be an occasional "pleasing poetic conceit . . . but these poems are for the most part unrelievedly mediocre."[14] *Enigmes* with their solutions were published regularly in the *Mercure de France*. They were also popular in England, appearing regularly in the *Gentleman's Journal*, the *Muses Mercury*, and other periodicals. Matthew Prior produced pleasing examples, such as his 1693 "Enigma" whose answer is the Jack of Spades, and his 1740 "Riddle" whose answer is ice-skates. It ends thus:

> Swifter they move as they are straiter bound
> Yet neither tread the air, the wave or ground:
> They serve the poor for Use the rich for whim,
> Sink when it rains and when it freezes swim.

Tony Augarde identifies "enigma in its narrowest sense" as "simply a kind of riddle in verse," adding that "they have seldom made good poetry" (*The Oxford Guide to Word Games*, p. 15).

On the other hand, literary riddles also include such remarkable contemporary examples as John Hollander's "Riddle and Answer" (*Movie-Going*) and Geoffrey Hill's riddle poem in *Mercian Hymns* (11). John Fuller and Donald Hall have also written riddle poems, some of them for children. Hollander's follows the style of Old English verse, Hill's the style of Old English riddles. Hollander's poem begins: "I am

---

13 Goldberg, *Turandot's Sisters*, p. 10. For an excellent survey of riddles, wisdom questions, etc., drawn from literary sources, see pp. 13–41.
14 Cronk, "The Enigma of French Classicism," 271, 270, 279.

answerable if and only if I'm / not"—not a riddle at all, perhaps. (Wittgenstein: "*The riddle* does not exist. If a question can be framed at all, it is also *possible* to answer it."[15]) Not "answerable," either. Poetically, a riddle that is fully answerable is not much of a riddle. A trope that is fully answerable is not much of a trope. A poetic riddle is only answerable to its best nature if it is not answerable, in the sense that its answer does not close down a question, but goes on generating meaning.

> I am answerable   if and only if I'm
> not; and you can know my   nature only
> after an icy   ignorance of all the
> certain solutions   has come to assume
> the worth and the warmth   of wisdom.

"Icy   ignorance" is different from soft-headed ignorance, which presumably likes the comfort of certitude. Icy ignorance of all the certain solutions (as against uncertain ones) leads to wisdom. "Not icy, but I-see ignorance," we say. Donatus's textbook example provides an ice-water solution to a riddle. A solution in the abstract answers a riddle. A literal or material solution dissolves a riddle, at least if the riddle is ice and if an answer lives with warm wisdom.

Hill's short poem has as its answer Offa, the name of the king who "reigned over Mercia (and the greater part of England south of the Humber) in the years AD 757–796" (p. 127). "A common name," says the poem, and the note confirms that the name was indeed once common. Parts of the riddle remain opaque to me, though the imitative sounds of "laugh" and "cough" are clear.

In both 1986 and 1996, Dan Pagis set out a distinction between the literary riddle and the folk riddle. Folklorists, he argues, usually consider riddling situations "only as public occasions for the performance of folk riddles, and usually as background to understanding how these folk riddles are created and function in human life." The major difference in a literary riddle is the position of the riddler. "For the folk riddle, he is primarily a transmitter presenting traditional material, with his own additions and changes; while in the literary, 'learned' realm, the riddler is the author himself, who reserves the same rights over his own riddles as over his other works" ("Toward a Theory of the Literary Riddle," p. 83).

---

15 "*Das Rätsel* gibt es nicht. Wenn sich eine Frage überhaupt stellen lässt, so *kann* sie auch beantwortet werden." Ludwig Wittgenstein, *Tractatus Logico-philosophicus: The German Text of Logisch-philosophische Abhandlung: With a New Translation*, trans. D. F. Pears and B. F. McGuinness (London: Routledge, 1961), 6.5.

A similar distinction holds true when a writer like Sophocles includes a riddle in a literary work, even when it may be a folk riddle. The riddle enters a fictional world, which it reads and is read by in turn. Thus also with riddles within folk tales, as folklorists know (see Rudolph Schevill, p. 127 below).

Taylor invented the term "neck-riddle," which he calls a "well-established and enigmatic genre" in his collection, *English Riddles from Oral Tradition* (p. 1). A neck-riddle, following Taylor, is a riddle set by someone whose life is at stake and who will die if the riddle is solved. Hence clever neck-riddles are based on secret, personal knowledge, unavailable to the powers that be. Taylor's term may usefully be expanded to include any riddle where one's life depends on answering it, whether it is set by oneself or another. Beyond the impossible question, the great difference between the neck-riddle and the "true riddle" is in the relation of riddler to riddlee. Fowler's generic characteristics of emotional coloration or mood (8), characteristic occasion (9) and attitude (10) also apply here, for the mood, occasion, and attitude of the common riddle are all modified in the neck-riddle. The mood is menacing, the occasion is a trial by wits, the attitude of the riddler is legalistic or murderous.

Any riddle that requires such esoteric knowledge to answer it is not a true riddle, Taylor argues, and that includes Samson's famous one in Judges 14. The judgment is longstanding. In the seventeenth century, the astute scholar Gerardus Joannes Vossius argued that Samson's riddle was not a true *aenigma*, and Benjamin Keach quoted him with approval in 1682.[16] (Current commentators sometimes repeat this argument as if it were a startling modern discovery.) Samson's riddle is well known: "And he said unto them, Out of the eater came forth meat, And out of the strong came forth sweetness. And they could not in three days expound the riddle."

It seems self-evident that this is not a true riddle in that no logic or wit will provide the answer, but only private knowledge. Yet there is Richard Wilbur's evidence before us:

After I had learned the secret of Mr. Richter's folk riddle [like Samson's, but birds in a horse's skull rather than bees in a lion's carcass], I continued to ask it of people, and was astonished, on one occasion, when a Wesleyan student solved it at once. How did he do it? He had been raised on a ranch in Montana, and was no stranger to nests built in animal skulls. ("The Persistence of Riddles," p. 340)

---

16 "id quod Samson proposuerat, aenigma non erat," Vossius, *Institutiones oratoriae* (1643), Book IV, p. 205.

If our inner landscapes were filled with Georgia O'Keeffe figures, we too might solve Samson's riddle without difficulty. All the more so, if such a sight commonly elicited some form of the Samson riddle: "Well, well, meat out of the eater again, I see."

A true riddle is often defined as one whose question contains sufficient evidence for the answer, even if the evidence is given in an obscure way. (The definition goes back at least to Robert Petsch in 1899, whose "fundamental distinction between real and unreal riddles has been maintained to this day."[17]) The answer may depend on someone being sufficiently wise or quick, but nonetheless a solution to a true riddle is possible without outside aid. To be sure, wisdom and quickness depend partly on experience in a specific language and culture. Thus with Samson's riddle. Even wide expertise in folk riddles will not suffice in a strange situation. Roger D. Abrahams records being set up by a group of children on the island of Nevis, where riddling is very active. The answers to a series of riddles depended on knowing local names for genital parts, and knowing the local decorum of word-play on them. "Great laughter ensued, telling me that only the smallest child gets caught by that one. . . Only after some major status-reduction on my part and protestation of innocence would they believe that I didn't know 'son' refers to the scrotum as enlarged by elephantiasis" (*Between the Living and the Dead*, p. 18).

Taylor offers a definition of the true riddle that is tighter than an evidence-based definition. It also accords with the centuries-old rhetorical definition of enigma as an obscure or hidden similitude, a closed simile. True riddles, says Taylor, are descriptions of objects in terms intended to suggest something entirely different. He excludes insoluble puzzles, both neck-riddles and other "clever questions," including those that depend on "acquaintance with a detail of Biblical history" (presumably catechal questions). He also excludes arithmetical puzzles, and simple conundrums, for example, those using puns (*English Riddles from Oral Tradition*, p. 1). A coded communication is not a true riddle, but rather a puzzle using an arbitrary key. Nor is the esoteric and arbitrary riddle a true riddle, its answer being available only to initiates. The true riddle in Taylor's sense establishes a central definition for the riddle genre, through its historical longevity and its rhetorical good sense.

---

17 Scott, "Some Approaches to the Study of Riddle," p. 116, citing Petsch, *Neue Beiträge zur Kenntnis des Volksrätsels*, Palaestra IV (Berlin, 1899), p. 5.

At the same time, riddles other than "true" riddles can be very useful for literary purposes. For Wilbur, fairness is not an important criterion in judging the merits of a riddle. A riddle, he argues, "is much more than a puzzle, and we do not evaluate it in terms of sufficiency of evidence or ease of solution. The only thing we ask, as Alice said to the Mad Hatter, is that people not make up riddles which have no answers at all" ("The Persistence of Riddles," p. 340). As with true and mistaken etymology, so with true and other riddles, as defined by Taylor, the Opies, and others: a writer qua writer does not care greatly about this distinction. Conundrums using puns, riddles using schemes, cryptic encoding, and more: these kinds of riddle can also be valuable devices. We need to exercise a little caution with the term "true riddle." A more neutral adjective might help. As with the "true" in "true rhyme," an apparently useful adjective can unwittingly intimate a prejudice. In an article just preceding his 1951 book, "The Varieties of Riddles," Taylor uses the term "descriptive riddles or riddles in the strict sense" for what he later called "true riddles." Perhaps he should have stuck with the first term.

The illustrated emblem-riddle is another example from among the sub-genres of the complex genre of riddle. This is to follow Pagis's suggestion with reference to Hebrew emblem-riddles, and to expand a little on Rosalie Colie's admirable analysis of the emblem poem as a hybrid genre. Colie observes how it combines adage, epigram, and picture, and she notes "the enigmatic potentialities of the form":

It is important to note how this tiny form mixed genres and even arts–and how cryptic its parts were, implying far more than was said. With its gnomic grammatical involution of significance into one phrase, the adage offered one version of much in little; the epigram's syntactical economies challenged ingenuity precisely by its terseness. The addition of figures to such abbreviated forms . . . might present a problem thrice made intricate and esoteric. Certainly early emblem-books exploit the enigmatic potentialities of the form.

(The Resources of Kind, p. 37)

How many adages in the emblems take riddle form? Some emblems should also be defined as a hybrid of epigram, picture, and riddle. Riddle and proverb or Greek *gnomon* are longstanding associates, linked grammatically and rhetorically since Aristotle.

Would a riddle-ballad, incidentally, be a sub-genre of riddle or of the ballad? The riddle-ballad is a type known only in English and German traditions, a very interesting observation made by Taylor in his *Problems in German Literary History of the Fifteenth and Sixteenth Centuries.*

RIDDLE AS MODE

The class of modes as distinct from genres exhibits no consistent external form and no consistent length, yet it is a discernible type of writing. Modes are defined by adjectives rather than nouns.[18] "Pastoral," for example, uses well-known conventions, but they may appear in a number of different genres. "A few short kinds [or genres] have generated well-established modes, with corresponding adjectival terms applied to style (aphoristic, proverbial)" (Fowler, *Kinds of Literature*, p. 108). This, I think, is also true of the genre of the free-standing riddle. It would be helpful to use the adjective "riddling" when the riddle is present as a mode rather than a genre.

"The riddle is essentially a charm in reverse," Frye says; "it represents the revolt of the intelligence against the hypnotic power of commanding words." Charm poetry works with a rhetoric that is "dissociative and incantatory; it sets up a pattern of sound so complex and repetitive that the ordinary processes of response are short-circuited. Refrain, rhyme, alliteration, assonance, pun, antithesis: every repetitive device known to rhetoric is called into play" ("Charms and Riddles," p. 126). Frye cites the *Midsummer Night's Dream* song, "Never harm / Nor spell nor charm," as well as Spenser's stanzas on Morpheus from *The Faerie Queene*. Charm poetry (which I think Frye preferred personally) is familiar from Theocritus to Spenser through Keats to Tennyson and Swinburne. Its rhetoric is familiar from advertising techniques. It is "shown at its subtlest in Keats and Tennyson and at its clearest in Poe and Swinburne, [and] dominated taste until about 1915" (ibid., p. 142). Riddle poetry follows what Renaissance specialists call the "line of wit." We can trace it from the Old English riddles through Donne to Browning, Dickinson, Hopkins and Eliot–and its rhetoric, very occasionally, in advertising techniques.

Charms and riddles may work in contrary ways, but they also have an affinity for each other. "Charms and riddles . . . are psychologically very close together, as the unguessed or unguessable riddle is or may be a charm." As for modern writers, far from confining themselves to one of these, "a poet interested in charm techniques is likely to be interested in riddle techniques also, if only because both present technical problems." Frye mentions Poe, who is par exellence a charm poet, but also liked

---

18 I am following Fowler's definition of "mode" because it is empirically useful. The definition differs in two earlier books, Frye's *Anatomy of Criticism* (see the Glossary) and Genette's *The Architexte* (p. 61, and see pp. 70–1n).

riddles and wrote acrostic poems. *Finnegans Wake* offers "a kind of language that could be read either as oracular dream language or as associative wit" (ibid., pp. 137–8, 141). (Frye here introduces two more terms into the discussion, "oracle" and "dream," both closely connected with riddle, as with charm.) Eliot also knew very well how to write charm poetry, as witness his song "Under the bamboo" from *Sweeney Agonistes* and his "New Hampshire," "Virginia," and "Cape Ann" from "Landscapes."

When Frye speaks of the line of charm poetry, he is speaking mainly of charm as mode and not as genre. Charm as genre would resemble riddle as genre, in that a separate charm or explicit charm-poem like the second Idyl of Theocritus would show many characteristic traits of a genre. Certainly an external structure (2), size (4), values (7), emotional coloration or mood (8), occasion (9), attitude (10), style (14), and the reader's task (15) are distinct for the charm. For the most part, Keats and Tennyson do not write such charms, though Tennyson's refrain in "The Lotos-Eaters" comes close. On the analogy of "riddling," much of this "charm" poetry would be called "charming," if the word had not developed in other directions. Such charm poetry (or charming poetry) exhibits charm as mode.

When charm poetry is in the ascendant, riddle or enigma is widely assumed to be antipathetic to lyric poetry. The assumption is illogical but pervasive. In the nineteenth century, expectations of charm poetry meant that lyric and riddle were set against each other, for all that riddle is said to be one of the roots of lyric. Thus one criticism of Browning, where the alternatives are very clear: "Why he should turn away from themes in which everyone can find answer to his sympathies, and from modes of the lyric which find their echoes wherever hearts and ears know aught of music – is an enigma no less painful than perplexing, the unriddling of which is possibly reserved for no contemporary."[19] Mallarmé, according to Henri Clouard, suffered from "never feeling his work swept on in any wide-reaching lyric invention . . . His system paralyzes feeling in the presence of insoluble riddles, and annihilates lyricism."[20] Mallarmé himself had a different view: "One must always have enigma [énigme] in poetry; this is the aim of literature" (ibid., p. 19). To Valéry, the enigmas

---

19 *Browning: The Critical Heritage*, ed. Boyd Litzinger and Donald Smalley (London: Routledge and Kegan Paul, 1970), p. 157.
20 Quoted in *Representative French Lyrics of the Nineteenth Century*, rev. edn., ed. George Neely Henning (Boston: Ginn, 1935), p. 421.

of Mallarmé were themselves a revelation: "But what intellectual effects on us at that time were caused by the revelation of the least of Mallarmé's writings, and what moral effects!" (p. 637). This whole dispute is a question of taste, in Frye's precise word, and not a question of merit.

On the face of it, proverb and riddle sound very different. Riddles ask questions but proverbs assert. Riddles upset what is usual; proverbs offer conventional wisdom. Riddles entrance children; proverbs sound parental or avuncular, as if instructing or admonishing or occasionally comforting. Riddles can be a game or a contest; proverbs seem to preclude games by coming at once to a conclusion. Riddles like unusual language; proverbs strive for plainness. Proverbs sound clear and persuaded, and tell us: this is the way things are. Or they seem to do so, by their rhetorical force. The fact that proverbs say quite contradictory things, so that one proverb can cancel out another, has never eliminated them. ("Look before you leap." "He who hesitates is lost.") Whatever the situation, we seem to like gnomic utterances. There is something about these short pithy sayings that seems to reassure us by providing words and summing up things, even if the words offer conventional wisdom and can be found to suit any situation.

Yet, as with riddle and charm, there are also likenesses between riddle and proverb. Both are ancient forms that sometimes belonged to wisdom literature. Proverbs and proverbial gnomic sayings have long been associated with riddles, and with reason, despite their obvious differences. Aristotle's *Rhetoric* II.xxi.8 includes a passing remark on riddling statements within a discussion of maxims. Donatus and many another included both *paroemia* and *aenigma* as two of the seven species of allegory. Formally, this makes sense. Proverbs can be re-phrased so as to make them riddles, and vice versa. Erasmus links "proverbial sentences and . . . proverbs" with enigma, for "In [allegorical] proverbs, allegory sometimes results in enigma." "The horseleech hath two daughters" (Prov. 30: 15) is often cited as a riddle, yet it also functions as a proverb, provided the answer is known. Scripture tied the two together, at least for some kinds of enigma. Solomon, the famed resolver of *aenigmata*, was also the accepted author of the Book of Proverbs and of Ecclesiastes, which comes with its own well-known set of proverbial gnomic sayings. ("The sun also ariseth." "To every thing there is a season, and a time to every purpose under the heaven: A time to be born, and a time to die." "Remember now thy Creator in the days of thy youth.") The proverb like the riddle can act as a free-standing generic form or else as a mode.

The selfsame person who delights in enigmas may delight in proverbs. Wallace Stevens is a case in point. He is a poet who wrote at least one riddle poem proper, who knows how the trope of enigma works, and who decidedly likes the riddling mode. He also liked proverbial sayings, and put together his own collection, "Adagia."

As for constructional types, see the following chapter.

RIDDLE AND THE HIERARCHY OF GENRES

Reactions to riddles and the riddling mode depend not only on current taste, but also on generic and rhetorical assumptions. And, while the notion of hierarchy in relation to genre sounds almost quaint today, the old hierarchies still have influence.[21]

For Hegel, there is no question that genres come ranked in a hierarchy. The symbol, "strictly so-called, is *inherently* enigmatical [an sich räthsel-haft]". This is to use the word as a synonym for "mysterious" in the sense of a perennial mystery such as the mystery of great art. The riddle, on the other hand, for Hegel "belongs to conscious symbolism [gehört der bewussten Symbolik]," a lower form of art. "Symbols in the strict sense are, both before and after, unsolved problems, while the riddle is absolutely solved."[22] Works of Egyptian art and even the Grecian Sphinx are exceptions, but only because their riddles give answers that lie "in the absolute meaning, in the spirit, just as the famous Greek inscription calls to man: Know thyself" (*Aesthetics*, p. 361). The sharp distinction here and elsewhere is of a piece with Hegel's sharp distinction between fable, parable, proverb and the like and the "proper species of *poetic* art, namely, lyric, epic, and drama" (p. 382). There is a kind of class system in his literary taxonomy that corresponds with the class of their makers. Even the parables of Holy Writ do not appear quite upper class, a fact that would not surprise their maker. They too are "trivial in content" and important only because of the comparison with the doctrine of the Kingdom of Heaven (p. 391). Once again, we are seeing enigma in her double guise. Hegel places her either in the heavens or in the kitchen, either the "inherently enigmatical symbol" or else the mere riddle that is "absolutely solved" (p. 397). This is not the literary distinction between

---

21 See "Hierarchies of Genres and Canons of Literature," in Fowler's *Kinds of Literature*, pp. 213–34.
22 Hegel, *Aesthetics*, trans. Knox, vol. 1, p. 397 (*Vorlesungen über die Aesthetik*, vol. 1, p. 526). On the original, which is based on transcriptions of Hegel's lectures and his lecture notes (1823, 1826, 1828–9), see Knox, Translator's Preface, pp. v–viii.

trope and scheme, or the folklore distinction between a true riddle and other types. It appears to be based on content.

The riddle's "appearance in history lies principally in the East, in the intervening and transitional period between more obtuse symbolism and more conscious wisdom and generalization. Whole peoples and periods have delighted in such problems. Even in the Middle Ages in Arabia and Scandinavia, and in the German poetry of singing contests at the Wartburg, for example, it plays a great part" (p. 398). Riddles also belong to the tradition of wisdom in the Hebrew Scriptures and scriptural traditions, especially those associated with Solomon. Hegel does not mention them. More time on the delight of Arabian and Scandinavian and medieval German riddles might have mitigated the extremes of this argument.

Erich Auerbach's classic essay "Figura" works against a Hegelian sense of genre. He addresses longstanding theological disputes about how to read scripture, especially the allegorical method as against a more historically rooted, rabbinical method. The two different ways of reading are laid out in the typological context of Christian theology. Among others, Daniel Boyarin distinguishes very usefully between Origen's allegorical method and rabbinical interpretation in midrash. Origen, as he says, reads from concrete to abstract, while midrash moves from abstract to concrete (pp. 109–10).[23] James Kugel also contrasts "allegorical exegesis of the Bible and its (more Semitic) competitor, midrash." In midrash, unlike allegory, attention never shifts from the text. Kugel adds that, ironically, Christian exegesis is "sometimes more 'Jewish' than Philo" (*The Idea of Biblical Poetry*, pp. 135–8). Hegel decidedly does not belong to the rabbinical or the typological way of reading. These ways of reading would pass only if they were abstracted and placed in the service of Hegel's *Geist* or Spirit.[24]

As for riddle taking the form of fable, Aesop's views and doctrines may be "ingenious and clever, but . . . as it were, a subtle investigation of trifles. . . Instead of creating free shapes out of a free spirit [Aesop wrote fables]. . . hidden as it were in a riddle which is at the same time always being solved. In the slave, prose begins [Im Sklaven fängt die Prosa an], and so this entire species is prosaic too."[25] Annabel Patterson observes that Hegel gave philosophical authority to the tradition that fables originated

23 Boyarin, "The Song of Songs, Lock or Key," pp. 105–16. The distinction between a literary form and a hermeneutic figure, which Boyarin takes over from Gerard Bruns, seems doubtful to me. It might help if the terms "taxonomy," "topos," and "typology" were more differentiated.
24 Knox's note on p. 401 of vol. 1 calls the treatment of allegory "needlessly obscure"; perhaps it is an error in transcription.
25 Hegel, *Aesthetics*, trans. Knox, vol. 1, p. 387.

in a slave culture; she cites an earlier instance of this argument in Samuel
Croxall's 1722 *Fables of Æsop and Others.*[26] Fowler suggests that "we ought
also to be a little skeptical toward easy correlations of genres with
immediate social concerns" (*Kinds of Literature*, p. 36), a point that
Patterson bears out. She shows how Aesop's fables and their tradition
can function on behalf of both the political status quo and political
resistance. ("'Aesopian writing' [is] a medium of political resistance in
eastern Europe" ["Fables of Power," p. 273].) So also with the riddle.
Certainly, there is social and political influence on generic matters. Yet
generic schemata are not per se either retrogressive or revolutionary.

Riddle in the first instance proclaims itself as a low genre on the social
scale, without the cachet of ode or elegy, to say nothing of epic. Or, for all
that, the cachet of enigma. In one way, that seems fair enough. A riddle
for most people is a trivial joke, momentarily amusing. Epics are never
trivial. Yet the riddle is also an honest unpretentious fellow, incapable of
puffery, whereas some self-styled modern epics are puffed ad nauseam.
There is something to be said for a genre and mode that are hard to fool
or fool around with.

RIDDLE WITHIN OTHER GENRES

Context conditions the way we read everything, including not only
literary riddles but also folk riddles. Riddles that appear in written works
by known authors, say, in *Oedipus Rex*, obviously function within the
context of these narratives. Riddles that appear in folk-tales also function
within a given context, which may alter the sense of a riddle. Rudolph
Schevill notes that *The Arabian Nights* puts the old riddle-challenge of
drinking the sea "into the mouth of a rogue or sharper."[27] It is quite
otherwise in Plutarch's "Banquet of the Seven Sages," where swapping
riddles is leisure enjoyment for wise people. Here the king of Egypt has
been challenged by the king of the Ethiopians to answer the drink-the-sea
riddle. He has written for help to one of the seven wise men, Bias, who
replies: "'Let him tell the Ethiopian to stop the rivers which are now
emptying into the ocean depths, while he himself is engaged in drinking
up the ocean that now is; for this is the ocean with which the demand is

26 "Fables of Power," pp. 271–5. Patterson notes that Croxall is reacting against Sir Roger
L'Estrange's *Fables of Aesop*, which proceed from Stuart sympathies.
27 Schevill, "Some Forms of the Riddle Question," p. 213. In Burton's *The Book of a Thousand
Nights and a Night*, the tale of "The Sandal-Wood Merchants and the Sharpers" occurs on night
604 (vol. V, see p. 115).

concerned, and not the one which is to be'" (151d). A royal challenge or a con-man's game? And with what consequences?

We may suppose that folk riddles are somehow autonomous, yet here too context is crucial. The folklorists' world, while not fictitious, is nonetheless governed by a fictive construct. Certain assumptions prevail in telling folk riddles at a given time and place. This fictive construct is not always recorded or examined, especially the story inside which the riddler is speaking. The story in play may be the standard one about the learned folklorist inquiring of simple folk and receiving a straightforward answer. Or it may be different. Abrahams' record of how a group of children in Nevis enjoyed reversing roles, and playing their own games with the learned visitor, is a case in point.

If a riddle does not come with a context, we provide one from our own store, for example, when and how to ask a riddle. Roberto Benigni uses this as a device in his film *Life Is Beautiful*. There, an Italian doctor likes to exercise his wits through riddle contests with a correspondent. Benigni, playing the comic lead of a waiter, helps this patron solve the riddles and provides more. Transfer the context to a concentration camp where the doctor works for the Nazis. Benigni, now an inmate, finds an occasion to whisper to the doctor an old riddle, whose answer is "a secret." The doctor then contrives a time when, he says, he must speak to Benigni in secret. Their short conversation takes place under cover of a dinner where a few inmates are acting as servants. Full of anticipation, Benigni and the audience await the doctor's response to the "secret" riddle. It is this. The doctor has received another riddle from his correspondent and needs the help of his old acquaintance, the riddle-master, to help him solve it. Benigini leaves him without speaking. Riddle upon riddle upon riddle – the greatest being that of the doctor's character. Benigni uses close-up camera shots focusing on the eyes of the doctor and the inmate, so that an allegory of sight and blindness hovers over the narrative. The selfsame riddle will have a different answer, even though the words themselves may be exactly the same. It is the resonance of those words as they interact with a larger fictive construct that matters. The riddle informs the larger fiction, and it in turn informs the riddle.

Generically, riddles do not sit comfortably with ordinary mimetic writing, except as amusement or wit. The social pastime of setting riddles can itself be part of a realistic fiction, where it may produce fine effects as in Thackeray's acted charades in *Vanity Fair*. As a structural force, riddles belong more naturally to fairy-tale or myth rather than the realistic novel. Where a work has mythic or legendary dimensions, as in *Oedipus Rex* or

Pericles or *Turandot,* a riddle can function memorably in the plot. Otherwise it usually functions on the edge of ordinary mimesis or in an auxiliary way. "At its generic core, riddle simply cannot comprehend narrative time; plot is not a meaningful category in riddle's concept of reality."[28] This may help to account for the tonal variety, implicit or explicit, in defining or commenting on riddles.

Yet the great writers of realistic fiction are also aware of the uncanny. Take, for example, Jane Austen's riddles in *Emma,* her one novel where riddles play a part. Are they simply part of an evening's entertainment, with their own due ironies and misreadings? Yes, of course – but, but.

Consider how Mr. Woodhouse frets in his mildly obsessive way because he can remember only one stanza of a familiar riddle. It is just right that he cannot remember the whole riddle, given his hypochondriac's trepidation at the very mention of the word "cold."

> Kitty, a fair but frozen maid,
>   Kindled a flame I yet deplore,
> The hood-wink'd boy I called to aid,
> Though of his near approach afraid,
>   So fatal to my suit before.[29]

Nor can he remember the solution, except that it is "very clever." And "frozen"? Is this part of Mr. Woodhouse's great worry over chills? No doubt, but there are reverberations, at a distance. This is also the father who wants his daughters to remain with him unchanged, or as others might put it, frozen, like Blake's Thel. What are we to say of a father who can only envision a static life, a frozen life, for himself and for his young daughter too? "Emma a fair but frozen maid"? The standard ice-water riddle is propounded as a mother-daughter puzzle, where mother bears daughter who in turn bears mother. Mr. Woodhouse's wife bore a daughter, who in turn takes over her mother's role in running the household. Considered as a self-enclosed plot, the ice-water riddle would suit Mr. Woodhouse very well, and indefinitely. The "Kitty" riddle is connected with Emma's mother ("Your dear mother was so clever at all those things! If I had but her memory!"), one of the very few direct references to Emma's mother in the entire novel. She knew the full riddle

---

28 Dorst, "Neck-riddle as a Dialogue of Genres," 423.
29 *Emma,* chap. 9, where most of the novel's riddles are concentrated. Emma says that the riddle was copied from *Elegant Extracts,* but the editor of the Oxford Austen could not find it there (see *Emma,* p. 489n); the earliest entry was apparently in *The New Foundling Hospital for Wit* (1771, Part 4).

and its solution, while aimiable Mr. Woodhouse, stuck in stanza 1, is simply reminded of his elder daughter ("she was very near being christened Catherine").

The answer to the full four-stanza riddle is a chimney-sweep. It is a literary riddle, for it is ascribed to the actor David Garrick. Needless to say, the erotic implications of Garrick's riddle do not surface in Mr. Woodhouse's mind. But such intimations also stir delicately in the ambience of Kitty, whether daughter or chimney. ("Lady, lady, does your chimney burn?" W. S. Merwin once wrote, in a twentieth-century variation of Garrick.) How far do the resonances of such a small riddle bear on the main plotting of a novel like *Emma*? In one sense, not far at all, given the good will that Austen allots to Mr. Woodhouse and Emma and Mr. Knightley. In another, immensely far, because such troping goes on generating meaning, like the tropes of good poetry. Lesser novelists do not give out such resonances.

When a riddle does function as a structural principle, it sometimes points toward enigma as masterplot, as we have seen. The Book of Revelation or the Apocalypse, a great enigma, governs the narrative of the Christian Bible and leads toward the ending. Apocalyptic writing demonstrates the riddle in one of its generic functions. But the governing enigma does not need to be the great masterplot outlined in chapter 3. Detective stories also work with the structure of a riddle to be solved by the end. "The whodunit demands a solution to a riddle, making it a member of that oldest allegorical type, the *aenigma*" (Fletcher, p. 6). Occasionally an actual riddle becomes part of the plot. John Buchan uses a triple riddle to propel much of the plot of *Greenmantle*. (In comparison, the riddle he inserts in *The Three Hostages* is quite ineffectual.) Josephine Tey centers *The Singing Sands* on a riddle that is retrieved accidentally from the murder victim, and serves admirably both as a red herring and a pointer to the murderer:

> The beasts that talk,
> The streams that stand,
> The stones that walk,
> The singing sand,
> . . .
> That guard the way
> To Paradise.

Most detective stories have little to do with a Pauline or Sphinxine or Plutarchan or other sense of enigma, though occasionally a detective-story

writer introduces some larger background. When however, a great novel-
ist combines enigma as masterplot with the detective-story structural
riddle, the result can be astonishing. This is what happens in *The Brothers
Karamazov*, a book that is at once an ordinary detective story and an
extraordinary metaphysical novel. Borges is the modern master of this
potent mixed genre.[30]

Dreams and riddles seem to have a natural affinity with each other, and
for good reason. Both invite interpretation, and have done so since the
earliest records we possess, whether in the *Odyssey* or the Pentateuch or
native North American dream rituals. Enigma is defined rhetorically as a
hidden similitude, and this is the premise on which dream interpretation
is based. The dream is something other than actual life, with a hidden or
obscure significance, but what? The dream interpreter works like a riddle-
master, clarifying the strangely fashioned story that has played out in our
heads. Dreams remain a mystery: they are not subject to our volition, for
all that they live inside us.

The affinity of dream and riddle turns up generically in the use of
riddles within dream narrative and dream vision. As with other genres
where verisimilitude does not reign supreme, dream literature is a
congenial place for enigma. Some of our best-known dream visions
include famous riddles. Dante set one at the end of the *Purgatorio* that
remains unsolved to this day. Carroll included riddles of many types in
his dream romances, *Alice's Adventures in Wonderland* and *Through the
Looking-Glass*.

Joseph's early dreams are sent to one who will become patriarch and
prophet, and he is granted the gift of reading dreams. Henry Peacham
classifies under Enigma the Egyptian dream-riddles in Genesis, which
makes Joseph one of the earliest riddle-masters, earlier even than the
preeminent riddle-master of the Hebrew Scriptures, Solomon. The
dreams that Joseph interprets in Genesis are allegorical, but they do not
take the form of enigma or riddle. Pharaoh's seven fat kine and seven lean
kine, and his seven full ears of corn and seven blasted ears, are one and the
same allegory of seven years of good crops followed by seven years of
drought. Freud rightly calls Joseph's method of intrepretation "symbolic."
He draws attention to Aristotle's remark that the best interpreter of

---

30 *The Brothers Karamazov* is not included as a metaphysical detective novel as defined in *Detecting
Texts: The Metaphysical Detective Story from Poe to Postmodernism*, ed. Patricia Merivale and Susan
Elizabeth Sweeney (Philadelphia: University of Pennsylvania Press, 1999). Borges is included, and
is well treated.

dreams is the person who can best grasp similarities (*Interpretation of Dreams*, pp. 11–12).

The dreams we dream are unlike the enigma in waking life because they are never works of art. Though fictitious, the dream is not a short story or a play because no artistic imagination or conscious will has touched and shaped it. Most dreams have little interest except for the dreamer, and often not much then.

Contexts for dream-interpretation vary widely. In Homer's epic romance, dreams come from the supernatural world, but human beings must decide whether the dream is benign or malign. Dreams that delude come through the gate of ivory, and those that are true come through the gate of horn (*Odyssey* XIX.562–7).[31] The two gates turn on wordplay, as if actual concrete matter concealed its functions by a rebus. ("Ivory" in Greek is *elephas*, and the verb *elephairo* means "to cheat." "Horn" is *keras*, and the verb *kraino* means "to fulfill.") If sent by a god or *daimon* who is benevolent, then the dream will help. If sent by an inimical power, it can destroy (OCD, "dreams"). In classical literature, dream interpreters are important from Homer onwards, and one book of dream interpretation survives, Artemidorus' *Oneirocritica*, where interpretation consists of a set symbolic reading of given objects.[32] The dream-book of Achmet (*Biblion oneirokritikon*) from the tenth-century Arab world works in the same way.[33] Freud calls this method the "cipher method" because the objects always have the same import. His own method differs, because it requires the dreamer to do the work of interpretation (*Interpretation of Dreams*, p. 12). Iroquois dream-riddles are interpreted in ways that avert danger and fulfill desires. The Jesuit Father Rageneau described their functions astutely and sympathetically in 1649. (See further in chapter 10.) But his fellow Jesuit, Claude-François Ménestrier, was wary in 1694. "Des Songes [On Dreams] & de leur Interpretation" is one of many chapters in *La philosophie des images énigmatiques* where the good Father tries to correct

---

31 Thus also in Plato, *Charmides* 173a; Virgil, *Aeneid* VI.893–6; and Horace, *Odes* III.27.41. The legend may have originated with the pun. Penelope uses the adjective *ainos* when describing her dream in *Odyssey* XIX.568. W. B. Stanford commends the translation "uncanny" in his *The Odyssey of Homer* (London: Macmillan, 1948); A. T. Murray prefers "strange" (Cambridge, Mass.: Harvard University Press, Loeb, 1919). On the adjective *ainos*, more commonly rendered as "dread" or "horrible," and the noun *ainos*, the etymon for *ainigma*, see Appendix, p. 258 below.

32 Artemidorus, the *Oneirocritica*, trans. Robert J. White as *The Interpretation of Dreams* (Park Ridge, NJ: Noyes Press, 1975).

33 Steven M. Oberhelman, *The Oneirocriticon of Achmet: A Medieval Greek and Arabic Treatise on the Interpretation of Dreams* (Lubbock, Tex.: Texas Tech University Press, 1991).

LA
PHILOSOPHIE
DES
IMAGES ENIGMATIQUES,
OU IL EST TRAITE'

Des
{
Enigmes,
Hieroglyphiques,
Oracles,
Propheties,
Sorts,
Divinations ,
}
{
Loteries ,
Talifmans,
Songes,
Centuries de Nof-
tradamus,
De la Baguette.
}

Par le P. CL. FRANÇOIS MENESTRIER
de la Compagnie de JESUS.

A LYON,
Chez HILAIRE BARITEL, ruë
Merciere , à la Conftance.

M. DC. XCIV.
AVEC PRIVILEGE DU ROY.

Figure 4. Title-page, Claude-François Ménestrier, *La Philosophie des images énigmatiques* (1694).

error and delusion. He does not encourage reading dream-riddles or dreams as riddles.

RECENT GENRE STUDY

Recent genre study suggests a few areas worth exploring in relation to riddle and enigma. Chief among them is the perception of various genres over time. Where do we find "alterations in the perception of genre"[34] and why? Riddle and enigma provide a very striking example, both as genre and as mode.

Plain-style advocates are apt to dislike riddles and enigmas. Although they may offer high-sounding reasons for this, preferences for plain or elaborate styles are matters of taste, both personal and general. Such taste varies enormously from one era to another. Take, for example, the assumptions in Demetrius' *On Style*. The trope of enigma compliments the reader or listener. "It seems like a slur on your hearer," Demetrius writes, quoting Theophrastus, "to tell him everything as though he were a simpleton" (*On Style* IV. 22). James Merrill makes a similar point about literary allusion: "Some readers (I am among them) are flattered by an author's assumption that they've read the same poems as he, or know by heart the same music. Others complain of elitism. This means we can't expect them to consult a reference book."[35]

It is true that rhetoricians warn constantly about over-ingenuity in using the trope of enigma or riddling language. But this warning is usually aimed at orators, and rhetoricians themselves use somewhat different critieria for imaginative literature. Then too, ideas of what constitutes over-ingenuity differ markedly from time to time and place to place. Geoffrey Hill was once asked in an interview, "Your poetry has been described as 'persistent games-playing with words.' Would you reject this as a criticism?" Hill replied:

There's a tendentious emphasis in the kind of suggestion you refer to, as though games-playing with words were a perversity indulged by poets alone, while the rest of the world goes its innocent and straightforward way. It seems to me that any writer contemplating the world of commodity and policy sees the entire conduct of commerce and nations ruled by patter. It fools nobody and yet it fools everybody.[36]

---

34 Duff, *Modern Genre Theory*, Introduction, p. 18.
35 Merrill, "Comments," *University of Toronto Quarterly* 61 (1992), 390.
36 "Interview: David Sexton talks to Geoffrey Hill," *Literary Review* (Feb. 1986), 28–9.

Augustine's North African congregations had far higher rhetorical expectations than readers and congregations nowadays.

[Augustine's] hearers might have had less sophisticated reasons for enjoying the sermons of their bishop. For, seen in this light, the Bible became a gigantic puzzle – like a vast inscription in unknown characters. It had all the elemental appeal of the riddle: that most primitive form of triumph over the unknown which consists in finding the familiar hidden beneath an alien guise. The African, particularly, had a Baroque love of subtlety. They had always loved playing with words; they excelled in writing elaborate acrostics; *hilaritas* – a mixture of intellectual excitement and sheer aesthetic pleasure at a notable display of wit– was an emotion they greatly appreciated. (Brown, *Augustine of Hippo*, pp. 253–4)

Similarly with the Elizabethans. To quote James Reaney, the Canadian poet and playwright: "Perhaps the whole problem is best described in a statement by one of my high-school teachers, Miss Rose McQueen, when she announced that 'in Elizabethan times it was fashionable to be clever; to-day, it is not.'"[37]

Victorians could be impatient with riddles and enigmas, at least in the wrong places. Despite the existence of such great riddlers as Lewis Carroll, Ruskin was irritated when Goethe and others spoke darkly in enigmas about those moral precepts that he, Ruskin, saw so clearly in the work:

It is a strange habit of wise humanity to speak in enigmas only, so that the highest truths and usefullest laws must be hunted for through whole picture-galleries of dreams, which to the vulgar seem dreams only. Thus Homer, the Greek tragedians, Plato, Dante, Chaucer, Shakespeare, and Goethe, have hidden all that is chiefly serviceable in their work . . . under types which have rendered it quite useless to the multitude.[38]

"Riddle Redundant" was the title of an 1883 parody of Browning's "Wanting is–What ?"[39] When charm poetry seems the natural way for poetry to behave, then riddle poetry is in trouble, and this happens often enough in the nineteenth century and beyond. It is a matter of taste, to repeat Frye's precise word.

In the early twentieth century, enigma began to come into her own. "Charm poetry, shown at its subtlest in Keats and Tennyson and at its clearest in Poe and Swinburne, dominated taste until about 1915, after which a mental attitude more closely related to the riddle began to supersede it" (Frye, "Charms and Riddles," p. 142). Eliot and Pound,

37 Reaney, "'Cutting Up Didoes,'" *University of Toronto Quarterly* 61 (1992), 373.
38 Ruskin, *Munera Pulveris*, III, "Coin-Keeping," section 87, *Works*, vol. XVII, p. 208.
39 Anonymous, *Punch*, 21 April 1883.

master polemicists, led the attack on charm poetry. Eliot called it oratory, and produced some risible examples. But he also disliked some of the best kind, Tennyson's, for example, and he abhorred Swinburne.

Several strands of argument become interwoven in attacks on enigma's ingenuity. First, the confusion of what is obscure with what is difficult, a perennial confusion in the perception of genre. Second, the matter of esoteric riddles, specifically designed to block outsiders. Third, the question of responsibility toward an audience, an acute question for preachers, on which see chapter 2.

Discussions of obscure writing, to say nothing of obscure enigmas, are bedeviled by the frequent use of "obscure" to mean simply "difficult." Higher mathematics is obscure to someone with only high-school training, but is more properly called "difficult." Some highly wrought forms of writing may be beautifully crafted, but can be read only by those advanced beyond high-school verbal training. Such writing is not obscure; it is difficult. A related question is how we write about difficult and complex subjects, including some human emotions, sensations, and thought processes. How can these be made clear? Or does the careful, delicate tracing of such processes, like an intricate medical procedure, necessitate some intricate writing? Valéry listed "the inherent difficulty of the [writer's] subjects" as the first cause of obscurity in writing.[40]

Sometimes such intricacy is attained through apparent shadow or darkness or "obscurity." Rosamond Tuve, commenting on such shadowed images, notes how Renaissance discussions of "poetry's power to *realize clearly*" have little to do with "facile lucidity." She is especially helpful in reminding us not to equate clarity with certain styles. The pleasures of such challenges are laid out by Chapman, and quoted by Tuve, in a passage that should be standard reading on the question: "Obscuritie in affection of words, & *indigested* concets [conceits], is pedanticall and childish; but where it shroudeth it selfe in the hart of his subiect, utterd with *fitnes* of figure, and *expressive* Epithetes; with that darknes will I still labour to be shaddowed" (1595).[41] I have already quoted Peacham on how sometimes "darknesse of speech causeth delectation" (1593).

---

40 Valéry, "Naissance de 'La Jeune Parque,'" *Œuvres*, ed. Jean Hytier (Paris: Gallimard, Pléiade, 1957), vol. 1, p. 1621. See also Jarrell, "The Obscurity of the Poet," and T. S. Eliot, "Conclusion," *The Use of Poetry and the Use of Criticism*.
41 Tuve, *Elizabethan and Metaphysical Imagery*, pp. 32, 31.

The wider question of esoteric riddles concerns secret or hidden knowledge deliberately coded to keep outsiders away. In literary works, this is a rarity, though some Alexandrian poets favored it, for example, Callimachus. In other areas, political, alchemical and so on, riddles proved useful in keeping certain matters private. Thus in Plato's *Letters* (II.312e), in Renaissance alchemists, and so on. The work of Theognis of Megara appears to play a double game, first offering "'riddling' or coded discourse . . . [to intensify] an exclusivist sense of inside/outside while reaffirming . . . a fellowship of like-minded comrades." Such "riddling possibilities" sometimes move into the political arena.[42] Esotericism need not use verbal riddles at all, of course, but simply conceal knowledge of some doctrines or some rites. Pausanius refuses to elaborate on rituals in the Mysteries beyond a certain point ("other rites which are not to be spoken of"),[43] just as modern Masons keep some rituals secret. The word "mystery" covers such thinking and activities.

Recent genre study is also interested in the relation of genre and gender. One pertinent question concerns riddle-masters such as Oedipus or Solomon. Why are there no corresponding female riddlers and riddle-masters, a question raised in connection with enigma as masterplot (chapter 3)? They abound in fairy-tales and popular legend, to be sure. And mythical narratives do find a place for female wisdom figures such as the Sibyls or Penelope. But the wit and intelligence required for a riddle-master are commonly assigned to males. It is as if the elevated status of myth and major legend could not accommodate the clever princess or the clever peasant-girl, while a genre lower in the hierarchy can. Athenaeus records a riddle set by Sappho, but Sappho is widely admired for her exceptional gifts, not just in this realm. The mysterious Queen of Sheba is not remembered primarily for her roles as riddler and riddle-master, or her Sibylline knowledge. (One possible exception is Duncan Grant's charming 1912 painting of reciprocal conversation with Solomon, "The Queen of Sheba." The reciprocity is indicated by the language of hands.)

Plutarch includes extensive praise for Cleobulina in his symposium, "The Dinner of the Seven Wise Men":

"Have you not heard of the wise and far-famed . . . Cleobulina . . . the cleverness and skill she shows in her riddles (*ainigmata*); for it is a fact that some of her conundrums (*proballomenon*) have found their way to Egypt . . . these she uses

---

42 Walker, *Rhetoric and Poetics in Antiquity*, pp. 256–7. Walker is drawing on Figueira and Nagy, eds., *Theognis of Megara: Poetry and the Polis*.
43 Pausanias, *Guide to Greece*, Book II.12 (vol. 1, p. 158).

like dice as a means of occasional amusement, and risks an encounter with all comers. But she is also possessed of wonderful sense, a statesman's mind. . ."

("Dinner," *Moralia* 148D, Loeb)

When one dinner-guest speaks of her riddling as amusement fit for girls, Aesop laughs at him, for he is unable to solve a riddle she tossed out earlier. In keeping with the good-humored mood of the dinner, the dinner-guest himself bursts out laughing at the wit of the answer (ibid., 154B–C). Perhaps the question is why such figures as Cleobulina have vanished from general knowledge. Or would a revival of symposium literature also revive such figures?

Modern genre theory is also interested in the transformations of genre, but the riddle as a free-standing genre is so small that transformation is unlikely. Yet while so small, it remains a potent genre and potent mode. Nowadays it may even appear sometimes as if all genre and mode aspire to the condition of enigma. To embed hidden similitudes, to disrupt expected troping, to play with parallel enigmatic masterplots: writers like to make use of a riddling mode within and for different genres. Writers have also rediscovered older genres, among them, schematic and constructional ones that belong to the species of enigma. As usual, riddle and enigma may be small, but they come with large possibilities.

CHAPTER 6

Riddle as scheme: a case for a new griph-class

People are still interested in crossword puzzles and riddles. I don't like crossword puzzles because poetry has more relevance. If you would present highbrow poetry as a superior type of riddle with a definite answer, it might catch on with a good many people. Yes, the highbrow critics would feel a little lost.

(W. H. Auden)[1]

About the year 200, Athenaeus of Naucratis in Egypt put together his series of dinner-table conversations, *The Deipnosophists*, often translated as *The Learned Banquet*. It belongs to the genre of symposium literature, whose prose form is commonly cast in dialogue or discussion among well-read thoughtful speakers, skilled at conversation. "Certain forms and themes like the epigram, the *skolion* [drinking-song], riddles, and chain poems are characteristic" (OCD, "symposium literature"). Athenaeus is especially cherished now, because his invaluable symposium includes quotations from some 1,250 writers, otherwise mostly lost to us.

A whole section of this multi-volume work is given to riddles (x.448b–459b), especially in the form of the *griphos*. The word *ainigma* appears only rarely after the introductory remarks. Occasionally, the word *problema* describes various riddling questions (see Appendix, pp. 263–5 below). In *The Learned Banquet*, *griphoi* are associated with dinner-table amusements, complete with forfeits. (Drinking a glass of salted wine is the worst forfeit in Athenaeus, who does not enlarge on the consequences.) What are these *griphoi*? One speaker cites Clearchus of Soli as an authority: "'A riddle [*griphos*] is a problem put in jest, requiring, by searching the mind, the answer to the problem to be given for a prize or forfeit.' And again in the treatise *On Riddles* [*Peri griphon*], Clearchus says there are seven kinds of riddles" (x.448c). The speaker quotes only three of the seven kinds, but these three locate a *griphos* as a type of cryptic-crossword or

---

1 *Table-Talk of W. H. Auden*, ed. Alan Ansen (New York: Sea Cliff Press, 1989), p 25.

Scrabble riddle. The first type depends on one letter. The riddlee may be challenged to give "the name of a fish or plant beginning with *a*," or words with or without a certain letter "like the riddles called the *s*-less; whence even Pindar composed an ode against the letter s, putting forth, as it were, a kind of riddle in lyric poetry" (x.448c–d). This type of griph remains a popular favorite. A 2002 challenge in Warren Clement's column in the Toronto *Globe and Mail* offered just such a riddle: what word has the most consonants per single vowel? (The winner was the word "strength.") A second type turns on a change of syllable, "where, for example, we are to name something . . . that has the lion as its leader, like Leonides" (x.448c, and cf. English Lionel or Leonard). Or (type 3) the riddle may turn on an entire noun, where the riddlee is asked to name a word with two syllables where the form has a low or a pompous implication, etc.

When Donatus wrote about the trope of *aenigma*, he decided to drop two words for "riddle" in favor of one. Something was thereby lost. His predecessor, Sacerdos, offered the same seven species of allegory, but the riddle came as a pair, *aenigma sive griphus*, enigma or griph. *Griphos* in Greek writing appears as part of the same pair often enough. Plutarch, for example, says that the sphinx wove together her enigmas and griphs (*ainigmata kai griphous plekousan*, "weaving her riddles and puzzles" [Loeb], *Bruta animalia ratione uti* 988a). If English had kept both terms, we would have two classes of riddle, sometimes overlapping but distinct enough to be useful. In fact, a French writer, Alfred Canel, suggested in 1867 that the word *griphe* should be retrieved as the generic name for small riddles. (The word was still current in popular usage in his natal province of Normandy at the time he wrote, though it was obsolete in English by 1796.) Under *griphe*, he would have classified "énigmes, charades, logo-griphes, anagrammes, casse-têtes [brain-teasers, literally "crack-pates"] et rébus" – a useful grouping, though a shortened or sub-divided list would have been even more useful.[2] Too bad that Canel's suggestion did not take hold. Instead, he had to settle for "Devinades." A number of these *devinades* work with schemes, those surface rearrangements of words that are present in poetry, though not sufficient in themselves to make poetry.

Four of the specialized terms for this species of enigma, "griph," "logograph," "rebus," and "charade," merit some attention. The first has roots in antiquity, the second branches from the first in the sixteenth century, the third is also a sixteenth-century word (and a vogue in

---

2 Canel, *Recherches sur les jeux d'esprit*, vol. 1, p. 337.

sixteenth-century France), while the fourth suddenly appeared in 1770 in France and also became a vogue. The way in which all four work is basic to the workings of language, and the rebus may even be said to initiate writing in the Western world.

Despite such a history, the tonal variety among definitions and commentaries for these smaller species can be astonishing. Oddly enough, the smaller the type of riddle, the greater the heat. Even etymology can provoke high dudgeon, as witness Leo Spitzer's anger with his fellow philologists over the etymon for "charade" (see p. 151 below).

DEFINITIONS

The word γρῖφος (*griphos*) meaning "riddle" goes back to Aristophanes, as we have seen, and comes down through Philodemus, Demetrius and others into Athenaeus, and later. *Griphos* came over into Latin as *griphus*, which Lewis and Short call an unusual term, though the *Oxford Latin Dictionary* does not. It is not frequent in any case. Gellius mentions it in his *Noctes Atticae* (*Attic Nights*), written about two decades before Athenaeus. The term is used by a braggart of the Stoic school who claims that he alone can unravel (*dissolvere*) the logical tricks of the genus *griphos* (I. ii.3–4), among others. Gellius has little interest in *griphos*, that tricky Greek creature, or in a later Latin equivalent, *scirpus*. This last, he says, is what the Greeks call *ainigma*, though it seems more like an invented Latin term corresponding to *griphos* – a calque on *griphos*, as Martin L. West says (OCD, "riddle"). (See also p. 188 below.) Elsewhere, Gellius gives the example of an old favorite from Varro, a neat little riddle on minus once and minus twice (XII.vi). The answer is Terminus, god of endings (Ter-minus, punning on *ter* meaning "three" and *minus* as in English).

The fourth-century rhetorician and consul Ausonius (d. 390) wrote a long riddle, which he called *Griphus Ternarii Numeri* (Griphus on the Number Three). Despite the word "griphus," it is not a griph-type riddle at all, but like an Old English riddle poem, where the title names some object or creature, and the poem piles up an exhaustive list of characteristics and examples in cryptic form. So here, the ninety-line poem (Ausonius notes this triform number) draws from all domains, with great ingenuity, ending with the climactic *tris deus unus* (three persons and one God). Ausonius is deprecatory about such a trifle (*inter nugas . . . ignobilis*), though this sounds like a modesty topos. Some time after Ausonius, the word *griphus* disappeared from general use in Western Europe until the early sixteenth century. But from that time on, the word *griphus* was available; by century's end, it was appearing regularly. The excellent Greek scholar Joachim Camerarius was using both words by 1540 in his *Elementa Rhetoricae* ("Multae sunt formae aenigmatum & gryphorum" [pp. 326–7]). Clearchus of Soli, known through Athenaeus, was often cited as an authority.

Entries for *griphus* in the first Latin–English dictionaries suggest that there is little early differentiation between *aenigma* and *griphus*, except posssibly by Elyot. That is, the English language, now rapidly expanding,[3] made no initial effort to distinguish comic riddles from enigmas, perhaps not very aware of Greek practice. In 1538, Elyot included *gryphus* in the first edition of his Latin–English dictionary, and it came with a double signification: "Gryphus, a grype or gryffon. also a captious, an insoluble, or diffuse argumente, a ryddyll." *Aenigma* is defined as simply "a derke question, harde to be understanded." Perhaps Elyot wished to separate a griphus-riddle from an enigma-riddle in the sense of a large, solemn mystery. Robert l'Estienne (Stephanus) in his 1552 *Dictionariolum Puerorum Tribus Linguis* . . . listed: "Aenigma . . . a darke and obscure sentence, harde to coniecte or gesse, A question and sentence insoluble . . ."; "Griphus . . . a darke & obscure question or sentence and hard to bee copied." Richard Huloet, *Abecedarium Anglico-Latinum* (1552), entered gryphus under "Riddle or captious question." Similarly with Thomas Cooper (1565) and John Rider (1589).[4]

Griphus does not attract much attention in the classical and post-classical rhetoricians, and definitions vary a good deal. Among Aristotle's different types of enigma are joking riddles, for example, riddles with a change of letter (*Rhet.* III.xi.6). These sound like *griphoi* as defined by Clearchus, but Aristotle does not use the word. Demetrius' definition is not helpful: "Such want of sequence is called 'griphus'" (*On Style* III.152–3, Loeb). Other Greek rhetoricians such as Philodemus and Pollux mention the term, without expanding on it.[5] The sense of *griphos* or *griphus*

3 See Landau, *Dictionaries*: "The entire stock of English words in the fifteenth century was less than a fifth of what it is today. It was therefore necessary to turn to other languages to provide descriptions of things for which no English word existed. The interest in Renaissance learning naturally made the classical languages, particularly Latin, a favorite source" (p. 37). The expansion reflects the growing predominance of vernacular languages in Europe; lexically, it marks the first stage of standardization.

4 Thomas Cooper's *Thesaurus Linguae Romanae et Britannicae* (1565), which absorbed and expanded Elyot, listed *aenigma* as "a darke or harde question: a ryddle," and *griphus* as "a nette: a riddle: an intricate or dark sentence." John Rider, *Bibliotheca Scholastica* (1589), gave both *aenigma* and *gryphus*, with *scrupus* for good measure, under "A Riddle, or darke sentence." (For *scrupus*, read *scirpus*; the spelling in the Renaissance varies.)

5 Pollux was a contemporary of Athenaeus, also from Naucratis in Egypt.

remained wobbly in Renaissance rhetoricians. Despite Clearchus, Julius Scaliger defines *griphi* vaguely as ambiguities (*ambages*) in 1561. Even Vossius cites sources, rather than trying to define the word.[6] In the mid-seventeenth century, the Abbé Cotin defined a *griphos* as a riddle on a serious subject ("ceux que les anciens appelloient γριφος qui auoient pour leur sujet des choses graves & serieuses, comme on peut voir dans les Nuicts Attiques," Preface, n.p.). Such an odd definition argues that the lexicographers' early melding of *aenigma*-words and *griphus*-words held sway for some time.

Late in the century, Claude-François Ménestrier devoted a chapter to the *griphus* in *La philosophie des images énigmatiques* (1694, pp. 55–68). He outlines the types of *griphe* in Clearchus, then gives subsequent examples, including some ingenious anagrams from the *Mercure Galant* and a rebus on *griphe*. The most pleasing enigmas, he adds, are those based on "la similitude ou la ressemblance de diverses choses" – a reminder to his readers not to forget about enigmas that use tropes. Nearly a century later, the word *griphus* was still in use in J. F. Facius, *De Aenigmate et gripho* (1789), where it refers to classical *griphi*.[7]

The word "griph" (sometimes "gryphe" or "griphus") even came into English for a while, though most of the OED's quotations (1652–1796) refer to classical riddles. Pope used the word in 1726, but as a Latin term, not a naturalized English word. ("The Hebrews as well as Greeks had a custom of entertaining themselves at their festivals, with these *griphi convivales*" [*The Sixth Book of the Odyssey*].) But the word survives to this day as a suffix of "logogriph," whose signification is much the same as that of "griph." "Logogriph" merely spells it out.

While the word "griph" in English, along with its cognates in other Western European languages, became generally obsolete, the word "logo-griph" stuck. A logo-griph is simply a word-riddle of the *griphos* type, usually following the description of Clearchus. The first use of Latin *logogriphus* that I have found is in Scaliger's posthumous 1561 *Poetices Libri Septem*. The fact that he offers no account of the word argues that "logogriph" was already current.[8] *Logogriphus* comes over into English,

6 The sources are Gellius, Ausonius, and Apuleius in II Florid. (Vossius, *Etymologicon linguae Latinae* [Amsterdam, 1695], "griphus").

7 J. F. Facius, *De Aenigmate et gripho* (1789). Archer Taylor, who had not seen a copy, lists J. K. Facius in his *Bibliography*, but the copy at Princeton shows J. F. on the title page.

8 Presumably the title of one section of the *Carmina* (1395), "Aenigmata et Logogryphi," by Philip of Harveng [d. 1183] was added by a later editor (*PL* CCIII).

French, Italian, Spanish, and Portuguese in vernacular forms, and survives to this day. Though the term is specialized, it even turns up in standard desk dictionaries like Cassell's Italian or Chambers Twentieth-Century Dictionary. Bishop Hall provided the first recorded English use in 1597–98. (He disdained logographs as did Ben Jonson forty years later.) The first recorded French use was by Naudé in 1623 (*Trésor de la langue française*, citing Littré),[9] so that the OED's "logograph . . . ad. F. *logographe*" may be mistaken.

A logograph in German is a *Worträtsel* (word-riddle), as in Gustav Gerber's 1885 *Die Sprache als Kunst*. Gerber's examples sound like the *griphoi* of Athenaeus, and include Latin logographs from Scaliger (pp. 385ff.). The logograph also exists in Turkish and Persian. It appears more than once in Orhan Pamuk's 1990 novel, *The Black Book*. (A journalist, for example, constructs logographs "to get around the censor and the press prosecutor."[10]) In Persian, the word for logograph is *Mima*. Joseph von Hammer described them in his 1818 *Geschichte der schönen Redekünste Persiens* in a section on "Chronographen, Räthsel und Logographe."[11] They are more demanding than the logographs listed above, for it is not enough to transfer the letters of a word; the arts of punctuation, inversion, and so on are also brought into play as part of the solution. "Logograph" in a Persian dictionary would be defined differently.

This is a species of riddle that remains a widespread favorite today, especially in its anagrammatic or acrostic forms, as witness the daily cryptic crossword puzzles in newspapers or the weekly crossword puzzles in the *New York Times,* the *Times Literary Supplement,* and elsewhere. In 1758, a correspondent of the *Mercure de France* protested the degradation of logographs among the moderns, "who have debased [avili] this genre," so esteemed among the ancients. Clearly he wished to restore the logograph along the lines of a Persian *Mima*. The logographs offered by the *Mercure* included the anagrammatic type: how many words can be

---

9 *Trésor de la langue française.* (The *Trésor* follows W. von Wartburg, *Französisches Etymologisches Wörterbuch,* fasc. 44 (1950), v, 399/2.) The word is not in Edmond Huguet's *Dictionnaire de la langue française du seizième siècle* (Paris: Didier, 1946). The OED may have its possibly mistaken view about the English word as an adaptation of the French on such evidence as that of G. Mieze, ed., *The Great French Dictionary* (London, 1688), which explains the word (s.v. "Logogrife"), but has no entry in the English–French part. I owe this last surmise to E. G. Stanley, as I also owe the information about Wartburg.

10 Pamuk, *The Black Book,* pp. 66, 88. On the tradition of Turkish riddling, see Andreas Tietze, *The Koman Riddles and Turkic Folklore* (Berkeley: University of California Press, 1966).

11 Hammer, *Geschichte der schönen Redekünste Persiens,* pp. 33–4. The Persian word for riddle/*Rätsel* is *Laghs*.

made of this single word? (In English, for example, the word "create" gives you at least eighteen other words: a, at, cat, rat, rate, ate, art, cart, eat, ear, tea, tar, car, acre, tear, crate, erect, trace.) But a properly made logogriph, this man argued, provides true riddle to be solved subsequently.[12] The difference can be seen in crossword-puzzle anagrams today. Most solutions require simple ingenuity, and there is an end to it. But the best anagrams are also witty, sometimes even metaphorical, and solving them brings a quick smile.

The word "rebus" in modern times dates from 1512 in France, and from 1605 in England (OED). It is usually defined as the ablative plural form of Latin *res* or "thing," though this derivation has been challenged. In his very popular *Les Bigarrures*, Etienne Tabourot called rebuses "riddles as speaking pictures [*équivoques de la peinture à la voix*]." But the name disappointed him: "Isn't it too bad that such a witty invention [une si spirituelle invention] is called by the word Rebus, which is general to all things and means 'things'?" They are "Rebus de Picardie" because the Picards delight in them more than any other Frenchmen do (vol. 1, fol. 6r–v). Gilles Ménage, in his etymological dictionary (1650, 1694), says that the full name is "rebus de Picardie" because the *clercs* of Bazoche used to invent libels based on actual events. These they called "De rebus quae geruntur" (On things that are done or happen), and they read the *libelles* in processions during Carnival. Ménage records in 1650 that the police in Boulogne eventually banned *des rébus de Picardie* because they defamed so many well-known families. According to Camden, the English picked up the word from their garrisons at Calais and other places bordering Picardy (Chambers, *Cyclopaedia* [1728], "rebus").[13] Canel prefers the simpler explanation that words are represented by things: "pour les choses" or *rébus*. Hence the name. For indeed a rebus is defined as a picture that substitutes for a word by means of a puzzle. An eye drawn on the page signifies "I," in a verbal and visual pun.

French scholars have several objections to the derivation of "rebus" from Latin *res* by whatever means. First, Renaissance *res* is not simply identical with "thing" as object, but also and often with "words as subject or content."[14] Second, not one libel has been found in the archives of

---

12 Anon., *Mercure de France* (Dec. 1758), 60–3.
13 Schenck, in her 1973 book on the rebus, *Das Bilderrätsel*, lists the authorities who have accepted this etymology ("Etymologie des Wortes 'Rebus,'" pp. 55–6). Gerber, *Die Sprache als Kunst*, p. 392n, refers also to Ochmann, *Zur Kenntnis der Rebus* (Oppeln, 1860), who draws on Tabourot.
14 "The term *res*, meaning *subject–matter*, seems to become confused with *res* meaning *things*" (A. C. Howell, "*Res et Verba*: Words and Things," *ELH* 13 [1946], 131).

Picardy or beyond, despite many assiduous searches by scholars. Third, an early source spells the word "resbus" or "resbuz," and this from the pen of the good Latinist Geoffroi Tory, who was unlikely to insert an *s* in the middle of *rebus*. I have yet another reason. Though I have not seen it noted, the second edition of Ménage in 1694 is a good deal more tentative about the origin of rebus. "On prétant [prétend] qu'on les nomme *Rébus*. . ." instead of "On les appelle *rebus*" ("It is claimed they are called Rebus" instead of "They are called rebus").[15] Jean Céard and Jean-Claude Margolin prefer Pierre Guiraud's etymology of *rébus-rebours* whereby the old rebus saw the world *à rebours* or upside-down. Their thorough analysis[16] also notes how the word "rebus" has spread through European languages; modern Hebrew adapted it by 1975 through a phonetic equivalent.

Rebuses are obviously related to visual riddles, including blazons, devices, and emblems – forms much in favor in the sixteenth century. The rebus, said Camden, "was in wonderful Esteem among our Fore-fathers; and he was no-body who could not Hammer out of his Name an Invention by this Wit-craft, and Picture it accordingly" (Chambers [1728], "rebus"). Chambers adds that the rebus eventually grew out of fashion at court, despite its antiquity, though it was greatly esteemed in its day. His examples include the Abbot of Ramsey who engraved in his seal a ram in the sea. He also quotes the standard example of a dedication by Cicero, where the drawing of a chick-pea is added to the names Marcus Tullius. (The Latin word for chick-pea is *cicer*.) Canel similarly reports the French passion for the rebus in the form of emblems and devices in the sixteenth century. "It was, as may be seen, a rage [une fureur]" (p. 390), especially in Picardy. This was less due to the natural wit of the Picards, Canel adds, than to the sun and soil of Picardy, which produced rebuses as naturally as other regions produce apples – a very proper observation for a man from Normandy.

Like others, he observes the older history and varied use of the type. In a Book of Hours of about 1500, for example, the word *louange* (praise) is

---

15 Gilles Ménage, *Les origines de la langue françoise* (Paris: Augustin Courbé, 1650), which takes over Tabourot's definition; *Dictionnaire Etymologique ou Origines de la langue françoise*, 2nd edn. (Paris: Jean Anisson, 1694), "rébus." The addition of the accent in the later edition shows the gradual naturalizing of the word. Céard and Margolin cite the 1650 edition, but quote from the later edition, wrongly assuming that it is identical (pp. 279, 292n).

16 Céard and Margolin, *Rébus de la Renaissance*, pp. 277–94. Taylor's *Bibliography* says that a 1903 study of rebus is "of cardinal importance" (p. 148) but I have been unable to see it: O. Thorel, "Les Rébus de Picardie: Etude historique et philologique," *Mémoires de la société des Antiquaires de Picardie*, 4th sér., 4 (34) (1903), 499–700.

represented by a wolf (*loup*) and an angel (*ange*). The devotional manual could even be used by the illiterate when keyed this way. That is, the rebus could provide access rather than bafflement. The same principle sometimes applies to Hieroglyphic Bibles, though often no rebus is involved but simply a substitute picture. A picture of a hand may substitute for the word "hand," a device that is an illustration rather than a small puzzle like the charade-like rebus of "louange."[17] It is also true that not all rebuses could be deciphered by the illiterate.

The device remained a favorite. Benjamin Franklin and Lewis Carroll alike composed ingenious and charming letters using rebuses. (See, for example, Tony Augarde's examples in his *Oxford Guide to Word Games* [pp. 88, 89].) Sometimes the position on the line or the size of the font gives a word ("over" or "under," large A or small A).

> Tils   vent   bien
> Trop   sont   pris
> Trop subtils sont souvent bien surpris.
> (Tabourot, *Les Bigarrures*, quoted in
> Gerber, *Die Sprache als Kunst* p. 391)

That is, "Those too subtle are often quite surprised," playing on *sub* and *sous* (under) and *sur* (over). Sometimes the substitution is not a pun, but a pictorial form of a word, as in New York as the Big Apple. James A. Kelso includes them in a wide, earlier definition, "a riddle put in the form of a picture or of things in words or syllables." "According to Plutarch, Alexander the Great, during the siege of Tyre, saw in a dream a satyr (Σάτυρος) who could be caught only with difficulty. The wise men interpreted the dream for him very quickly: Σάτυρος = Σὰ Τύρος" ("Riddle," p. 766). That is, a *satyros* is a *Tyros*, a satyr stands for Tyre.

Though the word "rebus" is not ancient, the principle goes back very far. Commentators often connect them with Egyptian hieroglyphics (from 3000 BCE), which consist of objects represented by pictures, a chain of rebuses, as Canel puts it (*Recherches sur les jeux d'esprit*, pp. 387–8). But Jared Diamond is closer to the mark when he connects the principle of the rebus to the earliest apprehension of Western writing itself. In the Sumerian alphabet of pre-3000 BCE (Mesopotamia), there is a seminal linking of the aural and visual representations of language. "It's easy to draw a recognizable picture of an *arrow*, hard to draw a recognizable picture of *life*, but both are pronounced *ti* in Sumerian, so a picture of an arrow came to mean either *arrow* or *life*. . . Linguists term this decisive

---

17 See, e.g., Clouston, *Hieroglyphic Bibles.*

innovation, which also underlies puns today, the rebus principle."[18] What is now a "riddle" is actually a principle of writing, but so completely absorbed as a convention that its earliest form now seems a novelty.

"Charade" is derived from eighteenth-century French *charade*, but beyond that the origin is doubtful (OED). Sébastien-Roch-Nicolas Chamfort first defined it in *Le Grand vocabulaire françois 1767–1774* (quoted below by Leo Spitzer). By 1798 it was listed in the French Academy's authoritative *Dictionnaire de l'Académie*. It had rapidly become a vogue. It crossed the Channel by 1776 ("Pray send me some *charrades*," OED), and flourished in England as well as on the Continent. In 1777 a sardonic *Treatise on the Charade* by a so-called Sieur Rondeaulet was translated into English by one Tobias Rigmerole, and published in London. In the same year, when charades were a new-fangled French device barely out of diapers, Sheridan included them in *The School for Scandal*. "I back him at a rebus or a charade against the best rhymer in the kingdom," says Crabtree of Sir Benjamin Backbite (i.i), thereby claiming that his nephew is both quick-tongued and up to date. (Perhaps Sheridan recalled that rebuses were earlier accounted an occupation for fools, at least by some: "Scribblers . . . Rhimers, Anagrammatists, Acrosticians, Rebus-Men, Punsters, and Blank Versifiers," *The Fool* ii.96, 1746.)

In fact, the principle of the charade (a syllable-puzzle) goes back very far. Spitzer notes Lavine's syllable-division of her lover's name as *e-ne-as* in the medieval *Roman d'Eneas* (p. 83n). There is also an old Arab charade on the name "Samarkand," recorded in a well-known collection by Muhammed ibn Ahmad Ibshihi (1388–c. 1446).[19] For all that, the rebus on "louange" could equally well be presented without pictures. In 1711, long before the word itself, a recognizable charade was offered in *Delights for the Ingenious*.

> From the mate of the cock, winter-corn in the ground
> The Christian name of my friend may be found:
> Join the song of a cat, to the place hermits dwell in,
> Gives the surname of him who does music excel in.

In 1711 this was not called a charade, but a rebus. "This rebus," says *Delights*, "is upon the name of M. Henry Purcell" (Hen-rye Purr-cell).[20]

---

18 Diamond, *Guns, Germs and Steel*, p. 220. For the rebus as part of phonography, and for variations in Egyptian, Chinese, and Aztec, see Ducrot and Todorov, *Encyclopaedic Dictionary*, p. 196.

19 Muhammed ibn Ahmad Ibshihi, cited in Taylor, *Literary Riddles* (where the name is spelled Abshihi), p. 20.

20 *Delights for the Ingenious* (1711), quoted in Augarde, *The Oxford Guide to Word Games*, p. 21.

But all these examples actually come late in the history of the charade. The *Greek Anthology* records a charade on "Rhodes": "My first is the 'moo' of a cow: / My second the creditor's cry: / And my whole the name of an island" (xiv.16). The moo of a cow is ῥο (*ro*), δός (*dos*) means "give," and the whole is ʹΡΟΔΟΣ (*Rodos* or Rhodes).[21]

Charades quickly became very popular, and lived on as a favorite parlor-game. French riddle collections rapidly began to include charades, for example, *Enigmes, charades et logogriphes* (1784), *Manuel des oisifs . . .* (1786), and *Le Sphinx aux Oedipes présens et à venir* (1803). English collections were no less prolific. In London in the 1790s, there appeared Thomas Hookham's *A New Collection of Enigmas, Charades, Transpositions, &c.* (1791), Peter Puzzlewell's *A Choice Collection of Riddles, Charades, Rebuses &c.* (1792), Charles Hutton's *The Diary Companion . . . containing answers to last year's enigmas, rebuses, charades. . .* (1795), Thomas Whiting's *The Poetical Delights: containing enigmas, charades, rebuses, &c. with their answers: Selected from an extensive correspondence* (1797), *Amusing Recreations, or A collection of charades and riddles on political characters and various subjects* (London: Vernor and Hood, 1798), and Peregrine Puzzlebrains' *Christmas Amusement: or, the happy association of mirth and ingenuity: being an elegant collection of original riddles, charades &c. Culled from the vase of fancy at Conundrum Castle* (1799). In 1797, a periodical was established called *The Masquerade: A Collection of new Enigmas, Logogriphs, Charades, Rebuses, Queries and Transpositions.* Alas, it survived only until 1800. Collections continued to pour out after the turn of the century.

In 1806, charades were still new enough to need explaining, or so Samuel Tizzard thought in his *New Athenian Oracle.* The game was stricter than it is now.

To inform those who are not used to this species of wit, it may be proper to observe, that Charades are a kind of Rebus, imported from the French, and have this property, namely, that the subject, or word in question, called the *whole*, must be a noun substantive of two syllables; and each of the syllables, called the *first* and *second part*, must also be a noun substantive; also each syllable separately, and the whole compound word, is to be described, or enlarged upon, by some elegant allusion.[22]

21 Forster, "Riddles and Problems from the Greek Anthology": 45. The OCD ("anthology") gives a date of about 940 for the *Palatine Anthology*, which formed the basis of the *Greek Anthology*.
22 Tizzard, *The New Athenian Oracle*, head-note to "Charades," p. 56.

George Crabbe's 1810 poem, "The Borough," records that "his fair friends . . . Oft he amused with riddles and charades" (III.105). Jane Austen admired Crabbe's work, and would have encountered the word there. But many an English collection of riddles before 1810 also included them. *The Masquerade* thanked contributors for their submissions. Were the Austen family among them?[23] They enjoyed riddles and charades, and a small collection of their inventions was published in 1895.[24] (Of the twenty-three composed by nine of the Austen family, three are by Jane Austen, and, like the others, they are neat and amusing.) "M^r & Mrs Digweed [took] kindly to our Charades, & other Games," Austen recorded in 1816.[25] The play with a courtship charade in *Emma* is play with a game still fresh.

In this well-known example, Mr. Elton employs a charade to say coyly what he cannot say openly: "Court" plus "ship" = "courtship." The wrong woman duly copies a censored version into her riddle collection. Mr. Elton's courtship charade causes confusion all round. Harriet Smith is not bright enough to decipher it, until Emma tells her what the answer is and what it implies. Quick-witted Emma is blind to Mr. Elton's pretensions, quite misreading the primary meaning of this charade. Mr. Elton delightedly rushes ahead.

What has happened? A folklorist might observe that a basic folktale type is faintly elicited here: the clever peasant girl and/or the clever princess who find ways to help a desirable suitor answer a crucial riddle. (Cf. "the cycle of the Clever Peasant-Girl [Die kluge Bauerntochter]" mentioned by Taylor and others.[26]) If you wish an ironic take on the standard folk-tale, what could be better than Austen's sweet but dim peasant girl, clever but self-deceived princess, and socially ambitious crude suitor?

What has happened in literary terms? The answer to the courtship charade in *Emma* depends on an ability to read schemes and tropes, here including the pun.[27] Harriet is at sea with schemes and tropes both.

---

23 "To Correspondents. The Favors received from Bath, Salisbury [etc.] . . . are acknowledged gratefully" (2 [1798]). Mrs. Austen and her daughters stayed with a friend in Bath in November 1797 (*Jane Austen's Letters*, p. 361n).

24 *Charades &c. Written a hundred years ago by Jane Austen and Her Family* [1895].

25 *Jane Austen's Letters*, 8 Sept. 1816, p. 320. Cf. also p. 202. Austen, incidentally, is credited in the OED with inventing the compound word "riddle-book" in *Emma* in 1816. Keats picked it up in 1820 for "The Eve of St. Agnes" (xv), where, needless to say, the function is very different. There were "books of riddles" long before Austen, but not "riddle-books."

26 Taylor, "The Riddle," p. 147.

27 Puns were, in fact, known to earlier rhetoricians as figures of speech, most commonly paronomasia.

Emma and Mr. Elton easily read the answer to the "courtship" charade, for they are good at reading rhetorical schemes. But the essential trope of "courtship" requires more context than either Emma or Mr. Elton realize. Is "courtship" a synecdoche, a part for the whole? If so, what whole? "Courtship" takes its place in one whole plot in Emma's mind, and quite a different whole plot in Mr. Elton's. Or is courtship an example of the old trope of enigma, an enigma doubly deployed as a scheme?

Acted charades developed a little later. Augarde records an 1821 letter from Maria Edgeworth, in which acted charades are apparently mimed. The amusement sounds novel: "We acted *words* – charades last night.. . . *Coxcomb.* Mr Smith. Mr Ricardo . . . crowing. Ditto . . . combing hair. Mr Ricardo solus – strutting coxcomb very droll. *Sinecure.* Not a good one" (p. 24). Thackeray's Becky Sharp is memorable in her charade, and *Vanity Fair* (1848) is listed in the OED as recording the earliest example, which takes place a generation before. ("At this time, the amiable amusement of acting charades had come among us from France; and was considerably in vogue in this country," chap. 51.)

But low views of the charade prevailed in part of the word's signification. Something is said to be a "charade" when it is farcical. One of George Eliot's speakers uses the word this way in her poem "A College Breakfast-Party" (ll. 85–8):

> Why, rhetoric brings within your easy reach
> Conclusions worthy of – a butterfly.
> The universe, I hold, is no charade,
> No acted pun unriddled by a word. . .

Nor does Sébastien's etymology for "charade" help: he suggested a Provençal origin, meaning "chatter," conversation to kill the time.

Yet a charade has to do with writing, to follow Spitzer, who is indignant about his fellow philologists and their easy acceptance of Sébastien's etymon. Only their general disdain for riddles and even for myth, he argues, could explain their all-too-easy acceptance of Provençal *charrado* as the etymon for "charade." He quotes Sébastien: "This word comes from the Languedoc idiom, and means originally talk intended to kill time [tuer le temps]: one says in Languedoc, 'Let's go make charades' for 'Let's go pass the time after dinner' or 'Let's go spend the evening at so-and-so's,' because, in after-dinner gatherings, people of this region entertained themselves in idle talk [dire des riens] as a pastime." Spitzer adds Mistral's example, "Mistral's noun 'causerie . . . sorte d'énigme': a development from 'idle talk as a means of passing the time' to 'riddle, puzzle.' But to me," he stresses, "such a semantic development is gravely suspect" (Spitzer, "Charade," pp. 77–8).

For why ignore the perfectly good Old French words *charait, charaie, charaute, charaude* as etymons for *charade*? These are words signifying a written "character" or letter. They suggest charade as a type of letter-riddle. But, Spitzer laments, "The mythical approach to the world which the riddle presupposes has been replaced today by the scientific approach – with the result that the the riddle has lost its seriousness in modern civilization where it has become either a game for children or a social pastime for their bored elders" (p. 80). Bad science follows, for the philologists have been lax in allowing their presuppositions to govern their judgment. Whether Spitzer is right or wrong, his argument reminds us of the effect of originary explanations. Philologists too are subject to the genetic fallacy.

FUNCTIONS

The folklorist Roger D. Abrahams, comparing the effects of folk-riddles and of poetic techniques, notes the "devices of rhyme, alliteration, balance and contrast."[28] He is especially helpful because he is stressing how schemes work in riddles, even though he does not call them that. The dictionary significations of "enigma" and "riddle" allow room for both tropes and schemes, both the good metaphors of memorable riddles, and the fun and games of schematic ingenuities.

Several of Canel's species, such as charades, logogriphs, and anagrams, chiefly take the form of schemes, not tropes. If the surface patterning of schemes can include the look of words and homonymic puns (I–eye), then a rebus also works on the same principle. I want to take up Canel's suggestion, and extend it. I want to propose that riddles in literature that play with schemes rather than tropes might be classified as griph-type riddles. This means that some riddles that do not qualify as true riddles for folklorists would be perfectly respectable schematic riddles for literary purposes. By the same token, some devices now hard to classify and often omitted as mere novelties would have a literary home. The distinction between trope and scheme seems to me to mark out neatly the general area of these riddles. Analysts of small forms like the rebus sometimes

---

28 Quoted by Charles T. Scott, "Some Approaches to the Study of the Riddle," p. 114.

observe that no metaphor is involved in the way that metaphor is involved in large enigmas. (Sometimes this takes the form of saying that small conundrums are monosemous, while large enigmas are polysemous.[29]) My own distinction finds a rhetorical place for the rebus and its like.

If the trope of enigma acts as a closed simile and turns on similitude, how does the scheme of a griph-riddle function? Again, similitude is at work, but now an internal similitude, so to speak. This kind of similitude draws from the multitude of likenesses within the make-up of words, say, in letters or syllables. Homonymic puns work on the same principle, using an apparently accidental similitude of sound. (A satyr can provide a figure for Tyre in Greek.) Other schemes re-arrange words or parts of words. Of course, just as all horses are animals, but not all animals horses (Augustine again, *De trin.* xv.ix.15), so also with schemes of the griph class. Not all schemes are riddling. This is very clear with rhyme schemes. Only a hidden or esoteric metrical scheme would be so classified. On the other hand, an acrostic or anagram or rebus or charade is by definition riddling, though a writer may not exploit the riddling possibilities very far.

Schemes do not in themselves reverberate as tropes do. We would not say that the answer to a griph-type riddle is also an enigma. Not at all. When we have solved the griph or logogriph or rebus or charade, there is an end of it. Fun, yes, and sometimes suggestive. Anagrams on proper names can appear to reveal a truth, all the more if proper names are thought to possess magic qualities in themselves. Louis XIII even established an official Anagrammatist in the same class as the Poet Laureate. A Thomas Billon was appointed at a salary of 1,200 livres. The position did not survive long. Still, flattery helps at court, and ingenuity likes exercise. Louis was a skilled falconer and "Louis XIII, Roi de France et de Navarre" was transposed into "Roi très-rare, estimé dieu de la fauconnerie," a 36-letter-and-digit anagram. An admirer of "William Ewart Gladstone, Midlothian," devised a 31-letter anagram, "It is a title we allow him, Grand Old Man" (newspaper clipping, found in an old book). Anagrams even made their way on to tombstones, as if the character or lot of the deceased lay concealed within the name. One tombstone in East Coker, Eliot's ancestral village and burial-place, has both an acrostic and an anagram on Robert Paul (Apt Labourer).[30]

29 Enigma, "by its metaphoric structure . . . makes use of the long way. . . . The rebus, on the contrary . . . of the short and trivial way (if one may say so!) of the proper meaning" (Céard and Margolin, pp. 102–3).
30 Wheatley, *Of Anagrams*, pp. 91, 122–7.

In his chapter on "Des Griphes," Ménestrier mentions that some explicators of riddles in the *Mercure Galant* signed their names in anagrams. Some followed Hebrew practice and reversed letters so they read from right to left, as in Roma and Amor. Poets also liked to hide their names this way. Jean Bouchet became "A bien touché" (*i* and *j* were interchangeable). Pierre Roussin became "Prière sur Sion." Someone even devised an anagram on "Claude Ménêtrier" as "Miracle de Nature," to which Ménestrier penned a graceful deprecatory reply in verse (Wheatley, *Of Anagrams*, pp. 94–5). The device is still current today. The professional life of Margaret Atwood is handled by the organization O. W. Toad.

Schemes can also be mnemonic devices that tag something in our memories. But only if a scheme moves toward a condition of trope will it continue to generate meaning. Good writers can make schemes work this way, including rhyme schemes. Here is Richard Wilbur speaking from a poet's workbench:

It is precisely in its power to suggest comparisons and connections – unusual ones – to the poet, that one of the incidental merits of rhyme may be said to lie. Say to yourself *lake, rake,* and then write down all the metaphors and other reconciliations of these terms which occur to you within one or two minutes. It is likely to be a long list, extending from visual images of wind furrowing the water, to punning reminiscences of Lancelot and Guinevere . . .[31]

The same is true of riddling rhyme schemes, as witness James Merrill's poem "Pearl" below.

The general principle of griph-riddles as art goes back very far in Western literature. Clearchus' first example of a *griphos* is Pindar's "ode against the letter *s*," written without the *s* or sigma.[32] Pindar put "as it were a kind of riddle in lyric form, since many had taken offence at him because he was unable to abstain from the letter *s* and they did not approve of it" (Athenaeus x.448c–455c). (The problem of a voiceless sibilant is more apparent in recited poetry, as also in singing.) This kind of *griphos* is still in play today. The French group of writers called OULIPO reveled in such games; they identified the device of omitting one letter by its proper name, a *lipogramme*. (In English, the word "lipogram" was introduced in 1711 by Addison, according to the OED. It is still in use today.[33]) Georges Perec, the best-known member of OULIPO, wrote a novel without the letter *e*, called *La Disparition* (*The*

---

31 Richard Wilbur, "The Bottles Become New, Too," *Quarterly Review of Literature* 7 (1953), 191.
32 Pindar, frag. 79, *Poetae Lyrici Graeci.*
33 Joseph Addison, *Spectator* no. 62 (1711); Mark Ford, *Times Literary Supplement* (29 August 2003), 24.

Disappearance) in 1969. In 2001, the Canadian poet Christian Bök published a prize-winning collection, *Eunoia*, a series of ingenious and accomplished prose-poems where each section uses only one vowel ("Duluth dump trucks lurch, pull U-turns," from chapter U). As with rhyme, the challenge is not merely to do it, but to make art of it.[34] Useful forms have a long shelf life. They may be re-discovered and resuscitated, or discovered *ab ovo* and assumed to be new and post-modern. Either way, they can provide a stimulus for good work.

Anthologists of these small species of riddle incorporated them in larger collections of schematic forms. The full title of Canel's 1867 book is *Recherches sur les jeux d'esprit, les singularités et les bizarreries littéraires, principalement en France*, and it is a treasure-house for poets who enjoy playing with such forms. So is Etienne Tabourot's much earlier collection, *Bigarrures* (Paris 1572). As separate creatures, some griph-type schematic riddles would constitute what Alastair Fowler calls constructional types, a "quasi-generic grouping." Both Canel and Tabourot would provide fine starting-points for a study of schemes and of a few constructional types, that "vast although neglected subject" (Fowler, *Kinds of Literature*, pp. 126–9).

We tend to underestimate schematic forms as art. The riddles that Athenaeus records from Clearchus sound like what they are in *The Learned Banquet*: after-dinner amusement. They are decidedly at the small end of the scale. Yet Clearchus, the authority, offers a literary example for *griphos* from no less an author than Pindar. Pindar's *griphos* reminded dinner guests indirectly of questions of art. So also, with some older kinds of challenges that Clearchus lists, such as capping quotations or naming cities all beginning with the same letter. He contrasts such amusements with those of his contemporaries:

"The solution of riddles is not alien to philosophy, and the ancients used to make a display of their knowledge by means of them. For in propounding riddles in their drinking-bouts they were not like the people of to-day who ask one another, what is the most delightful form of sexual commerce, or what fish has the best flavour . . ." (Ath. x.457d)

No, these worthy ancients (as ancients tend to be) enjoyed displaying their familiarity with Homer through play with his lines.

For writers, and especially poets, the play of language is bread and meat. They enjoy schemes in themselves, but then so do we. Schemes of

34 *Times Literary Supplement* column, "NB," for 30 August 2002 also mentions Isidro de Robles's 1666 *Varios Efectos de Amor* (five stories, each lacking a particular vowel), and so on.

the riddling kind have been favorites from the ancients to this day. "The gaiety of language is our seigneur," as Stevens put it ("Esthétique du Mal" XI), and the gaiety of language governs many a popular puzzle, if not quite with seigneurial force. Literary critics all too often underestimate a reader's sheer pleasure in schematic skill. All the more in riddling or griph-type schematic skill.

George Herbert can make poetry of anagrams arranged like a charade, as in the last lines below. But his schemes in "Jesu" (*Complete English Works*, p. 109) are not hidden. We may say that the name lay buried in words, as if letters and puns are always ready to tell us something. Herbert has unearthed it for us at the start, in his wonderfully lucid art, rather than burying it deeper for us to dig up.

> JESU is in my heart, his sacred name
> Is deeply carved there: but th' other week
> A great affliction broke the little frame,
> E'en all to pieces, which I went to seek:
> And first I found the corner, where was *J*,
> After, where *E S*, and next where *U* was graved.
> When I had got these parcels, instantly
> I sat me down to spell them, and perceived
> That to my broken heart he was *I ease you*,
> And to my whole is *J E S U*.

A griph-type scheme propels Mark Strand's "great dog" poem ("Five Dogs (2)"), where a missing term must be inferred.

> Now that the great dog I worshipped for years
> Has become none other than myself, I can look within
> And bark, and I can look at the mountains down the street
> And bark at them as well.
>
>   . . .
>
> I roam around and ponder fate's abolishments
> Until my eyes are filled with tears and I say to myself, "Oh Rex,
> Forget. Forget. The stars are out. The marble moon slides by."

Strand's move from the standard joke on "dog" as a reversed "God" over to an elegiac meditation on the death of God is a hazardous one, likely to be fatal in the hands of a lesser writer. The challenge lies especially in the control of tone. Too flippant and the scheme will go out of control. Too easily melancholic and it will dissolve in dampness. It is St. Paul's enigma as masterplot that is mourned here. The griph of Aristotle's joking riddle or Clearchus' after-dinner amusement is called into unusual service. Yet just as Herbert could make of Jesus' name a griph-type riddle capable of becoming a trope, so also here, but through a plot reversal. The standard joke has become an entire narrative.

Acrostics (where initial letters of a given unit follow a pattern) have been practiced regularly from at least the time of the Hebrew Scriptures.[35] In poetry in English, initial letters of a line often spell out a name. Edgar Allan Poe used acrostics to bury his addressees' names in the poems, "A Valentine" and "An Enigma." Not too deep, however, for the titles invite a reader to look further and so does the last line of "An Enigma" ("Of the dear names that lie concealed within 't"). To find the addressees' names requires looking at the first letter of the first line, the second letter of the second line, and so on. The Poe who wrote classic mystery stories was also attracted to the minor mysteries of poetic schemes. Acrostics with a name spelled out vertically in the first letter of each line are easy enough to read, though not always apparent at first. Poe has buried the names of his addressees deeper than usual.

With John Ashbery's bush in his poem "Susan" (from *Hotel Lautréamont*), we may hear a griph-type scheme already turned into trope, if we listen. That bush is an ordinary bush, growing and then dormant, until it encounters someone who can change it ("celebrate it," in fact) into "trope." Into topiary, more like, which in turn evokes a tropiary, a place where gardener-poets turn literal vegetable bushes (and just possibly human erotic ones, as well) into figures. Nature and art work together in both contexts. The tropiarian clips a bush into some ornamental shape. The poet clips a bush into a metaphor. A topiary-tropiary is schematic echo, as puns often are, here with one term implied. It is also a griph-riddle, a buried scheme that works by changing one letter.

John Hollander relies on both a scheme and allusive echo in the opening stanza of "The Mad Potter" (*Harp Lake*):

> Now at the turn of the year this coil of clay ·
> Bites its own tail: a New Year starts to choke
> On the old one's ragged end. I bite my tongue
> As the end of me – of my rope of stuff and nonsense
> (The nonsense held, it was the stuff that broke),
> Of bones and light, of levity and crime,
> Of reddish clay and hope – still bides its time.

---

35 See, e.g., F. H. Woods, "Acrostic," James Hastings, ed., *A Dictionary of the Bible* (Edinburgh: T. & T. Clark, 1898). See also David Armstrong on "sacred acrostics" in the Roman Catholic and Orthodox Churches, citing A. Dietrich and F. Dornseiff, in *Philodemus and Poetry: Poetic Theory and Practice in Lucretius, Philodemus, and Horace*, ed. Dirk Obbink (New York: Oxford University Press, 1995), pp. 210–11n.

It is as if the Muse were the nymph Echo, to whom the poet cried, before this poem began: "Give me a trope," to which she replied, "rope." Whereupon the poet said, "Well, you *can* trope on a rope." You can build pots out of a rope of clay. The snake with its tail in its mouth, the Ouroboros, can be a rope. You can develop the common trope, "I'm at the end of my rope," which for a poet means "at the end of trope" as well. And the relation of trope and rope? What is a rope but a beheaded trope, as if the Queen of Hearts from *Alice in Wonderland* had arrived with her usual sentence, "Off with his head" – an Atropos figure of sorts. Fortunately there is Alice, who replies to the Queen's "Sentence first – verdict afterward." "Stuff and nonsense!" says Alice.[36] A whole series of entwined tropes in that "rope of stuff and nonsense" are wittily and cogently suggested by Hollander's scheme and allusive echo. One part of the scheme is a griph-type riddle as defined by Clearchus: it depends on the change of one letter in "trope." For Ashbery, it was the letter *r*, for Hollander, the letter *t*. What makes both passages riddling is that one term is silent and must be inferred by the reader.

Debra Fried has raised the question of whether esoteric or hidden metrical schemes may be riddles of sorts. I think so. Envelope rhymes (e.g., abcdeedcba) are not always very apparent, especially when the sequence is extended. They can remain hidden until some link alerts us. Merrill's envelope rhyme in his "Pearl," for example (*A Scattering of Salts*, 1995), takes fifteen lines before reaching the poem's central two-word line, "Of grit," and starting to move out again. It is possible to read the entire poem without being aware of the rhyme. Such buried rhyme might well qualify as a griph-type schematic riddle. I recall a student's outburst of enthusiasm at seeing the sheer skill of this envelope rhyme.

Writers know how to make schemes metamorphose into tropes, the sine qua non of poetry. Merrill's envelope rhyme is a case in point, for the poem treats a small boy's fascination with his mother's single pearl, worn on a chain around her throat. The rhyme moves toward its short center line, then out again. It suggests a trope on the pearl as center of the boy's mesmerized gaze and of a series of reflections that may be traced and re-traced. Ashbery's bush trope itself moves toward a scheme, where the scheme of "topiary" clarifies the trope. This is a scheme that grows out of

---

36 Chapter 12. The exchange follows the King's under-appreciated joke: "'It's a pun,' the King added in an angry tone." Troping his work as a rope of stuff and nonsense is just right for the mix of tone in Hollander, as is the verdict that the nonsense held, etc. "The nonsense held" partly because Alice herself provides the stuff for this wonderful trope in the so-called nonsense book by Carroll.

a trope. Or rather, a scheme that takes an overt trope (shaping a work of art is like shaping a bush) and makes a griph-type riddle of it (trope to topiary). Many skillful griph-type schemes do not announce their presence, but mask it, at least at first. Ashbery's riddle-scheme only gestures quietly toward itself when the trope is announced. Hollander's "rope" as beheaded "trope" silently awaits a memory from *Alice in Wonderland*. Strand's elegiac dog poem silently depends on the hoary old chestnut of "God"–"dog."

Schemes may sometimes appear to be

> "just an excuse for you to leave your posts,
> toying with anagrams, while the real message
> is being written in the stars."
> (John Ashbery, *Girls on the Run* 11)

Merrill knew better, and so do Ashbery, Hollander, and Strand, masters of the pleasure of schematic forms.

CHAPTER 7

Case study II
Mapping riddles: Lewis Carroll and the Alice books

> In both worlds, one of the most important and powerful characters
> is not a person but the English language. Alice, who had hitherto
> supposed that words were passive objects, discovers that they have a
> life and a will of their own.
>
> (W. H. Auden, "Lewis Carroll")

Lewis Carroll is not a riddling writer in the sense of working with the
trope of enigma. He is not in the line of riddle writers such as Donne,
Browning, Hopkins, and Eliot. He is not trying to invent powerful
hidden similitudes to be puzzled out, then pondered. Nor does he offer
uncanny haunting enigmas. At least, not in the first instance. The strength
of what he does lies elsewhere. For the most part, he offers puzzles or
logical paradoxes or schematic riddles of the griph type. Some even work
with pretty feeble puns, the kind to make children hoot and adults groan.
Still, these puzzles and paradoxes and riddles can move toward tropes in
the most unexpected ways. So also can the personified riddles, the riddle-
masters, the mirror-riddles, the arithmetical riddles and more. Charm and
proverb, those generic siblings of enigma, also appear regularly and with
the same effect.

I want to look at some of Carroll's resonances, as well as some of his
overt effects, suggesting that the Alice books provide us with something
like a topography of enigma, including griph. If enigma and griph had a
country of their own, here is what it might look like. Here is how various
personified riddle types might behave. Here is how they might relate to
events and people in our more familiar everyday world. This is the Land
of Enigma, in Auden's sense of the English language as "enigma" inhabiting a country. We perforce see it from a young girl's perspective, in
Carroll's imaginative tour de force. And after all, it is only right that
puzzles and paradoxes and griphs, as well as personified riddles, riddle-
masters, mirror-riddles, arithmetical riddles and more populate this place.
A child faces such challenges and tasks and people regularly. The great

haunting tropes of enigma, say, the challenge to Oedipus, belong normally to an adult world. Not exclusively though. A child may also be aware of such larger riddles. They will hover in the background of even a happy childhood, reverberating now and then. It is just such reverberations that Carroll can elicit from the characters of his Land of Enigma.

Take, for example, the Gryphon and what comes of the puns there. They are schemes, but with surprising consequences.

The Gryphon is a personified riddle, so to speak. Why did he go to the classical master for lessons? To learn Greek and Latin, and thereby to learn his own name, which puns on Greek *griphos* and *gryps*, both sometimes rendered in Latin by the same spelling, *gryphus*. Whether this was a schoolboy joke in Carroll's day or whether it was known through Ariosto or whether Carroll himself heard it freshly, I do not know. But there is the pun, in chapter 9, where the Mock Turtle and the Gryphon continue their discussion of education. The Gryphon says:

> "I went to the Classical master, though. He was an old crab, *he* was."
> "I never went to him," the Mock Turtle said with a sigh. "He taught Laughing and Grief, they used to say."
> "So he did, so he did," said the Gryphon, sighing in his turn; and both creatures hid their faces in their paws.

Latin and Greek, Laughing and Grief: all familiar, and strange too. The whole matter of translating and learning is caught here: into and from and between Latin and Greek, into and from and between laughing and grief, together with crossings of the two pairs. Yes, learning Latin and Greek is a matter of laughing. (*Swimmo, swimmere, sinki, drownum* used to be a standard Latin-class joke in my day, together with some ruder ones.) A matter of grief too, on occasion. Then, as happens in Carroll, there is the unexpected larger resonance, when we reflect on the curious connecting of laughing and grief. And then, to clinch the whole matter, the third pun. For what else is a laughing grief but a *griph-* (pronounced *grief*, as in the first syllable of *griphos*), and how odd that the root of the Greek word for a joking riddle should sound the same as the English word for sorrow.[1] And how odd that Latin *gryphus* should be the same word in some spellings for both a riddle and a fabulous creature.

Certainly John Tenniel sensed the doubleness of the pun and the creature. In his first illustration, the Gryphon is sleeping, solitary and

---

1 If the first syllable of *griphos* was pronounced in Carroll's day so as to rhyme with "strife," then the point about sorrow is lost. But a griffin point is gained, for the syllable then sounds like the German word for griffin, *Greif.*

fierce, with a high hill or mountain in the background. It's as if the creature were inhabiting its legendary mountain near the Hyperboreans and guarding its hoard of gold from the one-eyed Arimaspians. ("If you don't know what a Gryphon is, look at the picture," says Carroll – fortunately now Tenniel's picture, and not his own: see Fig. 5.) Ariosto said they inhabited Norway, which was the northern extremity of his inhabited European world. Wherever you choose to place these fierce creatures, it must be at the edge of the world, in a place almost legendary, a Wonderland. In Tenniel's next two illustrations, the Gryphon is shown with Alice and the Mock Turtle, sitting on its hind quarters and dancing on its hind legs. It is a doleful domestic pet or stuffed animal, though its dolefulness is deceptive. The Gryphon, having the nature of a *griphus*, is not given to taking things seriously, including the imperious Red Queen and the sad Mock Turtle. Alice finds the Red Queen fierce, and she pities the Mock Turtle, thus responding to each as each would wish. The Gryphon simply says, "What fun!" as he watches the Red Queen.

"What *is* the fun?" said Alice.

"Why, *she*," said the Gryphon. "It's all her fancy, that: they never executes nobody."

The first version of the Gryphon comes with only one pun on education, the "tortoise"/"taught us" pun. All the rest of that conversation, including the extended Greek and Latin punning I have noted, was added later. In fact, the first version of the Gryphon, as illustrated by Carroll, looks like another creature among the many Alice has already met. He might be some extinct creature like the Dodo, though out of old legend and heraldry. He looks scrawny and ineffectual, a decided oddity. Carroll commends his reader's attention to the drawing, but no child would surmise from it what a griffin is. Things changed in the published version, where we may also see how Carroll's schematic riddles move toward troping. Not that "tortoise" and "taught us" is a dead pun, considering the look of some teachers or the slow pace of some teaching and learning – a pace that may nonethless win the race with a hare (especially a March Hare?).

As for the Mock Turtle,

"What is his sorrow?" she [Alice] asked the Gryphon. And the Gryphon answered, very nearly in the same words as before, "It's all his fancy, that. He hasn't got no sorrow, you know."

The Gryphon knows about fancy, being himself a creature of fancy. He also likes punning a lot. He should. He *is* a pun, after all – a pun that Alice

Liddell's father, of Liddell and Scott's *Greek–English Lexicon*, would recognize. Is it because he is merely a pun that Carroll makes him lower-class, a status marked by his faulty grammar? The Gryphon's classical education was apparently rudimentary.

If this Graeco-Latin punning sounds improbable, we have only to look at the fine punning on Latin grammar in the White Queen's famous saying, "'The rule is, jam to-morrow and jam yesterday – but never jam today'"(chap. 5). Quite right too, because Latin *iam* ("now") is used only with the future and past tenses, never with the present tense. (In Latin, *i* and *j* are interchangeable.[2]) "Latin teachers . . . tell me that the Queen's remark is often used in class as a mnemonic for recalling the proper usage of the word."[3] In the present tense, "now" is rendered as *nunc*, as we may know from musical settings of biblical Latin ("Nunc dimittis . . . Lord, now lettest Thou thy servant depart in peace"). "*Jam* to-morrow and *jam* yesterday – but never *jam* today." "Now" and "then" work the same way in English. Through a punning schematic riddle, the grammatical *jam* rule becomes a domestic fable that can expand into a political fable all too readily.

Or take a different kind of example, this latter-day version of the Grecian Sphinx, that triform creature who sits high on a cliff, propounds a riddle to all who pass, and kills those who cannot answer her riddle. In a number of Attic vase paintings from the fifth century BCE, she sits on a pillar looking down on one man and sometimes more. Her famous riddle is, of course, "What has four legs, two legs, and three legs and speaks with one voice?" Or sometimes: "What has four legs in the morning, two at mid-day, and three in the evening?" The answer is humankind. In the Oedipus story, he finally provides the answer, and the Sphinx, mortified, throws herself off the cliff and dies. Oedipus becomes king – for a time, that is.

My latter-day riddler sits "on the top of a high wall" (the adjective "high" is added to the original version of this creature's story). He (for the sexes are reversed) demands: "Tell me your name and your business," which certainly sounds like some legendary or fairy-tale challenge to approaching strangers. Or, for that matter (moving to ordinary mimesis), a version of "Who goes there?" or a curt no-nonsense greeting. This

---

2 In fact, Lewis and Short (first edn. 1879) list the word as "jam," though the *Oxford Latin Dictionary* follows the more usual spelling of "iam." What Latin dictionaries would Carroll have followed?

3 *See* Gardner, ed., *The Annotated Alice: The Definitive Edition*, p. 196.

Figure 5. Lewis Carroll's drawing of the Gryphon and the Mock Turtle, *Alice's Adventures under Ground* (London 1886).

questioner is exceedingly impatient when the traveler through his domain cannot tell what her name means. No Oedipus or "Swollen-Foot" she. He, on the contrary, has a "speaking name," a riddle in itself. She also reverses things by asking *him* riddles, though quite unintentionally.

Figure 6. John Tenniel's drawing of the sleeping Gryphon, Lewis Carroll, *Alice's Adventures in Wonderland* (London, 1866 edn.).

"Don't you think you'd be safer down on the ground?" [she] went on, not with any idea of making another riddle, but simply in her good-natured anxiety for the queer creature. "That wall is so *very* narrow!"

This only makes my latter-day Sphinx growl. (He does so twice, though he's not in leonine form like his original, who is quite safe on high walls.) "What tremendously easy riddles you ask!" he "growled out." And then: "Now, take a good look at me! I'm one that has spoken to a King, I am" – and indeed he has, though not to Oedipus.[4] Conversation is impossible, for everything becomes a riddle with this sphinxine creature. But things proceed smoothly enough when he can have his way and interpret all riddles, including (says he) "all the poems that ever were invented – and a good many that haven't been invented just yet." For as with words, and as with his female riddlee, "The question is . . . which is to be master – that's all."

---

4 For Oedipal resonances in the Red King's story in *Through the Looking-Glass*, especially as mediated through Borges' fiction, see Irwin's *The Mystery to a Solution*, index, "Red King."

In short, if we want to see in a nutshell something of the structure and function of the Sphinxine riddle, we could do worse than reread the sixth square or chapter of *Through the Looking-Glass*. Humpty-Dumpty's anxiety even causes him to repress the obvious foot-riddle about himself, though attention to his crossed legs and to the horses just following this chapter might alert us.

Humpty Dumpty was sitting, with his legs crossed like a Turk, on the top of a high wall – such a narrow one that Alice quite wondered how he could keep his balance. . . he crossed one knee over the other and clasped his hands around it . . . [chap. 6] Then came the horses. Having four feet, these managed rather better than the foot-soldiers. [chap. 7]

Oedipus, to quote the classical scholar Frederick Ahl, "disposed of the Sphinx . . . by solving the riddle of the feet. Logically, he, like the Sphinx, is destroyed when someone 'solves' the riddle of his own feet" (*Sophocles' Oedipus*, p. 28). What has two legs and no legs and speaks with one voice? Well, a man who is an egg, or vice versa. And what is Humpty Dumpty so anxious about? The Sphinxine riddle tradition of eat-or-be-eaten, and we'd be anxious too if we were eggs.

Harold Bloom calls Humpty-Dumpty a "pompous egghead," and so he is, though not for Carroll as the word apparently dates back only to 1907. He is also entirely an egg, and so the personified form of one favorite topic for a riddle. The nursery-rhyme where Humpty-Dumpty was born is itself an indirect riddle, whose answer is "an egg." Egg riddles are great favorites; the form of an egg offers a good deal of scope to a riddler. (It contains a full creature or a world in little. It is yellow like the sun and white like the moon. And so on.[5]) Humpty-Dumpty is a personified riddle who prefers to act as a riddle-master. We might say the same thing of the Sphinx.

The word "master" takes its signification from its context, as for example: (1) in a craft or an art, on a scale of apprentice, journeyman, master; (2) in a class structure, as someone in charge of servants or slaves. "Master" in a class structure may well have temporal mastery over the plot of any given story or life. It is also true that a question of mastery suffuses all our uses of words, as Carroll intimates through Humpty-Dumpty. It perforce suffuses masterplots themselves. What kind of mastery depends on context.

5 See the egg-riddles in chapter 8 and Taylor's section on egg-riddles in *English Riddles from Oral Tradition*.

Alice as female quester neatly evades Humpty Dumpty's attempt to engage her in a riddling contest. Her instincts are wise enough to know that you are better off keeping right outside a riddler's terms and frame of thought. The inside–outside trope of enigma can be its most dangerous. The best riddle-answers turn the question back on the questioner. They resemble the well-known Zen Buddhist dialogue:

SOLEMN DISCIPLE: Can a dog have a Buddha-nature?
MASTER: Bow-wow.[6]

It bears repeating that these are the kinds of intimations that Carroll's work generates. What interests me in the Humpty-Dumpty resonance and many another is Carroll's sure sense of limits. Carroll is not alluding to the Grecian Sphinx and her famous riddle. Even the word "echoing" is too strong. A resonance, a reverberation, a reminder that comes and then vanishes: again and again the genius of the Alice books is to set these delicately in motion. They are not merely fanciful, but neither are they firm. They live on a scale from certain (the *jam* pun and the Gryphon scheme-trope) through probable to just possible. This is not a scale in relation to Carroll's intentions, but a rhetorical scale measuring reasonable limits to our inferences from a trope.

For an example of a just-possible scheme, this time through a proverb, we might look at the Duchess. The proverb is riddle's rhetorical sibling, and it too has a place in the Alice books, most memorably in the Duchess's incessant moralizing. She does not moralize in her kitchen, but her chief form of conversation on social occasions is to repeat the refrain "And the moral of that is . . ." followed by some maxim. Near the beginning of the Gryphon chapter, the Duchess and Alice are conversing: "'The game's going on rather better now,' she [Alice] said by way of keeping up the conversation a little. ''Tis so,' said the Duchess: 'and the moral of that is – "Oh, 'tis love, 'tis love, that makes the world go round!"' 'Somebody said,' Alice whispered, 'that it's done by everybody minding their business.'" That somebody is the Duchess herself three chapters previously. Alice, trying to protect the baby from its mother's barrage of pans and dishes, cries out, "Oh, *please* mind what you're doing!" The Duchess growls, "If everybody minded their own business . . . the world would go round a good deal faster than it does."

---

6 Compare Blake's quatrain, "The Question Answered," and see John Hollander's explication in his "Poetic Answers" (*Melodious Guile: Fictive Pattern in Poetic Language* [New Haven: Yale University Press, 1988], pp. 49–50).

"Doing our own business" is offered as one possible definition of temperance in Plato's *Charmides*, as translated by Carroll's colleague Benjamin Jowett. Socrates is discussing the ideal of temperance (*sophrosyne*), and with good reason, given Charmides' own physical attractions.

[CHARMIDES:] I heard from someone, "Temperance is doing our own business" . . .

[SOCRATES:] I should be surprised if we are able to discover their truth or falsehood [i.e., of the quoted words], for they are a kind of riddle [*ainigma*]. . . I am quite certain that he put forth his definition as a riddle. (161b–162b)

And so on, through a passage including several references to enigmas in a dialogue centered on a riddle of sorts – the charm of Charmides and what to do about it. Socrates refutes this definition of temperance by showing that the world would not go round better if everyone simply did their own business. The idea of the Duchess offering – growling out – a prescription for temperance is charming. Reading Charmides and Socrates against Alice and the Duchess is equally charming.

Carroll does not begin with riddles, but rather with the riddle's other rhetorical sibling, the charm. Since charms are incantatory and lull the mind to rest, they help to build a mimesis of someone falling asleep. So with the start of it all in the Alice books. Alice falls asleep and into her dream by a long fall down that rabbit-hole, a fall remarkably free from claustrophobia or a sense of entrapment. A fall that also enacts the metaphor of "falling" asleep. She falls down a "well" that echoes and rhymes and puns on its own name, as well as on "fall–fell," as if in a charm or a slide into sleep: "a very deep well. . . well. . . fell. . . well. . . 'Well,' thought Alice to herself." (Though she has fallen asleep outdoors, the well resembles an Oxford don's study, elongated, rather as if Alice had fallen asleep in such a room. There are the "book-shelves and cupboards . . . maps and pictures hung upon pegs," together with a jar of orange marmalade.) "Down, down, down" echoes another charm-like refrain, before Carroll begins his soporific "'Do cats eat bats? Do cats eat bats?' and sometimes 'Do bats eat cats?' for, you see, as she couldn't answer either question, it didn't much matter which way she put it. She felt that she was dozing off, and had just begun to dream" – to dream a dream within her dream, that is. It is an excellent technique to make the outer dream sound actual.

After this, few charms appear, though the White Queen uses a charm-like technique on Alice in the last chapter of *Through the Looking-Glass*, as Frye points out. Alice is being examined for her fitness to be a Queen, having moved up to the eighth rank of the chessboard as a pawn.

"Can you do Addition?" the White Queen asked. "What's one and one and one and one and one and one and one and one and one and one?

"I don't know," said Alice. "I lost count."

"She can't do Addition," the Red Queen interrupted.

"The White Queen is not employing a charm," Frye observes, "but she illustrates the overwhelming of sense by sound, which is where charm starts" ("Charms and Riddles," p. 124). "Too high a speed of utterance" here prevents understanding.

The small schematic riddle of Alice's "Antipathies" enters her dream-fall as she muses on falling right through the earth to the other side. "She was rather glad that there *was* no one listening, this time, as it didn't sound at all the right word." The passing joke on the unspoken word "Antipodes" comes with some troping power, for Alice's view of the Antipodes is anything but antipathetic. Even among people in the Antipodes who "walk with their heads downward," as in old travelers' tales, she retains her sense of courtesy. How far the British at large regarded the Antipodes with antipathy is another matter. But Carroll stays away from such riddles for a time, while he puts in place the essentials of his dream-world. In the first version of chapter i in *Alice's Adventures under Ground*, the Antipodes joke does not appear at all.

Carroll ends the chapter first by shrinking Alice, then by enlarging her. Children must cope with changes in size, but not this rapidly, and not so as to cause the fear that "'it might end, you know . . . in my going out altogether, like a candle. I wonder what I should be like then?' And she tried to fancy what the flame of a candle is like after the candle is blown out, for she could not remember ever having seen such a thing." Any possible dread in Alice's simile ("Out, out, brief candle!") passes easily by, but Carroll will return to it in *Through the Looking-Glass*. ("'If that there King was to wake,' added Tweedledum, 'you'd go out – bang! – just like a candle!'") This is the first of several changes in Alice's size, and it leads very naturally to reflections on her odd environment in chapter 2: "'How queer everything is to-day! And yesterday things went on just as usual. I wonder if I've been changed in the night. . . But if I'm not the same, the next question is, Who in the world am I? Ah, *that's* the great puzzle!'"

And so it is, of course, the enigma of identity being a standard philosophical question. It lies behind the Sphinx's riddle. How can the infant we once were, the adult we now are, and the aged person we will become (we hope) – how can all these speak with one voice? How do we retain one identity through so many changes in our lives? Carroll stays away from any sphinxine or philosophical heaviness, here by moving Alice on to the question of other possible identities, perhaps Ada, perhaps Mabel. (Mabel elicits firm ideas from Alice: she refuses to be less intelligent and especially less well off than she is in her present life.) The question of identity moves out on a tangent, but it will reappear in different contexts all through the first Alice book.

In chapter 5, the question of Alice's identity is mitigated by considering it in relation to a butterfly's metamorphosis – not a parallel that ordinarily helps with the human riddle of identity. To be sure, the parallel is often invoked to describe eternal life, a life utterly different in kind from earthly existence. We can no more imagine this, so the argument goes, than a caterpillar can imagine what life will be like when it has turned into a butterfly.

Not that Alice's Caterpillar is much of an example.

"Who are you?" said the Caterpillar.

This was not an encouraging opening for a conversation. Alice replied, rather shyly, "I – I hardly know, sir, just at present – at least I know who I was when I got up this morning, but I think I must have been changed several times since then."

And so on through a conversation that leads to metamorphosis, something quite natural for the caterpillar, but, says Alice, "would feel very queer to *me.*"

"You!" said the Caterpillar contemptuously. "Who are *you?*"

Alice now responds by saying ("very gravely," Carroll remarks), "'I think you ought to tell me who *you* are, first.'" Though the Caterpillar, a born contrarian, answers, "'Why?'", the burden of identity has shifted. Shape-changing occurs not only to the Caterpillar as a matter of course, but also to other Wonderland creatures as a matter of course.

In the next chapter, Alice calmly reflects that the Duchess's baby she has been tending "'would have made a dreadfully ugly child: but it makes rather a handsome pig, I think.' And she began thinking over other children she knew, who might do very well as pigs, and was just saying to herself, 'if one only knew the right way to change them' – when she was a little startled by seeing the Cheshire Cat sitting on a bough of a tree a few yards off." By now, Alice can control her own size; she has moved pretty rapidly to the thought of acting like some Circe, the goddess who changed men into pigs at her pleasure. Carroll keeps the thought momentary, a child's passing fancy (or his own, as some critics think). The grinning Cheshire Cat interrupts any further Circe-fancies. Like the

Caterpillar and the pig-baby and Alice herself, the Cheshire Cat is a shape-changer. But by now, the question of identity does not follow from Wonderland's odd metamorphoses. Alice remains composed when the Cheshire Cat twice vanishes, not by jumping down and running away, but by suddenly dissolving from sight, like a ghost. After the third reappearance, she makes a request:

"I wish you wouldn't keep appearing and vanishing so suddenly; you make one quite giddy."

"All right," said the Cat; and this time it vanished quite slowly, beginning with the end of the tail, and ending with the grin, which remained some time after the rest of it had gone.

Here is a manifestation to evoke the Sphinx's riddle and questions of identity, but Alice takes it all quite calmly, including the Cat's interpretation of her request. What Alice means to convey is that she wishes the Cat would appear and disappear like a normal cat, like her own Dinah, of whom she is so fond. This Cat has the agility of a ghost, not a cat. When the Cheshire Cat does accede to Alice's request, it retains its own identity, vanishing like the "you" who is the Cheshire Cat and not like Dinah.

The question of identity itself has been metamorphosing from the hint of a metaphysical question at the start through the Caterpillar's contemptuous interview, where its question properly elicits the answer to the Sphinx's riddle, "A human being." Given the Caterpillar's tone and bearing, the question sounds less enigmatic or philosophical than social, as if the creature were interrogating Alice about her status.

Carroll introduces the shape-changing of creatures long before the Duchess's baby son-pig in chapter 6. From the start, it is associated with cats, partly by a charm-refrain where the word "cat" itself changes shape (cats-bats, bats-cats, ma chatte, Cat-erpillar, Cheshire Cat). In chapter 3, it is associated with a cat through the Mouse's tale-tail, that is, a shape poem. (Carroll's original tail-tale shape poem in *Alice's Adventures under Ground* began with a cat.) Martin Gardner's invaluable *Annotated Alice* quotes Charles Peirce on the technique he called "art chirography" (p. 35), a technique known from the shape poems of the ancient Greeks through the Renaissance to the early twentieth century and to our own day. Is such a technique a form of the griph riddle? I think so. Normally, shape poems are not riddling, but they do have affinities with the rebus. A rebus often gives a pictorial equivalent of one word. A shape poem also often gives a pictorial equivalent of one word (the "Axe" poem by Simmias of Rhodes [c. 300 BCE], Herbert's "The Altar," Apollinaire's

Calligrammes, Hollander's "Swan and Shadow").[7] But it is done differently. A shape or pattern poem makes all the poem's words on the page conform to a pictorial outline rather than accepting the conventional box shape with a justified left margin. Carroll improves the occasion by punning on "bend-*not*-knot," tangling the tale-tail even more.

In chapters 6 through 9, Alice becomes more and more at home in the Land of Enigma, or, as the Cheshire Cat defines it, the place where everyone is mad.

> "Visit either you like: they're both mad."
> "But I don't want to go among mad people," Alice remarked.
> "Oh, you can't help that," said the Cat: "we're all mad here. I'm mad. You're mad."
> "How do you know I'm mad?" said Alice.
> "You must be," said the Cat, "or you wouldn't have come here."

Worries about her own identity dissolve, especially after she realizes in chapter 8, "'Why, they're only a pack of cards, after all. I needn't be afraid of them!'" – a moment at which she is close to waking. In chapter 9, she is still frightened of the imperious Queen, but by the end, she is sure of her identity and can answer back, intervene, and protest. She has also started growing again at a prodigious rate ("a mile high," objects the King), something she now accepts nonchalantly.

The riddle of identity also appears indirectly and intermittently in *Through the Looking-Glass*. Here Alice does not change shape. Her environment does, including both time and place. Nor does Alice ask the question of who she is. Nonetheless, the riddle of identity recurs, now in scenes where it is linked with a question of power. It resurfaces in the most terrifying scene of the Alice books (or so it was for me as a child), the discussion of the Red King's dream in chapter 4:

> "He's dreaming now," said Tweedledee: and what do you think he's dreaming about?"
> Alice said "Nobody can guess that."
> "Why, about you!" Tweedledee exclaimed, clapping his hands triumphantly. "And if he left off dreaming about you, where do you suppose you'd be?"
>
> "Where I am now, of course," said Alice.
> "Not you!" Tweedledee retorted contemptuously. "You'd be nowhere. Why, you're only a sort of thing in his dream."

---

7 Hollander, *Types of Shape*. See also Higgins, "Pattern Poetry," which notes that pattern poetry "was taken as suitable only for comic verse" at the time of Carroll's "The Tale of the Mouse" (p. 890); and Hollander, "The Poem in the Eye."

"If that there King was to wake," added Tweedledum, "you'd go out – bang! – just like a candle!"

Alice protests, to no avail. Tweedledum is adamant that she is "'only one of the things in his dream. You know very well you're not real.'" "'I *am* real!' said Alice, and began to cry." Finally, in Dr. Johnson's fashion of kicking a stone to refute radical idealism, Alice wisely says to herself, "'I know they're talking nonsense,'" and sensibly has done with it.

Of course, she is not "real," in the sense that fictional characters are not real. But then, what kind of reality do they possess that they live in our heads, sometimes with more life than actual persons? Carroll leaves us with the question. And of course she *is* part of a dream, or rather a dream-romance. As with Alice's dream-within-a-dream in the first Alice book, so here with the dream-within-a-dream. It helps to give the mimesis of this odd mirror-world a sense of actuality. It is also raised to the power of who-is-dreaming-whom. As Gardner notes, a common mirror-image puzzle lies behind this question. "An odd sort of infinite regress is involved here . . . like two mirrors facing each other, or that preposterous cartoon of Saul Steinberg's in which a fat lady paints a thin lady who is painting a picture of the fat lady who is painting a picture of the thin lady, and so on deeper into the canvases."[8]

The question remains with Alice, reappearing at the opening of chapter 8. ("'Only I do hope it's *my* dream, and not the Red King's! I don't like belonging to another person's dream.'") It remains with her when she wakes up, and Carroll chose to end his book with it, except for the closing verses.

"Now, Kitty, let's consider who it was that dreamed it all . . . You see, Kitty, it must have been either me or the Red King. He was part of my dream, of course – but then I was part of his dream too! . . . Oh, Kitty, *do* help to settle it! . . . " But the provoking kitten only began on the other paw; and pretended it hadn't heard the question.

Which do *you* think it was?

This makes for a somewhat ineffectual ending, as Carroll slides away from his powerful fiction. The first Alice book does not fare much better. Carroll has a little trouble waking up from his great dreams.

Carroll mentions riddles by name in only three episodes of *Alice's Adventures in Wonderland* and *Through the Looking-Glass*. The Mad

---

8 *The Annotated Alice: The Definitive Edition*, ed. Gardner, p. 189. See also Irwin, *The Mystery to a Solution*, on dreams within dreams and on infinite regress (index, *Through the Looking-Glass*).

Hatter sets his famous riddle at the Mad Tea Party. Humpty Dumpty turns every statement into a riddle. The White Queen sets a riddle of sorts at the eighth-square banquet where Alice becomes a queen.

The Mad Hatter's riddle of the raven and the writing desk has no single answer, though several workable answers do exist. The Mad Hatter, who sets the riddle for Alice, says there is no answer at all, and Alice protests (chap. 7).

> "Have you guessed the riddle yet?" the Hatter said, turning to Alice again.
> "No, I give it up," Alice replied. "What's the answer?"
> "I haven't the slightest idea," said the Hatter."Nor I," said the March Hare.
> Alice sighed wearily. "I think you might do something better with the time," she said, "than wasting it in asking riddles that have no answers."

Richard Wilbur agrees. Although he allows even unfair riddles some possible merit, "The only thing we ask, as Alice said to the Mad Hatter, is that people not make up riddles that have no answers at all" ("The Persistence of Riddles," p. 340).

Carroll eventually provided a "fairly appropriate" answer in 1896, though it was his answer and not the Mad Hatter's. "The Riddle, as originally invented, had no answer at all." But of course. If the Mad Hatter had concealed the real answer from Alice at that mad tea-party, his character would have to be reread. Gardner gives the details, including Carroll's 1896 answer: "Because it can produce a few notes, tho they are *very* flat; and it is nevar put with the wrong end in front." He adds:

Note the spelling of "never" as "nevar." Carroll clearly intended to spell "raven" backwards. The word was corrected to "never" in all later printings, perhaps by an editor who fancied he had caught a printer's error. Because Carroll died soon after this "correction" destroyed the ingenuity of his answer, the original spelling was never restored.

Only in 1976 was the original spelling discovered, after much ink had been spilled devising ingenious answers.[9] Edgar Allan Poe's "The Raven," with its famous refrain, "Quoth the Raven, Nevermore," was published in 1845, twenty years before *Alice's Adventures in Wonderland.* Poe, a master of charm effects, could not but have heard the reverse "Raven / Never" in his own poem. This is a griph-type riddle, but a rather flat one, appropriately enough.

---

9 *The Annotated Alice: The Definitive Edition,* ed. Gardner, pp. 71–3; the original spelling was drawn to public attention by Dennis Crutch in *Jabberwocky* (winter 1976).

Generically, the two Alice books are romances, as Robinson Duckworth recognized on the river-trip where *Alice in Wonderland* began. "I rowed *stroke* and he rowed *bow* in the famous Long Vacation voyage to Godstow, when the three Miss Liddells were our passengers, and the story was actually composed and spoken *over my shoulder* for the benefit of Alice Liddell, who was acting as "cox" of our gig. I remember turning around and saying, 'Dodgson, is this an extempore romance of yours?' And he replied, 'Yes, I'm inventing as we go along.'"[10] Perhaps it helped that Alice sat behind him as he invented this new world.

The two romances take the form of dream-romances, though, as Auden and others have noted, they differ from one another. Auden observes how the ground-rules change with *Through the Looking-Glass*.

What Alice finds so extraordinary about the people and events in these worlds is the anarchy which she is forever trying to make sense and order out of. In both books, games play an important role. The whole structure of *Through the Looking-Glass* is based on chess, and the Queen of Hearts' favourite pastime is croquet – both of them games which Alice knows how to play. To play a game, it is essential that the players know and obey its rules . . . Anarchy and incompetence are incompatible with play. . . in Wonderland, they behave as they choose and the game is impossible to play. In the Looking-Glass world, the problem is different. It is not, like Wonderland, a place of complete anarchy . . . but a completely determined world without choice.

("Lewis Carroll," p. 289)

In both worlds, griph-type riddles offer *in nuce* some "sense and order." The sense and order may be curious or ludicrous, but sense and order they are. Seeing and solving *griphi* can provide a small, limited corner of sanity.

William Empson acutely observes that "*Wonderland* is a dream, while the *Looking-Glass* is self-consciousness" ("The Child as Swain," p. 341). John Hollander expands on why the first Alice book is more essentially dreamy: "its concentration on the dreamer, her falls and changes of size, and the kinds of situation she encounters . . . [*Through the Looking-Glass*] has more the form of a romance . . . it has a quest-story (ephebe-pawn to move through chessboard squares to be queened). . . its episodes are mapped by its scheme . . . its actual regions and places are more allusively allegorical . . . *Through the Looking-Glass* also has an allusive relation to the earlier book . . . This multiple allusiveness . . . is typical of . . . major

10 Robinson Duckworth (the "Duck" of chapter 3), from *The Lewis Carroll Picture Book*, ed. Stuart Dodgson Collingwood (London, 1899), quoted in *Alice in Wonderland*, ed. Gray, p. 272.

romances like *The Faerie Queene*" ("The Poetry of Nonsense," p. 201). To be sure, *Alice's Adventures in Wonderland* is also governed by a quest story, at least for the first seven of its twelve chapters. It is the quest for the lovely garden, glimpsed in chapter 1: "Suddenly," in the way of both dreams and romances, "she came upon a little three-legged table, all made of solid glass; there was nothing on it except a tiny golden key." The key, seen through a glass all too clearly, opens the door to "the loveliest garden you ever saw. How she longed to get out of that dark hall, and wander among those beds of bright flowers and those cool fountains." But Alice is much too large for the tiny entryway into the small garden. Then, when the magic of romance provides a drink to reduce her size, she cannot reach the key. Like some garden typical of Eden, this one can be glimpsed but not entered in a normal human state. (It enters into the apprehension of Eliot's rose garden in *Burnt Norton.*) Like some Fellows' Garden in an Oxford college, this one is inaccessible to a general public; it requires a key. And while it looks delectable when you are kept outside, it proves much less so inside, where you discover that those in charge go in for general bullying, impossible games, and arbitrary trials. It *was* a Fellows' Garden after all, and not the Earthly Paradise.

If the most crucial trope for an enigma is the inside–outside trope (see chapter 8 below), then dream-narrative, and especially romance, makes an ideal generic home. The dreamer is outside the dream, yet often inside it as well. The dream's riddling nature can be brought out from the dream for examination. But the insider–outsider world of Oxford is only one set of boundaries at play in this dream-romance.

Is Carroll troping on the mistaken reading of Paul's famous text when he has Alice actually go *through* the mirror in *Through the Looking-Glass*? This would be to trope by literalizing. As far as I know, it is the first example of a person actually penetrating through and behind a mirror. Critics sometimes mention George Macdonald, who speculated in 1858 on a mirror world: "'What a strange thing a mirror is! . . . For this room of mine, as I beheld it in the glass, is the same, and yet not the same. It is not the mere representation of the room I live in, but it looks just as if I were reading about it in a story I like'" (*Phantastes*, chap. 13). But his protagonist observes this strange independent mirror-world from the outside, as if in mirror-divination. He does not enter it. Carroll has also described literally a child's fascination with how mirrors work. Many another child must have peered into the edges of a mirrored room, nose against the glass, trying to locate the exact edge of that second room. (I certainly did, well before knowing about Alice.) Mirrors like riddles raise questions about boundaries.

Paul's text seems to me to echo faintly, at least for a moment, even when we know that a number of "Looking-Glass" books existed prior to Carroll's. Such books use the longstanding trope of a mirror that reflects virtue to be emulated ("those worthy Mirrors of their Age")[11] or else sin to be expurgated. They are heavily didactic. Ronald Reichertz reprints excerpts from several, for example, Abraham Chear, *A Looking Glass for Children* (1673) and *The Laughable Looking Glass for Little Folks* (1857), which at least uses comedy for its moral instruction.[12] The echo also remains even when we know that Carroll began with the working title of "Behind the Looking-Glass." Carroll was much too devout to be joking about this text. (He once protested several jokes based on biblical texts in a fledgling comic magazine.[13]) Yet, once the formulation of *through* any kind of glass was chosen, Paul's text seems unavoidable. If the title of his second book intimates that we may go through a present barrier into some different world, Carroll would not be averse. For Carroll, children could be aware of worlds blocked to adults, and even be holy in their imputed innocence. Fortunately, this sense does not impinge on the Alice books themselves. But it does mean Carroll would not automatically discard a title that echoed at a distance the well-known Pauline verse. This is not making a joke with the phrase, but letting it intimate something for the adult reader. A far-off allegory of movement through life as through a chess-game might stir faintly. More to the point, Paul's mirror of this world, apprehended as if in an enigma, might well resemble the Looking-Glass world. It does not include as strong an intimation of the earthly

---

11 Abraham Chear, quoted in Ronald Reichertz, *The Making of the Alice Books: Lewis Carroll's Uses of Earlier Children's Literature* (Montreal: McGill-Queens University Press, 1997), p. 171.

12 Reichertz, *The Making of the Alice Books*, p. 54; see Appendix 4, pp. 171–88, on representative Looking-Glass books from 1673 to the 1870s.

13 "I wrote . . . remonstrating on the use of Bible phrases in several articles of the first number [of *Comic Times*]," journal entry, 24 Aug. 1855, in *Lewis Carroll's Diaries*, ed. Edward Wakeling, 9 vols. (Luton: Lewis Carroll Society, 1993), vol. I, p. 123. Carroll quotes the second part of 1 Corinthians 13: 12 in a letter to a friend that discusses immortality: "then shall we know even as we are known," from a letter of 14 February 1886, *The Letters of Lewis Carroll*, ed. Morton N. Cohen, 2 vols. (London: Macmillan, 1979), vol. II, p. 620. This is the only reference to this Pauline verse, according to the indices of the *Letters* and the *Diaries*. Despite his devoutness, Carroll did not escape censure from vigilant piety. An Essex vicar wrote to the *St. James Gazette* to protest Carroll's parody of Isaac Watts, "'Tis the voice of the sluggard," because it echoes "the voice of the turtle" in Song of Songs 2: 12 (*The Annotated Alice: ed. Gardner, The Definitive Edition*, ed. Gardner, p. 106).

paradise as Alice's garden. But it does include the woods where things have no names, and these woods come with a distinctly paradisal sense. Not the lion lying down with the lamb, but the fawn and human child entwined in a loving embrace – until they emerge and the fawn remembers its own name, in one of the briefly shadowed moments of the Alice books:

So they walked on together through the wood, Alice with her arms clasped lovingly round the soft neck of the Fawn, till they came out into another open field, and here the Fawn gave a sudden bound into the air, and shook itself free from Alice's arm. "I'm a Fawn!" it cried out in a voice of delight. "And, dear me! You're a human child!" A sudden look of alarm came into its beautiful brown eyes, and in another moment it had darted away at full speed.

The near-mirroring of two sets of chessmen at the start of a game connects all Carroll's mirror-play with his governing scheme. He plays on glass and mirroring in the first Alice book as well. The little golden key is a literal key, yet Carroll invests it with a hovering sense of allegory. This is the key that will let you into the earthly paradise, your secret garden, the place you long to be. At first, Alice is too big, child that she is. The key fits. She does not. When Alice finally does fit, the key proves unattainable. She fits, the key fits, but she cannot get to it to put it to use. "When she went back to the table for it, she found she could not possibly reach it: she could see it quite plainly through the glass, and she tried her best to climb up one of the legs of the table, but it was too slippery" (chap. 1). "Through the glass" now means a barrier, not a dim adumbration of that better world, as in St. Paul.

It is in this opening chapter that resonances of a masterplot involving the story of Eden reverberate slightly, no more. In the Alice books, possibilities of various masterplots suggest themselves throughout, briefly shadowing or brightening Carroll's story, then dissolving. The two dream-romances keep well away from explicit reference to the masterplot that governs some of the great Western dream-visions. No Christian or sphinxine or other masterplot lays out its allegory in the Alice books. Hints and resonances are something other. When Carroll came to write *Sylvie and Bruno*, he did not maintain this distance, and the book suffers badly from its doctrinal infusion. It is in *The Hunting of the Snark* that Carroll comes closest to evoking some sense of masterplot, while still retaining full control of his genre.

Carroll's extraordinary resonances are part and parcel of his extraordinary command of rhetoric. What rhetoric is so supple and tactful, so sure in tone as Carroll's through virtually all of the two Alice books? "Tone" is a critical term that we tend to use casually, partly because it is hard to define. Yet it is the most difficult requirement for a writer, according to T. S. Eliot: "Whether one writes a piece of work well or not seems to me a matter of crystallization – the good sentence, the good word, is only the final stage in the process . . . the words come easily enough, in comparison to the core of it – the *tone* – and nobody can help one in the least with that."[14] For James Merrill, "voice" is simply the democratic word for "tone." "'Tone' always sounds snobbish, but without a sense of it how one flounders!" (*Recitative*, p. 26). He then adds the most useful remark about tone that I know. Tone follows from the writer's manners toward the reader.

Manners are for me the touch of nature, an artifice in the very bloodstream. Someone who does not take them seriously is making a serious mistake . . . And manners – whether good or bad – are entirely allied with tone or voice in poetry. If the manners are inferior the poem will seem unreal . . . Manners aren't merely descriptions of social behavior. The real triumph of manners in Proust is the extreme courtesy toward the reader, the voice explaining at once formally and intimately. . . Proust says to us in effect, "I will not patronize you by treating these delicate matters with less than total, patient, sparkling seriousness."

(ibid., p. 33)

Alice is much aware of manners, for she is a well-brought-up child. Again and again, she demonstrates her conscious concern with manners, and her instinctive sense of what underlies their conventions, true courtesy. Commentators often mention Victorian manners, inferring a social world that Carroll builds on. This is useful historically, but the manners that interest me even more are Carroll's own as a writer. His exquisite touch is like Proust's: at once formal and intimate, utterly without patronizing (a rare gift in writing for children), "total, patient, sparkling seriousness." Something in that original small audience of the three young Liddell sisters, with or without the friendly Robinson Duckworth, elicited Carroll's sure touch.

Carroll is a powerful and uncanny writer who adopts his simple guise in *Alice's Adventures in Wonderland* and *Through the Looking-Glass*. Such simplicity becomes the simplicity of great art, here a trap for the unwary. Carroll's two great books are dream-romances, in which he himself finally emerges as the unlikely all-conquering knight. Not so much as the wonderful self-parody of the White Knight, smiling foolishly, falling off

---

14 *The Letters of T. S. Eliot*, vol. 1, 1898–1922, ed. Valerie Eliot (London: Faber and Faber, 1988), 1 June 1919, pp. 298–9.

his horse, and full of lunatic inventions. Rather, as the author Lewis Carroll. Challenger after challenger tries to pin him down with a psychological or philosophical or other lance. Carroll defeats them all, smiling deprecatingly in his photographs, falling metaphorically off his horse, full of ingenious inventions including enigma as scheme and trope. Like all great artists, he tests his readers more than they can test him. Unlike many great artists, he appears easily comprehensible, and to the foolish, easily explained. Though he would have laughed at the epithet, Carroll can be a terrifying author.

CHAPTER 8

Figures for enigma

What a wonder, he thinks, that the long, bitter, heart-wrenching history of the planet should allow curious breathing spaces for the likes of mere toys and riddles; he sees them everywhere. Games, glyphs, symbols, allegories, puns and anagrams, masquerades, the magician's sleight-of-hand, the clown's wink, the comic shrug, the somersault, the cryptogram in all its forms, and especially . . . the teasing elegance and circularity of the labyrinthine structure, a snail, a scribble, a doodle on the earth's skin with no other directed purpose but to wind its sinuous way around itself. . . He also loves the secret knowledge that a maze can never be truly symmetrical. These small oddities keep him reverent, awe-struck, faithful.

(Carol Shields, *Larry's Party*, chap. 8)

LIGHT AND DARK, FOLDS, KNOTS, NETS AND TRAPS, LOCKS
AND KEYS, LABYRINTHS AND MAZES, CHINESE BOXES,
SOLVING AND DISSOLVING AND RESOLVING

Traps, mazes, nets, knots, and the like, together with the language of darkness versus light: these are part of the common lexis or diction of enigma. Joshua Poole gives a comprehensive list of epithets under "riddle" in *The English Parnassus*, much as a modern thesaurus does: "dark, knotty, perplexing, puzzling, posing, subtle, hard, profound, obscure, doubtful, ambiguous, secret, grave, scrupulous, mysterious, concealed." All these terms are standard in descriptions of enigma and riddle, except for "doubtful" and "scrupulous," now obsolete in this connotation. Donne's small compendium of such terms for enigma has already been quoted: "Poore intricated soule! Riddling, perplexed, labyrinthicall soule!" (Sermon XLVIII, 1628/9). Wordsworth knows the lexis and uses it in the "perplexing labyrinths" of the stream of human life in *The Excursion* ("Despondency," III.982). The context alters from Donne to Wordsworth: an atheist, a despondent. A sermon, a meditative narrative poem. But the lexis and troping are the same, though they need a full context to read them well.

A good deal of the standard lexis for enigma is implicitly figurative, and some is explicitly so. "Intricate" and Donne's "intricated" are derived from Latin *in* with *tricae* ("trifles, nonsense," and figuratively "tricks"). "Perplexed" is etymologically related to braids, from Latin *plexus*, the past participle of *plectere*, "to plait." Tricks or braids? These etymological tropes are related but they are not the same, nor are the riddles and enigmas they figure forth, at least if the writer knows what he or she is doing.

Tropes for riddle and enigma most often liken them to some physical object. Of the common tropes, several entrap the reader or the desired answer. Several hide the answer (enveloping, wrapping, locking up). Several obscure the answer rather than hiding it completely (clouds, veils). Several complicate it to an extreme (knots, tangles, braids). The tropes for solving enigmas can be as interesting as the tropes for enigma itself, and these include the word "solve." Different types of trope imply different processes. A key acts like the sudden opening of a door or the sudden ability to read encrypted language via a master code. Ariadne's thread is different: the process is more gradual.

In what follows, I want to examine some common tropes for enigma, as well as the occasional scheme. Recognizing standard tropes helps us to see variations and revisions of them. They may tell us what type of enigma or what masterplot is in play, if any. As with all tropes, they condition the way we think and feel about the problem to hand. This is true for critics, folklorists, and theorists alike, in our own writing.

We also need to exercise a little caution. Many of these tropes are not exclusive to what is enigmatic and riddling. To repeat Augustine once more: "As every horse is an animal, but not every animal is a horse, so every enigma is an allegory, but not every allegory is an enigma" (*De trin.* xv.ix.15). Just as not every animal is a horse, so not every trap is a riddle. Or every net or knot or lock. Special care is needed with terms like "cloud" and "veil," which are also standard terms in writing about mystery at large.

In descriptions of enigma, the most common lexis and troping by far is that of light and dark. Down through the centuries, poets and rhetoricians and novelists and others routinely speak of enigma as "dark" or "obscure." Johann Buchler's 1548 *Parnassus Poeticus* provides a list of modifiers for the Latin word *aenigma*. The list reads: "caecum, durum, latebrosum, tenebrosum," that is, "blind (i.e. dark or unintelligible or concealed), hard, obscure, shadowy." Wallace Stevens's brilliant pun "obscurer selvages" implicitly comments on its own riddle-form, on which see chapter 9.

"Obscure" belongs to a whole family of synonyms that describe riddles and enigmas: veils, clouds, mists, and so on. More than "describe." This is a lexis that comes with its own range of possible troping. What kind of veil and where and behaving how? What kinds of cloud and mist, and where and behaving how? We have already seen such lexis in Paul's expression "under the veil," used of the Hebrew Scriptures. Dante uses the trope of the veil for enigmatic writing: "the doctrine that is hidden under the veil [velame] of the strange verses" (*Inferno* 9.62–3, Singleton). But not all veils belong to the troping of enigma. During Matelda's physics lesson in Eden (*Purgatorio*, canto 28), she dispels the cloud (*disnebbiar*) from Dante's mind (28.81) or clears away the mist (*nebbia*) that offends him (28.90). Is this the familiar lexis of enigma? Yes and no. Matelda readily answers these puzzles, and there is little sense of tension, sin, danger, or even witty challenge. It is a matter of learning about a perfect place.

Thomas Aquinas distinguished three kinds of darkness (*obscuritas*) within St. Paul's *in aenigmate*: (1) the obscurity of primordial chaos; (2) the obscurity of all created things, in comparison with God; (3) the obscurity due to sin, after the fall of mankind (*Sententiae* II, ds 23, qu 2, ar 1, ra 3). In the *Summa*, he repeats that unfallen mankind did indeed see God "per essentiam" or "sine medio et sine aenigmate" (without mediation and without enigma). But he now argues that the unfallen Adam saw God face to face in one sense (*medium videri*), but not in another (*medium demonstratis*, *Summa* II, qu 94, ar 1, ra 3). After the fall, Adam saw in a much darker enigma.

In any trope of darkness, the question is what causes it, and whether the darkness is temporary or even delectable, to use Henry Peacham's word. Does the darkness confine us, even imprison us, and where? As if underground, as if in a cell, as if in necessary mortality? Gregory of Nyssa speaks of "initiation into divine light via a divine darkness,"[1] a move from the area where enigma overlaps with mystery over into mystery proper and even the mystical. Gregory's *tenebrae* in this process are initiating transitory shadows, beyond ordinary knowledge.

1 Cited in Geoffrey Hartman, "Adam on the Grass with Balsamum," *Beyond Formalism: Literary Essays 1958–1970* (New Haven: Yale University Press, 1970), p. 136.

Light and whiteness, by contrast, are commonly assumed to be a great good, though not inevitably. For Melville, the troping of white and light works paradoxically to terrify in "The Whiteness of the Whale," chapter 42 of *Moby-Dick*. The troping of darkness and light, then, will not tell us much about the kind of riddle and enigma facing us. These tropes are too large and all-embracing for that. Dark and light must be read in context. Keys and locks do not switch about this way, nor do their riddles. You want to attain the key and open the lock, period. Unless of course, there is a further trap.

Clouds and veils more often figure as part of the lexis and troping of mystery than of enigma. In James Thomson's *The Four Seasons*, for example, "Summer" ends thus: "But here the cloud, / So wills Eternal Providence, sits deep." In a sonnet by Fulke Greville that anticipates apocalyptic revelation, biblical language provides the final answer. The veils are rent: "Vain thought, the word of power a riddle is, / And till the veils be rent, the flesh new-born, / Reveals no wonders of that inward bliss. . ."[2] If this is biblical enigma, it is figured differently from Paul's, for Paul's enigma allows dim perception, somewhat as if in an ancient mirror. John Bunyan follows Augustine's sense of godly riddles in the preliminary verse to *The Pilgrim's Progress* Part II, where a cloud is the trope for a riddle or dark similitude:

> Whereas some say a cloud is in his [Bunyan's] head,
> That doth but show how wisdom's covered
> With its own mantles, and to stir the mind
> To a search after what it fain would find,
> Things that seem to be hid in words obscure,
> Do but the godly mind the more allure;
> To study what those sayings should contain,
> That speak to us in such a cloudy strain.

Bunyan has an author's pragmatic sense of what will attract a reader, for he continues:

> I also know a dark similitude
> Will on the fancy more itself intrude,
> And will stick faster in the heart and head,
> Than things from similes not borrowed.[3]

---

2 Fulke Greville, Sonnet CIII ("O false and treacherous probability"), ll. 9–14; on Victorian uses of analogy, language, and teleology in this trope, see Shaw, *The Lucid Veil.*

3 Bunyan, *The Pilgrim's Progress*, p. 227. The full title to both parts of *Pilgrim's Progress* includes the phrase, "Delivered under the similitude of a Dream."

Like Peacham, Bunyan knows that darkness can be delectable. Nor does he equate clear language with a minimal use of tropes. A tinker who has absorbed the language of the English Bible can be more sophisticated about figures of speech in 1684 than a Royal Society scientist on a language-cleansing rampage.

Clouds and veils may be turned to another kind of troping: the necessary clouding of the divine for human eyes and minds. Otherwise its unmediated force would kill us. Thus the veiling of the face before God in the Hebrew Scriptures. Thus the Christian doctrine of accommodation. A classical version is found in the legend of Zeus and Semele.

Galileo ends one of his verse riddles with this most common troping for enigma:

I inhabit dark shadows [tenebre oscure], and if I pass from the shadows [ombre] into bright light my soul quickly slips away with the coming of the day and my tired limbs fall away, and I lose my being with my life and with my name.[4]

Answer? A riddle.

Beyond light-and-dark tropes, well-known tropes for enigma include folds and enfolding and enveloping. Dante knows the figures well.

"So may thy lineage find at last repose,"
I thus adjured him, "as thou solve this knot [solvetemi quel nodo],
Which now involves ['nviluppata] my mind."
(*Inferno* 10.94–6, Cary)

The Carlyle–Wicksteed translation also uses the word "involve": "solve the knot which has here involved my judgment." Other translators prefer "entangled" (Singleton), "perplexed" (Ciardi), and so on. The translations may reflect whether or not the translator remembers the language of Virgil. "Entangled" and "perplexed" are good, standard terms in the lexis of enigma, with some immediate troping force in "entangled." But "envelop" and "involve" evoke Virgil's Sibyl and her enigmas. For one of the great classic riddlers, the Sibyl of Cumae, is said by Virgil in a well-known passage to speak "dread enigmas" in this way:

Talibus ex adyto dictis Cumaea Sibylla
horrendas canit ambages antroque remugit,
obscurus vera involvens.. . .

---

4 Cited by Bryant in his *Dictionary of Riddles*, no. 616; I have altered the translation slightly.

(In such words the Cumaean Sibyl chants from the shrine her dread enigmas and echoes from the cavern, wrapping truth in darkness . . . [*Aeneid* 6.98–100, Loeb; my italics].)

Enigma is commonly troped as "wrapped" or "enveloped" or "folded," no doubt thanks to Virgil. Thus Bacon's "enigmatical folded writing" (OED "folded"). Thus Churchill's well-known 1939 remark: "I cannot forecast to you the action of Russia. It is a riddle wrapped in a mystery inside an enigma." Thus John Maynard Keynes, talking about Newton as a solver of riddles: "he himself [Newton] wrapt the discovery of the calculus in a cryptogram." Dante's " 'nviluppata" is just right for an enigma.

Involucrum or wrapping (from *involvo*) can be pejorative, but not in Augustine: "'Perhaps it has been set down more darkly, in order that it might generate many meanings, and that men might come away from it the more enriched, finding something enclosed that could be opened in many ways, more than if they had found it, already open, in one way only.' "[5] By now, this sounds like familiar Augustinian territory, expanded somewhat into an area of mystery. Working out enigmatic language enlivens and enriches the mind, here the mind of a believer searching the Scriptures. This Augustinian way of reading is inherently poetic, as I have argued, for it is the way we read tropes that go on generating meaning. We open a trope, here the trope of enigma, "in many ways."

Folded thoughts ask for untying, loosening, explication, and so on into all the troping of conceptual knowledge. Sometimes of other knowledge too, including sexual, as in Nahum Tate's memorable figure: "Untie your folded thoughts / And let them dangle loose as a bride's hair" (1707, OED, "folded"). Jacques Derrida has written ingeniously and exuberantly of a whole family of *pli* words, enjoying the potential sexual play in the word-root.[6] Tate was there before him. So was Tennyson, with fuller design and ability in troping.

In Tennyson's "folded" in "A Dream of Fair Women," sexual touch is kept indirect, delicate, and intense. Tennyson is working with mystery, but his lexis is worth examining for its uses of "dissolved" and "folded." As the speaker wakes from his dream (ll. 261–3),

> . . . the white dawn's creeping beams
> Stolen to my brain, dissolved the mystery
> Of folded sleep.

5 From Augustine, *Ennar. in Ps.* CXXVIII; see Dronke's argument in *Fabula*, pp. 56–7n.
6 Derrida, "The Double Session" II, in his *Dissemination*, pp. 227–39.

"Folded" as in mystery itself, "folded" as in eyelids folded down (l. 1: "before my eyelids dropt their shade"), "folded" as in some sleeping postures of the body. "Folded" also in the extended senses of safety (as in a sheepfold) and of sleep's own enfoldings (of the day's activities, of dreams). The preposition "of" also works in two ways, for "mystery" refers to the great dream itself, which sleep has included. But then sleep itself is a mystery of sorts, as the preposition "of" also implies. Sleep and dream dissolve together. Stevens also knows this lexis: "There he saw well the foldings in the height / Of sleep, the whiteness folded into less . . ." ("The Owl in the Sarcophagus" III).

A knot is a long-standing figure for enigma. Here is Juvenal: "You must go to the toga-clad herd for a man to untie the knots and riddles of the law" (. . . qui iuris nodos et legum aenigmata solvat, Satire III.49–50, Loeb). Lewis and Short call this "an allusion to the Gordian knot" ("nodus" B.2), but the allusion is surely to the trope in general. Knots have long been connected with the law: "many knotty [enodandos] points of law," writes Gellius (*Noctes Atticae* XIII.x.1, Loeb, 1927) and there are references in the *Codex Justinianeus* (1.14.12.4). The trope offers a figure for both the riddle and the process of solving it. For a knot-like riddle, we need patience and observation. A knot is also a happily limited figure. Light and darkness can be vast, an entire enigmatic or riddling world. A knot this vast is rare. Knots in the figurative sense can have a somewhat wide meaning of "something difficult" such as a "knotty problem," though here the metaphor is close to dead. But a knot is usually more circumscribed, a particular problem, perhaps small and diverting, perhaps more challenging. *Untying the Knot* (ed. Hasan-Rokem and Shulman) is the title of a fine 1996 collection whose sub-title gives the specific subject: *On Riddles and Other Enigmatic Modes.*

Lewis Carroll embodied a series of mathematical puzzles in Knots, "like the medicine so dexterously, but ineffectually, concealed in the jam of our early childhood" (Preface, *A Tangled Tale*). The answers appear under Alice's remark about the knot (actually a "not") of the Mouse's tail-tale: "Oh, do let me help to undo it!" (*Alice's Adventures in Wonderland*, chap. 3). Knots appear frequently nowadays in mathematical titles, but they largely have to do with knot theory in mathematics.[7]

---

7 "Knot theory studies the possible types of knots and their deformability properties." Such knots have the ends of the string joined. See E. J. Borowski and J. M. Borwein, *Dictionary of Mathematics* (London: Harper Collins, 1989).

It is true that beautifully symmetrical knotted shapes can take on symbolic force, where enigma moves toward mystery. Dante not only uses a knot, a *nodo*, for a perplexing riddle as above. He also chooses it for the perfection of divine harmony in the closing lines of his vision. Eliot adapted the lines to close *Four Quartets*, with his "crowned knot of fire" into which "tongues of flame are in-folded." The word "in-folded" works against the "enfolded" of enigmatic *involucrum* or *involvens*. Eliot knows and deploys expertly the figurative lexis of enigma.

An enigmatic knot asks to be untied, perhaps unfolded. A Gordian knot invites immediate cutting, not untying. Waller summarizes Alexander's feat: "Such praise the Macedonian got / For having rudely cut the Gordian knot" ("To the King").[8] Shakespeare's Henry V, a formidable swordsman, goes one better by declining the sword in favor of an ingenious brain, unloosing rather than cutting through (*Henry V* I.i.45–7):

> Turn him to any cause of policy,
> The Gordian knot of it he will unloose,
> Familiar as his garter.

If you tie your garter in a Gordian knot just for practice in statecraft, you will make a formidable politician as well as swordsman.

Riddle-knots may just as readily give pleasure. "Now winter-nights enlarge . . . Some knotted Ridles tell," Thomas Campion wrote about 1605 in his *Third Book of Ayres* (*Works*, p. 147).

Riddles seem intrinsically net-like because of the double meanings of the words *griphos* (*griphus*) and *scirpus* and "riddle." For Greek *griphos* and Latin *griphus* have a second meaning. They also signify a "fishing-net." Similarly with the term *scirpus*, a "rush, bulrush," figuratively a "riddle" from the intricacy of woven rushes. In Antiphanes' play, *Ganymede*, a witty slave manages a double pun, first on the word *periplokai* (both "perplexing questions" and "also the entangling folds and plaitings of a net"), then on *griphos* (both a riddle and a fishing-net; Athenaeus x.459a). The noun "riddle" also signifies "a coarse-meshed sieve, used for separating chaff from corn [grain]," etc. (OED). (In late Old English, the word is "hriddel," the earlier form being "hridder.") Samuel Johnson was magisterial about the two different meanings of "riddle" in his *Dictionary*. "There is something of whimsical analogy between the two senses of the word

---

8 Cited in *Brewer's Dictionary of Phrase and Fable*, centenary edn., rev. Ivor H. Evans (London: Cassell, 1970), "Gordian knot."

riddle: as, we say, to sift a *question*: but their derivations differ." (Johnson had a low view of puns.)

In his standard guide to popular English and Scottish ballads, Francis Child cites examples of "The Clever Lass" folk-tale, linking it "with oriental stories of great age." In all variations, the king sets the clever peasant girl several riddles, and one is the demand that she come to him neither dressed nor naked. She answers this riddle by coming to him wrapped in a fishing-net (vol. 1, pp. 8–9). Perhaps the clever peasant girl knows Greek, and knows that a *griphos* is both a riddle and a fishing-net. She is offering the king both the riddle and its catch or answer (herself), as both in fact desire. Here is one example, incidentally, where literary knowledge has something to offer the folklorist, for the longstanding double meaning is not mentioned in commentary I have seen.

Seamus Heaney's "The Riddle" shows what a poet can do with the two meanings of English "riddle." The title itself sets a small riddle: what is the riddle? In the first two couplets, that is easy. It's a garden sieve. In stanza 3, Heaney asks us to look again at that garden sieve. We may think only of what is retained: the fish lifted out of the water, the grain sifted from the chaff. But sifting soil or flour is different. What is it that we lose or gain when we sift? Memory must perforce sift what we keep and what we let go. Memory's sifting tool remains a riddle in both senses. After the work of memory, more and more sifting follows, including the sifting editorial task of poetic thought working with imagination. Heaney closes his collection *The Haw Lantern* with this poem. The collection opens with the fine poem "Alphabets," itself something of a riddle poem on the puzzling shapes and sounds of English letters as first encountered by a young child. The strange letters also have a physicality when we first meet them as children, a physicality that shifts to abstraction when we learn to read easily. The alphabet from A to Z and the arrangements of letters chosen by riddling, whether sifting or enquiring: these frame Heaney's whole collection.

Mark Twain tropes wonderfully on the lines of longitude and latitude as a net: "When I'm playful I use the meridians of longitude and latitude for a seine, and drag the Atlantic Ocean for whales. I scratch my head with the lightning and put myself to sleep with the thunder" (*Life on the Mississippi*, chap. 1). This is the Lord God in playful mode. Not so much as in Proverbs where Wisdom plays before him (Prov. 8: 31). Rather it is as if the God from the Book of Job were amusing himself in a leisurely way. If all riddles are in the hands of God, then Paul's enigma itself could be troped as a great net. It is a pleasing thought that God is a fisherman of sorts, especially since he is said to be the father of fishers of men. So also in Jay Macpherson's concluding poem to the final section of *The Boatman*, which is called "The Fisherman: A Book of Riddles," and ends thus:

> But God the Lord with patient grin
> Lets down his hook and hoicks him in.

"Pseudo-Saadya, an anonymous Jewish commentator of the tenth century, characterized the Song of Songs as a 'lock to which the key has been lost.'" Thus Daniel Boyarin, opening a persuasive argument that rabbinical writers of the midrash "regarded the holy song as a mashel, a hermeneutic key to the unlocking of the Torah."[9] What interests me especially are the five examples, in parable form, of how the Song of Songs is working. We move from the main trope of the key to other tropes, all including in their stories the wise man, Solomon. He has provided the master key with the Song of Songs, and further provides a rope (twice), a sickle, and handles (twice). For the Song of Songs may be read as: (a) a rope to help enter into and exit from a palace; (b) a sickle to mow a thicket of weeds; (c) handles for a basket of fruit; (d) handles for a pot of boiling water; (e) a rope to lower into a well of sweet, cold water.

The tropes divide between attaining something very desirable or even necessary (water) and getting rid of something undesirable or hazardous. There are two ropes, the first like the usual thread or clue of some Ariadne–Theseus story. The second provides the vertical rather than the horizontal form of this. There are two sets of handles, and the trope of "getting a handle on something" or starting to comprehend it better suggests itself here. The sickle is unusual, though not when compared with the pun on sieves or riddles or creels in the words *griphus, scirpus,* and "riddle." The brain sorts possible answers to riddles, abandoning impossible ones. So also, in cutting down weeds. The trope has gone back one stage, from the harvested grain in the riddle-sieve to the field where the harvest grows.

Writing "keys" to understanding a sacred text is commonplace. In 1682, for example, Benjamin Keach published ΤΡΟΠΟΛΟΓΙΑ [*Tropologia*]:

---

9 Boyarin, "The Song of Songs, Lock or Key," p. 105. "Mashel" is often translated as "parable," following the Septuagint *parabole*. For links among midrash, mashel, riddle (*hida*), and figures of speech, as well as astute remarks about interpretive approaches, see Kugel, *The Idea of Biblical Poetry*, pp. 135–46.

A Key to open Scripture Metaphors. The troping goes back centuries. "Origen notes that, thanks to its darkness, the Scripture resembles a great many locked rooms in a single house. There is a key next to every door, but it is not the key for that door." Origen says he received this tradition " 'from the Hebrew,' and that it relates to the whole of the Scriptures."[10] Of course, so-called riddles or enigmas within a sacred text may simply be puzzling passages that are quite clear to an expert. Or the lock–key metaphor may be no more than a claim by the author.

For puzzles set by codes or ciphers or cryptographs, the trope of a key commonly applies, though by now it is a dead metaphor. The OED (6) divides it into a general solution to something mysterious and a specific tool such as a cipher. This signification is not listed as "figurative." Still, John Buchan uses it first as trope, then as a cipher key:

> The name Julia Czechenyi flashed across my memory. Scudder had said it was the key to the Karolides business, and it occurred to me to try it on his cypher. It worked. The five letters of "Julia" gave me the position of the vowels. . . "Czechenyi" gave me the numerals for the principal consonants. . . In half an hour I was reading with a whitish face and fingers that drummed on the table.
> (*The Thirty-Nine Steps*, chap. 3)

Arthur Conan Doyle uses a random substitution cipher in "The Adventure of the Dancing Men." Edgar Allan Poe's "The Gold Bug" also uses such a cipher, including numbers and printer's symbols. Lewis Carroll named his 1868 cipher after Blaise de Vigenère, the sixteenth-century writer on, and inventor of, numerous ciphers. Carroll's Vigenère cipher uses a 26-by-26 squared matrix, and applies a key word. John Hollander ends his spy sequence, *Reflections on Espionage*, with this cipher, through which the reader can discover the fate of the main character, Cupcake.

A puzzle of this kind in a literary work is rhetorically a scheme. Hollander incorporates this scheme-coding and scheme-decoding into poetic narrative, as Poe and Conan Doyle and Buchan do into prose narrative. As with other schemes, larger reverberations can move this kind toward trope.

A literal labyrinth or maze is a riddle laid out spatially for various purposes, from small pleasures through to challenge. Physical structures may be stone or paved or turf, floral or topiary; they may be situated underground, in a church, and so on. Literal labyrinths and mazes have their own fascinating history and their own specialists. Hermann Kern's

---

10 Stroumsa, "Moses' Riddles," p. 243.

definitive 1982 study, *Labyrinthe: Erscheinungsformen und Deutungen 5000 Jahre Gegenwart eines Urbilds,* has recently been translated as *Through the Labyrinth: Designs and Meanings over 5,000 Years.*[11] There is even a periodical for labyrinth devotees called *Caerdroia* (Kern, *Labyrinthe,* p. 21).

Literal labyrinths are related to geometrical rather than verbal riddles. As riddles in space, they have to do with shape and visual thinking, like plane geometry. They are closer to jigsaw puzzles than to cryptic-crossword puzzles, and they belong broadly to the class of visual riddles. Not that the line is hard and fast between these verbal and visual riddles. I am not thinking so much of enigmatic emblem poems as of odd visual and verbal conjoinings. Sometimes, in solving anagrams, the letters re-arrange themselves as other words when you simply look at them. No conscious working out of alternatives takes place. Riddle-solving also sometimes works this way. (Very occasionally I can add a column of double figures this way, but only with the right combination of cal-culation and intuition, attention and relaxation. Others can do so easily.) The link in the brain between reading words spatially and reading words for sense is operating here. The mathematical example indicates that reading numbers can work the same way. As for Saul Steinberg's play with visual and verbal, that is the subject for a full-scale study.

A labyrinthine riddle is by implication intricate, winding, and tortuous. It is likely to be drawn out, rather than a quick pick. It tempts us toward many a false start and dead end. It tries repeatedly to frustrate us. It is multiple, and demands multiple small solutions before the final answer. Beyond that, only the context will say what kind of labyrinthine riddle is in play. The word "labyrinthine" by association offers the sense of being enclosed, enveloped, or wrapped in darkness. So famous is the Cretan labyrinth, with its story of the Minotaur and Theseus and Ariadne, that a verbal enigma can draw on this resonance with only the slightest hint. Sometimes it thereby pulls toward enigma as masterplot. John Ashbery makes forceful use of this trope in "Never Seek To Tell Thy Love," as noted in chapter 3. The literary troping of the labyrinth seems to be commonly sinister, either a type-2 malevolent (Sphinxine) riddle or a type-4 infinite-regression riddle. Either a labyrinth that raises the specter

---

11 In English, Matthews' older *Mazes and Labyrinths* is well known and still useful, though he confuses the terms "labyrinth" and "maze" (Kern, *Through the Labyrinth,* p. 316n). Doob's *The Idea of the Labyrinth* draws on both visual and literary sources. For a good short survey, see Ferber, *A Dictionary of Literary Symbols,* "labyrinth."

of the dark unanswered riddle with a dark hostile riddler, or a labyrinth enacting the unanswerable riddle with no riddler whatever.

Curiously enough, this meaning of "labyrinthine" is purely literary in origin, as Kern makes clear. It is the maze that is multicursal (with many paths), tortuous, confusing, and sometimes sinister. Ancient labyrinths are shown as unicursal. "All depictions of labyrinths up to the Renaissance show only one path, therefore, there is no posssibility of going astray. . . This visually simple concept, however, has been eclipsed by the more complex notion of a 'maze' (at first a mere [sic] literary construct) since antiquity. . . these two distinct notions have been obfuscated over time."[12] The literary tradition of a labyrinth as confusing goes back to late antiquity (third century), while references to the Theseus story with its labyrinth are found some six centuries earlier.[13]

A labyrinth pattern that is unicursal can be a challenge, but the challenge belongs to the quest it figures forth. Here any enigma present is mostly subsumed into its larger rhetorical class, allegory. Church labyrinths, for example, are allegorical but not enigmatic per se.[14] They reverse the Cretan myth, substituting redemption in place of the Minotaur. (See the fine examples in Kern, *Labyrinthe*, chap. 8, "Church Labyrinths," pp. 143–65.) They include those called a *chemin de Jérusalem* or *daedale*; the center is called *ciel* or *Jérusalem*. Kern notes, however, that interpretation of the function of church labyrinths is mostly from hearsay and comes late, possibly from the eighteenth century (p. 146). One medieval example on the cathedral at Lucca is said to be centered on the battle of Theseus and the Minotaur, but the central motif has been erased by human fingers tracing the labyrinth lines over hundreds of years.[15] St. Bernard's labyrinth is made of words and is a challenge to the wits, but not at all scary. Like some riddling catechisms, its purpose is didactic. So, of course, with many a metaphor of the labyrinth. Penelope Doob quotes Ambrose on "labyrinths of error" (*The Idea of the Labyrinth*, p. 75), and the figure is commonplace (see Jerome, below).

12 Kern, *Through the Labyrinth*, p. 23. Translators have inserted the word "mere"; Kern is too good a scholar for that. The German reads: "Dieser visuell eindeutige Begriff wurde schon seit der Antike von der – zunächst nur literarisch formulierten – Vorstellung 'Irrgarten' überlagert" (p. 13); "zunächst" in this context means simply "at first." Kern also defines a "meander" pattern.

13 Kern cites Callimachus (3rd century BCE) and possible earlier references (*Through the Labyrinth*, p. 26).

14 Doob notes the peaceful co-existence of two models of *laborintus* in the Middle Ages: a visual unicursal model and a written multicursal one.

15 Ruskin, *Works*, vol. XXVII, p. 401, drawing on Julien Durand (1857).

Figure 7. Labyrinth design, Lucca, from John Ruskin, *Works*, vol. XXVII, p. 401.

The OED gives "maze" as a synonym for both a literal and a figurative labyrinth.[16] It cites Whitlock in 1654: "Some [authors] Maze their Thoughts in Labyrinths, and thus Invoke no Reader, but an Oedipus" ("maze," verb, 4b). In landscape gardening, however, a "labyrinth" brings pleasure. Kern dates the earliest such example from the fourteenth century; the OED gives the earliest English example as 1611. In 1792, A. Young compared a garden labyrinth to a rebus, using the word "rebus" in the loose older sense of any visual riddle. "The labyrinth [at Chantilly] is the only complete one I have seen, and I have no inclination to see another; it is to gardening what a rebus is to poetry" (OED, "labyrinth" 1b). In Carol Shields' 1997 novel, *Larry's Party*, garden mazes enchant the title character, who finds his vocation in building them. He has read Matthews's book.

16 The etymologies for "labyrinth" and "maze" are quite distinct (see OED, OCD).

As with riddles generally, literal mazes can offer amusement, from the Hampton Court maze right down to party favors where a mini-maze for the palm of a hand can be traced by a tiny weighted ball. Manual dexterity plus reading spatial pattern is the challenge. If you miss a crucial turn, your ball drops out of sight as if down some Gothic trap-door. But not to fear: it reappears at once to start the game over again. Mazes can also be enjoyed with the right guide, for example, the great masters of romance such as Spenser. Thus the tribute by Thomas Warton Jr. in *The Pleasures of Melancholy* (ll. 60–3) to Spenser's sure steps "thro' bewild'ring Fancy's magic maze" (l. 62). For all that, mazes may simply imply a "thicket" or landscape "whence it is hard to get out again," as Spenser glosses his adjective "mazie" in the December *Eclogue*. Similarly with a labyrinthine entanglement in *Don Quixote*: "Don Fernando thanked heaven for its mercy in extricating him from the intricate labyrinth [intricado laberinto] in which he had been on the verge of losing both his good name and his soul" (Book 1, chap. 37).

Mazes can also figure forth a masterplot, as in Pope's "a mighty maze! but not without a plan" (*Essay on Man* 1.6). An accidental maze, arbitrary, random, and subject to chance: Pope's negative evokes such a maze only to dismiss it. For his contemporary, Mark Akenside, science toils in a maze ("On Lyric Poetry," *Odes* 1.xiii), but a maze with a hazard: "He asks a clue for Nature's ways; / But evil haunts him through the maze" (Akenside, "To Cheerfulness," *Odes* 1.vi). What this poor "pensive sage" must learn is "To trace the world's benignant laws" (ibid.). In the age of the great Newton, Akenside reads Nature's laws as benignant and not indifferent, let alone malignant. Newton's own famous trope has nothing of the maze about it. It is of sea and seashore, and a child playing there – a trope of plenitude, more vast than enigmatic, though mysterious enough. "I do not know what I may appear to the world; but to myself I seem to have been only like a boy playing on the seashore, and diverting myself in now and then finding a smoother pebble or a prettier shell than ordinary, whilst the great ocean of truth lay all undiscovered before me."

Life's journey can be troped as a walk wandering through a maze. The *Boy's Own Paper* for 5 January 1884 uses the figure of maze and thread, with the clue provided not by Ariadne but by Christ:

> Resolve it shall be so! It lies
> Within your power to make the days
> Be good or evil; he who tries
> Can find the clue to thread life's maze.

You ask what is the magic clue
 Which keeps you safe from every ill?
Follow the Christ, the good, the true,
 And let the year bring what it will!

Resolution, determination, persistence: lassitude must have been tempting in the latter part of the nineteenth century. The addition of "magic" adds the power of a charm to a solution of the riddle, a threading of the maze. But the main troping is not a nineteeth-century invention. It appears to be a topos, as witness Jerome: "We endure labyrinthine errors and guide our blind footsteps by the thread of Christ."[17] Kern, *Labyrinthe* includes a section, "Das Labyrinth der Welt" (The Labyrinth of the World, pp. 295–342), with examples of Christian pilgrimages, love's labyrinth, and so on. Emblem books, many drawing on Andreas Alciatus (1492–1550), include labyrinths. In one example from Francis Quarles, a woman holds a staff with a cord that is grasped by an angel at a distance (*Complete Works*, vol. III, pp. 79–80, 155). In another from Herman Hugo, a pilgrim with staff reaches across a deep-cut winding labyrinth of turf toward a celestial center (*Pia Desideria* Antwerp, 1632 edn.). The plot of Ariadne and Theseus and the Minotaur is once again at work, in a Christian revision. Not so in the famous original, where the Minotaur awaits you at the center, and will devour you, unless you are Theseus and have entranced the Minotaur's half-sister, Ariadne.

In a contrary move, known territory can be rendered labyrinthine to outsiders by simply removing familiar landmarks. In *The Black Book* (1990), Orhan Pamuk refers to "Field Marshal Fevrzi Çakmak who . . . conceived of pulling down all the minarets in order to rob the Russians of landmarks, and of evacuating Istanbul and proclaiming it a ghost town, thereby turning it into a labyrinth where an occupying enemy would be lost" (p. 164). The military strategy takes on troping force as part of Pamuk's theme of familiarity made strange. Similarly with the ancient *lusus Troiae* or Game of Troy, if it once served as an initiation ritual, blocked to outsiders. It consisted of a series of choreographed steps following a labyrinth pattern, and is reported to have been "originally performed during funeral rites." The ritual was adapted by the Romans as a mock war-game on horseback, but the original function of this labyrinth may have been apotropaic, warding off evil or enemies.[18]

---

17 Preface to Book 2, Commentary on Zacharias, cited in Doob, *The Idea of the Labyrinth*, p. 64.
18 See Kern, *Through the Labyrinth*, chap. 5, "Lusus Troiae: The Game of Troy," pp. 77–83. He notes that the labyrinth is an apotropaic symbol in India. Old labyrinth designs also appear in Colorado and Utah among Hopi, Zuni, and other aboriginal cultures.

Vtinam dirigantur viæ meæ ad custodiendas iustificationes tuas! Psal. 118.

Figure 8. Pilgrim in a labyrinth, from Herman Hugo, *Pia Desideria* (1632 edn.), p. 148.

Chinese boxes provide very different possibilities of troping on the physical shape of an enclosing pattern. So do Russian dolls. So do onions. Then too, many a pleasing box is designed to open only with the right touch or a push on the right panel. But this brings us closer to lock-and-key models.

The trope of Chinese boxes first appeared in the United States in the early nineteenth century, according to the OED. Robert Sands (1799–1832), a lawyer and writer, published a story in 1829 titled "A Simple Story." The setting is "a certain village," and the tone and plotting are Hawthorne before Hawthorne. The plot turns on strangers in a small town, attempts to penetrate their taciturnity, and efforts by the town bureaucracy to aid their penury. "The executive committee were not inactive; but, strange to relate, unless they patronized some of the members of one or all of the three Societies, thus compacted like Chinese boxes, there was never a soul in the place upon the causes and actual extent of whose poverty and destitution they could report" (vol. II, p. 244).[19] This riddle is more a matter of bureaucratic barriers than mystery, enigma, or riddle, though Sands's satiric eye on small-town paralysis is part of a very mysterious story.

Chinese boxes are simply nesting boxes that come from China. Rather than a convenience, Sands's Chinese nesting boxes work to obstruct communication. Each box is self-enclosed, and nothing gets from one to another. This is a flowchart that does not flow. These Chinese boxes make something appear puzzling that really is not so. They are a smoke-screen, a pretense, a non-riddle masquerading as a riddle like the Wizard of Oz. (John Hollander has raised the further question of what differences there are between bureaucracy as Chinese boxes and bureaucracy as Byzantine boxes or Machiavellian boxes.) It is the adjective that gives Chinese boxes their riddling flavor, and the adjective appears elsewhere about this time with the same implication. The Bodleian Library lists a collection of riddles called *Chinese Nuts, or New Riddle Book: Consisting of Enigmas, Rebusses, Charades, and Conundrums*, published some time between 1820 and 1839.[20] "Nuts" as hard conundrums has longstanding authority, but exactly when does "Chinese" begin to add mystery to the conundrum? The OED sheds no light. It would make an interesting exercise to find out, for both lexical and cultural reasons.

Any challenge to the wits can take the trope of a nut to be cracked. Thus the OED: "in allusion to the difficulty of cracking hard-shelled nuts: a. A question difficult to answer or a problem hard to solve" ("nut" 4a). The illustrative quotations run from Elyot in 1545 to Stevenson in 1886 in

---

19 Later collected in *The Writing of Robert C. Sands*, vol. II, pp. 44–61; the sentence quoted is identical there, apart from minor changes in spelling and capitalization.
20 *Chinese Nuts, or New Riddle Book . . .* (London: J. Fairburn, n.d., Bodley shelfmark Vet. A6 e.1855).

Dr. Jekyll and Mr. Hyde; Webster cites Dos Passos. No quotation refers specifically to riddles, though one from 1863 reads "He especially liked his mental nuts." But collectors liked the trope of cracking a nut for the activity of tackling and solving puzzles, sometimes including riddles. The Bodleian catalogue also lists, for example, *A Bag of Nuts Ready Cracked, or, Instructive Fables, Ingenious Riddles, and Merry Conundrums,* 11th edn., by "the celebrated and facetious Thomas Thumb, Esq." (1786), *Nuts To Crack; or Quips, Quirks, Anecdote, and Facete of Oxford and Cambridge Scholars* (1835), *Nuts and Nutcrackers, illustrated by "Phiz"* (1845), *Nuts To Crack for the Merry, Witty, and Wise* (1860), and *Nuts To Crack: A Book of Puzzles and Quizes* (1961). Nuts are likely to be enjoyable riddles, designed to amuse. The inside-to-outside movement works well. A moment of pressure between the fingers or within a strong fist or with a nut-cracker, and voilà, the meat. The required pressure depends on how tough the riddle is, and some take more than one guess or squeeze. Then the meat offers itself suddenly with little further ado. It may even be nourishing though it is small.

Tennyson's word "dissolved" in "A Dream of Fair Women" is just right: the dissolving of night and dream into daylight, and the dissolving also of mystery. Not solving or resolving, but dissolving. All three verbs turn up in the resolution of riddle and enigma. Tennyson's mystery is not the kind of mystery we solve. Tennyson in fact wants more of it, and he tries to get back into his dream. No use. There are dreams that come mysteriously, that we want to retain, not wishing white dawn and morn.

A 1537 Latin grammar solves the sphinx's riddle with the verb "dissolve": "Id postremum Oedipus dissoluit" (At last, Oedipus solved it).[21] Henry Cockeram uses the verb in its anglicized form in 1623: the sphinx "slue all that could not dissolve her riddle."[22] The 1611 Bible uses it in a related context in Daniel: "I have heard of thee, that thou canst make interpretations, and dissolve doubts" (5: 16; Vulgate, *ligata dissolvere*). The OED lists it as archaic rather than obsolete, offering its last illustration from Tennyson: "Thou hast not between death and birth / Dissolved the riddle of the earth" ("The Two Voices"). While the phrase "dissolving riddles" may sound odd, "dissolving doubts" sounds less so. It is the use of the verb to give a firm clear answer to a specific challenging question that has become out of date.

---

21 Despauterius, *Commentarii Grammatici*, Book II, p. 79.
22 Cockeram, *The English Dictionarie*, Appendix, s.v. "Monsters." Cf. also OED 1607 quotation.

Often a solution will dissolve a riddle altogether, in the sense that it collapses and loses all interest. Thus in the anonymous Swedish riddle quoted by Archer Taylor: "When one does not know what it is, it is something; but when one knows what it is, then it is nothing" (*Literary Riddle*, p. 4). Thus also in Dickinson (poem 1222):

> The Riddle we can guess
> We speedily despise –
> Not anything is stale so long
> As Yesterday's surprise –

But these examples refer to riddles that are not well troped.

Throughout this family of "solving" words, the underlying metaphor remains. No doubt the standard rhetorical example of "mater me genuit" reinforced the use of *dissolvere* for answering a riddle by also applying it literally, ice dissolving into water. For T. S. Eliot, "the enigma of the fever chart" needs a firm "resolve," not the less satisfactory "solve" or "dissolve" (*East Coker* iva):

> The sharp compassion of the healer's art
> Resolving the enigma of the fever chart.

To "resolve" an enigma sounds a little strange, though we resolve problems, conflicts or questions. But then, this is Christ the surgeon at work, resolving the metaphysical enigma of life's fitful fever. Solutions themselves work in different ways, so that solution is quite rightly troped in different ways.

MIRRORS, ENIGMAS, AND SEEING THROUGH A GLASS DARKLY

The mirror is not a trope for enigma, yet enigma and mirror seem to have a natural affinity for each other. Both make use of light. A mirror does so literally in order to work at all, and enigma figuratively in its lexis of light and dark. Both make use of inside and outside, a mirror literally, and an enigma figuratively. Both mirror and enigma are double, the mirror in its imaging and enigma in its before-and-after question-and-answer shape. Both mirror and enigma have a capacity for trick uses. There are mirror riddles, of course, as in this example from the Greek Anthology: "If you look at me I look at you too. You look with eyes, but I not with eyes, for I have no eyes. And if you like, I speak without a voice, for you have a voice, but I have only lips that open in vain."[23] There is mirror-writing, a

---

23 From Book xiv, cited in Bryant, *Dictionary of Riddles* (no. 685).

simple-reversal riddle, familiar from the first chapter of Carroll's *Through the Looking-Glass.* As for riddling mirrors, we might call some trick mirrors or distorting mirrors "riddling," but here we start to stretch the term – a hazard to be watched in discussions of enigma and riddle. Still, the common association of mirror and enigma probably has more to do with the Apostle Paul than with all the links just given.

The troping of mirrors on their own, quite apart from enigma, is vast. (See, for example, the extensive 1973 study by Herbert Grabes, *The Mutable Glass: Mirror Imagery in Titles and Texts of the Middle Ages and the English Renaissance.*) Similarly with the use of mirrors in the history of painting. "Self-Portrait in a Convex Mirror" is both an intriguing painting by Parmigianino and an intriguing poem by John Ashbery. The unusual perspective reminds us that a flat mirror is nonetheless a mirror, and not actuality. By extension, it reminds us that realism in painting and in writing is an artistic convention, and not actuality. Both mirror and convention are mysterious enough to evoke thoughts of enigma, but then so is actuality. We are not dealing with verbal riddles here, but rather with mysteries of representation.

Peering into a mirror-world, or eliciting spirits from a mirror-world is another matter. Divination by means of mirrors was known to various cultures, including Greek and Mayan.[24] Anne Hébert makes very fine use of such a mirror-world in "Vie de Château," when the ghostly dead emerge from it:

> Vois, ces glaces sont profondes
> Comme des armoires
> Toujours quelque mort y habite sous le tain
> Et couvre aussitôt ton reflet
> Se colle à toi comme une algue
>
> S'ajuste à toi, mince et nu,
> Et simule l'amour en un lent frisson amer.

(See, these mirrors are deep / As armoires / Always, someone dead lives there behind the silvering / And quickly covers your reflection / Sticks to you like seaweed // Adjusts himself to you, thin and naked, / And simulates love in a slow bitter shudder [ll. 10–16].)

---

24 See, e.g., the note on magic mirrors and divination in Gellius, *Noctae Atticae* (note to XVI.xviii on optics, Loeb). See also Burkert on divination by looking into flowing water (*Greek Religion*, p. 393n). Mayan divination mirrors are depicted on objects from Guatemala or Mexico, though they are not common (Museum of Fine Arts, Boston, cylinder vase, 778; Royal Ontario Museum, Toronto, item 957.105, 550–850).

Paul's text must surely be the best known of all his well-known texts, a favorite in secular contexts, even among those with no idea where it began. Wilkie Collins' aged house-steward, Gabriel Betteredge, knows full well where the expression comes from: " 'My lady's horror of him might (as I have since thought) have meant that *she* saw his drift (as the scripture says) "in a glass darkly". I didn't see it yet – that's all I know' " (*The Moonstone*, chap. 13). That was in 1868. Current websites using "glass darkly" include fantasy-genre sites, attracted to a good phrase floating in the air of popular allusion. How many of the numerous titles using "Through a Glass Darkly," "In a Glass Darkly," or simply "A Glass Darkly" are aware of their origin? Paul, with the assistance of the Geneva Bible, has contributed an English-language trope to the common tongue for over four hundred years. It shows no signs of vanishing. Latinate and Greek forms go back centuries before. The reception of Paul's text would be a study in itself, for the text has led an entire life of its own.[25]

Paul's mirror is itself of much interest.[26] His *esoptron* (ἔσοπτρον) is an unusual mirror: the common term is *katoptron*.[27] It is not a modern mirror. Ancient mirrors were usually of polished metal (occasionally of semi-precious stone) and they required frequent polishing.[28] Corinth was famous for the manufacture of them. As noted, exegesis that supposes we see through this mirror as if through a window is mistaken.[29] Tyndale's 1534 translation makes Paul's text clearer ("in a glass"), as does Luther's 1522 translation ("einen Spiegel"). So had Wyclif's, even earlier ("Forsoth we seen now by a myrour," "bi a myrour").[30] So had the Vulgate, much earlier ("per speculum"). But the 1611 Authorized Version drew on the Geneva Bible for this verse. Despite all this, the misreading of "a glass" as "a window" is widespread, and was so even when the word "glass" more commonly meant "mirror." The misreading remains stubbornly

25 Grabes is helpful in *The Mutable Glass*, pp. 88–9, 111, and *passim*.
26 On Paul's use of mirrors, Victor Pöschl et al. list, among other titles, Norbert Hugedé, *La Métaphore du miroir dans les Épîtres de Saint Paul aux Corinthiens* (1957) in their *Bibliographie zur antiken Bildersprache* (Heidelberg: C. Winter, 1964), p. 386.
27 For the difference, see Kittel, *Theologisches Wörterbuch*, *esoptron*, especially p. 696n. Liddell and Scott list the word as *eisoptron*.
28 So necessary was regular polishing that a sponge with pumice-stone was often attached. Some glass mirrors began to appear in the late Roman Empire, but they are not silver-backed like modern mirrors (OCD, "mirror," "glass").
29 In fact, windows were not likely to be glazed in Palestine in Paul's day. See OCD, "glass." Some glazed windows are reported from Pompeii (ibid.).
30 *The Pauline Epistles*, ed. Margaret Joyce Powell, Early English Text Society, extra ser. 116 (Millwood, NY: Kraus Reprint, 1973; orig. pub. 1916).

prevalent – an unconscious tribute to the power of metaphor. More knowledge of Paul's rabbinical forebears would have helped; they used both mirror and riddle as tropes for prophetic revelation.[31]

Carroll made his title clear by adding to "glass": *Through the Looking-Glass*. He tropes brilliantly on the mistaken reading of Paul's famous text when he has Alice actually go *through* the mirror. This is to trope by literalizing. Ruskin exploits the mistaken reading for purposes of his own masterplot: "no more as in the Gothic times, through a window of glass, brightly, but as through a telescope-glass, darkly. Your cathedral window shut you from the true sky, and illumined you with a vision; your telescope leads you to the sky, but darkens its light, and reveals nebula beyond nebula, far and farther, and to no conceivable farthest – unresolvable."[32] Ruskin's chapter "The Dark Mirror" from *Modern Painters* expounds on man made in the image of God, and quotes both Genesis 1: 26 and 1 Corinthians 13: 12. So does Augustine in his great exegesis, but he does not fold enigma into the trope of the mirror as Ruskin does. Enigma in Ruskin becomes adjectival, simply modifying the mirror, which is the essential trope in Ruskin's allegoresis.[33]

Many a troping remains close to Paul. Thus in Langland's *Piers Plowman*[34] or Mary Wollstonecraft's 1788 novel, *Mary* (chaps. 4, 18). Much more often, the text simply implies some mystery, perhaps just a frisson. Sheridan le Fanu titled his fine 1872 collection of ghost stories *In a Glass Darkly*. Other authors are not so discriminating. For a book on cinema and religion (2002), the old phrase is suggestive, but for a book on conflict prevention, management and termination (2001)? "Face to face" takes on a dimension not imagined by the Apostle Paul.

The text is easy to parody. In Thomas Love Peacock's satirical novel *Crotchet Castle* (1831), Mr. Trillo puts the case for building an opera-house, where "justice may be done to sublime compositions (*producing part of a manuscript opera*)."

MR SKIONAR: No, sir, build *sacella* [chapels] for transcendental oracles to teach the world how to see through a glass darkly (*producing a scroll*).
MR TRILLO: See through an opera-glass brightly.
REV. DR FOLLIOTT: See through a wine-glass, full of claret: then you see both darkly and brightly. (chap. 6)

---

31 See Kittel, *Theologisches Wörterbuch*, *ainigma*.
32 Ruskin, *Lectures on Art* VII, "Colour," section 179, in *Works*, vol. XX, p. 171.
33 Ruskin, *Modern Painters*, Part IX, chap. I, *Works*, vol. VII, pp. 259–62.
34 See Simpson, " 'Et vidit Deus cogitationes eorum.' " He mentions Augustine's commentary in *De trinitate*.

The Reverend Dr. Folliott is one of those clergy who likes to live comfortably, St. Paul or no St. Paul.

In the sixteenth century, Paul's text could be adapted for a way of looking at the natural world. One commentator on Euclid in 1570 saw the Book of Nature as providing a mirror of the divine. John Dee thought that, when we see "the creatures of God, both in the heavens above, and in the earth beneath . . . as in a glasse, we beholde the exceding maiestie and wisdom of God." He is extending the Pauline text to make a claim for mathematicians and their colleagues. For Tennyson, three centuries later, "the outward world, where the ladders and symbols are, is surely more of a veil which hides the Infinite than a mirror which reveals it."[35]

Tennyson was fully aware of the interactions of both riddle and charm with glass or mirror. Take, for example, these lines from "Merlin and Vivien" in *Idylls of the King*:

> And Merlin locked his hand in hers and said:
> "O did ye never lie upon the shore,
> And watch the curled white of the coming wave
> Glassed in the slippery sand before it breaks?
> Even such a wave, but not so pleasurable,
> Dark in the glass of some presageful mood,
> Had I for three days seen, ready to fall.
> And then I rose and fled from Arthur's court
> To break the mood. You followed me unasked;
> And when I looked, and saw you following still,
> My mind involved yourself the nearest thing
> In that moon-mist: for shall I tell you truth?
> You seemed that wave about to break on me
> And sweep me from my hold upon the world,
> My use and name and fame."[36]

Vivien, replying, ignores the word "glassed" ("the coming wave / Glassed"), as well she might. Tennyson emphasizes the word in three ways: by enjambment, by placing it first in the line, and by varying the iambic stress with it. The word is asking for attention, and we can hear why two lines later, when it reappears with a Pauline echo of seeing darkly or in a riddle. Again, the word is emphasized by placement in the line and reversal of the iambic stress: "Dark in the glass of some presageful mood, / Had I for three days seen." Merlin's magic mirror was famed, a

35 Quoted in Norman Page, ed., *Tennyson: Interviews and Recollections* (London: Macmillan, 1983), pp. 182–3. See also Shaw, *The Lucid Veil*.
36 *Poems*, vol. III, p. 404 (ll. 288–302).

glass that could show the future (see Spenser's *Faerie Queene* III.iii). Vivien wants neither his magic glass nor a reminder of St. Paul. She elides "glass" and retains the word "dark" only to speak of Merlin's "dark mood." "See you not, dear love," she entreats, moving Merlin's prophetic gaze from his mirror to her, that she fears he does not wholly trust her. And in the immemorial way of seducers, she demands proof of trust: here, his secret knowledge. Merlin, like any good wizard, is privy to the secret codes of both riddles and charms, and Tennyson wonderfully conjoins them here. Vivien deflects Merlin's gaze from a sea that is like his own enigmatic mirror, for seeing and reading riddles requires an alert mind. She lulls his mind with her charm in order to find out his charm. It takes six hundred lines and more, but she does it. Merlin's mind was right when it "involved" her, as that good Virgilian reader Tennyson implies (*Sibyl involvens* . . .).

Tennyson is one of the great charm poets, and this book of the *Idylls* is centered on charm, both Vivien's feminine charm and Merlin's great secret charm. It is when Merlin is worn out and drowsy, no longer seeing clearly, that the secret slides out, almost casually, it seems. The glassy wave *was* Vivien after all, and she has figuratively shattered Merlin's prophesying glass.

Hollander's *Reflections on Espionage* works with the master trope of the poet as spy and a double sense of "reflections." The observing, the spying, that goes toward the making of poems is reported by an outsider in Browning's "How It Strikes a Contemporary" and an insider in Hollander's *Reflections*. Alas, the speaker, Cupcake, is not enough of an insider, as his encoded fate on the back page makes clear. The entire series is full of brilliant griph-type schemes. In "5/1 To Image," Hollander plays on seeing and mirroring and speaking, starting with *spec-* or *skep-* words meaning "look, see": first, Latin *specere*, whence "aspect, species, speculation, specula, expect," then Greek *skeptomai*, whence "scope." The dance then turns to "skeptical in all our unwisdom," where the Greek root is *skepsis*, "inquiry or doubt," a different kind of *skep-*looking. Indo-European *spek-* (whence Germanic *spekh-*) moves seeing toward speaking and spying. The move from "*spec-*" or "*spek*" words to "*skep-*" is a mirror-like reversal of letters 2 and 4. These "specs" do not lead to wisdom literature, but rather downward to "specious" and "despicable." An extended family of words and sounds invites thoughts about origins and strange connections. "Seeing through a glass, darkly," indeed.

As for Borges, his great sonnet "Oedipus and the Enigma" also conjoins enigma and mirror (*espejo*):

. . . with afternoon there came a person
Deciphering, appalled at the monstrous other
Presence in the mirror, the reflection
Of his decay and of his destiny.
We are Oedipus. . .

INSIDE, OUTSIDE, AND INSIDE OUT

To me, this is the most important troping of enigma, more important even than light/dark troping. The inside/outside trope concerns the functioning of enigma, rather than one specific object. It governs several of the groups of tropes listed above. In the form of "insiders" and "outsiders," it is a constant trope in narratives where riddles are at work. It may be found in the Gospel of John.[37] The Apostle Paul suggests the importance of the inside/outside trope to his young congregation at Corinth: *en ainigmati, in aenigmate*, "*in* an enigma." One story about the Grecian Sphinx is that she eats those who cannot answer her riddle, a graphic illustration of the inside/outside logic of enigma. If you can't answer it, it swallows you.

This is also one trope that governs the workings of mirrors. It is a curious visual phenomenon, when we stop to think about it, that we appear to be inside a solid reflecting surface that we can see out there. Other creatures can also appear to exist there, as if the mirror were water and we were peering into another world. Where mirror and enigma are both involved, the inside/outside troping can take on special force. Thus throughout Carroll's riddling in *Through the Looking-Glass*.

The inside/outside trope acts so as to place the reader. As with the two meanings of "riddle," *griphos* (*griphus*) and *scirpus*, so here. In all these words, the brain's process of solving riddles may be likened to draining or panning out or sifting or winnowing what you don't want from what you do, as you search for answers. Is this a purely lexical line of inheritance, or is it a continuing trope, a metaphor that went on appealing to word-smiths? Leo Spitzer reads a more sinister definition of "net" – a net in which the riddlee is caught. *Griphos* "suggests the snarl in which the *examinandus* is caught by the insidious riddle." He cites Quevedo as well as the Sphinx ("Charade," p. 79n). Yet *griphoi* in Greek literature tend to be comic riddles. Henri Estienne, who was "Interpreter to the French

---

37 See John Ashton, "Riddles: Insiders and Outsiders," e.g., p. 396, part of an illuminating discussion of this Gospel in relation to the apocalyptic.

King for the Latine and Greek Tongues," read the *griphus*-net more lightly in 1650: "at Banquets . . . the understandings of the Feasters are caught (as it were in nets) by obscure questions" (*The Art of Making Devises*, p. 6).

The question is how to read figurative meaning. If the riddle is a net, is it a trap or is it an exercise for the brain? It all depends on where you are. Are you caught inside the riddle? Or are you in process of answering the riddle, safely outside its clutches, at least for the moment? This dynamic of inside and outside seems to me the dominant trope of enigma's behavior.

In the standard rhetorical example for enigma, the ice-water riddle, there is no inside/outside trope at work (though a ship trapped by ice could add a footnote about literal ice and its power to entrap). There is a fine example of the ice-water mother-daughter riddle in Old English.

The monster came sailing, wondrous along the wave; it called out in its comeliness to the land from the ship; loud was its din; its laughter was terrible, dreadful on earth; its edges were sharp. It was malignantly cruel, not easily brought to battle but fierce in the fighting; it stove in the ship's sides, relentless and ravaging. It bound it with a baleful charm; it spoke with cunning of its own nature: "My mother is of the dearest race of maidens, she is my daughter grown to greatness, as it is known to men, to people among the folk, that she shall stand with joy on the earth in all the lands."[38]

The answer to this riddle is an iceberg.

The ice-water riddle is clear and engaging, but on second thought, a little spooky, like many riddles of generation. What is a little *unheimlich* here is the trope of inside and outside: inside the womb, then born to the outside, then in turn giving birth, but not to a new baby. Rather, to the mother who bore you. Schoolboys do not reflect very far on tropes, and few schoolgirls learned much Latin or, for that matter, might have reflected very far either. Some mother-child riddles like ones on Jocasta are much more sinister, but this one escapes by its move over into natural phenomena. Jesus uses this same trope of outside and inside and outside the womb, also playing literal versus figurative, in his discussion with the learned Nicodemus. "You must be born again . . . " (John 3: 3).

To answer an enigma is to solve or dissolve or even resolve it. It is to move to where we contain the enigma instead of it containing us. To answer an enigma may also be to turn it inside out. Northrop Frye

---

38 Quoted in Frye, "Charms and Riddles," pp. 146–7.

identifies this as the most radical move of all: "When Mallarmé says that the poet does not name or point, but describes the mood evoked by the object, he seems to suggest a method of riddle-writing without guessing, which appears to destroy the whole point of the riddle. It may be, though, that he is also suggesting a way of getting past the deadlock we encountered" and to a series of better-formulated questions. Frye is talking about getting past the inside/outside trap. It is a move he himself uses at the end of "Charms and Riddles": "As Paul says, we see now in a riddle in a mirror, but we solve the riddle by coming out of the mirror, into the world that words and things reflect." This interesting movement – inside out and outside in – may also be seen in the aphorism/narrative move in a 1990 "Response" by Frye.[39]

Paul Celan's extraordinary use of the compound *Sprachgitter* (Speech-grille) suggests yet more. *Sprachgitter* is the title of Celan's third collection of poetry, published in 1959. The word is "a compound offering a wide spectrum of translations. . . the barred window or grating though which the cloistered spoke to outsiders. . . language as a grid which filters the expression of ideas. For fishermen, the *Gitter* is a trap or a net" (*Last Poems*, p. xviii).[40]

It is a word Celan uses to describe the operations of his own poetic language, in a poem about strangeness and strangers. . . The word is a compound of two nouns whose relation is ambivalent. *Sprach* refers to language; *Gitter* means some kind of lattice, fence or woven mesh. For people living cloistered lives, *Gitter* is the grillework or *fenestra locutaria* through which they speak to those outside. For fishermen, it means a net or trap. . . Does Celan use *Gitter* to imply passage, blockage or salvaging of speech? Mesh can do all of these. Celan may mean all of these.[41]

In most troping of nets, the crucial point is whether we are inside and caught, or outside and draining or panning out or sifting or winnowing.

39 "The way I begin a book is to write detached aphorisms in a notebook, and ninety-five percent of the work I do in completing a book is to fit these detached aphorisms together in a continuous narrative line. . . it is possible that many of my readers tend to find their way back to the original aphoristic form, finding me more useful for detached insights than for total structures" "Response," *Eighteenth-Century Studies* 24 (1990–91), special issue on Frye, 249.

40 Did *Gitter* also once bear the meaning of an enigma? The connection may be quite fortuitous, but the sound is tantalizing etymologically: it comes close to the Old English early form of "riddle," *hridder*, a winnowing tool, a kind of grille. In turn, this word echoes Hebrew *hida* ("riddle"), perhaps quite by accident.

41 Carson, *Economy of the Unlost*, pp. 30–1, and note p. 30n on the usage, which goes back to Jean Paul. See also Felstiner, *Paul Celan*, p. 107, and Jerry Glenn, *Paul Celan* (New York: Twaine, 1973), pp. 100–5.

In the examples of Frye and of some of Saul Steinberg's drawings, there is a paradoxical inside out and outside in. Celan's *Gitter* suggests something other, neither inside nor outside.

For him, language comes hard, as if dragged through the grate or mesh, struggling out. It is a question of how he is to write faithfully in German, when it is both the language of the great German classics and the language of the Nazis. In Celan's troping, both the words inside the *Gitter* and the words pulled through are reached with great difficulty. There is no easy passage, no easy freedom. This troping of a speech-riddle (to read *Sprachgitter* that way) comes much closer to the great, haunting enigmas like the Sphinx's. There is no easy position, no matter where we are situated.

CHAPTER 9

Case study III
The structure of reality: enigma in Wallace Stevens's later work

"The accuracy of accurate letters is an accuracy with respect to the structure of reality."

("Three Academic Pieces"[1])

It is necessary to propose an enigma to the mind. The mind always proposes a solution.

("Adagia"[2])

Wallace Stevens proposed enigmas to his mind all his life. They inform his poetry from start to finish, chiefly as trope but also as masterplot, as riddle poem, and at least once as a personified muse figure. Enigma as masterplot became a topic for reflection in Stevens's later work, as he sculpted the shapes of the word "enigma" in both poetry and prose. He decidedly belongs to the riddling line of poetry, though he could also write fine charm poetry. He loved proverbs and adages, so that he also lives in the tradition of poetry descending from the ancient genre of the proverb. These three generic pulls within Stevens's work suggest that he was drawn to those *formes simples* that André Jolles grouped together, and that Northrop Frye and Alastair Fowler after him have examined. As for the trope of enigma, it flourishes in Stevens's work. His temperament – witty, inquiring, demanding, sensuous and fastidious at once – drew him to the form. In this, he bears comparison with his friend Marianne Moore.

Some of our favorite poems come from Stevens's first collection, *Harmonium*, in 1923, where his fondness for riddling effects is very evident. The trope of enigma is present in the opening poem, "Earthy Anecdote," where a strange "firecat" challenges "bucks clattering over Oklahoma." The poem challenges readers too, as it evades any certain

---

1 Wallace Stevens, *The Necessary Angel* (hereafter *NA*), p. 71.
2 Stevens, *Opus Posthumous* (hereafter *OP*), p. 194. Other abbreviations are: *CP* (*Collected Poems*), *L* (*Letters*).

allegorical reading, yet opens out into numerous questions – questions of genre and fictive constructs, of Oklahoma history and memory, of first-ness in place and in writing, of names. "The Snow Man" works more with logical paradox than the trope of enigma. "The nothing that is not there and the nothing that is": this is what the snow man/no man sees. One of Stevens's two valedictory poems at the end of this collection is a small riddle-poem titled "Tea." At first glance, it appears a charming short exotic poem with an Imagist flavor, and not much more. But when we remember Stevens's ongoing work with the topos of leaves, together with the fact that we drink a brew made of tea leaves – perhaps also the fact that Stevens was a tea-fancier – we start reading the poem quite differ-ently. It transforms itself into a leave-taking poem, an invitation to ingest Stevens's work.

The effects of *Harmonium* are remarkable, yet Stevens's major writing still lay ahead, including his work on enigma. After this first book, he set about crafting an even more distinctive style of his own, that most demanding task for a writer. When he returned to poetry with *Ideas of Order* (1935), a new plainness became evident, even at the expense of some subtlety and the lush exotic voice of *Harmonium*. In part, this was because of the times, the difficult 1930s. In part, it was because Stevens sought a fuller, more authentic voice, and not just for the 1930s. When he moved into the extraordinary work of the forties and fifties, enigma came into its own. Now enigma's scope moves even beyond the play and wit of Stevens's early writing.

One example from the 1940s, "the obscurer selvages" ("Esthétique du Mal" v), even describes how it works as a trope. The canto deals with grief, and the ceremonies that help us in times of sorrow. It sets bound-aries that keep these ceremonies authentic for Stevens: "Within what we permit, / Within the actual. . . within what we permit, in-bar . . . against the suns / Of ex-bar . . ." (v.3–4, 19, 20–1). For this, says Stevens, we "willingly forfeit the ai-ai // Of parades in the obscurer selvages" (v.12–13). What are these obscurer selvages? They make general sense in a hazy way, as yet another kind of boundary. They mark the edge of a swath of woven material, preventing it from unraveling. But "parades in the obscurer selvages"? "Obscurer" indeed, a reader might mutter.

But Stevens is not a hazy writer. The phrase lies in wait for a time when we are re-reading the opening lines of Dante's *Divine Comedy*. There, in *Inferno* I.1–5, Dante the pilgrim is lost in the middle of life's way, lost in a dark wood, a "selva oscura." The word *selva* is repeated in line 5, where it is followed by *selvaggia*: "selva selvaggia," a savage wood.

Nel mezzo del cammin di nostra vita
Mi ritrovai per una selva oscura,
Ché la diritta via era smarrita.

Ah quanto a dir qual era è cosa dura
Esta selva selvaggia. . .

(In the middle of the journey of our life I came to myself in a dark wood where the straight way was lost. Ah, how hard a thing it is to tell what a wild . . . wood this was. . . . [Carlyle-Wicksteed][3])

The echoing effects are remarkable: "selva oscura . . . selva selvaggia." T. S. Eliot's acute ear heard them, and he played with them in the title of the third *Quartet*, *The Dry Salvages*. Stevens's acute ear also heard them. He joins the adjectives, *oscura* and *selvaggia*, but he shifts *selvaggia* to a like-sounding noun, "selvage." He is indirectly responding to Dante. For Dante's dream-vision of hell and purgatory and heaven is not in the middle of life's journey for Stevens, but on the edge of things, the selvages. Dante is a figure that Stevens greatly admires, but he cannot share his perspective. In this hidden riposte, he is responding more immediately to a Dantean tradition manifest in Eliot's *Dry Salvages*, which was published not long before "Esthétique du Mal." Nor do Stevens's selvages hint through their etymology at salvation, as Eliot's echoing does in *Dry Salvages*.[4] I doubt that Stevens knew the old rhetorical definition of the trope of enigma, but his trope does happily describe itself: an "obscurer" similitude, a closed simile until we open it, woven into the edges of his material.

It is tempting but misleading to call every riddling effect in Stevens's work a "riddle" or "enigma." Similarly it is misleading to call a Stevens poem with unexpected tropes a "riddle poem." But genuine riddle poems there are, such as the late poem, "Solitaire under the Oaks" (*OP* 137). The poem has little to do with the early figure of a "solitaire" in Stevens's poem "The Place of the Solitaires," or with his use of the words "solitary" and "solitude." Rather, we need to read "Solitaire under the Oaks" as if it were an Old English riddle poem asking "Who am I?"

---

3 The lines are so famous that translation is always a challenge. "Wild" often translates *selvaggia*, though with mixed effect. Cary's influential 1814 translation chooses two adjectives, "how savage wild / That forest," while Robert Pinsky's 1994 one sticks to "savage."

4 See "The Senses of Eliot's Salvages," in my *Against Coercion*, pp. 120–7. Stevens, incidentally, knew professionally about dealing with salvage through his work at the Hartford Accident and Indemnity Company (Peter Brazeau, *Parts of a World: Wallace Stevens Remembered* [New York: Random House, 1983], p. 31).

> In the oblivion of cards
> One exists among pure principles.
>
> Neither the cards nor the trees nor the air
> Persist as facts. This is an escape
>
> To principium, to meditation.
> One knows at last what to think about
>
> And thinks about it without consciousness,
> Under the oak tree, completely released.

A clue to the answer lies in the title-pun on the word "solitaire" as both a solitary person and a card-game. The answer itself puns on *des cartes* (playing cards) and the philosopher René Descartes. Curious that the name of the great philosopher should mean "playing cards." And what card game would Monsieur Cards play? Solitaire, of course, the quintessential Cartesian card game. If we adopt the common view that Cartesian philosophy isolates us as self-conscious thinking subjects, and divides us from the rest of the natural world, then it makes us into *solitaires*. "Cogito ergo sum," "I think, therefore I am." What is the evidence for Descartes's presence? Why else use the words "principium" and "meditation," thereby echoing two of Descartes's best-known titles, *Principia philosophiae* and *Les Méditations*? The poem also offers a way out. All this in eight lines, as if to demonstrate Stevens's mastery of this genre and of compact riddle effects.

Stevens's poetry is inhabited by numerous invented characters. They are figures with speaking names by which we infer what they are like and how they will probably act. "Berserk" appears in a dream poem, with expected effect ("Anecdote of the Prince of Peacocks"). The delectable Nanzia Nunzio in "Notes toward a Supreme Fiction" is a messenger of sorts, related to a papal nuncio and to the various angels in the poem. (*Angelus*, like *nuntius*, means "messenger.") She is also related through her language to the biblical spouse of the Song of Songs. Canon Aspirin in the same poem has a name and nature not too difficult to surmise, though richer than we might expect. The name is allegorical, like a name out of Spenser or Bunyan, rather than riddling. This is someone at the least canonical in behavior and thought, perhaps religious. He also aspires, and may soothe headaches, including his own (we hope). When the Canon's language proves to be Miltonic, and, when we recall that Stevens once copied out lines about aspiring from Browning, we know we are on the right track. (Browning's lines are from "Rabbi ben Ezra": "What I aspired to be, / And was not, comforts me"; Stevens copied them in a 1909 notebook.[5]) None of these names can be said to use the trope of enigma. Their similitude is not hidden, even if their full wit and appropriateness takes time to appreciate.

Other proper names have remained hidden for some time. They trope on a name, but not in any obvious way. They require unriddling, for they are using hidden similitude. Thus with the name of Professor Eucalyptus from "An Ordinary Evening in New Haven." Stevens is punning on the two words "apocalypse" and "eucalyptus," as did Borges in his story, "Death and the Compass." The point of this becomes apparent, once we have heard echoes from the Apocalypse in the poem. Stevens is rewriting the sense of a "New Haven" and a "New Heaven" as they were apprehended by the first founders of New Haven. How might a visitor to the city see it in 1949, walking its streets, imbued with a sense of its history back to colonial days? Stevens's long sequence focuses in part on last things, things having to do with apocalypse and the Apocalypse. An apocalypse is a sudden unveiling as in the last book of the Bible. "Eucalyptus," like "apocalypse," has the Greek stem meaning "hidden" or "veiled," whence the nymph Calypso and similar *–calyp* words. The eu-calyptus tree is so named for its well-covered flower, which appears in due time, gradually becoming uncovered. The point is that this uncovering is governed by natural processes, not supernatural. Similarly, the tree's name does not derive from any transcendent or legendary source; it is an eighteenth-century botanical invention. This difference is crucial in Stevens's poem. If we see *in aenigmate* for the time being, it is in an enigma offered by nature, not by divine forces. Stevens is pressing back against a biblical sense of apocalypse. For him, it is now not accurate "with respect to the structure of reality," though it was for New Haven's founders.

As for St. Paul's famous text, "For now we see through a glass, darkly; but then, face to face," Stevens writes against it in all three sections of "Notes toward a Supreme Fiction." In Part I.v, Adam and Eve "found themselves / In heaven as in a glass; a second earth." Not Eden as the first-created unfallen earth, but Eden as in the Genesis narrative, where, Stevens implies, the author fashions heaven out of what he knows of earth. Not ascertaining what we may of heaven through a glass, by means of a mirror, but the other way around. Eve "made air the mirror of herself." Part II, "It Must Change," ends with an earthly vision of transformed nature, of seraphs and saints as part of this world:

5 *Souvenirs and Prophecies: The Young Wallace Stevens*, ed. Holly Stevens (New York: Knopf, 1977), p. 220.

> It is ourselves, the freshness of ourselves,
> And that necessity and that presentation
> Are rubbings of a glass in which we peer.

We ourselves direct the play of this "Theatre / Of Trope." We ourselves govern the structures of what "we see" or rather of what we peer at, as we search that newly cleared glass. Part III, "It Must Give Pleasure," includes references to Christian worship, to St. Jerome (as translator of the Bible into Latin), and to visions of heaven. Stevens goes on to design his own form of the marriage of earth and heaven, the "mystic marriage" that is nonethless very earthly, between Bawda and the great Captain (III.IV).

> They married well because the marriage-place
> Was what they loved. It was neither heaven nor hell.
> They were love's characters come face to face.

Not the characters of St. Paul's hymn to love that is centered in God, and his vision of seeing face to face after the mirror and enigma. But earthly characters, both as personifications and as letters on the page.

The great riddle-master of the Hebrew Scriptures also enters Stevens's poetry of the 1940s, though more in his general capacity as a wisdom figure. Stevens loved wisdom literature and made his own collection of adages, the "Adagia," and his own commonplace book, *Sur Plusieurs Beaux Sujects*, with its deliberately archaic title.[6] Among the biblical books of wisdom, he found the symbols in the Book of Ecclesiastes pleasurable: "they give us the pleasure of 'lentor and solemnity' in respect to the most commonplace objects" (*NA* 78, 1947). The Ecclesiast, or the Preacher of Ecclesiastes, traditionally Solomon, concludes canto XIX of "An Ordinary Evening in New Haven":

> What is the radial aspect of this place,
> This present colony of a colony
> Of colonies, a sense in the changing sense
>
> Of things? A figure like Ecclesiast,
> Rugged and luminous, chants in the dark
> A text that is an answer, although obscure.

The rabbi figure runs throughout Stevens's poetry, a figure cherished as a wisdom figure. The 1949 poem, "Things of August," opens Part v with

---

6 *Sur Plusieurs Beaux Sujects: Wallace Stevens' Commonplace Book*, ed. Milton Bates (Stanford: Stanford University Press for the Huntington Library, 1989). Modern French spells "subject" as *sujet*. He admired the *Adages* of Erasmus, liking him for "a certain chic. He would be horrified to know . . . that it is THE EPITOME OF ADAGES that I go for" (*L* 409, 1942).

these spirited lines (*CP* 492): "We'll give the week-end to wisdom, to Weisheit, the rabbi, / Lucidity of his city, joy of his nation . . ." As with the word "enigma," so with wisdom writing and references to wisdom. They multiply in the later work.

In 1947, Stevens opened his lecture "Three Academic Pieces" with the sentence quoted in the first epigraph. "Accuracy . . . accurate . . . accuracy": the little scheme draws attention to itself like Stevens's thrice-repeated *app-* sounds in "apparition apparelled in / Apparels" from "Angel Surrounded by Paysans." In what ways are letters accurate? Do we think of "accurate letters" as a near-oxymoron, and, for that matter, the "accurate songs" in "Notes toward a Supreme Fiction" I.ix as a near-oxymoron? If so, why? I want to look at Stevens's work with the word "enigma" in his late poems and essays, reflecting on how it is "accurate . . . with respect to the structure of reality."

There are some words that turn up only at certain times in Stevens's work. One such is the word "enigma." Other words run all through the work, but gather with concentrated force at certain times. The word "figure" does this, offering intense critical interest from about 1942, the year of "Notes toward a Supreme Fiction," to 1949, the year of "An Ordinary Evening in New Haven." The term "figure," including especially figures of speech, provides one organizing principle for three or four of the seven essays that constitute *The Necessary Angel.* The entire collection opens with figuration: "In the *Phaedrus,* Plato speaks of the soul in a figure."

The word "enigma" does not appear at all in Stevens's poetry until 1947, when he was in his sixties. From 1947 until his death in 1955, it turns up in four major poetic sequences, as well as the short version of the fourth one. Each use is distinctly different. The four major poems are as follows: "Credences of Summer" (1947), "The Auroras of Autumn" (1948), "An Ordinary Evening in New Haven" (1949), and "The Sail of Ulysses" (read in 1954). The very short version of "The Sail of Ulysses," titled "Presence of an External Master of Knowledge," was published in 1954.[7] The dates of the word "enigma" may be slightly extended, from the 1943 essay already quoted in chapter 3 to a preface published after Stevens's death in 1955. To these instances, we may add two undated

---

7 "Credences of Summer" was actually written by July 1946 (*L* 530). "The Auroras of Autumn" was first published in the *Kenyon Review,* Winter 1948. Eleven cantos of "An Ordinary Evening in New Haven" were read in November 1949, at which time all the poem was complete.

examples, one from Stevens's list of titles for possible poems and one from the "Adagia" quoted in the epigraph to this chapter.

Of course, Stevens could use the word "enigma" more generally and casually, apart from his work, and did so in a few letters written about this time. "On the other hand, the sort of poem I have in the winter number of *The Kenyon Review* ["Variations on a Summer's Day"] . . . also has its justifications. In a world permanently enigmatical, to hear and see agreeable things involves something more than mere imagism . . . " (*L* 346, 29 Dec. 1939). The enigmatical world of December 1939 included a Western world mostly at war, as Stevens was well aware. In 1940, he suggested in a telegram to his friend Henry Church: "Do have Allen Tate if convenient. We can have a trial bout with this enigma." Whether the enigma was the Chair of Poetry under discussion, or Allen Tate himself, I cannot tell (18 Oct. 1940).[8] After Church's death, Stevens wrote that his friend appeared to many to be an enigma, because of the seeming paradoxes in his life and behavior. Stevens intimates that he was not (*L* 571, 1947).

Early in the year after he published "Notes toward a Supreme Fiction" and delivered the lecture "The Figure of the Youth as a Virile Poet," Stevens wote to Hi Simons, a congenial critic and regular correspondent:

> I ought to say that I have not defined the supreme fiction. . . The next thing for me to do will be to try to be a little more precise about this enigma. . . In principle there appear to be certain characteristics of the supreme fiction and the NOTES is confined to a statement of a few of those characteristics. As I see the subject, it could occupy a school of rabbis for the next few generations.
>
> (*L* 435, 1943)

"The next thing for me": and so it was, from 1943 until the end of his life. In all the examples from the poetry of this period, enigma is read in this capacious sense, where the possibility of some masterplot is present. The question is: what kind or kinds?

Stevens compiled a list of enchanting titles for poems, most of which remained only titles. One proposed subject for which he never wrote a poem is "On the Resolving of Noble Enigmas."[9] The word "Noble" connects the phrase with Stevens's 1942 essay, "The Noble Rider and the Sound of Words." About this time, I surmise, Stevens was thinking about the resolving of noble enigmas, or, say, sublime enigmas, if I am right that the word "noble" in his essay signifies something close to the

---

8 Wallace Stevens papers, Huntington Library, quoted by permission of the Huntington Library.
9 George S. Lensing, "*From Pieces of Paper*: A Wallace Stevens Notebook," *Southern Review* 15 (1979), 881.

word "sublime." Noble or sublime enigmas would decidedly include the Apostle Paul's much-troped one in 1 Corinthians 13: 12. Paul's enigma is resolved, of course, and in the most complete way. I take it that noble enigmas not only get solved but also resolved, in the emphatic form of the verb in English, as in Latin. "Resolve," like Latin *resoluere*, includes the sense of bringing things to an end, as a simple "solve" or *soluere* does not.

Stevens uses the word "solve" only once in his poetry, in part 23 of *The Man with the Blue Guitar* (1937). The word, like the entire section, has to do with final, teleological matters, "all / Confusion solved." It is only after this that the word "resolve" appears in Stevens's poetry, and all four uses also have to do with momentous questions. It is as if, having written "all / Confusion solved," he later decided that "resolve" was the better word and used it thereafter. The example from "Connoisseur of Chaos" is well known:

> After all the pretty contrast of life and death
> Proves that these opposite things partake of one,
> At least that was the theory, when bishops' books
> Resolved the world. We cannot go back to that.
> The squirming facts exceed the squamous mind,
> If one may say so.

The word also appears in two poems of 1947, "The Owl in the Sarcophagus" (*Horizon*, 1947) and "Of Ideal Time and Choice," the last of "Three Academic Pieces" (*Partisan Review*, 1947). Its last appearance is in the posthumous poem "The Sail of Ulysses" (*OP* 127–8), where "misgivings [are] dazzlingly / Resolved in dazzling discovery." The dazzling discovery is that we possess "no map of paradise." All four uses of "resolve" come at the end or beginning of enjambed lines, as if the very positioning of the word in a poetic line troped its signification concerning ends and beginnings.

Not all enigmas ask to be resolved, of course. Certainly not Stevens's 1943 "enigma" in his lecture, "The Figure of the Youth as Virile Poet." The word appears twice in the last section of the essay, both times in an italicized speech. Stevens's essay is describing an artist, a masterful artist, perhaps some future Milton, but a Milton for our own day. So it has always been, he surmises: "*a younger figure emerging, stepping forward in the company of a muse of its own, still half-beast and somehow more than human, a kind of sister of the Minotaur. This younger figure is the intelligence that endures.*" For Stevens, such a muse must come from "*the spirit out of its own self, not out of some surrounding myth.*" It will know how to delineate "with accurate speech the complications of which it is composed" (*NA* 52–3).

We all undergo a purification (to use Stevens's word, *NA* 60) when we return to an "agreement with reality" (*NA* 59). Then we can say:

No longer do I believe that there is a mystic muse, sister of the Minotaur. This is another of the monsters I had for nurse, whom I have wasted. I am myself a part of what is real, and it is my own speech and the strength of it, this only, that I hear or ever shall. (*NA* 60)

As observed in chapter 3, the speech is an article of faith declaring independence from any muse external to ourselves, such as Milton's. Stevens uses "we," thereby including his readers in this credal act. For him, and for many, a Miltonic muse and a Miltonic or Christian structure of things is now not accurate "with respect to the structure of reality."

Stevens closes his essay with a revised version of this speech, which is what the "figure of the youth, in his character of poet" (*NA* 66) is thinking. "He is thinking of those facts of experience of which all of us have thought and which all of us have felt with such intensity, and he says:

Inexplicable sister of the Minotaur, enigma and mask, although I am part of what is real, hear me and recognize me as part of the unreal. I am the truth but the truth of that imagination of life in which with unfamiliar motion and manner you guide me in those exchanges of speech in which your words are mine, mine yours. (*NA* 67)

This revision interests me especially because Stevens does not abandon his muse-figure; he re-invents her. She is now "inexplicable," now a "mask," and notably now an "enigma." Given Stevens's late work on the word "enigma," the loose general sense of "the mystery of creation" will not suffice. What shape does his 1943 enigma have? A hidden shape, masked, inexplicable. Not a "noble enigma" that will be resolved.

Stevens's uses of "enigma" after 1943 show that he continued to brood over the word, still figuring it forth, still troping it. In 1947, the word "enigma" appears for the first time in his poetry, in that fine homecoming poem "Credences of Summer." In part IV, set in Stevens's natal state of Pennsylvania, his troping catches the summer languor of those wide, wide Pennsylvania valleys when the sun is hot and the wind balmy and the car wants to drive itself forever up and down the roads. But Stevens says it as it needs saying:

> One of the limits of reality
> Presents itself in Oley when the hay,
> Baked through long days, is piled in mows. It is
> A land too ripe for enigmas, too serene.

> There the distant fails the clairvoyant eye . . .
>
>   . . .
>
> Things stop in that direction and since they stop
> The direction stops and we accept what is
> As good.

All is ripeness here, as if St. Paul's incomplete *in aenigmate* does not apply. Paul's completion of both *speculum* and enigma belong in "the distant," at the end of time. But in Stevens's warm summer Pennsylvania landscape, "the distant fails the clairvoyant eye." "Things stop." A strong sense of reality has encompassed all enigmas. The land is not only too ripe, but also too serene. In 1942, Stevens used the phrase "serenely gazing" to describe the behavior of his leaping angel, a composite Miltonic figure ("Notes toward a Supreme Fiction" III.viii).[10] Now, in 1947, Stevens reclaims the word once again, for a kind of sight that does not press toward a final face-to-face seeing. Yet it is a clear seeing, a "clairvoyant eye."[11] It is, for Stevens, a reality, if limited, a reality without enigma, where human life is good in itself.

In 1948, Stevens again thought about the word "enigma" for use in a poem, but he troped it very differently indeed in "The Auroras of Autumn" viii–ix:

> So, then, these lights are not a spell of light,
> A saying out of a cloud, but innocence.
> An innocence of the earth and no false sign
>
> Or symbol of malice. That we partake thereof,
> Lie down like children in this holiness,
> As if, awake, we lay in the quiet of sleep,
>
> As if the innocent mother sang in the dark
> Of the room and on an accordion, half-heard,
> Created the time and place in which we breathed . . .[ellipsis *sic*]
>
> IX
> And of each other thought – in the idiom
> Of the work, in the idiom of an innocent earth,
> Not of the enigma of the guilty dream.

I do not know what "the enigma of the guilty dream" is. Is there always an enigma when guilt is involved? Not under civil or criminal law, where one

---

10 "Serenely," in Stevens' full context, recalls Milton's "drop serene" in his Invocation to Light (*Paradise Lost* III.25); "drop serene" translates *gutta serena*, Milton's own type of blindness.

11 All three late uses of "serene" have to do with seeing. The other comes in the 1944 "Esthétique du Mal" vi.16.

is guilty or not guilty, but, say, in a dream. Is this a dream as read by Freud? Is it a dream at all in the ordinary sense? Or is it a dream in the sense that an untrue or less true or transitory way of being might be called a dream? ("We fly forgotten as a dream / Dies at the opening day," says the old hymn.) Why this axis of innocence and guilt? The only other use of the word "guilt" in Stevens' poetry comes in the late poem, "One of the Inhabitants of the West," and it is not a dream.

In "The Auroras of Autumn," Stevens imagines an "idiom" in which we are truly at home on this earth, for once not exiles, not inhabiting it a "in the idiom . . . of the enigma of the guilty dream." Whatever this idiom, it is not, for Stevens, an idiom accurate with respect to the structure of reality.

A fine use of "enigma" appears in "An Ordinary Evening in New Haven" in 1949:

> It is fatal in the moon and empty there.
> But, here, allons. The enigmatical
> Beauty of each beautiful enigma
>
> Becomes amassed in a total double-thing.
> We do not know what is real and what is not.
> . . .
> This faithfulness of reality, this mode,
> This tendance and venerable holding-in
> Make gay the hallucinations in surfaces. (x.1–5, 16–18)

Here, enigma follows the scheme of chiasmus: "The enigmatical / Beauty of each beautiful enigma." It is emphatically neither Pauline enigma nor its dark opposite, Sphinxine enigma. It might be called self-enclosed self-mirroring enigma, but it sounds playful. This is not a sunny land too ripe for enigmas, but a land of the sun that includes "morning and evening . . . evening feast and the following festival." A chiastic or self-enclosed enigma has much potential for being sinister or ironic in some structures of reality. This is how Eliot saw the ever-recurring cycle of the seasons in *The Waste Land*. Enigma as chiasmus might sound as if traps us in cyclic ignorance. But Stevens's "total double-thing" apparently works differently.

Stevens is playing with inside and outside, here and elsewhere in this poem. "It is fatal *in* the moon and empty there. But *here*, allons" ("An Ordinary Evening" x.1–2, my italics, here and later). Or, in the canto just preceding (ibid. IX.11–16):

> We seek
> Nothing beyond reality. *Within* it,

> Everything, the spirit's alchemicana
> *Included,* the spirit that goes roundabout
> And through *included,* not merely the visible,

> The solid . . .

Or, in a canto near the end (ibid. XXVIII.14–18):

> A more severe,

> More harassing master would extemporize
> Subtler, more urgent proof that the theory
> Of poetry is the theory of life,

> As it is, *in* the intricate evasions of as,
> *In* things seen and unseen, created from nothingness,
> The heavens, the hells, the worlds, the longed-for lands.

Stevens's sense of how we live and move and have our being within a world that our heads create is powerful. Perhaps that is why he insists so strongly that this world must be informed by the world outside our heads, what he calls reality. However enigma works, it must be accurate "with respect to the structure of reality," just as accurate in its way as a physicist's accuracy is in a physical way.

The last example of "enigma" in Stevens's poetry comes in the closing lines of his long posthumously published poem, "The Sail of Ulysses." Enigma this time comes as "*an enigma's flittering*" (*OP* 131):

> *The great sail of Ulysses seemed,*
> *In the breathings of this soliloquy,*
> *Alive with an enigma's flittering . . . [sic]*
> *As if another sail went on*
> *Straight forwardly through another night*
> *And clumped stars dangled all the way.*

"Presence of an External Master of Knowledge," the very short version of this poem that Stevens released for publication (24 lines as against 172), also closes with these six lines. Five of the six lines have their words slightly altered, the exception being the line on enigma, "*Alive with an enigma's flittering. . . .*"

Three things interest me about this example. First, the poem includes a personified figure of enigma from classical literature, something not seen since 1943. It is the Sibyl, descended generally from the ancient riddling

Sibyls, and more specifically from Stevens's 1943 personified "Inexplicable sister of the Minotaur, enigma and mask." She descends also from Heraclitus. In 1943 Stevens wrote to Henry Church:

[Jean] Wahl wrote to me the other day. Among other things, he said . . . "I read these lines by Heraklitos: 'And the Sibyl with raving lips and uttering things solemn, unadorned and unembellished, reaches, over a thousand years with her voice because of the god in her.' I am bound to say that I feel the most intense desire to have a copy of Heraklitos after that quotation, but he is not easy to find." (12 October 1943)[12]

The reference in Heraclitus is "the earliest reference to the Sibyl in extant literature."[13]

Stevens's Sibyl in "The Sail of Ulysses" is different. She is an everyday Sibyl, like the ordinary sublime of "An Ordinary Evening in New Haven." It is easy to see why the Sibyl in Heraclitus would draw Stevens, at least insofar as she utters things solemn but unadorned and embellished.[14] Here is his own Sibyl, as described by Ulysses at the start of part VIII of "The Sail of Ulysses":

> "What is the shape of the sibyl? Not,
> For a change, the englistered woman. . .
> It is the sibyl of the self
> . . . the sibyl's shape
> Is a blind thing fumbling for its form,
> A form that is lame, a hand, a back,
> A dream too poor, too destitute
> To be remembered, the old shape
> Worn and leaning to nothingness,
> A woman looking down the road,
> A child asleep in its own life.
> As these depend, so must they use. . ."

Stevens also writes this Sibyl against the famous twentieth-century Sibyl who lives in the antechamber to *The Waste Land* – writing, as he put it elsewhere, of plain reality, not grim reality (*L* 636, 1949).

---

12 Wallace Stevens papers, Huntington Library, quoted by permission of Huntington Library.
13 Fragment 34 in *The Art and Thought of Heraclitus: An Edition of the Fragments with Translation and Commentary*, ed. Charles H. Kahn (Cambridge: Cambridge University Press, 1979), pp. 124–6. Kahn translates: "Plutarch; 'The Sibyl with raving mouth', according to Heraclitus 'utters things mirthless' and unadorned and unperfumed, and her voice carries through a thousand years because of the god <who speaks through her>."
14 Her "raving lips" would probably not appeal to Stevens any more than they apparently did to Heraclitus (ibid., p. 125).

The shape of Ulysses' voyage, as outlined in chapter 3, also interests me greatly. Stevens is not seeing darkly or *in aenigmate*, though moving in darkness, propelled by a sail that is "Alive with an enigma's flittering." What shape would this voyage and this enigma take? It seems to me that Stevens, in this powerful death-poem, has worked out an alternative to Pauline enigma. Not an enigma resolved in a final eschatological revelation at the end of time. Not that teleology, and not teleology at all in the strict sense. Not a dark sphinxine resolving either, or a random, puzzling and hence sinister or disappointing resolving. This is still an end-directed plot, but the end is long-term rather than final.

Third, I am interested in the word "flittering." The sail itself seems both animated and inspired by Ulysses' own breath, as Stevens works his late magic of inventing a world both within and without, or rather a world of the imaginative state where within and without are one. Propelling his own voyage, by his own breathing spirit, Ulysses steers his course, himself like some angel-winged boat bearing the redeemed to Purgatory, and like many another wondrous vessel of which we read.[15] Now Stevens has found the word he wants for a late, or even final, all-encompassing enigma. Not dark enigma, not enclosing enigma: flittering. It is a word used three times elsewhere of lightning,[16] but this is starlight. It is a word used at once of lightning and of poetry and metaphor in "Notes toward a Supreme Fiction" II.ix and in "The Bouquet."

In a late essay, Stevens includes remarks on enigma, as apprehended by Mallarmé and Valéry ("Two Prefaces," *OP* 297), or rather as seen through Alain's remarks on Mallarmé and Valéry:

[Alain] said that of all the indicators of thought the most sensitive were poets, first because they take risks a little further than logic permits; also because the rule they adopt always carries them a little beyond what they hoped for. Mallarmé and Valéry announce a new climate of thought. They want clear enigmas, those that are developable, that is to say, mathematical . . . Among other things, this is surely a gloss on Mallarmé's famous saying, "Il toujours doit avoir énigme en poésie . . ." (There must always be enigma in poetry).

Stevens goes on to quote Valéry's Socrates in *Eupalinos*:

---

15 It is also a vessel that includes implicitly Stevens's own art, his craft. The pun is a favorite. Cf. Ursula K. Le Guin's title for her book on writing skills, *Steering the Craft*.
16 In "The Comedian as the Letter C" and "The Bouquet," and see the reference to "Notes" just following.

What is there more mysterious than clarity? . . . What more capricious than the way in which light and shade are distributed over hours and over men? . . . Orpheuslike we build, by means of the word, temples of wisdom and science that may suffice for all reasonable creatures. This great art requires of us an admirably exact language. (ibid., p. 298)

So it is that the dark saying or enigma, *in aenigmate,* may give way to "clear enigmas" – and these clear enigmas yet retain a mystery – all through "an admirably exact language."

Figures of enigma in Stevens's work from 1943 to 1954 tell a story, of which the chapter titles might be:

1. "On the Resolving of Noble Enigmas" or thoughts about old-style Pauline enigma.
2. The perpetual enigma of a muse–figure – an enigma no artist would wish to see resolved.
3. Ripeness beyond enigmas, but on earth, not heavenly.
4. The idiom of the enigma of the guilty dream set aside, with no resolving needed.
5. Enigma revived, alive. It is the "great sail," "the sharp sail of Ulysses [that] seemed, / In the breathings of that soliloquy, / Alive with an enigma's flittering."

We can watch Stevens taking that crucial word, that figure, that end-directed plot, and turning it over and over, until by the time of "The Sail of Ulysses" he has worked out his own pattern of enigma. It is a pattern that is accurate for him.

"The accuracy of accurate letters is an accuracy with respect to the structure of reality." If we still think of "accurate letters" or "accurate songs" as a near-oxymoron, it might help to listen to Stephen Jay Gould:

We often think, naively, that missing data are the primary impediments to intellectual progress – just find the right facts and all the problems will dissipate. But barriers are often deeper and more abstract in thought. We must have access to the right metaphor, not only to requisite information. Revolutionary thinkers are not, primarily, gatherers of fact, but weavers of new intellectual structures.[17]

When Stevens writes of finding an analogy for a "structure of reality," I think this is the kind of example he has in mind. Through his own "accuracy of accurate letters," the trope of enigma can figure forth a "structure of reality."

17 Stephen Jay Gould, "For Want of a Metaphor," from his *The Flamingo's Smile: Reflections in Natural History* (New York: Norton, 1985), p. 151.

CHAPTER 10

From protection to innocent amusement: some other functions of enigma

I would far rather be given the solution first and the riddle afterwards.

(Sancho Panza)[1]

PROTECTION, HEALING, ORACLES, STATECRAFT

Some functions of riddling are direct practical functions, where the rhetorical strength of an enigma is not a primary concern. Sophocles' great play works with a classic riddle, but the Iroquois riddle quoted by Father Ragueneau below is neither very difficult nor very interesting. It is not the art of such enigmas that matters, but their efficacy. Take, for instance, W. G. Archer's account of the Uraons in India. They use

"kennings" or summary riddles . . . at night as substitutes for the names of certain animals – "a rope" for a snake, "the long-tailed one" for a tiger, "the woolly-coated one" for a sheep. . . The use arises from the tabu against using a correct name after dark – the tabu springing from a sense of the identity of a thing and its name, and the apprehension that to name an animal may either cause it harm if it is a domestic one or cause it to do harm if it is a wild one. For Uraons such "kennings" or summary riddles are as useful as insurance and as important as a gun or a club.[2]

This is the riddle as protection. It is related to taboos on certain names, and wariness about revealing one's name to strangers. A name is simply too powerful, and a riddle can guard it. Some names are never to be pronounced aloud, and some are to be said only in certain times and

---

1 As quoted in Hegel, but apparently not by Cervantes (Hegel, *Aesthetics*, trans. Knox, vol. 1, p. 397).
2 Archer, *The Blue Grove*, p. 179. He also cites S. C. Roy, *The Oraons*, p. 361. An Old English kenning does not name an object directly, but uses a figure that becomes standard. The sea is a "whaleroad" or a "home for fishes." Few kennings would qualify as true riddles, though Trypho did include them as one class of *ainigma*.

places. In the Hebrew Scriptures, God's own sacred name is not to be pronounced; Yahweh and other names of God provide substitutes.

The rhetorical function in such examples is contrary to the main rhetorical functions of enigma. Rather than seeking the answer and solving the riddle, the riddle remains. Its answer is known to insiders, but not voiced. The unresolved riddle acts as a barrier, a defense against inimical forces. The forces may threaten physical harm or (for the name of God) sacrilege. Thus in Charles Williams's homiletic detective thriller *Many Dimensions*, centered on a miraculous stone bearing the Tetragrammaton, the four Hebrew letters of God's name.

On the other hand, some threats may be avoided through answering riddles. Dream-riddles often function this way, and are especially interesting in the Iroquois tradition, where dreams were (and may still be) exceedingly important. Anthony Wallace calls the Iroquois theory of dreams "basically psychoanalytic": "Father Ragueneau in 1649 described the theory in language that might have been used by Freud himself." Wallace judges that "the seventeenth- and eighteenth-century Iroquois' understanding of psychodynamics was greatly superior to that of the most enlightenened Europeans of the time." On the fourth day of the extensive Midwinter Ceremony, for example, secret medicine societies practiced their rituals, mostly curing rituals. "Men and women also on this day propounded their dream-riddles, and the guessers offered miniature talismans representing the tutelary revealed in the dream."

Each person or a group announced his "own and special desire or 'Ondinonc' – according as he is able to get information and enlightenment by dreams – not openly, however, but through Riddles. For example, someone will say 'What I desire and what I am seeking is that which bears a lake within itself'; and by this is intended a pumpkin or calabash. . . Another will intimate that he desires an Andacwandat feast – that is to say, many fornications and adulteries. His Riddle being guessed, there is no lack of persons to satisfy his desire."[3]

Iroquois dream-riddles belong to a larger ceremony of healing. Wallace is astute about their function in maintaining the health of Iroquois society, including the mental and emotional health of the warriors. As with the riddle-dreams in Genesis, whose correct reading by Joseph will help to heal Egypt of famine, so here. So also in Sophocles' ancient Thebes, where the sphinx's riddle must be solved to heal Thebes of its

---

3 Wallace, "Dreams and the Wishes of the Soul," pp. 53, 61–5 passim.

plague.[4] So also with modern psychoanalysis, where reading dreams correctly will help to cure or alleviate.

Robert Sands, apparent inventor of the phrase "Chinese boxes," was intrigued with native life and drew on Father P. de Charlevoix's records to describe another riddle custom:

Previous to entering the enemies' country, the warriors ran about their camp, proclaiming their obscure visions; and he whose riddle was not satisfactorily guessed, had the privilege of returning without comment or dishonour. . . These enigmas, as the author repeatedly remarks, were always ascribed to the inspiration of a genius.[5]

This is a neck-riddle in advance, so to speak, permitting a warrior to opt out of battle honorably, or so Charlevoix reported.

The ancient oracles also had a practical function. In legendary oracles, priests and priestesses were forbidden to reveal the god's specific knowledge of the future. They could speak only in riddles. Joseph Fontenrose argues that historical answers at Delphi were not ambiguous and obscure; these are characteristics of legendary oracles (quoted in Ahl, *Sophocles' Oedipus*, p. 26). Michael Wood also observes that some answers from the oracle were quite clear, for example, "Do not fence off the isthmus; Do not dig." In Herodotus, political leaders regularly consult the oracles, much as Macbeth consults the witches. Such consulting was not simply for religious reasons. Delphic priests amassed a good deal of useful information about the Greek world and beyond, simply because the oracle was constantly being visited.[6]

Plutarch sharply differentiates the enigma of the E at Delphi and the *ainigmata* of the oracles: "people were coming to look with suspicion upon metaphors, riddles and ambiguous statements [*metaphoras . . . ainigmata . . . amphibolias*], feeling that these were secluded nooks of refuge devised for furtive withdrawal and retreat for him that should err in his prophecy."[7] He especially attacked charlatans at the shrines of the Great Mother and of Sarapis ("Oracles at Delphi," 407c). Vague and obscure *ainigmata* offered by the oracles were different in kind from the *ainigma* of the E at Delphi. Oracles could mislead their petitioners and

---

4 Bernard Knox comments on the medical language in *Oedipus Rex* and on Oedipus as physician (*Oedipus at Thebes*, p. 139 and passim).
5 "Thine the riddle, strange and dark" (*The Writings of Robert C. Sands*, vol. 1, p. 371).
6 H. D. F. Kitto, *The Greeks* (London: Penguin, 1951), pp. 82–3.
7 "Oracles at Delphi" 407a–b, cited in Stroumsa, "Myth as Enigma," p. 273.

cause calamity. The learned men interpreting the E at Delphi were not engaged with riddles as if they were soothsayers.

The riddle within a religious rite does not function as practical magic, not directly, at any rate, and not at all in one's own religion, only in other people's. In James Kelso's 1918 entry on "Riddle," the last category is titled "Riddle in religious ceremonies." It sets the tone in the first sentence: "The strangest use of riddles to the modern mind is in connection with religious rites and ceremonies." Kelso notes some uses of riddles at the time of death or of harvest, in Greek oracles, at Dionysian festivals, and notably in the Vedic hymns. (These last are commonly cited as the oldest riddles we possess, for example, in the *New Princeton Encyclopedia of Poetry and Poetics.*) But while the riddles themselves are worthy of admiration, their use in religious rite is not. And yet, under "types," Kelso includes (2a, enigma proper) scriptural examples from the Christian Bible, including Ezekiel and the conversations of Jesus with Nicodemus. Nor does he consider that parts of Christian ritual, for example, reciting the Apostles' Creed, could readily be cast in question-and-answer form so as to correspond rhetorically to the Vedic riddle hymn. Some portions would sound decidedly enigmatical to a person unfamiliar with Christian doctrine. "The strangest use of riddles to the modern mind" is strange only in someone else's religion.

Political riddles may be defined as, first, riddles based on current politics. Thus, for example, the cat-rat riddle quoted by Josephine Tey in *The Daughter of Time*:

> The Cat, the Rat, and Lovel our Dog
> Rule all England under a Hog.

The answer to this Tudor riddle is the Plantagenet, Richard III, whose badge was a white boar (the Hog); in his reign, William Catesby was Speaker of the House of Commons and Richard Ratcliffe was a Commissioner of Peace with Scotland. The function of this political riddle in its day was to deride the conquered Plantagenets. No genuine riddling was involved. Everyone knew the answer. In 1881 David Fitzgerald classified this as a historic riddle ("Of Riddles," p. 188), which is what political riddles become after their occasion is forgotten.

Another example offered by Fitzgerald (ibid.) is an epitaph for a Royalist from the time of the Revolution:

> Here lies wise and valiant dust,
> Huddled up 'twixt fit and just . . .
> One in extremes loved and abhorred;

> *Riddles lie here*, or in a word
> Here lies Blood, and let it lie,
> Speechless still and never cry.

Thus also presumably the broadside, *A Riddle of State, or, the Parliament Triumphant. To the tune of, The pink petticoat lac'd round* (London, 1689, hence just after the "bloodless revolution"). Thus also many another political broadside. Hester Thrale Piozzi in her *British Synonymy* of 1794 quotes Lord Bacon's enigmatical prophecy on Hempe: *H*enry, *E*dward, *M*ary, *P*hilip, *E*lizabeth, after which England ended and the United Kingdom began with James I ("riddles," vol. II, p. 221). Some ingenious political riddles do come with a certain rhetorical force. See, for example, Matthew Prior's 1710 lampoon on Godolphin, "The Riddle," working with the sphinx's riddle (quoted in chapter 1 above). But most political riddles are content with crude allegory. Swift, a master political satirist, exchanged riddles in letters to friends and boasted of his prowess at them, but they remained largely private rather than political. Thus, for example, in "The Dean of St. Patrick's to Thomas Sheridan" (1718):

> As for your new rebus, or riddle, or crux,
> I will either explain, or repay it by trucks;
> Though your lords, and your dogs, and your catches, methinks,
> Are harder than ever were put by the Sphinx.
>
>   And thus I am fully revenged for your late tricks,
> Which at present is all from
>
> Dean of St. Patrick's

Riddles may also be used to conceal information for political purposes. As with Uraon hunters and their kennings to avert danger, so also in the political arena. No open taunting here; the riddle is closer to its traditional rhetorical function as an obscure allegory, a closed simile. Slaves may want to hide information and sentiments from their masters, or masters from their slaves. The spirituals of southern African-Americans in the days of slavery sometimes offered a temporal as well as a purely spiritual reading. The two readings are not necessarily contradictory, and some slave-owners were uneasy about spirituals. "Swing low, sweet Chariot, / Coming for to carry me home," for example, refers to death in the common trope of passing over the River Jordan and a memory of the biblical chariot that carried Elijah heavenward. But it also refers to the northern constellation we call the Big Dipper, and the British call the Wain or Chariot. Crossing an earthly type of the River Jordan and going north meant freedom in this life, not simply freedom from this life. The spiritual does not pose a question in riddle form, but offers a double allegory. (Older rhetoricians would say a double allegory of the species enigma.) Political riddles may be part of an end-directed masterplot, as with this African-American spiritual where both temporal and teleological ends are encompassed. But they are not in the first instance end-directed; they very much have to do with means.

So convenient is the riddle for concealing politically seditious thinking that a riddle written below a painting in Dijon in the seventeenth century caused much disquiet, until it was solved. The "ambiguous nature of the riddle made it ideally suited to the propaganda of potentially seditious material." The answer proved to be innocuous. ("Multum Tardat Divio Rixam" was interpreted as "Moult-tarde Dijon-noise," in a play on Dijon mustard.) As Jennifer Montagu also points out, the technique is the same as in Rabelais' prophetic riddle at the end of *Gargantua* Book I (see p. 52 above), and also in any riddle with an apparently obscene answer and an innocent solution (Montagu, "The Painted Enigma," p. 309).

On the other end of the social scale, those in charge may conceal in riddles what they do not wish everyone to know. Thus in Plato's *Letters*:

you say that you are not satisfied with the demonstration of the nature of the first principle. I must state it to you in riddles, so that in case something happens to the tablet "by land or sea in fold on fold," he who reads may not understand. . . Take precautions, however, lest this teaching ever be disclosed among untrained people . . . (*Letters* II.312e, 314a)[8]

What follows in the *Letters* is very general but hardly riddling in the usual sense, certainly not like the trivial dinner-table riddles that Plato despised.

Spies make use of puzzles rather than riddles in their cryptography. They make use of secret knowledge when they use a password. Sometimes the password depends on pronunciation, like "shibboleth" in Judges 12: 1–6. (The Dutch under Nazi occupation tested suspected German agents by asking them to pronounce the name of a Dutch town, Scheveningen.) Sometimes private rather than secret knowledge is required, for example, the private family knowledge that can confirm one's identity. Penelope sets Odysseus a riddle-challenge without telling him what she is doing, when she asks the maid to move their marriage-bed. The genuine Odysseus would know that the bed cannot be moved, for it is part of a great tree (*Odyssey* XXIII.173–204). Concealment of a name for espionage and similar purposes may have little sense of riddling.

---

8 Plato, *Letters*, trans. L. A. Post, in *Collected Dialogues*.

Diplomatic language could also take the form of a riddle that both conceals and reveals. Setting and answering riddles was apparently once a skill required of upper-level Foreign Service personnel. The practice goes back centuries, and there was a good deal of advantage to it. Much could be implied without being recorded explicitly. It was even possible to avoid words altogether.

The Emperor Marcus Aurelius finds that his revenues are steadily decreasing and sends messengers to Judah, the patriarch, for counsel. Instead of giving a verbal reply, the latter takes the imperial emissaries out to his garden, where he uproots the larger plants and replaces them with smaller. The royal ambassadors return without any message, but report the strange actions of the rabbi to their royal master, who fully comprehends the symbolism of the act and follows the advice given to him in this strange manner. (Kelso, "Riddle," p. 766)

That is, the Emperor promptly gets rid of his senior administrators, replacing them with younger men. This is more allegory than riddle. (Kelso calls it a rebus, using the term for an allegory that is acted out.) A parallel story is told of Tarquin Superbus, but the heads of his garden plants are lopped off (Bryant, *Dictionary of Riddles*, p. 15). Tarquin was known for his ruthlessness, and, sure enough, executions followed.

One of the oldest riddles is a diplomatic one, cited in Aristotle: "what Stesichorus said to the Locrians, that they ought not to be insolent, lest their cicadas should be forced to chirp from the ground" (*Rhet.* II.xxi.8–9, Loeb). The riddle's context is political, for it carries the threat of war. Cicadas will have to chirp from the ground if your enemy lays waste your land and cuts down your trees. (If they are olive trees, your economy will be ruined.) The riddle was repeated over the centuries, all the way down to an echo in John Hollander's "Afternoon and Afterwards." The first refrain about sailboats in the poem is logical and easy. But the second?

> The cicadas sing upon the ground
> (*As much as to say, the trees are felled*)

If writers do not signal a riddle as such, another layer of riddling is added, a double concealment. Thus here, where lines 3–4 lie waiting for the right occasion, as for example, when a reader has been looking at Aristotle's *Rhetoric* or Demetrius' *On Style*.[9] Cicada sound has elicited the memory of that ancient riddle in Hollander's poem, as if several ears had heard the self-same song over some twenty-four centuries. As with Keats's

---

9 Demetrius, *On Style* II.99–100, Loeb, where it is ascribed to Dionysius.

nightingale ode, insect song overleaps history, and conjoins listeners otherwise far apart. As riddle, the answer and function have changed, but how far? Cicadas now chirp from the ground. What battle to lay waste what land is echoing here in Long Island?

Churchill's famous 1939 description of the former Soviet Union evokes this tradition of diplomatic riddling, for it offers the entire country as a triple enigma, wrapped onion-like in layers of riddling. ("I cannot forecast to you the action of Russia. It is a riddle wrapped in a mystery inside an enigma.") Kenneth Burke highlights the words *sub integumento* (under concealment) and *involucrum* (wrapped) in St. Bernard's description of how Virgil enfolds the understanding of truth under a fabled narration. He observes both words in Alan of Lille, and his remarkable eye notes how Jeremy Bentham refers to "*tegumen* and *res tegenda* in his remarks on the use of 'eulogistic coverings' as rhetorical concealments of motives." Burke's own interest is in "the *social* implications of the enigmatic, in keeping with Marx on 'ideology,' Carlyle on 'Clothes,' and Empson on 'Pastoral.'" He conflates "enigma" and "mystery," and associates both with magic. "Rhetorically considered, the acceptance of the 'enigma' as an element in a symbol's persuasiveness has led us to note the place of 'magic' or 'mystery' both as a passive reflection of class culture and as an active way of maintaining cultural cohesion."[10] Churchill's well-known description is also political, though the politics differs considerably from Burke's.

Riddle contests may be the sport of kings, as in the ancient contests mentioned in Plutarch's "Dinner of the Seven Wise Men" (see chapter 5). Josephus records that both Hiram and his father, kings of Tyre, engaged in riddle-contests with Solomon, who usually – but not always – won. "A great deal of money," according to Josephus, flowed back and forth over the border, depending on who won. Another account says that Solomon won all the contests, discovering the "hidden meaning" of "sophisms and enigmatical sayings" (Josephus, *The Antiquities of the Jews*, pp. 222–3). He needed no seven wise men, being himself a wise judge in Israel and the writer of wisdom literature.

Riddle contests can also be more threatening, like Samson's in Judges 14 or the Sphinx's on the road to Thebes. J. R. R. Tolkien, a scholar of Old English literature, invents a neck-riddle contest in chapter 5 of *The*

10 Burke, *A Rhetoric of Motives*, pp. 173–4. He is drawing on Richard McKeon's survey of medieval rhetoric.

Hobbit, "Riddles in the Dark." ("If precious asks, and it doesn't answer, we eats it, my preciouss" [*sic*, p. 68].) The contest includes some classic riddles such as an egg riddle, a time riddle, and so on, relating them to the above-ground and underground habitats of the two contestants. The hobbit "knew, of course, that the riddle-game was sacred and of immense antiquity, and even wicked creatures were afraid to cheat when they played at it. But he felt he could not trust this slimy thing . . . And after all that last question [a Samson-like riddle] had not been a genuine riddle according to the ancient laws" (p. 74). This is riddle as means of war, a duel of wits with deadly consequences. We have left far behind a pleasant social pastime – conversational to-and-fro, repartee, game, challenge, battle of wits. This different kind of combat takes us all the way through to the neck-riddle, even the neck-riddle involving an entire group or people.

INNOCENT AMUSEMENT: COLLECTORS AND COLLECTIONS

There are thousands of riddle collections and collectors, from ancient times to the present, and in so many cultures that the challenge must be to find a culture lacking riddles. "No other species of oral lore, not even the proverb, has been collected so often . . . Printed riddle books, too, such as the one Alice Shortcake borrowed from Master Slender, have been popular for four centuries (latterly only with children)."[11] Riddles come at every level of difficulty, like chess games on the computer. There are renowned collections, just as there are renowned single riddles and renowned riddle-masters. The oldest printed riddle book is said to be from Strasbourg, published in 1505 (Röhrich, "Rätsel"). The first printed collection of English riddles was the *Demaundes Joyous*, published in 1511 by Wynkyn de Worde. De Worde took twenty-nine of his fifty-four riddles from *Demandes joyeuses en manière de quolibets*, omitting most of the obscene French riddles. But obscene riddles are said to have helped cure Henry VIII of dangerous melancholy, and various Elizabethan riddle books do include them. It all depends on the temper of the times.[12]

Who collected riddles? The clergy, from early on, in England and France and elsewhere. (These included prominent clergy like St. Aldhelm

---

11 Opie and Opie, *The Lore and Language of Schoolchildren*, p. 73. Master Slender's "Book of Riddles" is in Shakespeare's *The Merry Wives of Windsor* I.i.201–5.
12 For an engaging account of obscene and scatological riddles in the Renaissance, see John Wardroper's Introduction to *The Demaundes Joyous*, *passim*.

and Tatwin, Archbishop of Canterbury, both in the eighth century.) In the seventeenth century, the remarkable Mexican Sister Juana Inés de la Cruz (1651–95) wrote a small collection. Women collectors are common, from the eighteenth century on, as a title-check of rare-book libraries will demonstrate. Those interested in national literatures collected them, and still do. Folklorists with a professional interest recorded and collected them, and still do. Anthropologists and travelers recorded them, and still do. Children collected them, and still do, or did in 1959: "A curious feature about riddles is the way many children, when they hear them, like writing them down and making collections of them" (Opie, "Riddles," p. 73).

A sampling of just a few well-known Western riddle collections would begin with those written by Symphosius in late antiquity, move to Aldhelm's and Tatwin's, as well as the Old English riddles in the *Exeter Book*, then Claret's in the Middle Ages, then Reusner's in the Renaissance and many another. These collections not only pass on the best-known (sometimes the best) riddles, but also occasionally provide an excellent introduction to the subject. Mark Bryant's 1990 *Dictionary of Riddles* is in this last tradition, and, true to form, provides a good introductory history of riddle collections (pp. 12–51). Archer Taylor's excellent and throrough account of literary riddle collections makes up most of *The Literary Riddle before 1600*. Nicholas Reusner's collection, *Aenigmatographia* (2nd edn., 1602), is one of the most remarkable, a generous anthology of classic riddle collections and some commentary. A near-contemporary discussion of *aenigma* by Lilius Gregorius Gyraldus opens the collection, and numerous examples follow. These are arranged mostly in loose chronological order: riddles from Cleobulus and Heraclitus and Homer, the Sphinx's riddle, Samson's riddle, the riddle of Jocasta, Virgil's riddle, Athenaeus, a dialogue by Jacobus Pontanus on *aenigma*, riddles from Athenaeus and Camerarius, Ausonius' Terminus riddle, Pythagoras' mystical sayings, riddles from Symphosius and Scaliger and Aldhelm, and more. One *logogriphus Germanicus* by Luther is given:

> Es ist ein Wort dass hat ein L.
> Wer es ansicht begehrt es schnell.
> Wann abr das L. wegt und ab ist
> Nichts bessers im Himl und erden ist.

(There is a word that has an l. Who looks at it desires it fast. But when the l is taken away, there's nothing better in heaven and earth. Answer: Goltt/Gott, i.e., Gold/God.)

Some earlier collectors disguised their names. They appeared anonymously in collections with no given author or by "a Lady" or "A Friend to Innocent Mirth." Or they appeared under their initials: W. B., Gent. or "the Revd. Doctor D—y." Some enjoyed fanciful pseudonyms: Asdryasdust Tossoffacan (1674), Thomas Thumb (1786), Peter Puzzlewell (1792), Peregrine Puzzlebrains (1799), Hilaire le Gai (1860).

Introductions to these various collections would make a study in themselves. When not perfunctory, most are concerned to justify their pursuit. They often stress how venerable the practice of riddling is, and how the most intelligent of the ancients enjoyed it. Sometimes scripture is enlisted on the side of riddling, using arguments familiar from Augustine through to John Bunyan:

> In things obscure, oft lies the greatest good;
> Gospel was so, before 'twas understood:
> This way our Saviour for our weakness deem'd
> The best, to make things pretious but esteem'd.
> (W. B., "Moral" of "A Riddler,"
> *Sphynx Thebanus*, 1664)

> And all th'Enigma shone in Joseph's breast,
> While he unfolded each abstruse decree,
> That foil'd th'Egyptian vers'd in mystery!
> (Peter Puzzlewell, "Introductory Address,"
> *A Choice Collection*, 1792)

Sometimes sacred riddles are carefully cordoned off from secular ones, as in Abbé Cotin's "Discours sur les énigmes." (Why make more obscure what is already obscure? Shouldn't these matters be clarified as far as possible?) Some collectors mention mental exercise as a benefit. Applying logic or exercising the wits is usually offered as a good in itself. This seemed self-evident centuries before observations of the brain's activities confirmed it. Nowadays "use-it-or-lose-it" advice routinely includes kinds of riddling as one type of mental stimulation.

Most collections from the nineteenth century to the present are for children or young people, and some became popular. *The Riddle Book. For the entertainment of all young masters and misses*, a 23-page pamphlet by the Reverend Patrick Delany, was printed four times from 1817 to 1825. The author identified himself only as "the Revd. Doctor D—y." Some, however, are aimed at an adult audience, as were many earlier ones. The frontispiece to Peter Puzzlewell's *A Choice Collection of Riddles, Charades, Rebusses, &c.* (London, 1792) illustrates the social pastime

Frontispiece.

The Solution of a Riddle.

Figure 9. Frontispiece titled "The Solution of a Riddle" from Peter Puzzlewell, *A Choice Collection of Riddles, Charades, Rebusses, &c.* (London, 1792).

of riddling in the persons of several well-dressed men and women gathered around a table in a drawing-room. A woman holding a book, presumably Puzzlewell's, is in charge. It is titled "The Solution of a Riddle." Charles Sorel's *Les Récréations galantes* from a century earlier (Paris 1671) was decidedly not for children. The game of enigmas ("Jeu des Enigmes") is sometimes played with forfeits, as follows: "[The game of enigmas] is also played by having a man propose a riddle [un Enigme] to a woman; if she cannot solve it, he has permission to kiss her.

Afterwards, she proposes a riddle to him, and, if he cannot solve it, she condemns him to anything she pleases" (p. 87). The Game of Labyrinth also comes with forfeits, which seem to be the chief point of these *récréations galantes.*

The rhetorical force of collected riddles varies enormously, as we might expect. So does the rhetorical maturity of the collectors who write introductions. Still, any collection that wanted to survive did need some wit and humor, some clever turn to appeal to the taste of the day. A number of collectors wanted to do something more, notably to add to knowledge and stimulate the mind. Sometimes this is a mere advertising ploy, but not always. Samuel Tizzard's *The New Athenian Oracle, or Ladies' Companion . . . designed for the improvement of the fair sex* (London: A. Loudon, 1806) includes "questions in prose, on moral, philosophical and other subjects, together with a great number of enigmas, paradoxes, rebuses, charades, &c.: also . . . mathematical questions." The questions in all areas of knowedge are serious and reasonably advanced. As for stimulating the mind, the *Thesaurus Aenigmaticus* (1725–26) offers readers the chance

to try their Skill in resolving of Aenigmas and Questions, which will not only whet the Appetite of both Sexes to the Love of Literature in General, but occasionally provoke them to the reading much Poetry and History in particular; and at the same time put them into a serious and methodical way of Thinking on any Subject, which by all must be acknowledg'd no small Advantage to the Mind. (Preface)[13]

By far the most common motive given is amusement. Amusement of an evening, before the advent of undemanding television or isolating computer, could take the form of a challenge of wits. *Sphynx Thebanus, with his Oedipus,* the 1664 collection by W. B., Gent., proclaims itself on the title page as *Excellently suiting with the Fancies of Old and Young, and exceeding useful to advance a Cheerful Society and to continue and preserve Mirth.* ("Cheerful" is a biblical word, much commended there.) He also hoped "this little Treatise . . . prove digestive to the Mind, as Fruit and Cheese after Meat doth to the Stomach" (sig. A4v). An 1800 collection from Edinburgh calls itself *Winter Evenings Pastime: consisting of a choice & extensive collection of riddles, rebuses, charades, and Scots proverbs. Well calculated to "set the table on a roar".*[14]

13 *Thesaurus Aenigmaticus* (London: printed for John Wilford, 1725–26).
14 *Winter Evenings Pastime* (Edinburgh: Printed for T. Brown, North Bridge, by J. Moir, Paterson's Court, 1800).

Riddle collections offered for youngsters, especially those compiled by women or the clergy, often stress their innocent amusement. How early did the phrase "innocent merriment" become a catchword, so that Gilbert and Sullivan could use it in *The Mikado* with fine resonance. ("And make each prisoner pent / Unwillingly represent / A source of innocent merriment / Of innocent merriment.") "Innocent merriment," "innocent amusement," "innocent whatever" is the repeated aim of numerous riddle collections. Coleridge agreed: "I am perhaps not the only one who has derived an innocent amusement from the riddles, conundrums, tri-syllable lines, &c. &c. of Swift and his correspondents, in hours of languor when to have read his more finished works would have been useless to myself, and, in some sort, an act of injustice to the author."[15]

So often does the word "innocent" appear that a reader begins to wonder what non-innocent amusement is. Perhaps these collections wanted to distance themselves from what Henry Peacham called "unchaste or unclean" riddles – "of which sort there be many of our English riddles." Some riddle collections proclaim themselves fit for "people of high taste." Thus *A Key to the Witling* (London, 1750), *being proper answers to a compleat collection of the most celebrated conundrums now in vogue among people of high taste.* No author is listed or ascribed in the Beinecke Library catalogue. A few collectors were explicit: "they ought to be on modest Subjects . . . that Greek who made one on that the Latins call *Podex*, hath, methinks, entail'd a perpetual Disgrace on his Memory" (*Thesaurus Aenigmaticus*, 1725–26, "Of Ænigmas," p. ii). In 1791, an anonymous compiler pronounced her collection "perfectly free from everything that has a pernicious tendency, which is more than can be said for many works of genius" (*A New Collection of Enigmas*, p. v). The temper of the times can be inferred from riddle collections or analyses where the answers to rude riddles are not given. In a 1747 issue of *The Fool*, examples of the epigrammatic style are provided from gravestones. "The Third is truly Enigmatic . . . 'Here lies one bereav'd of Life, / Who was my Mother, Mistress, Sister, and my Wife'" But, says the author, "when brought to Light, [this] only tells a bad Story; I therefore shall not unriddle it" (*The Fool*, no. 75, 21 Jan. 1747, 186). Archer Taylor omits the riddles under "Erotic Scenes" in his 1951 collection. He "deemed it

15 Samuel Taylor Coleridge, *Biographia Literaria*, ed. James Engell and W. Jackson Bate (Princeton: Princeton University Press, Bollingen, 1983), chap 3, pp. 62–63.

sufficient to cite the answers to these riddles with the references to the places where they have been printed" (*English Riddles from Oral Tradition*, p. 687). The practice is akin to translating Greek works into Latin, but retaining the Greek for sexually suggestive passages. As noted in chapter 2, older rhetorical handbooks mostly assume a certain sense of decorum, thereby teaching it indirectly.

The hazard to innocence might not be rude or obscene riddles. The anonymous compiler of *A New Collection of Enigmas* (1791) promoted her book thus: "Many an hour is passed innocently in the amusement these trifles supply, that might otherwise be sacrificed to cards, which generally excite baneful passions" (p. vi). Earlier, the *Thesaurus Aenigmaticus* cast a wider net: "For what Exercise can be more beneficial to those, who will give themselves Leisure from Sports and Gaming" (Preface).

Collections are usually in a single language now, though Renaissance ones like Reusner's could be centered on riddles in the lingua franca of Latin, with others added in vernacular languages. A compiler may augment a single-language collection with foreign riddles (more risqué? more à la mode? more demanding?). Louisa Thompson's *"Guess if you can!"* advertises itself in its sub-title as *A collection of original enigmas and charades in verse: together with fifty in the French language by a lady* (London, 1851). Some riddles will not travel from one language to another. Arithmetical riddles (often excluded from true riddles) readily do so. (How can you remove 1 from 19 and get 20? Answer: xix − 1 = xx.) The twelve-plus-thirty half-black half-white riddle is in the *Arabian Nights*, and works perfectly well in English too (months of a year and days of a month, night and day). Riddles turning on verbal play do not.

Like other national matters, collections gathered according to nation or people can sometimes turn nationalist and generate heat, especially in the matter of folk riddles. In 1877, Eugène Rolland published his collection, *Devinettes et énigmes populaires de la France*, with a preface by Gaston Paris. By that date, German scholars were easily preeminent in the Western study of folk literature, including folk riddles. But, says Gaston Paris airily, with a *sangfroid* no doubt maddening to many German readers, the entire enterprise of Germanic scholarship on the subject of folk riddles is easily explained: the German sense of nationality is not yet established. In Germany and the Slavic countries, such studies are natural, given "nationalities [les nationalités] still hesitant, which have been seeking gropingly to form a historical consciousness [une conscience historique]." France, "strongly unified and deeply imbued with the ideas of civilization," could not possibly take the same interest in such matters (p. v).

Some cultures are fonder of riddles than others. The Greeks enjoyed them greatly. The Romans did not, though modern Italians appear to do so.[16] Sanskrit riddles from about 1000 BCE are closer to wisdom questions than to riddles.[17] An old Nordic riddling tradition survives in the *Elder Edda* and notably in the contest in the *Hervarar Saga*, with its rhythm of one formulaic response ("Good is your enigma, Gestumblindi; it is solved").[18] Both Jews and Arabs are heirs to vigorous and subtle riddling traditions. Nowadays there are journals devoted to riddles and at least one popular radio show, the Israeli program on riddles called "The Hanitzer Quiz."[19]

Two major medieval poets and riddle-masters, one Jewish and one Arab, were contemporaries. Jehuda Halevi was the outstanding Hebrew poet of southern Spain in his day (he died in 1139). "No festive occasion was considered complete that was not celebrated by Jehuda's muse. . . Besides these official epithalamia and epitaphs, Jehuda contributed to the social gatherings of which he formed part many short and witty poems, containing riddles, which were then the fashion." One sample reads:

> Happy lovers, learn our law,
>   Be joined in one, as we;
> Aught that parts us through we saw,
>   And again are one, you see.
>   [Pair of Scissors][20]

Joseph Jacobs calls such riddles "elegant trifles": no nineteenth-century disparagement of riddles in his 1896 account, but instead a measured enjoyment. Thus also the nineteenth-century Larousse *Grande Encyclopédie* concerning acted charades: "un de nos plus jolis jeux de société" (one of our prettiest social amusements). Leopold Löw and Israel Abrahams also mention the Jewish practice of riddle-setting in the Middle Ages, and Dan Pagis's study of some three hundred Hebrew riddles written from

---

16 In 1926, the gold medal for a worthy book on the subject of riddles was bestowed on the collection *Enimmistica* (Céard and Margolin, *Rébus de la Renaissance*, p. 97n, on the Fédération Enigmistique Italienne).

17 *Rig-Veda*, Book 1, hymn 164. See Taylor, *The Literary Riddle before 1600*, pp. 13–14; Caillois includes "Le Tournoi de la Vajasameyi Samhita," trans. Louis Renou, in his *Art Poétique*, pp. 167–70.

18 "Le Tournoi d'Enigmes de la Herverar-Saga," trans. and ed. Pierre Renauld, in Caillois, *Art Poétique*, pp. 171–88. For the riddles in English, see Bryant, *Dictionary of Riddles*, pp. 184–5 (no edition given); he refers to "an attractive variant" of the saga's riddle contest in the "Faroese Riddle Ballad" (p. 17).

19 It is run by Dan Hanitzer, and invites the audience to phone in solutions. One contest went on for several months. I am indebted to Jon Whitman for this information.

20 Joseph Jacobs, *Jewish Ideals and Other Essays* (London: David Nutt, 1896), pp. 107–8.

before 1650 to after 1850 has already been noted.[21] The riddle series in the Passover Haggadah is well known.

Among Arab riddle-masters, Jehuda's contemporary, the great poet al-Hariri (b. 1054 in Basra, d. 1122), was preeminent. His *Assemblies* (*Maqamat*) enjoyed great popularity; Bryant calls them "a classic of the Arabic tongue second only to the Koran itself" (*Dictionary of Riddles*, p. 28). Various types of riddle appear among the many genres of the *Assemblies*, some turning on puns or grammatical play. The twenty-fourth Assembly includes grammatical riddles, also a favorite type among Jewish riddlers. They are set by an enigmatic visitor, who alone can solve them. "Now by Him who has sent down grammar into speech to be as salt in food, and has veiled its risings from the perceptions of the vulgar": so begin the solutions.

Then he slipped away as slips the serpent, and sped with the speeding of the cloud. – And I knew then that he was the light of Serûj; the full moon of scholarship that passes through the signs of heaven. – And our end was grief at his departure and separation after he was gone. (al-Hariri, *Assemblies*, pp. 247–8)

Taylor provides several examples from al-Hariri, noting also that "the enigmatic art has long been popular among writers of Arabic, but rather few examples have been translated into western European languages."[22] Riddles are included in some stories in the *Arabian Nights*.

Sociologists are interested in the process of "socialization"; the literary reading of riddles is another matter. John McDowell, in his helpful *Children's Riddling*, puts it this way:

Socialization is concerned with the techniques, whereby first the family, later the peer group, and finally official and unofficial social authorities influence, contain, or control (depending on your ideological proclivity) the behavior of the individual. In the acquisition of riddling competence, the socialization process resides in the negotiation of riddling, the emergent adjustment of individual forays and strategies to socially sanctioned riddling etiquette. In learning to negotiate riddling, the child learns to formulate proper riddling vehicles, and eventually to produce the telling incongruity native to the genre, in order to participate actively as a valued riddler. (pp. 221–2)

David Fitzgerald recorded in 1881 how the Highland Scots and the Senegalese both enjoyed the pastime of riddle-setting. "Of less artificial

---

21 Löw "Räthsel und Witzesspiele," provides an updated list of those writing poetic riddle-literature. Abrahams observes that "It is almost impossible to differentiate between the riddle and the metaphor" (*Jewish Life in the Middle Ages*, p. 408).

22 *The Literary Riddle before 1600*, p. 31. Taylor provides an excellent short introduction to both Arab and Jewish literary riddle traditions (pp. 17–42).

societies may be instanced Scottish Highlanders, among whom riddle-setting, according to Mr. Alexander Mackenzie, is still one of the pastimes which beguile the tedium of the long nights of winter" ("Of Riddles," p. 179). A true picture of the pastime survives "in rude society" (ibid.) such as the Wolofs of Senegal, as described by Abbé Boilat. In 1877 Eugène Rolland quoted Boilat on the practice of riddle-setting among the Senegalese and how much they enjoyed it. "In the evening by moonlight or by a corner of the fire, gathered in a group, the Wolofs challenge each other through riddle questions with great bursts of laughter [de grands éclats de rire]." After a correct reply, everyone calls out "*Weuc neu deug!* (he has spoken true)." If the riddle is difficult, they hold their chins and call out "*Bissimilay Dhiame!* (in the name of the God of truth [Dieu de vérité])" (*Devinettes*, p. 168n). There is something here that the language of "socialization" misses, perhaps because the language of sociologists is so solemn. Is the practice of sociology itself a form of socialization? If so, it is apparently nothing like as much fun as riddle-setting among the Senegalese. But perhaps subversive sociologists enjoy themselves by holding secret riddle sessions as a socialization process.

The hundreds of riddle collections gathered, transcribed, and published over the centuries are chiefly meant for entertainment. Social norms are being taught, of course, a process that is clearer in less familiar societies. In Berber communities in North Africa, for example, rude or obscene riddles ("des énigmes 'grossières'") are propounded only in groups of the same sex, and they are rare. Youcef Allioui speaks of the Berber code of conduct in which vulgarity is shameful. Berber riddle contests are spirited, enjoyable, and formal occasions. The atmosphere, says Allioui, is indescribable:

Lined up in two facing rows, eyes sparkling with happiness, each person listens, feels and experiences [sens et ressens], "drinks in" each word. Each enigma is experienced as an event. It is awaited in silence and welcomed with emotion. Before asking oneself about the key to the enigma, one asks about its words. One also asks oneself about the context of its creation. One also loves the enigma for its poetry, its meaning. . . That is why I have written that "in enigmas, it is not guessing the object that matters most, but the rhyme, the assonance, the choice of words and especially the hidden sense that is only known to those who have been able to live the enigma [vivre l'énigme]." (pp. 245–6)

Here we have moved past a process of socialization to a process of absorbing language at an impressive level. Many a North American classroom does not reach this level of literary comprehension and enjoyment. Augustine's demanding North African congregations with their delight in *hilaritas* live on to this day in such communities.

Afterword: enigma, the boundary figure

> The unravelling of a riddle is the purest and most basic act of the
> human mind.
>
> (Vladimir Nabokov, *Speak, Memory*)

Enigma is a boundary figure in every aspect of its being. It always draws
attention to boundaries. Sometimes it invites action along or with a
boundary. In personified riddle, the boundaries of animal species are
crossed and common creatures change their shapes. In the most famous
Western story of a riddler, the Grecian Sphinx waits at the outer border
of Thebes, asking her question, a question that centers on the shifting
boundaries and crossings throughout a human life. Rhetorically, the trope
of dark similitude highlights strange joinings, odd borders, disrupted
boundaries. Familiar border-lines are reconfigured in funny or uncom-
fortable ways. Things change their look. In masterplots, larger boundaries
and shapes are in question, matters of life and death that bear on the
shape of a given life. Setting the boundaries for riddle as genre and
mode is always a challenge. Similarly with schematic riddles of the griph
type, in their ingenious rearranging of the usual categories. A simple
anagram changes the familiar order of letters in a single word, trans-
forming it into an unrecognizable scramble of letters. Solving an anagram
is a recognition scene in miniature. The common tropes for enigma rely on
boundaries for their force. Keys and locks, labyrinths and mazes, nets and
traps: always, there is a question of boundaries, a crucial troping of inside
and outside. Defining a word lexically is always a matter of boundaries.

Boundaries, borders, crossings. The most significant are birth and death,
the place of the opening riddle in chapter 2, Archer Taylor's Uraon birth-
and-death riddle. That is where I also want to end, but only after first
looking at our more casual forms of riddle.

Griph-type schematic riddles are easily the most common form of
riddle, certainly as a separate game apart from any literary treatment.

They are still boundary figures, though they do not have the force of birth-and-death riddles. They inhabit our more mundane, everyday world. Yet their familiar guise points toward a certain kind of thinking and behavior that helps to solve – or to live with – enigma's questions. We might well call this *metis* intelligence.

In 1974, Marcel Detienne and Jean-Pierre Vernant published an influential book on this topic, *Les Ruses de l'intelligence: la métis des Grecs*, translated as *Cunning Intelligence in Greek Culture and Society.* "*Metis* intelligence" is variously translated as "cunning intelligence," "practical intelligence," and so on. It is more than ordinary practical intelligence, however, for it is also wily, as need be. In Auden's poem "Under Which Lyre," Apollo is very practical indeed, but Hermes is wily. He has *metis* intelligence. It is more than street-smarts, for such intelligence can be highly learned, and it can work toward longterm goals. Though the *polutropos* man is a "man of the moment, a man of change: now one thing, now another," he is not an inconstant man. (For such a person, the term is *ephemeros* [*Cunning Intelligence*, p. 40].) Odysseus, commonly described as *polutropos*, literally "of many turnings," possesses *metis* intelligence. So do other sagacious rulers and riddle-masters like Solomon or Hiram. A recent book by Lisa Raphals argues for a Chinese equivalent of *metis* intelligence in the Confucian tradition. *Polutropos* includes the same word that gives us "trope," the class of figures of speech where ordinary meaning is altered or turned.

The tropes in Detienne and Vernant's description of *metis* intelligence sound very familiar: a knot, a labyrinth, weaving and twisting, snares:

The *poluplokos* octopus is a knot composed of a thousand interweaving arms; every part of its body is a bond which can secure anything but which nothing can seize. The fox, which is *poikilos*, lives in a labyrinth . . . The fox is a living bond which can bend, unbend, reverse its own position at will and, like the octopus, it is a master of bonds . . . To weave (*plekein*) and to twist (*strephein*) are key terms in the terminology connected with it. (pp. 40–1)

There is a further association of *metis* intelligence with the riddle, through the Greek word *griphos*, both as "a puzzle" and as "a fishing-net."

The sophist is also a master at interweaving for he is constantly entangling two contrary theses . . . Speeches like this are traps, *strephomena*, as are the puzzles set by the gods of *metis*, which the Greeks call *griphoi*, which is also the name given to some types of fishing-nets. With their twisting, flexing, interweaving and bending, both athletes and sophists – just like the fox and the octopus – can be seen as living bonds. (p. 42)

Detiennne and Vernant connect *metis* intelligence especially with early hunting and fishing for food for survival, though that connection has been disputed. They refer to literature from Homer to Oppian (p. 44).[1] The Uraons in India used specific kenning-riddles in hunting, as we have seen.

Metis intelligence also suggests an analogy for poets. Auden's trickster god, Hermes, in "Under Which Lyre" is clearly the patron of writers, and not his boring Apollo the bureaucrat. Writers, especially poets, belong more naturally to the many-troping Odysseus or the trickster type of hero than to the warrior Achilles or the *pius Aeneas* type.[2] Why? Because they are more astute about boundaries, about crossings. Because they know about tropes, small and large, to say nothing of schemes.

Enigma is a rhetorically a trope, and the power of troping is like a transformation of matter or energy, or like metamorphosis. Nor is this just an abstract "like." Thinking through a trope means thinking in a different way, expanding the brain, enlarging its energies. Thinking through a scheme does the same thing, in a lesser way. Why do people like cryptic-crossword, acrostic and similar puzzles?[3] In these games, we are challenged to make sense of things, to piece them together ("compose" in its root sense). Something in us finds the process of riddle-solving satisfying. Perhaps humans are riddle-solving and problem-solving creatures. Perhaps we like fictive or game encounters with riddle and enigma for atavistic reasons. The brain remembers or imagines life-threatening situations; it knows that riddle-solving keeps our wits alert.

Boundaries, borders, crossings. The association of riddle and enigma with birth and death is longstanding. Not so much with the results of birth and death, but rather with the process of crossing the boundary into life or into death.

Anthropologists record peoples where riddles are never asked except when there is a corpse in the village (among the Bolang Mongondo, Celebes), and others (in the Aru archipelago) where watchers by an uncoffined corpse expound riddles to each other (Kelso, "Riddle,"

---

1 The Loeb editor lists ten different words for kinds of nets in Oppian. A *griphos* "is the generic name for the draw-net or seine." See *Oppian, Colluthus, Tryphiodoros*, trans. and ed. A. W. Mair (London: Heinemann, 1928), p. xlii.
2 On the implications of such contrasting heroes for boys growing up, see Marina Warner's Reith Lectures, *Managing Monsters: Six Myths of Our Time* (London: Vintage, 1994), from "Boys Will Be Boys," pp. 24–31.
3 See, for example, Marcel Danesi, *The Puzzle Instinct: The Meaning of Puzzles in Human Life* (Bloomington: Indiana University Press, 2002).

p. 770). A remnant of this custom apparently survived in Brittany in the early twentieth century. There, "old men ... seat themselves on grave-stones and ask each other riddles after the friends of the deceased and the mourners have gone home" (ibid.). Similarly at wakes in Panama (see Robe, p. 3). Sphinxes were commonly guardians of graves, and their function was in part apotropaic. The great enigmas also often appear to have an apotropaic function, warding off death or monstrosity, including their threat to birth and generation. Thus with the famed Sphinx's riddle: an apparent monster proves to be merely a human, one of us.

The association of enigma with the processes of birth is just as prom-inent, perhaps more so. The school-book example of riddle over the centuries, the ice-water or "mater me genuit" riddle, tropes on mother and child. Other riddles also use tropes of generation. Henry Peacham offers this one: "I consume my mother that bare me. I eat up my nurse that fed me, then I die leaving them all blind that saw me. Meant of the flame of a candle, which when it hath consumed both waxe and waeke [wick], goeth out, leaving them in the darke which saw by it" (*The Garden of Eloquence*, "Aenigma"). As with the ice-water riddle, a normal genera-tive process is made to sound unnatural, until a simple answer solves everything. These are all metamorphoses of common elements, water and fire, commonly observed. Yet, like human procreation, whose workings are also well known, some sense of enigma lingers about the water and fire riddles. It *is* curious, even mysterious, to watch these transformations of matter. One of the oldest Western riddles is of this type: "Who becomes pregnant without conceiving? Who becomes fat without eating?" Answer: clouds. This is a semitic riddle recorded on a Babylonian tablet.[4] Simi-larly, Athenaeus tropes on day and night as giving birth, one to another (x.451–2) – not a transformation of matter but mysterious enough for all its familiarity. Similarly the well-known riddle "A father has twelve sons, each of them has thirty, half white, half black," which has as an answer: the year, the months, the days, the nights.[5]

Egg-riddles are old favorites. One German example reads:

> Es ist ein grosser Dom
> Der hat eine gelbe Blum
> Wer die gelbe Blum' will haben,
> Der muss den ganzen Dom zerschlagen.[6]

---

4 Bryant, *Dictionary of Riddles*, p. 1; Jäger, "Assyrische Räthsel und Spruchwörter," 277.
5 Quoted in, e.g., Rolland, ed., *Devinettes*, p. 1.
6 Gerber, *Die Sprache als Kunst* (1961), p. 492.

(There is a large, large dome / That has a golden flower. / Whoever wants the golden flower / Must dash to pieces all the dome.)

This example of the egg-riddle bears out Archer Taylor's judgment that eggs are not a fit poetic subject (see chapter 2). Jay Macpherson's poem "Egg" is of another order:

> Reader, in your hand you hold
> A silver case, a box of gold.
> I have no door, however small,
> Unless you pierce my tender wall,
> And there's no skill in healing then
> Shall ever make me whole again.
> Show pity, Reader, for my plight:
> Let be, or else consume me quite.

Macpherson's troping comes close to one of the ancient Babylonian riddles, for which Taylor suggests the solution: "A reference to a chest of silver and a casket of gold . . . is obviously an egg."[7] Egg-riddles encapsulate inside/outside troping. The egg is a sphere, a little world that contains a little world, possibly a new being. Cracking the shell is a birth process. Or we may break the shell and eat the inside, so that we ourselves contain this little world.

In the way riddle or enigma behaves, in the tropes we use of them, there is a likeness to the birth process. A question is answered. (What is the child like? or as in a riddle poem, "What am I? Name me.") Something obscure and in darkness is made clear and brought into the light. Something locked is opened, something hidden is revealed, and so on. The process involves a certain breaking of boundaries, and scholars who wish to be dramatic will even speak of the violence of certain literary forms. (See Claude Lévi-Strauss and Roger D. Abrahams below, on the riddle and incest.) Violence is part of childbirth, of course, including violent contrast of feeling, as all mothers know: great pain usually followed by great joy. When a mother delivers her child, a riddle is solved, but what remains is enigma (or poetry), the human life of a true enigma and the enigma of a human life. Nabokov, recalling the wonder of his newborn son, remarked on "an infant's first journey into the next dimension, the newly established nexus between eye and reachable object, which the career boys in biometrics or in the rat-maze racket think they can

---

7 Taylor, *The Literary Riddle before 1600*, p. 13. The ancient riddles are given in Jäger, "Assyrische Räthsel und Spruchwörter," 274–305.

explain . . . the riddle of the initial blossoming of man's mind" (*Speak, Memory*, p. 233).

Riddles have been connected with vegetable generation from the time of the Pentateuch. As noted, Peacham classifies under Enigma the Egyptian dream-riddles in Genesis, which turn on bounteous and then fatally scant crops (*The Garden of Eloquence*, "Aenigma"). Anthropologists record that riddles are sometimes asked at the time of harvest, to help ensure a bountiful harvest.[8] Dan Pagis also records a riddle by Jehuda Halevi: "What dies, cast upon the earth, is buried naked among men, / Yet lives again from in its grave, bears children, all emerging clad?" The answer is a seed, a grain of wheat: "the seed revives, sprouts, even bears many like itself and only afterward is buried, or sown. Moreover, it is buried naked, unlike human burial practice, yet its offspring are born clothed (in chaff, within the new wheat)" (Pagis, "Toward a Theory of the Literary Riddle," p. 78). Variations of the trope are common among the poets, and well known to us from Whitman, for example, who associates the trope with writing in the beautiful sixth section of "Song of Myself" (1881): "A child said *What is the grass?*. . . / . . . I guess the grass is itself a child, the produced babe of the vegetation."

Whitman's troping is beneficent, but most riddles about generation appear to turn on questions of unnatural generation, whether merely puzzling or ludicrously impossible or mildly spooky or monstrous and repugnant. The ice-water riddle and similar types set up a spectral possibility of generation gone awry, and then dispel the mini-nightmare. Some biblical riddles are of this type, where the normal human procreative process is made to sound unnatural. "Who was born before his father and died before his mother?" Answer: Abel.[9] Similarly with the Alsatian riddle "Wer gestorben und nit geboren sey?" (Who died and was never born?). Answer: Adam and Eve.

Sometimes the nightmare is not dispelled, as in the riddles whose answer is incest. One of the best known is the riddle from the romance of Apollonius of Tyre that Shakespeare uses in *Pericles* (1.i.64–71):

> I am no viper, yet I feed
> On mother's flesh which did me breed.
> I sought a husband, in which labour
> I found that kindness in a father.

---

8 See Kelso, "Riddle," p. 770, and Pagis, "Toward a Theory of the Literary Riddle," p. 98.
9 Quoted in Abrahams and Dundes, "Riddles," p. 134.

> He's father, son, and husband mild;
> I mother, wife – and yet his child.
> How may they be, and yet in two,
> As you will live, resolve it you.

In Shakespeare's play, this is a neck-riddle that Pericles answers obliquely, thus saving his life and endangering it all at once. The riddle frame for this play (already framed by Gower at the start of Act 1) invites us to attend to questions of sexual knowledge and generation in the main plot. An illicit and murderous father–daughter relation frames a miraculously redemptive father–daughter plot. A sense of impossible riddle informs the moving recognition scene between Marina and Pericles, the scene that so affected T. S. Eliot. The whole matter of lawful and unlawful generation, even more of natural and unnatural generation, is implicit throughout Shakespeare's play.

Sometimes the whole process of riddling is likened to incest. "Many commentators have referred to the relationship of the context of riddles with the 'incest-motive.' This seems especially appropriate in an understanding of the boundary-breaking activity of riddling, for nothing could confuse cultural categories more than the licensing of incest. . ." Roger D. Abrahams goes on to quote Claude Lévi-Strauss: "'like the solved riddle, incest brings together terms meant to remain separate: the son is joined with the mother, the brother with the sister, in the same way as the answer succeeds, against all expectations, in rejoining the question.'" But as Abrahams observes, Lévi-Strauss is arguing "by analogy, not homology."[10] The trope of incest sounds chiefly designed *pour épater le bourgeois*. Elli Köngäs-Maranda is more accurate in saying that "Riddles play with boundaries, but ultimately affirm them" (quoted in ibid., p. 22).

There are other riddles whose question concerns generation and whose answer is writing, and they go back over 2,500 years. Sappho, or so Athenaeus records, propounded the following riddle:

"There is a feminine being which keeps its babes safe beneath its bosom; they, though voiceless, raise a cry sonorous over the waves of the sea and across all the dry land, reaching what mortals they desire, and they may hear even when they are not there; but their sense of hearing is dull."

One riddlee, a male, suggests that the answer is the state (as mother) and her politicians (as babes). Sappho tells him not to talk nonsense.

---

10 Claude Lévi-Strauss, *Structural Anthropology*, vol. 11 (New York: Basic Books, 1976), pp. 22–4. Quoted in Abrahams, *Between the Living and the Dead*, pp. 20–2.

"The feminine being," she says, "is an epistle [the word *epistole* is feminine in Greek], the babes within her are the letters it carries round; they, though voiceless, talk to whom they desire when far away; yet if another happen to be standing near when it is read, he will not hear."

If this is the earliest troping of poetry as generative, then it first came in the form of a riddle and it first came from a female writer.[11] Goethe translated the version from the Greek Anthology in 1826: "Es gibt ein weiblich Wesen, / Im Busen trägt es Kinder. . ."[12] A similar riddle to Sappho's is offered by John Smith in *The Mystery of Rhetoric Unveiled* (1657): "*Cadmus* his daughters fram'd *Nilotis* quill, Whilst *Sepia* doth from *Cnidian* knot distill." The answer to this over-ingenious riddle, which is neater in Latin, translates as: "He writes love-letters in Greek." (Cadmus is inventor of the alphabet, the pen comes from reeds of the Nile, and so on [pp. 84–5].)

The association of riddle forms and generation and also writing – God's writing this time – is caught by Anthony Hecht in his remarkable poem "Riddles." It ends with a reference to a famous biblical enigma, the writing on the wall in the Book of Daniel. It begins almost whimsically, in a fine pun on a text from the Gospels that has become proverbial: "The wind bloweth where it listeth." Hecht's opening line (see below) also plays back against the poem's epigraph, "And the Spirit of God moved upon the face of the waters," with a touch as light as the wind's. The wind and the Spirit of God come voiceless from the natural world and the spiritual world. Hecht's verbal riddles trope these voiceless riddles through human language and art.

> Where the wind listeth, there the sailboats list,
>   Water is touched with a light case of hives
>   Or wandering gooseflesh.

In the Gospel echo, Jesus puns on the etymology of the word "spirit," which means "breath" or "wind" in both Hebrew and Greek (Gen. 1: 2: Hebrew *ruah* in the original, and Greek *pneuma* in the Septuagint). Life and breath also live in the etymology of "animates" in line 4, as Hecht extends his gaze, still as if at leisure.

---

11 Athenaeus says he is following Antiphanes. One of the numerous rumors about Sappho says she bore a daughter, while another says she was childless (*Sappho: A New Translation*, trans. Mary Barnard [Berkeley: University of California Press, 1958], p. 96).

12 Quoted in Biedermann, *Goethe als Rätseldichter*, p. 40.

> . . . The strange power and gist
>   Of whatever it is that animates our lives
>
> Scrawls with a lavish hand its signature
>   Of ripples gathered into folds and pleats
> As indecipherable, chiselled, pure,
>   And everlasting as the name of Keats.

With Keats, the face of the waters changes, moving to the outline of a single human being. (Keats wrote his own epitaph, carved on his gravestone in Rome: "Here lies one whose name was writ on water.") In the last stanza, we move from water and air to fire, as also from quotation and allusion to simple reference. The tone changes too, as Hecht's riddles gather in the reader and approach the condition of mystery, the mystery of ultimate judgment on our actions. Hecht does not quote the riddling words written on the wall by a mysterious hand at Belshazzar's feast, "Mene, mene, tekel, upharsin" or Daniel's interpretation.[13] A reference is as close as this poem wishes to come.

> [We] should be asking: "What do they portend?"
>   Other, please God, than those fiery words for coins
> That signified to Balshazzar the end
>   Of all his hopes and the issue of his loins.

Somehow, riddle and enigma have now come to encompass our world and our lives, quietly yet fully.

Writing, generation, birth, and death all come together in James Merrill's exquisite little riddle poem "b o d y." This is the type of riddle poem that offers its answer in its title, with the body of the poem providing the enigmatic characteristics. It is a small masterpiece, all in ten lines: a visual riddle, a punning riddle, a riddle linking the smallest of verbal units (a letter) with the largest of enigmas, a riddle pointing also to the first and last poems of Merrill's posthumous collection, *A Scattering of Salts.*[14]

> b o d y
>
> Look closely at the letters. Can you see,
> entering (stage right), then floating full,
> then heading off – so soon –

---

13 The literal meaning of the writing on the wall remains disputed. The three words are commonly said to signify "counted, counted, weighed, and assessed," or possibly "a Mina, a Mina, a Shekel, and Perases," that is, weights as coins. Hecht's preposition "for" covers both possibilities. See D. S. Margoliouth, "Mene . . . ," *A Dictionary of the Bible*, ed. James Hastings (Edinburgh: T. and T. Clark, 1900). The grammar causes difficulty as well.
14 They are titled "A Downward Look" and "An Upward Look" (pp. 3, 96).

how like a little kohl-rimmed moon
o plots her course from *b* to *d*

– as *y*, unanswered, knocks at the stage door?
Looked at too long, words fail,
phase out. Ask, now that body shines
no longer, by what light you learn these lines
and what the *b* and *d* stood for.

As a cryptic riddle poem, where we must ascertain that *b* = "birth" and *d* = "death," while *y* = "why," this is not very difficult. (The effect does pull second-person "you" and the verb "see" in line 1 toward the letters *u* and *c*, as if a submerged rebus was in play.) Merrill's lexis or diction is simple, mostly monosyllabic. The rhyme is also simple: four full rhymes for ten lines plus title, and one pararhyme ("full," "fail") that crosses stanzas and moves into a subsequent line with "fail / phase." Two imperative sentences frame the poem, providing some urgency; they contain one interrogative and one indicative sentence. Here the line lies so naturally over the sentence, and the line-length varies so unobtrusively that we hardly notice, but it is worth while working out the relations, together with the varied stress. The argument of lines 3 and 7, for example, is indirectly glossed by a scheme: these are the two shortest lines (six syllables each), though we do not experience them as short.

This is a visual riddle poem in its stage directions, with the letters *b* and *o* and *d* read as shapes. *O* moves across the stage, from the semi-circle or waxing half-moon of *b* (minus its upright) to the waning half-moon of *d*. (The shapes are familiar from newspaper weather forecasts giving the phases of the moon.) The *o* moves from left to right along the title line. Why then does Merrill say "entering (stage right)"? Because, in the theater, stage directions are given from the actor's perspective. The uprights on *b* and *d* represent sides of a stage, across which each of us moves a life, all the world being a stage. This is a griph-type riddle using letter-shapes as a scheme.

Merrill's title points toward the body of his poem, reminding us of a title as figurative head and the main text as body. There the poem stands on the page: head, neck (that white space), and body. So where *is* the body? Both places, much as our body is both in our head and what our head governs: our trunk and limbs. But the title does not say "body." It spells out "b o d y." "Riddle" in English is related etymologically to "reading," and this mini-riddle is a riddle of reading. Anyone understanding basic English knows what one's body is, but only someone who is literate will be able to understand spelled-out "b o d y." (This is how we conceal our speech from small children or savvy pets: we spell it out, we make a riddle of it.) The two functions point toward word and thing, and how we bridge that space with language. Given this entire collection, which is suffused with an acceptance of death, the title also reminds us of the time when body will relinquish language, will be only body.

If the ice-water riddle was for centuries the best-known teaching example of the trope of enigma, the most famous enigma in Western literature must be the Sphinx's. "What walks on four legs in the morning, two legs at noon, and three legs in the evening?" This is a riddle turning more on the philosophical problem of identity than on procreation. Yet questions of generation lurk behind it, and not only in Sophocles' story about what followed the first success of Oedipus as riddle-master.

For there is another possible answer to the sphinx's riddle and that is: you yourself, Madam Sphinx. Certainly a hybrid of woman, lion, and bird raises questions of legs. Natural creatures walk on four legs (a lion) or two legs (a bird or a woman). But what creature goes naturally on three legs? A three-legged creature, born as such, is a freak of nature or a monster, of the order of the sphinx, four-legged though she be. We know how the Minotaur came to be, but of the couplings that produce a sphinx we know nothing. (The parentage offered by Hesiod does not help.) Like Antiochus in Shakespeare's play, the sphinx poses a neck-riddle. Like Antiochus, she directs attention away from herself as a possible answer to the riddle. The standard answer to the sphinx's riddle, "humankind," works more neatly as answer. But the conjunction of four-footed and two-footed creatures needed to produce a sphinx gives pause. All the more so when the answer, "humankind," is centered on the cycle of generation, baby to adult to old person. It gives even more pause to compare the two answers, to inquire how much monster is included in humankind. Some such reflection lies behind Borges's extraordinary sonnet, "Edipo y el Enigma," noted earlier, and now quoted in full:

> Cuadrúpedo en la aurora, alto en el día
> Y con tres pies errando por el vano
> Ambito de la tarde, así veía
> La eterna esfinge a su inconstante hermano,
> El hombre, y con la tarde un hombre vino
> Qué descifró aterrado en el espejo
> De la monstruosa imagen, el reflejo
> De su declinación y su destino.
> Somos Edipo y de un eterno modo
> La larga y triple bestia somos, todo

Lo que seremos y lo que hemos sido.
Nos aniquilaría ver la ingente
Forma de nuestro ser; piadosamente
Dios nos depara sucesión y olvido.[15]

"Sucesión y olvido": the contrast is sharp between emptiness, the void of
olvido, and its contrary, issue or offspring. In Borges's uncanny retelling,
the sphinx's enigma is not only of identity but also of generation. Its
answer has produced another enigma, the enigma of ourselves and our
mirror images (*el espejo . . . el reflejo*). This second enigma is doubly
answered both through issue (the birth of our children) and through
oblivion (our own death). Yet the answer does not end the enigma: it
starts the story all over again. As Borges and Roberto Calasso and others
remind us, the answers to the great enigmas may themselves be enigmatic.

In one sense, riddles too may be generative. In Northrop Frye's essay
"Charms and Riddles," lyric poetry is said to be rooted in early, primitive
forms of writing. Roots, branches, seeds, etc., are frequent tropes in
literary history. Alastair Fowler uses the trope of human generation:
"Poems are made in part from older poems: each is the child (to use
Keats's metaphor) of an earlier representative of the genre and may
yet be the mother of a subsequent representative" (*Kinds of Literature*,
p. 42). He adds a useful caution. "We need to leave room for polygenesis
. . . and for remote influences" (p. 43). In both critics, we are hearing of
poetry itself as generation. Not the travails of the individual writer, but
rather the development of forms. What kind of life do the forms themselves possess? We tend to use inorganic and passive tropes for them. Yet
verbal forms live, grow, dance, procreate, die. Riddle or enigma, like

---

15 *Selected Poems*, p. 190; trans. John Hollander as "Oedipus and the Enigma" (ibid., p. 191):

> At dawn four-footed, at midday erect,
> And wandering on three legs in the deserted
> Spaces of afternoon, thus the eternal
> Sphinx had envisioned her changing brother
> Man, and with afternoon there came a person
> Deciphering, appalled at the monstrous other
> Presence in the mirror, the reflection
> Of his decay and of his destiny.
> We are Oedipus; in some eternal way
> We are the long and threefold beast as well –
> All that we will be, all that we have been.
> It would annihilate us all to see
> The huge shape of our being; mercifully
> God offers us issue and oblivion.

elegy, is a form with a peculiar affinity for the subject of generation. It can embody in its own workings the process of generation.

Boundaries, borders, crossings. Something of the form of the riddle, whether as simple scheme or as trope, catches a part of our existence, most richly in art, including literary art. Its own intrinsic metamorphoses, its own lingering mysteries: these trope our most riddling aspects of being, and not least enigmas of creation. As Michael Wood says of oracles, "But oracles don't puzzle the world, they mime the world's puzzles, and they are likely to appear wherever and whenever the world feels like a puzzle to us" ("Consulting the Oracle," p. 111). Enigma as trope not only mimes the world's puzzles, but also transforms and enlightens them, as it explores their hidden similitudes. As a boundary figure, enigma can embody the most challenging crossings in our lives. These include birth and death, as well as some mysterious metamorphoses of the natural world, and some mysterious crossings of art. Whatever our interest in riddle and enigma, it behoves us to watch these little words that preside over our crossing-places. There enigma sits, fierce or smiling or other, Sphinx or Apollo or stranger, along all our boundaries, waiting.

Appendix
Enigma, riddle, and friends among the lexicographers

Lexicographers have the unenviable job of trying to pin down enigma and riddle. They are concerned with exact meanings. So are good writers, whose antennae for exactness are extensively developed. Full lexical meaning in the great *Oxford English Dictionary* includes: (1) identification (grammatical part of speech, status such as "obsolete," etc.), (2) etymology, (3) signification or what we ordinarily call "meaning," and (4) illustrative quotations. Full literary definition includes even more.

The definitions in the OED work from all the quotations that are collected for each word, including many more than those printed (p. xxix). The procedure is important, for good dictionary definitions can appear to be not only authoritative, but also autonomous.[1] But the flow of influence is two-way, not simply downward from an authoritative source, however excellent. Good writers both consult dictionaries and help to make them, spoken practice influences dictionaries, and so on. The OED's illustrative quotations not only provide initial meaning. They also remind us to return to definitions and test their general signification against particular use. Writers also often want to know about correct word-roots, but they are especially interested in what tropes a given etymon might suggest, as it lives quietly in the back room like some aged grandparent. And false etymology may intrigue writers as much as it vexes etymologists. Elizabeth Bishop brilliantly plays the false etymology for "Christ" against the correct one in "Brazil, January 1, 1502."[2]

Lexicographers decide on the categories within the four main areas, and their schematization also deserves attention, because all taxonomies are interpretive. Taxonomies vary and change. As Stephen Jay Gould says, "The taxonomic order is a record of history."[3]

---

1 The process of isolating a given word, especially a noun, gives it a weight of separate existence, an effect quite different from a defined word within a running narrative. See Judith Anderson, *Words That Matter*.
2 See "Fables of War" in my *Against Coercion*, p. 59.
3 In *Science, Mind, and Cosmos*, ed. William H. Calvin et al. (London: Phoenix, 1996), p. 12.

WORD-ROOTS

The word "enigma" goes back to Greek αἴνιγμα (*ainigma*), which is part of the language from at least the time of Pindar and Aeschylus (fifth century BCE). Liddell and Scott define it first as "a dark saying, riddle," quoting from Pindar (see chap. 1). The word *ainigma* is not in Homer or in Hesiod, though the famous punning trick of Odysseus to the Cyclops was listed as an *énigme* by Abbé Cotin and others, and a saying from Hesiod was often classified as an enigma in Renaissance rhetoric. Riddle contests are also described in poems attributed to Hesiod (OCD, "riddle"). But the word *ainos* is in both Homer and Hesiod, and the etymology of *ainigma* is regularly said to be from *ainos*.[4] Liddell and Scott list *ainos* as a poetic and Ionic word for "tale" or "story." Martin L. West links the meanings more firmly in defining *ainos* as "a tale or fable containing a hidden lesson for the addressee" (OCD, "riddle").[5] The fact that the word αἶνος (*ainos*) meaning "tale, story" coincides so closely with αἰνός (*ainos*) meaning "dread, horrible" reinforces the etymology. For the great ancient enigmas of Aeschylus and Sophocles do bear this sense of lurking dread.

Greek *ainigma* came over into Latin as *aenigma* and thence into English as "enigma" by 1539, to follow the OED. Latin writers are much less interested in how the great enigmas work, as often noted. Nothing in classical and post-classical Latin literature corresponds to the sense of enigma in Aeschylus and Sophocles, partly because tragedy is not a genre in which Latin writers excel. The *Oxford Latin Dictionary*, Lewis and Short, and the *Thesaurus linguae latinae* alike demonstrate this tendency. Most citations of *aenigma* in the *Thesaurus*, for example, are from rhetoricians or patristic writers. Virgil's famous riddle in the *Eclogues* is an exception, though the OCD observes that it takes a Greek form. In the ecclesiastical Latin of patristic, medieval, and Renaissance writers, *aenigma* often comes close to *mysterium* or "mystery."

The word "riddle" is much older than "enigma" within English texts. Aelfric used it in the form of "redelsas" about 1000 to translate Latin *aenigmata* from Numbers 12: 8 in the Vulgate. In 1382, Wyclif translated Latin *problema* from Judges 14 as "riddle." For five hundred years and more, English "riddle" and Latin *aenigma* coexisted as approximate synonyms, before English began to naturalize "enigma." Early printed Latin–English dictionaries translate *aenigma* as "riddle," sometimes as "question" or "dark sentence." (Latin *obscura sententia* is synonymous with *aenigma*, as in Donatus.) Thomas Elyot lists it in 1538, Robert l'Estienne (Stephanus) in 1552, Thomas Cooper in 1565, and John Rider

---

4 Thus in OCD ("riddle"). See also Schultz, "Rätsel." König also gives this etymology, citing Hjalmar Frisk, whose three-volume *Griechisches Etymologisches Wörterbuch* (Heidelberg: Carl Winter, 1960) lists the word αἶνος and the derivatives therefrom.
5 Thus also Nagy on *ainos* as poetry of praise with a coded message, in his *The Best of the Achaeans*, pp. 238–41.

in 1589. John Florio in his 1598 Italian–English dictionary, *A Worlde of Wordes*, lists "Enimma, Enigma, a riddle or doubtful speech." Lexicons did not at first distinguish much between English "riddle" and "enigma," though usage would gradually mark out areas for "riddle" where "enigma" did not usually belong.

The word "riddle" does not appear as a separate entry in the seventeenth-century forerunners of the OED, the dictionaries of Robert Cawdrey, John Bullokar, Henry Cockeram, Thomas Blount, or Edward Phillips, though it does turn up in definitions of other words. These are dictionaries of hard words, and the meaning of "riddle" was clearly judged too well-known and straightforward to need defining. Shakespeare illustrates the point nicely in *Love's Labour's Lost* (III.i.71–2):

ARMADO: Some enigma, some riddle – come, thy l'envoy – begin.
COSTARD: No egma, no riddle, no l'envoy, no salve in the mail, sir.

A rustic like Costard knows well what "riddle" means, but "egma" is another matter. In Elisha Coles (1676), "riddle" is defined only as "an oblong sieve (to separate the seed from the corn)" and "riddeled" interestingly as "plaited, wrinkled." Nor is "riddle" listed in John Wesley's simple, short 1764 *Complete English Dictionary, Explaining most of those Hard Words, which are found in the Best English Writers*.

The word "riddle" originates in Old English *raedels* or *raedelse*, meaning "counsel, opinion, conjecture" and also "a riddle." In turn, the Old English words themselves are derived from the verb *raedan*, "to read" or "to rede." Ordinary reading and reading a riddle are linked etymologically in only English and Old Norse (OED, note to "read" as verb). How does it happen that "rede" is linked to reading only in English among the major modern European languages? Do the wonderful Old English riddles, such as those from the Exeter Book, help to explain this? Or is it a happy accident that simply emphasizes the inherent mystery of all language?

When the eminent literary philologist Leo Spitzer wanted to defend riddles against the charge of being trivial, he emphasized "the sense of considering or explaining something obscure or mysterious" (OED, "read" as verb) in many European vernacular terms for "riddle":

Indeed, if we consider the terms for "riddle" in the various languages, it is evident that here is generally a suggestion of the aim of arriving at truth: the truth which, sphinx-like, is ultimately underlying. Fr. *devinette* implies that there is a truth to be "guessed". . . Germ. *Rätsel* = Rat "advice"; Eng. *riddle* = OE *raedelse* "counsel, opinion". . . ("Charade," p. 79)

The notion is intriguing. For if the riddle is associated etymologically with counsel or advice in many European languages, why is Greek *ainigma* associated with dark or menacing stories? (Perhaps the question hovered in Spitzer's mind when he called the truth "sphinx-like.") One association points toward the enigmatic question or threat; the other points toward a response. Once again, we are seeing the inside/outside troping of riddle and enigma.

DEFINITIONS

Definitions of "enigma" and "riddle" face one major question. How does the lexicographer distinguish small joking riddles from large portentous enigmas?

One easy lexical division would be to reserve the word "enigma" for large riddles and the word "riddle" for smaller joking or ingenious riddles. Loosely, this is the division between Greek *ainigma* and *griphos*. Very loosely, it is a distinction in modern English usage, but only to a degree. It is necessary to say modern English usage, because seventeenth-, eighteenth-, and nineteenth-century riddle collections designed for sheer amusement often include the term "enigma." (See, e.g., titles listed in chapters 1 and 6.) Matthew Prior published an "Enigma" on the Jack of Clubs in the *Gentleman's Journal* for 1693. "Enigmas and their solutions appeared regularly in the *Gentleman's Journal*, the *Muses Mercury*," and elsewhere.[6] Similarly in France, with *énigmes* or small versified riddles.

The OED defines "riddle" in both editions as follows: (1) "A question or sentence intentionally worded in a dark or puzzling manner, and propounded in order that it may be guessed or answered, esp. as a form of pastime; an enigma; a dark saying." (2) "trans. [transferred sense] Something which puzzles or perplexes; a dark or insoluble problem; a mystery."

The first signification includes function or aim, which is useful, though the word "pastime" sits oddly alongside "enigma" (and the illustrative quotations include few pastimes). Chiefly, but not always, part 2 covers large riddles. The word "dark" turns up in both parts. Yet I think the lexicographers were right not to separate part 1 into two different significations, according to function. For in itself, a riddle will not tell you what its function may be. The enigma of the Sphinx was no pastime on the road to Thebes. But the Sphinx's riddle turns up as an independent folk-riddle in widely dispersed places from Africa to Asia.[7] Good riddles, like good jokes, travel far and fast. In part 2, "intentionally worded" indicates the distinction between a verbal or worded riddle and other kinds, such as visual riddles, a basic distinction.

The word "enigma" is defined as: (1) "A short composition in prose or verse, in which something is described by intentionally obscure metaphors, in order to afford an exercise for the ingenuity of the reader or hearer in guessing what is meant; a riddle. . ." (2) "fig. Something as puzzling as an enigma; an unsolved problem." Part 1 defines riddle poems very nicely. This time, the function is exercise rather than amusement, and what is exercised is ingenuity. As we have seen, Aristotle and others had a larger view of the profit and pleasure of enigmas. One quotation for part 1 refers to Joseph's prophetic dream in Genesis 37, so that,

---

6 *Literary Works*, vol. II, p. 1029, and see vol. I, pp. 124, 687.
7 See Taylor, *English Riddles from Oral Tradition*, pp. 20–4. He notes that "its simplicity suggests the possibility of independent origins for the Indonesian, Fijian, Samoan, and Hawaiian parallels, but any decision on this point is almost out of the question" (p. 20). For examples from Africa and elsewhere, see Apollodorus, *The Library*, trans. Frazer, note to III.v.8, p. 347.

once again, the illustrative quotations press beyond the given definition. Curiously, the definition of "riddle" offers more scope for the great enigmas like the Sphinx's in Sophocles than does the definition of "enigma."

In its categories, the *Trésor de la langue française*[8] offers an interesting comparison with the OED, for it separates *énigmes* that are amenable to solution (e.g., scientific questions) from ongoing riddles having to do with identity, final causes, etc. This latter category in effect offers uses of "enigma" that overlap with "mystery." Human answers to such mysteries are not expected in the way that human answers to most scientific problems are expected. Yet answers to the large ongoing enigmas will often determine exactly what we do with answers to scientific puzzles. In this sense, they are more powerful. Many are, in effect, enigma as masterplot. Unhappily, the adjectives for the large enigmas are more negative than hopeful: "une énigme inexplicable, inquiétante, insoluble, mystérieuse, profonde; cruelle, effrayante [frightening] énigme."

In the illustrative quotations of the OED, riddles and enigmas, both small and large, begin chronologically with those that are part of Jewish tradition as inherited and revised by Christianity. The Sphinx's riddle is *sui generis* as the only specific one with a definition of its own. "Riddle" as applied to mankind is late historically (meaning 14); the riddle or mystery of certain groups (women, for example) comes just a little earlier in the eighteenth century. A glance through book titles in any large library bears out the OED's general categories. Apart from the words "riddle" and "enigma" in titles of riddle collections or folk-riddle studies, the two words cover these same subject areas. They can signify a medical or scientific or artistic or linguistic problem: the enigma of cancer, of anorexia nervosa, of Van Eyck's double portrait, of the Rosetta Stone. They can signify perennial mysteries, incapable of ordinary solution: the enigma of evil, of suffering, of human significance. They can signify something between a problem capable of solution and an ongoing puzzle: the riddle of Eros, of the origins of human life, of the mind–body relation, of social justice. They can signify the puzzle of a country or a region: the Russian enigma, the Eastern enigma. They can signify the enigma of a single person, often a person of genius (Rabelais, Shakespeare, Gogol) or of mythic creatures (Sasquatch). They can signify a spy code, including the well-known one called "Enigma."

MYSTERY

The overlapping areas of "enigma," "riddle," and "mystery" remain a challenge, as in earlier dictionaries.[9] How do "enigma" and "riddle" shade over into

8 *Trésor de la langue française*, ed. Paul Imbs (Paris: Editions du centre national de la recherche scientifique, 1979).

9 The OED lists the major dictionaries preceding it as Cawdrey, Bullokar, Cockeram, Blount, Phillips, all seventeenth century; Kersey, Bailey, and notably Johnson, eighteenth century; Richardson and Webster, nineteenth century. For these dictionaries and others up to Johnson, see Starnes and Noyes, *The English Dictionary from Cawdrey to Johnson*.

"mystery"? How is "mystery" in turn defined? The word "mystery" in modern dictionaries sometimes includes religious mystery in a familiar orthodox way. Sometimes it is informed by eighteenth-century deistic ideas or by something a good deal vaguer. It is always worth inquiring.

The pre-eminent single lexicographer of the English language, Samuel Johnson, defines "enigma," "enigmatical," and so on, in familiar and unexceptionable ways in his famous *Dictionary*. "ENIGMA n.s. [aenigma, Latin; αἴνιγμα.] A riddle; an obscure question; a position expressed in remote and ambiguous terms" (1755). Johnson adds the words "darkly" and "cloudy" in his definition of "enigmatical."[10] Ambiguity is mentioned twice. Under "enigmatical," though not under "enigma," and there only in the illustration and not in the definition, the word "enigmatical" is applied to matters of religious faith. Johnson's preferred word for such enigmatical religious knowledge is "mystery." Every first definition and illustration of "mystery," "mysterious," and similar words concern religious mystery. The meaning of a medieval mystery play (so called first in 1744, says the OED) would not have puzzled Johnson, but a mystery story in the modern sense (so called first in 1908 by Chesterton, according to the OED) would have sounded strange to him. Not so Borges and other writers who connect the two categories of meaning, though the end-plots of Borges are very different from the mystery of the Trinity, at least in their effects.

A long entry in the first edition of Ephraim Chambers' *Cyclopaedia*, 1728, also associates mystery exclusively with matters of faith, chiefly Christian faith. "Heathens" are allowed their mysteries, though only some are judged respectable. Egyptian mysteries concealed under hieroglyphics are all very well. Grottos are something other. "The *Mysteries* of Paganism were celebrated in Grotto's, fitter to conceal Crimes than to hold religious *Mysteries* in."

The word "riddle" in Johnson's *Dictionary* shows no interest in "mystery." It confines its attentions to "enigma," "puzzling questions" or "dark problems" such as those the witches set for Macbeth or love games or conundrums. Earlier lexicographers also largely separated enigma and riddle from religious mystery, e.g., John Florio in 1598.

The word "mystery" meaning "a trade or art" has now vanished in English, though it is familiar from Shakespeare: "instruction, manners, mysteries and trades" (*Timon of Athens* IV.i.18) and "Do you call, sir, your occupation a mystery?" (*Measure for Measure* IV.ii.34). It derives from confusing two Latin words (OED, "mystery" 2). Johnson, following Warburton, suggested a different spelling for this kind of mystery: "it should . . . be written *mistery*, from *mestiero*, French, a trade" (cf. modern French, *métier*). The meaning of "mystery" as "trade" continued into the nineteenth century before finally dying out, except

---

10 He also offers a surprisingly loose definition of "enigmatically" as "a sense different from that which the words in their familiar acceptation imply." The definition has precedent, but is a category mistake; figurative use may also be so defined, but some figurative uses are not in the least enigmatic.

as irony. "Industrial espionage" is no doubt a separate coinage, but nonetheless joins the older sense of trade secrets and expertise as a mystery.

The OED includes within the "enigma" family a number of illustrations drawn from Christian doctrine, and within the "riddle" family a wide range of biblical and doctrinal illustrations. "Mystery" it sensibly disposes under the two main categories of "theological" and "non-theological."

The chief difference for me between "mystery" and "enigma" or "riddle" is that mystery need not imply an answer, because it need not be asking a question. Sometimes it simply elicits wonder or awe. Enigma commonly carries the sense of a question to be resolved.

FROM *problema* TO "PROBLEM": "RIDDLE" AND SCIENCE

Another Greek word for "riddle" also comes into Latin, then into English: πρόβλημα (*problema*), subsequently Latin *problema*, then English "problem." Liddell and Scott list "riddle" as the fifth signification, citing the Septuagint version of Samson's riddle contest in Judges 14. *Problema* meaning "riddle" looks like a comparative latecomer. The first signification is "anything put forward as a defence, bulwark, barrier" from a shield to a wall, literally "something thrown forward," with citations from Aeschylus, Sophocles, and others. The second is a "problem in geometry, etc." with citations from Plato, the third a problem in logic with citations from Aristotle, and the fourth more generally a "practical or theoretical problem." The earliest date for the Septuagint is the third century BC, that is, post-Aristotelian, so that its use of *problema* in Judges appears to be late and novel.

Why did the Septuagint translators choose *problema* to translate Hebrew *hida* in Samson's story, rather than *ainigma* or *griphos*? In fact, they were not being arbitrary. There are traces of *problema* meaning "riddle" in Greek Old and Middle Comedy. Athenaeus, who chiefly uses the word *griphos*, occasionally uses *ainigma* and *problema*. Yet Athenaeus is not drawing on the Septuagint use. He quotes the comic poet Hermippus, who won a victory in 435 BC, on an even earlier writer who propounded riddles (*problethenta*; Athen. x.451e). He also quotes a riddle from the *Problemata* of the Middle Comedy poet Antiphanes (first play in 385 BC; Athen. x.450c). He also quotes Clearchus of Soli: "'A riddle [*griphos*] is a problem [*problema*] put in jest, requiring, by searching the mind, the answer to the problem [*problethen*] to be given for a prize or forfeit'" (Athen. x.448c). (See also Schultz, "Rätsel,"cols. 88, 100.) One would give a good deal to have more of these comedies in full, rather than just in fragments.

How are all these meanings related? The literal meaning is "a thing thrown forward and hence a question put forward" (OED). In a riddle contest, is a challenge perceived as something thrown forward for which a defense is then erected? If *problema* meaning "riddle" is in fact the earliest meaning, not the latest, as Liddell and Scott suggest, was early work in geometry and logic so conceived? Did the universe itself seem to throw forward a challenge that required some answer, even some defense? The prize would be knowledge. For biological and medical problems, the prize would be knowledge and health and life itself. The forfeit would be the opposite. Or was early *problema* simply a term for something generally puzzling that could be solved, as against *ainigma*, which includes the great insoluble problems of human identity and destiny, injustice and evil? It is unusual to think of scientific investigation today as a riddle contest, yet in some ways it is.

Whatever the answer, the Vulgate Bible mostly followed the Septuagint's *problema* in Judges 14, though twice translating it as Latin *propositio*. Very likely the fame of this story accounts for the word "problem" as a synonym for "riddle" in medieval and Renaissance Latin and English use. Early Latin–English or all-English dictionaries retain the Latin sense of *problema* as a general word for something puzzling or riddling. In 1616, Bullokar in his *English Expositor* defines "probleme" as "a darke sentence, with a question ioyned unto it." The definition is indistinguishable from a definition of "enigma." But early in the seventeenth century, "problem" meaning "riddle" became obsolete. The OED's last quotation is from 1602 (though note Bullokar in 1616). One anomalous listing is from the 1689 *Gazophylacium Anglicanum*, an entry called "Riddle or Probleme." The word "problem" then reverted entirely to the old Greek types of logical, philosophical, or scientific question, as well as a general practical or theoretical question.

From at least 1570 in English, "problem" in Euclid's sense prevailed in mathematical, geometrical, and physical writing. Billingsley's well-known first translation of Euclid in 1570 provides the OED illustrations of "problem" for both geometry (OED 4) and physics and mathematics (OED 5). In such use, the term "proposition" (*propositio*) included the definition of "problem" (*problema*), following Euclid. "Propositions are of two sortes," Billingsley translates. "The one is called a Probleme, the other a Theorem. A Probleme, is a proposition which requireth some action, or doing: as the making of some figure [e.g. a triangle] . . . A Theorem is a proposition, which requireth the searching out and demonstration of some propertie or passion of some figure" (1570, for. ciiiv). The original Greek, as quoted by Proclus in the fifth century A D, gives *problema* where English "Probleme" appears.[11] When Cawdrey's 1604 *Table* defines "probleme" as "proposition, or sentence in the manner of a question," this is a general rather than a Euclidean signification. The first edition of Chambers' *Cyclopaedia* in 1728 classifies "problem" generally under "logic," and specifically under ethical, metaphysical, and scientific (e.g., algebra, geometry, mathematics) applications. In the 1786 edition, the words "riddle" and "aenigma" are connected with chemistry, but, tellingly, with alchemy as well (s.v. "Aenigma," 1728 "Enigma").[12]

---

11 *Euclid's Elements*, trans. Heath, vol. 1, pp. 128–9. The chapters on "Euclid in Arabia" and "Principal Translations and Editions of Euclid's Elements" are well worth pursuing.

12 The first edition of 1728 gives a compact entry for "enigma." By the fifth edition (1741), "enigma" has changed to "aenigma," apparently under a more pedantic editor. By 1786, two volumes had expanded into four, and "aenigma" had expanded accordingly.

Nowadays scientists speak of solving a problem, not solving a riddle or an enigma or a mystery. The one exception is when speaking of some longstanding classic problem, such as Fermat's Last Theorem, and even there, such language is more popular than professional. Leibniz refers to a classic problem, the Florentine enigma of Bincenzo Viviani, as *Aenigma architectonico-geometricum* in his 1692 solution, but he lived much closer in time to the old Latin meaning.[13] Keynes shows a fine sense of language when he says that Newton "looked at the whole universe and all that is in it as a *riddle. . .* a cryptogram set by the Almighty." Keynes not only retains the old general sense of "riddle," but also pays an appropriate compliment to this giant of science. Only the greatest scientists approach the enigmas of science, though their evidence comes from working on problems.

Roberto Calasso defines enigma as a mysterious formulation whose answer is likewise mysterious, an excellent definition of the great classic enigmas. "That is what distinguishes the enigma from the problem," he adds.

When a problem is resolved, both question and answer dissolve, are absorbed into a mechanical formula. Climbing a wall is a problem, until you lean a ladder against it. Afterward, you have neither problem nor solution, just a wall and a ladder. This is not so for the enigma. Take the most famous one of all, the Sphinx's . . . (pp. 343–4)

13 Gottfried Leibniz, *Aenigma architectonico-geometricum* (Hanover, 1692; repr. from *Acta Eruditorum*, June 1692).

Select bibliography

Abrahams, Roger D., *Between the Living and the Dead*, FF Communications no. 225 (Helsinki: Academia Scientiarum Fennica, 1980), Preface, pp. 8–23.
  "Introductory Remarks to a Rhetorical Theory of Folklore," *Journal of American Folklore* 81 (1968), 143–58.
  "The Literary Study of the Riddle," *Texas Studies in Literature and Language* 14 (1972), 177–97.
Abrahams, Roger D., and Alan Dundes, "Riddles," in *Folklore and Folklife: An Introduction*, ed. Richard M. Dorson (Chicago: University of Chicago Press, 1972), pp. 129–43.
Abrahams, Israel, *Jewish Life in the Middle Ages*, rev. edn. (London: Edward Goldston, 1932), pp. 148, 408–11.
Akenside, Mark, *The Poetical Works of Mark Akenside* (1845 edn.; repr. New York: AMS Press, 1969).
Ahl, Frederick, *Sophocles' Oedipus: Evidence and Self-Conviction* (Ithaca: Cornell University Press, 1991).
Alciatus, Andreas, *The Latin Emblems: Indexes and Lists* and *Emblems in Translation*, 2 vols., ed. Peter M. Daly (Toronto: University of Toronto Press, 1985).
Alexander of Villedieu, *Doctrinale*, ed. Dietrich Reichling (Berlin: A. Hoffman, 1893).
Allioui, Youcef, *Timsal énigmes Berbères de Kabylie: Commentaire linguistique et ethnographique* (Paris: L'Harmattan, 1990).
Ammons, A. R., *Corsons Inlet* (1965) in his *Selected Poems, Expanded Edition* (New York: Norton, 1987).
Anderson, Judith H., *Words That Matter: Linguistic Perception in Renaissance English* (Stanford: Stanford University Press, 1996).
Anon. [La Condamine?], "Lettre à l'Auteur du Mercure, sur le Logogryphe," *Mercure de France*, December 1758, pp. 60–3.
Ante-Nicene Christian Library: Translations of the Writings of the Fathers down to A. D. 325, ed. Alexander Roberts and James Donaldson (Edinburgh: T. & T. Clark, 1867–83).
Apollinaire, Guillaume, *Œuvres poétiques* (Paris: Gallimard, Pléiade edn., 1956).

Apollodorus of Athens, *Bibliotheca, The Library*, trans. Sir James George Frazer, 2 vols. (Cambridge, Mass.: Harvard University Press, Loeb, 1921), III.v.7–9, on the Sphinx's riddle.

Aragona, Raffaele, ed., *Enigmatica per una poietica ludica* (Naples: Edizioni Scientifici Italiane, 1996).

The Arabian Nights: see *The Book of a Thousand Nights and a Night.*

Archer, W. G., "Uraon Riddles," from his *The Blue Grove: The Poetry of the Uraons* (London: Allen and Unwin, 1940), pp. 177–95.

Aristophanes, *The Wasps*, in *The Acharnians, The Knights, The Clouds, The Wasps*, trans. and ed. Benjamin Bickley Rogers (Cambridge, Mass.: Harvard University Press, Loeb, 1924); *The Wasps*, ed. Douglas M. MacDowell (Oxford: Clarendon, 1971); *The Complete Plays of Aristophanes*, trans. Moses Hadas (New York: Bantam, 1962).

Aristotle, *The Complete Works of Aristotle*, rev. Oxford trans., ed. Jonathan Barnes (Princeton: Princeton University Press, Bollingen, 1984).

The "Art" of Rhetoric, trans. John Henry Freese (Cambridge, Mass.: Harvard University Press, Loeb, 1975).

The Poetics, trans. W. Hamilton Fyfe (Cambridge, Mass.: Harvard University Press, Loeb, 1932), with "Longinus," *On the Sublime*, and Demetrius, *On Style.*

Armour, Peter, "Griffins," in *Mythical Beasts*, ed. John Cherry (London: British Museum Press, 1995), pp. 72–103, 184–5.

Ashbery, John, *A Wave* (New York: Viking Penguin, 1984).

Girls on the Run (New York: Farrar, Straus, Giroux, 1999).

Hotel Lautréamont (Manchester: Carcanet, 1992).

Ashton, John, *Understanding the Fourth Gospel* (Oxford: Clarendon, 1991).

Athenaeus, from *The Deipnosophists*, commonly *The Learned Banquet*, trans. Charles Burton Gulick, 7 vols. (London: Heinemann, 1927–41; rev. edn. 1951), Book x.448–59.

Auden, W. H., *Collected Poems*, ed. Edward Mendelson (New York: Vintage, 1991).

"Lewis Carroll," in his *Forewords and Afterwords*, ed. Edward Mendelson (New York: Vintage, 1974), pp. 283–93.

Auerbach, Erich, "Figura," from his *Scenes from the Drama of European Literature*, trans. Ralph Manheim (1959; repr. Minneapolis: University of Minnesota Press, 1984), pp. 11–76; orig. pub. *Archivum Romanicum* 22 (1938), pp. 436–89, footnotes slightly different.

Augarde, Tony, *The Oxford Guide to Word Games* (Oxford: Oxford University Presss, 1984).

Augustine, *De trinitate, Corpus Christianorum series latina*, 50A (1968); *On the Trinity*, in *Nicene and Post-Nicene Fathers*, vol. III, trans. Arthur West Haddan, rev. William G. T. Shedd.

Œuvres de Saint Augustin, texte Bénédictine (Paris: Desclée de Brouwer, 1955).

On Christian Doctrine, trans. D. W. Robertson, Jr. (New York: Macmillan, 1958).

Opera Omnia, editio nova, ed. D. A. B. Caillou (Paris, 1842).

Ausonius: *Griphi Ausoniani Enodatio, per Fransciscum Sylvum Ambiantem unde Griphi verbis Io. Vacceus,* ed. François Dubois (Paris, 1516); *The Works of Ausonius,* ed. R. P. H. Green (Oxford: Clarendon, 1991).

Austen, Jane, *Charades &c. written a hundred years ago by Jane Austen and Her Family* (London: Spottiswoode [1895]).

    Emma, The Novels of Jane Austen, ed. R. W. Chapman, 3rd edn. rev. (Oxford: Oxford University Press, 1933, 1966), vol. IV.

    Jane Austen's Letters, ed. Deirdre Le Faye (Oxford: Oxford University Press, 1995).

Baldwin, T. W., *William Shakspere's Small Latine and Lesse Greeke,* 2 vols. (Urbana: University of Illinois Press, 1944).

Bartscht, Waltraud, "The Griffin," in *Mythical and Fabulous Creatures: A Source Book and Research Guide* (New York: Greenwood, 1987), pp. 85–101.

Bede, the Venerable, *De schematibus et tropis, Corpus Christianorum* 123A (1975), pp. 142–71; Gussie Hecht Tanenhaus, " Bede's *De schematibus et tropis* – A Translation, " *Quarterly Journal of Speech* 48 (1962), 237–53.

Benjamin, Walter, "Riddle and Mystery," in his *Selected Writings,* vol. I, *1913–1926,* ed. Marcus Bullock and Michael W. Jennings (Cambridge, Mass.: Harvard University Press, 1996), pp. 267–8.

    "Theologico-Political Fragment," in his *Reflections: Essays, Aphorisms, Autobiographical Writings* (New York: Harcourt, Brace, Jovanovich, 1978), trans. Edmund Jephcott, ed. Peter Demetz, from essays of 1955–72, pp. 312–13.

Betz, Hans Dieter, *Hellenismus und Urchristentum* (Tübingen: J. C. B. Mohr [Paul Siebeck], 1990).

    Plutarch's Theological Writings and Early Christian Literature (Leiden: E. J. Brill, 1975).

Beyer, Rolf, *Die Königin von Saba, Engel und Dämon: Der Mythos einer Frau* (Bergisch Gladbach: Gustav Lübbe, 1987).

Biedermann, Flodoard Freih. von, *Goethe als Rätseldichter* (Berlin: H. Berthold A. G. Abt. Privatdrucke, 1924; 41 pp.).

Bisi, Anna Maria, *Il grifone: storia di un motivo iconografico nell'antico oriente mediterraneo* (Rome: Centro di Studi Semitici, 1965).

Bloom, Harold, *Ruin the Sacred Truths: Poetry and Belief from the Bible to the Present* (Cambridge, Mass.: Harvard University Press, 1989).

Bloom, Harold, ed., *Sophocles' Oedipus Plays* (New York: Chelsea House, 1996).

Bonus, Arthur, *Rätsel* (Munich, 1907).

The Book of the Thousand Nights and a Night, trans. and ed. Captain Sir R. F. Burton, repr. and ed. Leonard C. Smithers, 12 vols. (London: H. S. Nicol, 1894).

Bök, Christian, *Eunoia* (Toronto: Coach House, 2001).

Borges, Jorge Luis, *Jorge Luis Borges: Selected Poems 1923–1967,* bilingual edn., ed. Norman Thomas di Giovanni (New York: Delacorte, 1972).

Boyarin, Daniel, "The Song of Songs, Lock or Key: The Holy Song as a Mashel," in his *Intertextuality and the Reading of Midrash* (Bloomington: Indiana University Press, 1990), pp. 105–16.

Brémond, Claude-François, "Pourquoi le poisson a ri," *Poétique* 45 (1981), 9–19.

Brogan, T. V. F., "Acrostic," NPEPP, p. 8.

Brooks, Peter, *Reading for the Plot: Design and Intention in Narrative* (New York: Knopf, 1984).

Brown, Peter, *Augustine of Hippo: A Biography* (Berkeley: University of California Press, 1969).

Brown, R. E., "Mystery (in the Bible)," *New Catholic Encyclopedia*, ed. Catholic University of America (New York: McGraw-Hill, 1967), vol. x, pp. 148–51.

Bryant, Mark, *Dictionary of Riddles* (London: Routledge, 1990); based on his *Riddles, Ancient and Modern* (New York: Peter Bedrick, 1984).

Buchan, John, *The Thirty-Nine Steps* (1915).

Buchler, Johann, *Parnassus Poeticus* (Venice, 1548).

Bunyan, John, *The Pilgrim's Progress*, ed. Roger Sharrock, rev. edn. (Harmondsworth: Penguin, 1987).

Burke, Kenneth, *A Grammar of Motives* (Berkeley: University of California Press, 1945, 1969), esp. Appendix D, "Four Master Tropes," pp. 503–17.

Burkert, Walter, *Ancient Mystery Cults* (Cambridge, Mass.: Harvard University Press, 1987).

    Greek Religion (Cambridge, Mass.: Harvard University Press, 1985), trans. John Raffan from *Griechische Religion der archaischen und klassischen Epoche* (1977), esp. "Oracles," pp. 114–18.

Caillois, Roger, *Art poétique* (Paris: Gallimard, 1958), from "L'énigme et l'image," pp. 151–64, and Annexes i-iii.

Calasso, Roberto, *The Marriage of Cadmus and Harmony* (New York: Vintage, 1993), trans. Tim Parks from *Le nozze di Cadmo e Armonia* (1988).

Camerarius, Joachim, *Elementa rhetorica* (Basel, 1540).

Campion, Thomas, *The Works of Thomas Campion*, ed. Walter R. Davis (New York: Doubleday, Norton, 1967 .

Canel, A. [Alfred], *Recherches sur les jeux d'esprit, les singularités et les bizarreries littéraires, principalement en France*, 2 vols. (Evreux: Auguste Herissey, 1867).

Carroll, Lewis, *Alice's Adventures under Ground* (New York: Dover, 1965).

    The Annotated Alice: The Definitive Edition, ed. Martin Gardner (New York: Norton, 2000); *Alice in Wonderland*, ed. Donald J. Gray (New York: Norton, 1971).

Cassander, Georgius, *Tabulae breves in praeceptiones rhetoricas* (Paris, 1553).

Cave, Terence, *Recognitions: A Study in Poetics* (Oxford: Blackwell, 1988).

Céard, Jean, and Jean-Claude Margolin, *Rébus de la Renaissance: des images qui parlent* (Paris: Maisonneuve et Larose, 1986).

Celan, Paul, *Last Poems*, ed. and trans. Katharine Washburn and Margret Guillemin (San Francisco: North Point, 1986).

    Poems of Paul Celan, trans. Michael Hamburger, bilingual edn. (New York: Persea, 1988).

Cervantes, Miguel de, *Don Quixote* (1605), trans. Edith Grossman (New York: HarperCollins, Ecco, 2003).

Chambers, E. [Ephraim], *Cyclopaedia: or, an universal Dictionary of Arts and Sciences . . .* (London, 1728).

Charles, Michel, "Claude-François Ménestrier: Poétique de l'énigme," *Poétique* 45 (1981), 28–52 (on Ménestrier's Preface).

Chastel, André, "Note sur la sphinx à la Renaissance," in *Umanesimo e simbolismo*, ed. Enrico Castelli (Padua: Cedam, 1958), pp. 179–82.

Child, Francis James, ed., *The English and Scottish Popular Ballads*, 5 vols. (Boston: Houghton, Mifflin, 1884–98; repr. New York: Dover, 1965)

Cicero, *De oratore*, trans. E. W. Sutton, completed with Introduction by H. Rackham (Cambridge, Mass.: Harvard University Press, Loeb, 1979).

Orator, trans. H. M. Hubbell (Cambridge, Mass.: Harvard University Press, Loeb, with *Brutus*, 1962).

Civil, M., "Sumerian Riddles: A Corpus," *Aula Orientalis* 5 (1987), 17–35.

Clampitt, Amy, *The Kingfisher* (New York: Knopf, 1983; London: Faber and Faber, 1983).

Classen, C. Joachim, "St. Paul's Epistles and Ancient Greek and Roman Rhetoric," *Rhetorica* 10 (1992), 319–44.

Clausen, Wendell, *A Commentary on Virgil's* Eclogues (Oxford: Clarendon, 1994), pp. 116–18 (on Virgil's riddle, *Ec.* 3.104–7).

Clement of Alexandria, "The Exhortation to the Greeks," *Clement of Alexandria*, trans. G. W. Butterworth (London: Heinemann, Loeb, 1919).

Stromateis (Miscellanies), ed. Alain le Boulluec, trans. Pierre Voulet as Clément d'Alexandre, *Les Stromates* (Book v), vol. 1 (Paris: Cerf, 1981).

Clouston, W. A., *Hieroglyphic Bibles: Their Origin and History* (New York: F. A. Stokes, 1894).

Colie, Rosalie L., *Paradoxia Epidemica: The Renaissance Tradition of Paradox* (Princeton: Princeton University Press, 1966).

The Resources of Kind: Genre-Theory in the Renaissance (Berkeley: University of California Press, 1973).

Conte, Gian Biagio, "Genre between Empiricism and Theory," in his *Genres and Readers: Lucretius, Love Elegy, Pliny's Encyclopedia* (Baltimore: Johns Hopkins University Press, 1994), trans. Glenn W. Most from *Generi e lettori: Lucrezio, L'elegia d'amore, L'enciclopedia di Plinio* (1991).

Cook, Eleanor, *Against Coercion: Games Poets Play* (Stanford: Stanford University Press, 1998).

"The Figure of Enigma: Rhetoric, History, Poetry," *Rhetorica* 19 (2001), 349–78.

Corpus Christianorum, series latina (Turnhout: Brepols, 1953–).

Cotin, Charles, "Discours sur les énigmes," in his *Recueil des énigmes de ce temps* (Lyons, 1655, 1661), n.p.

Couton, Georges, "Une peinture à lire: les tableaux énigmatiques," in his *Ecriture codée: Essais sur l'allégorie au XVIIe siècle* (Paris: Aux amateurs de livres, 1990), pp. 147–53.

Covarrubias Orozco, Sebastián de, *Tesoro dela lengua castellana o española* (1611; repr. Madrid: Editorial Castalia, 1994).

Cronk, Nicholas, "The Enigma of French Classicism: A Platonic Current in Seventeenth-Century Poetic Theory," *French Studies* 40 (1986), 269–86.

Cruz, Sister Juana Inés de, *Enigmas ofrecidos a la Casa del Placer*, ed. Antonio Alatorre (Mexico City: El Colegio de México, 1994) and note "Naturaleza de los 'enigmas'" (Introduction, pp. 39-53).

Curtius, Ernst Robert, *European Literature and the Latin Middle Ages* (Princeton: Princeton University Press, Bollingen, 1953), trans. Willard R. Trask from *Europäische Literatur und lateinisches Mittelalter* (1948).

Dante Alighieri, *La Divina Commedia, Inferno, Purgatorio, Paradiso: The Divine Comedy of Dante Alighieri*, 3 vols., trans. with commentary John D. Sinclair, rev. edn. (New York: Oxford University Press, 1961; first pub. 1939); *The Divine Comedy*, 3 vols., trans. with commentary Charles S. Singleton (Princeton: Princeton University Press, Bollingen, 1977).

Davies, J. M. Q., "*Emma* as Charade and the Education of the Reader," *Philological Quarterly* 65 (1986), 231–42.

Dee, M. I.[John], Preface, *The Elements of Euclid*, trans. H. Billingsby (London: Iohn Daye [1570]).

De la Mare, Walter, *The Complete Poems* (London: Faber and Faber, 1969).

Delplace, Christiane, *Le Griffon de l'archaïsme à l'époque impériale: étude iconographique et essai d'interprétation symbolique* (Brussels: Institut historique belge de Rome, 1980), with 321 illustrations.

De Man, Paul, *Blindness and Insight: Essays in the Rhetoric of Contemporary Criticism*, 2nd edn. (Minneapolis: University of Minnesota Press, 1983).

The Demaundes Joyous: A Facsimile of the First English Riddle Book (1511 edn.), ed. and intro. John Wardroper (London: Gordon Fraser, 1971).

Demetrius, *On Style*, trans. and intro. W. Rhys Roberts (Cambridge, Mass.: Harvard University Press, Loeb, with "Longinus" and Aristotle, 1932; additional notes 1973); *A Medieval Latin Version of Demetrius'* De Elocutione, ed. Bernice V. Wall (Washington, DC: Catholic University of America, 1937).

Demisch, Heinz, *Die Sphinx: Geschichte ihrer Darstellung von den Anfängen bis zur Gegenwart* (Stuttgart: Urachhaus, 1977), with 640 illustrations.

Derrida, Jacques, *La Dissémination* (Paris: Editions du Seuil, 1972).

Despauterius, Johann, *Commentarii grammatici* (Paris, 1537).

Detienne, Marcel, and Jean-Pierre Vernant, *Cunning Intelligence in Greek Culture and Society* (Chicago: University of Chicago Press, 1991), trans. Janet Lloyd from *Les Ruses de l'intelligence: La métis des Grecs* (1974).

Diamond, Jared, *Guns, Germs and Steel: The Fate of Human Societies* (New York: Norton, 1997).

Dickinson, Emily, *The Complete Poems of Emily Dickinson*, 3 vols., ed. Thomas H. Johnson (Boston: Little, Brown, 1960).

Donatus, Aelius, *Donat et la tradition de l'enseignement grammatical*, ed. Louis Holtz (Paris: Centre national de la recherche scientifique, 1981), *Ars grammatica: Ars minor, Ars maior*, also in Keil, *Grammatici latini*, vol. IV, pp. 355–66, 367–402.

Donne, John, *Complete Poetry and Selected Prose*, ed. John Hayward (London: Nonesuch, 1949).

Doob, Penelope Reed, *The Idea of the Labyrinth from Classical Antiquity through the Middle Ages* (Ithaca: Cornell University Press, 1990).

Dronke, Peter, *Fabula: Explorations into the Uses of Myth in Medieval Platonism* (Leiden: Brill, 1974), esp. "Image, Analogy, Enigma," Part I section ii, pp. 32–47; and "Mysteries and How to Cover Them," ibid., pp. 47–54.

Ducrot, Oswald, and Tzvetan Todorov, *Encyclopaedic Dictionary of the Sciences of Language* (Baltimore: Johns Hopkins University Press, 1979), trans. Catherine Porter from *Dictionnaire encyclopédique des sciences du langage* (1972).

Duff, David, ed., *Modern Genre Theory* (Harlow: Longman, 2000).

Dürrbach, F., "Gryps ou Gryphus," *Dictionnaire des antiquités grecques et romaines d'après les textes et les monuments* (Paris: Hachette, 1896).

Edmunds, Lowell, *"The Genre of Theognidean Poetry,"* in Figueira and Nagy, ed., Theognis of Megara, pp. 96–111.

   Oedipus: The Ancient Legend and Its Later Analogues (Baltimore: Johns Hopkins University Press, 1985).

   The Sphinx in the Oedipus Legend (Koenigstein: Hain, 1981).

Edwards, I. E. S., *The Pyramids of Egypt*, 2nd edn. (Harmondsworth: Penguin, 1961).

Ehlers, Johannes, *De Graecorum aenigmatis et griphis* (Prenzlau, 1875; 24 pp.).

Eliot, George, *The Writings of George Eliot*, vol. XIX, *Poems* (Boston: Houghton, Mifflin, 1908).

Eliot, T. S., "Conclusion," *The Use of Poetry and the Use of Criticism* (London: Faber and Faber, 1933, 1964), pp. 150–4.

   Four Quartets (London: Faber and Faber, 1944).

Empson, William, "The Child as Swain," from his *Some Versions of Pastoral* (1935), in Carroll, *Alice in Wonderland*, ed. Gray, pp. 337–65.

   Collected Poems, rev. edn. (New York: Harcourt, Brace, 1956).

Erasmus, Desiderius, *De duplici copia verborum ac rerum commentari duo* (Basel, 1514); trans. Donald B. King and H. David Rix as *On Copia of Words and Ideas* (Milwaukee: Marquette University Press, 1963).

Estienne, Henri, *The Art of Making Devises: Treating of Hieroglyphicks, Symboles, Emblemes, Ænigmas, Sentences, Parables, Reverses of Medalls, Armes, Blazons, Cimiers, Cyphres and Rebus*, trans. T. B., Gent (London: John Holden, 1650; repr. New York: Garland, 1979).

Euclid, *The Elements of geometrie of the most auncient philosopher Evclide of Megara. Faithfully (now first) translated into the Englishe toung*, trans. H. Billingsley (London: Iohn Daye [1570]); *The Thirteen Books of Euclid's Elements*, trans. from the text of Heiberg, ed. T. L. Heath, 2nd edn. (Cambridge: Cambridge University Press, 1956).

Euripides, *The Phoenician Women*, trans. Arthur S. Way, in vol. IV, *Bacchanals*, etc. (London: Heinemann, Loeb, 1912); *The Phoenician Women*, trans.

Elizabeth Wyckoff, in *Euripides V*, ed. David Grene and Richmond Lattimore (Chicago: University of Chicago Press, 1959).

Fahnestock, Jeanne, *Rhetorical Figures in Science* (New York: Oxford University Press, 1999).

Faral, Edmond, ed., *Les Arts poétiques du XIIe et du XIIIe siècle* (Paris: Honoré Champion, 1958).

Fenner, Dudley, *The Artes of Logike and Rhetoricke* (1584)

Ferber, Michael, "Labyrinth," *A Dictionary of Literary Symbols* (Cambridge: Cambridge University Press, 1999), pp. 102–4.

Figueira, Thomas J., and Gregory Nagy, eds., *Theognis of Megara: Poetry and the Polis* (Baltimore: Johns Hopkins University Press, 1985).

Fitzgerald, David, "Of Riddles," *Gentleman's Magazine* 251 (1881), 177–92.

Fletcher, Angus, *Allegory: The Theory of a Symbolic Mode* (Ithaca: Cornell University Press, 1964).

Foquelin, Antoine, *La Rhetorique françoise* (Paris: André Wechel, 1557).

Forster, E. S., "Riddles and Problems from the Greek Anthology," *Greece and Rome* 14 (1945), 42–7.

Fowler, Alastair, "Apology for Rhetoric," *Rhetorica* 8 (1990), 103–18.

"The Future of Genre Theory: Functions and Constructional Types," in *The Future of Literary Theory*, ed. Ralph Cohen (New York: Routledge, 1989), pp. 291–303.

Kinds of Literature: An Introduction to the Theory of Modes and Genres (Cambridge, Mass.: Harvard University Press, 1982).

Fraunce, Abraham, *Arcadian Rhetorike* (1588), ed. and intro. Ethel Seaton (Oxford: Blackwell, for the Luttrell Society, 1950).

Freud, Sigmund, *The Interpretation of Dreams* (Ware: Wordsworth, 1997), trans. A. A. Brill, 1932, from *Die Traumdeutung* (1900).

Jokes and Their Relation to the Unconscious, vol. VIII of *The Standard Edition of Sigmund Freud*, trans. and ed. James Strachey (London: Hogarth, 1905, 1960).

Fried, Debra, "Rhyme Puns", in *On Puns: The Foundation of Letters*, ed. Jonathan Culler (London: Basil Blackwell, 1988), pp. 83-99.

Friedrich, J. B., *Geschichte des Räthsels* (Dresden: Rudolf Kuntze, 1860).

Frye, Northrop, *Anatomy of Criticism: Four Essays* (Princeton: Princeton University Press, 1957).

"Charms and Riddles," in his *Spiritus Mundi: Essays on Literature, Myth, and Society* (Bloomington: Indiana University Press, 1976), pp. 123–47.

The Great Code: The Bible and Literature (Toronto: Academic Press, 1982).

Late Notebooks, 1982–1990: Architecture of the Spiritual World, 2 vols., ed. Robert D. Denham (Toronto: University of Toronto Press, 2000).

Gärtner, Hans Armin, "Rätsel," *Der Neue Pauly: Enzyklopädie der Antike*, ed. Hubert Cancik and Helmuth Schneider (Stuttgart: J. B. Metzler, 1996–), vol. X, cols. 754–8, with Barbara Böck (Alter Orient).

Gellius, *Noctes Atticae*, trans. John C. Rolfe as *The Attic Nights of Aulus Gellius*, 3 vols. (Cambridge, Mass.: Harvard University Press, Loeb, 1927).

Genette, Gérard, *The Architext: An Introduction* (Berkeley: University of California Press, 1992), trans. Jane E. Lewin from *Introduction à l'architexte* (1979).

Figures of Literary Discourse (New York: Columbia University Press, 1982), trans. Alan Sheridan from selections from *Figures* (1966–72).

Gerber, Gustav, *Die Sprache als Kunst*, 2nd edn. (Berlin 1885; repr. Hildesheim: Georg Olms, 1961), pp. 381–93 (on the *Worträtsel*), pp. 485–95 (on the *allegorische Rätsel*), and *passim*.

Goethe, J. W. von, *Correspondence between Goethe and Schiller 1794–1805*, trans. Liselotte Dieckmann (New York: Peter Lang, 1994).

Goldberg, Christine, *Turandot's Sisters: A Study of the Folktale AT 851* (New York: Garland, 1993).

Golding, Harriet, "Riddles and Enigmas in Medieval Castilian Literature," *Romance Philology* 36 (1982), 209–21.

Gombrich, E., "Aenigma Termini," *Journal of the Warburg and Courtauld Institutes* 1 (1937–38), 66–69; on Erasmus's use of the Terminus riddle.

Gorfain, Phyllis, "'Craft against Vice': Riddling as Ritual in *Measure for Measure*," *Asaph* 5 (1989), 91–107.

Grabes, Herbert, *The Mutable Glass: Mirror Imagery in Titles and Texts of the Middle Ages and the English Renaissance* (Cambridge: Cambridge University Press, 1983), trans. Gordon Collier, from enlarged edn. of *Speculum* (1973).

Gracián, Baltasar, *Agudeza y Arte de Ingenio* (Madrid, 1648).

Green, Thomas, and W. J. Pepicello, "Wit in Riddling: A Linguistic Perspective," *Genre* 11 (1978), 1–13.

Greville, Fulke, *Selected Poems*, ed. Neil Powell (Manchester: Carcanet, 1990).

Gubernatis, Angelo de, *Zoological Mythology: or, The Legends of Animals*, 2 vols. (1872; facsimile edn., Detroit: Singing Tree, 1968).

Hagen, Hermann, *Antike und Mittelalterliche Raethselpoesie* (Biel: K. F. Steinheil, 1869).

Hain, Mathilde, *Rätsel* (Stuttgart: Metzler, 1966).

Hammer, Joseph von (Hammer-Purgstall), *Geschichte der schönen Redekünste Persiens mit einer Blüthenlese aus zweihundert persischen Dichtern* (Vienna: Heubner und Wolfe, 1818).

Hardie, P. R., "Virgil: A Paradoxical Poet," *Papers of the Leeds International Latin Seminar*, vol. IX, ed. Francis Cairns and Malcolm Heath (Leeds: Cairns, University of Leeds, 1996), pp. 103–21.

Hariri, *The Assemblies of Al-Hariri*, trans. and ed. Thomas Chenery (London: Williams and Norgate, 1867).

Hasan-Rokem, G., and D. Shulman, eds., *Untying the Knot: On Riddles and Enigmatic Modes* (New York: Oxford University Press, 1996).

Heaney, Seamus, *The Haw Lantern* (London: Faber and Faber, 1987).

Hébert, Anne, *Œuvre poétique 1950–1990* (Montréal: Boréal, 1992).

Hecht, Anthony, *The Transparent Man* (New York: Knopf, 1990).

Hegel, G. W. F., *Aesthetics: Lectures on Fine Art*, trans. T. M. Knox (Oxford: Clarendon, 1975), vol. I, pp. 395–403, esp. "The Riddle," "Allegory";

Vorlesungen über die Aesthetik (Stuttgart: Fr. Frommanns [H. Kurtz], 1927).

Hein, Jean, *Enigmaticité et messianisme dans la "Divine Comédie"* (Florence: Leo S. Olschki, 1992).

Heraclitus, *The Art and Thought of Heraclitus: An Edition of the Fragments with Translation and Commentary*, ed. Charles H. Kahn (Cambridge: Cambridge University Press, 1979).

Herbert, George, *The Complete English Works*, ed. Ann Pasternak Slater (New York: Knopf, 1995).

Herder, Johann Gottfried von, *The Spirit of Hebrew Poetry*, 2 vols., trans. James Marsh, from *Vom Geist der hebräischen Poesie*, 1782–83 (Burlington: Edward Smith, 1833; repr. Naperville, Ill.: Aleph, 1971), vol. 1, Preface and pp. 200–210.

Hesiod, *Hesiod, the Homeric Hymns and Homerica*, trans. Hugh G. Evelyn-White (London: Heinemann, Loeb, 1914).

Hetherington, John, *Aeschylus* (New Haven: Yale University Press, 1986).

Higgins, Dick, "Pattern Poetry," NPEPP, pp. 890–1.

Highway, Tomson, *Dry Lips Oughta Move to Kapuskasing* (Calgary: Fifth House, 1989).

Hill, Geoffrey, *Mercian Hymns*, in his *Somewhere Is Such a Kingdom: Poems 1952–1971* (Boston: Houghton Mifflin, 1975).

Hoffmann, F. R., *Grundzüge einer Geschichte des Bilderräthsels* (Berlin, 1869).

Hollander, John, *Harp Lake* (New York: Knopf, 1988).

    Movie-Going (New York: Atheneum, 1962).

    "The Poem in the Eye," in his *Vision and Resonance: Two Senses of Poetic Form*, 2nd edn. (New Haven: Yale University Press, 1985), pp. 245–87.

    "The Poetry of Nonsense: Carroll's Quest Romance," in his *The Work of Poetry* (New York: Columbia University Press, 1997), pp. 200–9.

    Reflections on Espionage (New York: Atheneum, 1976).

    Types of Shape, rev. edn. (New Haven: Yale University Press, 1991).

Howe, Nicholas, "Aldheim's *Enigmata* and Isidorian etymology," *Anglo-Saxon England* 14 (1985), 37–59.

Howell, Wilbur Samuel, *Eighteenth-Century British Logic and Rhetoric* (Princeton: Princeton University Press, 1971).

Huizinga, Johan, *Homo Ludens: A Study of the Play Element in Culture* (London: Temple Smith, 1949).

Hüsing, Georg, *Die Iranische Überlieferung und das arische System* (Leipzig, 1909).

Irwin, John T., *The Mystery to a Solution: Poe, Borges, and the Analytic Detective Story* (Baltimore: Johns Hopkins University Press, 1994).

Isidore of Seville, *Isidori hispalensis episcopi Etymologiarum sive Originum libri XX*, ed. W. M. Lindsay, 2 vols. (Oxford: Clarendon, 1911).

Itzhaki, Masha, "The Riddles of Abraham ibn Ezra," in *Abraham ibn Ezra y su Tiempo/Abraham ibn Ezra and his Age*, ed. Ferando Díaz Esteban (Madrid: Asociación Española de Orientalistas, 1990), pp. 163–8.

Jäger, Martin, "Assyrische Räthsel und Spruchwörter," *Beiträge zur Assyriologie* 2 (1894), 274–305.

Jaeger, Werner, *Early Christianity and Greek Paideia* (Cambridge, Mass.: Harvard University Press, 1961).

Jakobson, Roman, "Subliminal Verbal Patterning in Poetry," in his *Language in Literature* (Cambridge, Mass.: Harvard University Press, 1987), pp. 250–61.

Jarrell, Randall, "The Obscurity of the Poet," in his *Poetry and the Age* (New York: Farrar, Straus, Giroux [Noonday], 1953, 1979), pp. 3–27.

Jauss, Hans Robert, "Theory of Genres and Medieval Literature," in his *Toward an Aesthetic of Reception* (Minneapolis: University of Minnesota Press, 1982), trans. Timothy Bahti from essays of 1969–80, pp. 76–109.

Javelet, Robert, "Per speculum, in aenigmate," in his *Image et ressemblance au douzième siècle*, 2 vols. (Strasbourg: Letouzey & Ané, 1967), vol. 1, pp. 367–88.

Jolles, André, "La Devinette," in his *Formes simples* (Paris: Seuil, 1972), trans. Antoine Marie Buguet from *Einfache Formen: Legende, Sage, Mythe, Rätsel, Spruch, Kasus, Memorabile, Märchen, Witz*, rev. edn. (Halle [Saale]: Max Niemeyer, 1956; orig. pub. 1930), pp. 103–19.

Joseph, Sister Miriam, *Rhetoric in Shakespeare's Time: Literary Theory of Renaissance Europe* (New York: Harcourt Brace, 1947, 1962); incorporates the following.
  Shakespeare's Use of the Arts of Language (New York: Columbia University Press, 1947).

Josephus, *The Antiquities of the Jews* in *The Works of Josephus*, trans. William Whiston (Peabody, Mass.: Hendrikson, 1987).

Joyce, James, *Finnegans Wake* (New York: Viking, 1939, corrected edn. 1958).

Jonson, Ben, *The Complete Masques*, ed. Stephen Orgel (New Haven: Yale University Press, 1969).

Kaivola-Bregenhøj, Annikki, *Riddles: Perspectives on the Use, Function and Change in a Folklore Genre* (Helsinki: Finnish Literature Society, 2001).

Keil, Henry, ed., *Grammatici latini ex recensione Henrici Keilii*, 8 vols. (Leipzig: B. G. Teubner, 1857–80; repr. Hildesheim: Georg Olms, 1961).

Kelso, James A., "Riddle," in *Encyclopaedia of Religion and Ethics*, ed. James Hastings (Edinburgh: T. & T. Clark, 1918), vol. x, pp. 765–70.

Kermode, Frank, *The Genesis of Secrecy: On the Interpretation of Narrative* (Cambridge, Mass.: Harvard University Press, 1979).
  The Sense of an Ending: Studies in the Theory of Fiction (New York: Oxford University Press, 1967).

Kern, Hermann, *Through the Labyrinth: Designs and Meanings over 5000 Years* (Munich: Prestel, 2000), trans. Robert Ferre and Jeff Saward from *Labyrinthe: Erscheinungsformen und Deutungen 5000 Jahre Gegenwart eines Urbilds* (1982) with addenda; copiously illustrated.

Keynes, John Maynard, "Newton, the Man," in *The Collected Works of John Maynard Keynes*, vol. x, *Essays in Biography*, ed. D. E. Moggridge (Cambridge: Cambridge University Press, 1971), pp. 363–74.

Kippenberg, Hans G., and Guy G. Stroumsa, "Introduction," *Secrecy and Concealment: Studies in the History of Mediterranean and Near Eastern Religions* (Leiden: Brill, 1995), pp. xiii–xxiii.

Kittel, Gerhard, *Theologisches Wörterbuch zum Neuen Testament* (Stuttgart: W. Kohlhammer, 1932), trans. Geoffrey W. Bromiley as *Theological Dictionary of the New Testament* (Grand Rapids, Mich.: W. B. Eerdmans, 1968–79).

Kircher, Athanasius, *Oedipus Aegyptiacus*, 3 vols. in 4 (Rome, 1652–54), vol. I, "Symbolica caput IV. De Aenigmate, Scirpo, Gripho, Logogripho."

Knowles, Rev. J. Hinton, "Why the Fish Laughed,"in his *Folk-Tales of Kashmir* (London: Trübner, 1888).

Knox, Bernard M. W., *Oedipus at Thebes* (New Haven: Yale University Press, 1957).

Knox, Dilwyn, *Ironia: Medieval and Renaissance Ideas on Irony* (Leiden: Brill, 1989).

König, J., "Aenigma," *Historisches Wörterbuch der Rhetorik*, ed. Gregor Kalivoda and Franz-Hubert Robling (Tübingen: Max Niemeyer, 1992), vol. I, cols. 187–95.

Kugel, James L., *The Idea of Biblical Poetry: Parallelism and Its History* (New Haven: Yale University Press, 1981).

"Solomon's Riddles," in his *The Great Poems of the Bible* (New York: Free Press, 1999), pp. 160–80.

Lamberton, Robert, *Homer the Theologian: Neoplatonist Allegorical Reading and the Growth of the Epic Tradition* (Berkeley: University of California Press, 1986).

Lampe: *A Patristic Greek Lexicon*, ed. G. W. H. Lampe (Oxford: Clarendon, 1961).

Landau, Sidney, *Dictionaries: The Art and Craft of Lexicography* (New York: Scribner, 1984).

Lassner, Jacob, *Demonizing the Queen of Sheba: Boundaries of Gender and Culture in Postbiblical Judaisim and Medieval Islam* (Chicago: University of Chicago Press, 1993).

Lausberg, Heinrich, *Elemente der literarischen Rhetorik* (Munich, 1949).

Handbuch der literarischen Rhetorik: eine Grundlegung der Literaturwissenschaft, 2nd edn., 2 vols. (Munich: Heuber, 1973).

Lawrence, D. H., *The Complete Poems of D. H. Lawrence*, 3rd edn., 2 vols., ed. Vivian de Sola Pinto and Warren Roberts (London: Heinemann, 1972).

Lévi-Strauss, Claude, "Structure des mythes," in his *Anthropologie Structurale* (Paris: Plon, 1958), pp. 235–42.

Lloyd-Jones, Hugh, *The Justice of Zeus*, 2nd edn. (Berkeley: University of California Press, 1983).

Löw, Leopold, "Räthsel und Witzesspiele," in his *Die Lebensalter in der Jüdischen Literatur* (Szegedin: Sigmund Berger, 1875), pp. 346–51.

Macpherson, Jay, *Poems Twice Told: The Boatman & Welcoming Disaster* (Toronto: Oxford University Press, 1981).

Macdonald, George, *Phantastes* (1858; repr. London: Dent, 1983).

Maier, Michael, *Septimana Philosophia qua aenigmata aureola* (Frankfurt, 1620).

Manuel, Frank, *The Religion of Isaac Newton* (Oxford: Clarendon, 1974).

Marks, Herbert, "Hollowed Names: *Vox* and *Vanitas* in the *Purgatorio*," *Dante Studies* 110 (1992), 135–78.

"Writing as Calling," *New Literary History* 29 (1998), 15–39.

Masen, Jacob, *Speculum imaginum veritatis occultae, exhibens symbola, emblemata, hieroglyphica, aenigmata*, 3rd edn. corrected (1681).

Matthew of Vendôme, in Faral, *Les Arts poétiques du XIIe et du XIIIe siècle*.

Matthews, W. H., *Mazes and Labyrinths: Their History and Development* (New York: Dover, 1922, 1970).

May, Georges, *La Perruque de Dom Juan ou Du bon usage des énigmes dans la littérature de l'âge classique* ([Paris]: Klincksieck, 1995).

Mayer, Cornelius, "Aenigma," *Augustinus-Lexikon*, ed. Cornelius Mayer (Basel: Schwabe, 1986–94), vol. I, cols. 140–41.

Mayor, Adrienne, *The First Fossil Hunters: Paleontology in Greek and Roman Times* (Princeton: Princeton University Press, 2000).

Mayr, Ernst, "The Idea of Teleology," *Journal of the History of Ideas* 53 (1992), 117–35.

McDowell, John Holmes, *Children's Riddling* (Bloomington: Indiana University Press, 1979).

McHale, Brian, *Constructing Postmodernism* (London: Routledge, 1992).

Melancthon, Philip, *De rhetorica libri tres* (1519); *Elementorum rhetoricae libri duo* (1531, 1542).

Melville, Herman, *Moby-Dick or The Whale* (1851; repr. London: Oxford University Press, 1920).

Ménestrier, Claude-François, *La Philosophie des images énigmatiques* (Paris: Hilaire Baritel, 1694).

Merrill, James, *Recitative: Prose by James Merrill*, ed. J. D. McClatchy (San Francisco: North Point, 1986).

A Scattering of Salts (New York: Knopf, 1995).

Migne, J. P., ed., *Patrologiae cursus completus, Series graeca*, 161 vols. (Paris, 1857–66).

Patrologiae cursus completus, Series latina, 217 vols. (Paris, 1844–).

Milton, John, *Complete Poems and Major Prose*, ed. Merritt Y. Hughes (Indianapolis: Bobbs-Merrill, 1957).

Minturno, Antonio, *De Poeta* (Venice, 1559; repr. Munich: Wilhelm Fink, 1970).

Montagu, Jennifer, "The Painted Enigma and French Seventeenth-Century Art," *Journal of the Warburg and Courtauld Institutes* 31 (1968), 307–35.

Moore, Marianne, *The Complete Poems* (New York: Macmillan Viking, 1967).

Moret, Jean-Marc, *Œdipe, la Sphinx et les Thébains: essai de mythologie iconographique*, 2 vols. (Geneva: Institut suisse de Rome, 1984), copiously illustrated.

Mortley, Raoul, *Connaissance religieuse et hermétique chez Clément d'Alexandrie* (Leiden: Brill, 1973), app. II, "La notion de l'énigme: αἴνιγμα, αἰνίσσομαι," pp. 229–32.

"The Mirror and 1 Cor. 13,12 in the Epistemology of Clement of Alexandria," *Vigiliae Christianae* 30 (1976), 109–20.

Mosellanus (Schade), Petrus, *Tabulae de schematibus et tropis* (1529; Nuremberg, 1540).

Mosès, Stéphane, *L'Ange de l'histoire: Rosenzweig, Benjamin, Scholem* (Paris: Seuil, 1992).

Müller, Hans-Peter, "Das Begriff 'Rätsel' im Alten Testament," *Vetus Testamentum* 20 (1970), 465–89.

Murphy, James J., "The Historiography of Rhetoric: Challenges and Opportunities," *Rhetorica* 1.1 (1983), 1–8.

Medieval Rhetoric: A Select Bibliography, 2nd edn. (Toronto: Centre for Mediaeval Studies, 1989).

Rhetoric in the Middle Ages: A History of Rhetorical Theory from Saint Augustine to the Renaissance (Berkeley: University of California Press, 1974).

Nabokov, Vladimir, *Speak, Memory: An Autobiography Revisited*, rev. edn. (New York: Pyramid, 1968).

Nagy, Gregory, *The Best of the Achaeans: Concepts of the Hero in Archaic Greek Poetry*, rev. edn. (Baltimore: Johns Hopkins University Press, 1999).

Nicene and Post-Nicene Fathers: A Select Library of the Nicene and Post-Nicene Fathers, ed. Philip Schaff (Edinburgh: T. & T. Clark, 1887–; repr. Grand Rapids, Mich.: Wm. B. Eerdmans, 1993).

Nicol, T., "Riddle," *A Dictionary of the Bible*, ed. James Hastings, (Edinburgh: T. & T. Clark, 1902), vol. IV, pp. 270–2.

Nigg, Joe, *The Book of Fabulous Beasts: A Treasury of Writings from Ancient Times to the Present* (New York: Oxford University Press, 1999).

Nolan, Edward P., *Now through a Glass Darkly: Specular Images of Being and Knowing, Virgil to Chaucer* (Ann Arbor: University of Michigan Press, 1991).

Ohlert, K., *Rätsel und Rätselspiele der alten Griechen*, 2nd edn. (Berlin, 1912).

Ong, Walter J., "Wit and Mystery: A Revaluation of Medieval Latin Hymnody," *Speculum* 22 (1947), 310–41.

Opie, Iona and Peter, "Riddles," in their *The Lore and Language of Schoolchildren* (Oxford: Clarendon, 1959), pp. 73–86, also 68–9 and *passim*.

Pagis, Dan, *Al sod hatum* or *A Secret Sealed: Hebrew Baroque Emblem-Riddles from Italy and Holland* (Jerusalem: Magnes Press, Hebrew University, 1986; in Hebrew apart from the Summary).

"Toward a Theory of the Literary Riddle," in *Untying the Knot*, ed. Hasan-Rokem and Shulman, pp. 81–108.

Pagninus, Sante, *Institutiones Hebraicae* (1526).

Pamuk, Orhan, *The Black Book* (New York: Farrar, Straus, Giroux, 1994), trans. Güneli Gün from *Kara Kitap* (1990).

Paris, Gaston, Introduction to Eugène Rolland, ed., *Devinettes et énigmes populaires de la France* (Paris, 1877), pp. i–xvi.

Pascal, [Blaise], *Pensées*, texte établi par Léon Brunschvicg (Paris: Garnier-Flammarion, 1976).

Patterson, Annabel, "Fables of Power," in *Politics of Discourse: The Literature and History of Seventeenth-Century England*, ed. Kevin Sharpe and Steven N. Zwicker (Berkeley: University of California Press, 1987), pp. 271–96.

Pausanias, *Guide to Greece*, trans. Peter Levi, 2 vols., rev. edn. (London: Penguin, 1979).

Peacham, Henry, *The Garden of Eloquence*, 1577, 2nd edn. 1593 (Gainesville, Fla.: Scholars' Facsimiles and Reprints, 1954).

Peacock, Thomas Love, *Crotchet Castle* (1831; with *Nightmare Abbey*, Harmondsworth: Penguin, 1969).

Perec, Georges, "Histoire du lipogramme," in OULIPO, ed., *La Littérature potentielle (Créations Re-créations Récréations)* (Paris: Gallimard, 1973), pp. 77–93.

Permjakov, Grigorij, "The Logical Structure of Some Russian Riddles," in *Semiotische Studien zum Rätsel*, ed. Wolfgang Eismann and Peter Gryzbek (Bochum: N. Brockmeyer, 1987), pp. 107–10.

Pernety, (Antoine Joseph) Dom, "Mémoire sur l'usage des Anciens & des Modernes de proposer des énigmes à deviner, ou à résoudre," *Nouveaux Mémoires de l'Académie royale des sciences et des belles-lettres de Berlin* (1773), 498–522.

Petsch, Robert von, *Neue Beiträge zur Kenntnis des Volksrätsels* (Berlin: Mayer & Müller, 1899), series *Palaestra* IV.

Plato, *The Collected Dialogues of Plato*, ed. Edith Hamilton and Huntington Cairns (Princeton: Princeton University Press, Bollingen, 1961).

Plutarch, "The Dinner of the Seven Wise Men," *Moralia*, trans. Frank Cole Babbitt (Cambridge, Mass.: Harvard University Press, Loeb, 1928), vol. II, pp. 348–449.
   "De E apud Delphi," *Moralia*, trans. Frank Cole Babbitt (London: Heinemann, 1936), vol. V, pp. 198–253.
   "Isis and Osiris," ibid., pp. 6–191; *Plutarch's De Iside et Osiride*, ed. and trans. J. Gwyn Griffiths (Cardiff: University of Wales Press, 1970), bilingual text with glosses.

Poe, Edgar Allan, *Poetry and Tales*, Library of America (New York: Literary Classics of the United States, 1984).

Pollux, *Pollucis Onomasticon*, ed. Ericus Bethe (Stuttgart: Teubner, 1967), vol. X of *Lexicographi Graeci*.

Poole, Joshua, *The English Parnassus* (Menston: Scolar Press, 1972; repr. 1657 edn.).

Pope, Alexander, *Pope: Poetical Works*, ed. Herbert Davis (Oxford: Oxford University Press, 1978).

Porzig, Walter, "Das Rätsel der Sphinx," *Lexis: Studien zur Sprachphilosophie, Sprachgeschichte und Begriffsforschung* 3.2 (1953), 236–9; on the Greek alchemical riddle.

Prior, Matthew, *The Literary Works of Matthew Prior*, 2nd edn., ed. H. Bunker Wright and Monroe K. Spears, 2 vols. (Oxford: Clarendon, 1971).

Pritchard, James B., ed., *Solomon and Sheba* (London: Phaidon, 1973).

Prümm, "Mystery Religions, Graeco-Oriental," *New Catholic Encyclopedia*, ed. Catholic University of America (New York: McGraw-Hill, 1967), vol. x, pp. 148–64.

Putnam, M. C. J., "The Riddle of Damoetas," *Mnemosyne* 18 (1965), 150–4.

Puttenham, George, *The Arte of English Poesie*, 1589, ed. Gladys Doidge Willcock and Alice Walker (Cambridge: Cambridge University Press, 1936).

Quarles, Francis, *The Complete Works in Prose and Verse*, ed. Alexander B. Grosart, 3 vols. (Hildesheim: G. Olms, 1971, from the 1635 edn.).

Quintilian, *Institutio oratoria*, trans. H. E. Butler, 4 vols. (Cambridge, Mass.: Harvard University Press, Loeb, 1921).

Rabelais, François, *The Histories of Gargantua and Pantagruel*, trans. J. M. Cohen (Harmondsworth: Penguin, 1955).

Rad, Gerhard von, *Wisdom in Israel* (London: SCM Press, 1972), trans. James D. Martin from *Weisheit in Israel* (1970).

Rademaker, C. S. M., *Life and Work of Gerardus Joannes Vossius (1577–1649)* (Assen, the Netherlands: Van Gorcum, 1981).

Ramacciotti, Valeria, *La chimera e la sfinge: immagini, miti e profili decadenti* (Geneva: Slatkine, 1987).

Rand, Nicholas, *Le Cryptage et la vie des œuvres: Etude du secret dans les textes de Flaubert, Stendhal*, [etc.] (Paris: Aubier, 1989).

Raphals, Lisa, *Knowing Words: Wisdom and Cunning in the Classical Traditions of China and Greece* (Ithaca: Cornell University Press, 1992).

Renou, Louis, "The Enigma in the Ancient Literature of India," trans. Elaine P. Halperin, *Diogenes* 29 (1960), 32–41.

Rhetores graeci, ed. Leonhard von Spengel (Leipzig: Teubner, 1853–56; repr. Frankfurt: Minerva, 1966).

Ricoeur, Paul, *Temps et récit*, 3 vols. (Paris: Seuil, 1983–85); trans. Kathleen McLaughlin and David Pellauer (vols. i and ii) and David Pellauer and Kathleen Blamey (vol. iii) as *Time and Narrative* (Chicago: University of Chicago Press, 1984–88).

Rivius, Joannes, *De Rhetorica libri tres* (London, 1552).

Robe, Stanley L., ed., *Hispanic Riddles from Panama* (Berkeley: University of California Press, 1963).

Röhrich, L., "Rätsel," *Die Religion in Geschichte und Gegenwart: Handwörterbuch für Theologie und Religionwissenschaft*, ed. Hans Frhr. v. Campenhausen et al. (Tübingen: J. C. B. Mohr, 1961), vol. v col. 767.

Rolland, Eugène, ed., *Devinettes et ènigmes populaires de la France* (Paris, 1877).

Rondeaulet, Sieur (pseud.), *A Treatise on the Charade*, trans. Tobias Rigmerole (London: T. Davies, 1777).

Rosenberg, Harold, "The Labyrinth of Saul Steinberg," in his *The Anxious Object* (Chicago: University of Chicago Press, 1964, 1982), pp. 163–8.

Rosmarin, Adena, "Theoretical Introduction" and "Defining a Theory of Genre," in her *The Power of Genre* (Minneapolis: University of Minnesota Press, 1985), pp. 3–22 and 23–51.

Ruskin, John, *The Works of John Ruskin*, ed. E. T. Cook and Alexander Wedderburn, 39 vols. (London: George Allan, 1903–12).

Sacerdos, Marius Plotius, *Artes grammaticae*, Book I, in Keil, *Grammatici latini* vol. VI, pp. 427–546.

Salusinszky, Imre, *Criticism and Society* (New York: Methuen, 1987).

Sands, Robert C., "A Simple Story," *The Writings of Robert C. Sands in Prose and Verse*, 2 vols. (New York: Harper, 1835), vol. II, pp. 44–61.

Santi, Aldo, *Bibliografia della Enigmistica* (Florence: Sansoni, 1952).

Scaliger, J. C., *Poetices libri septem* (1561).

Schechter, S., "The Riddles of Solomon in Rabbinic Literature," *Folk-Lore* I (1890), 349–58.

Schenck, Eva-Marie, *Das Bilderrätsel* (Hildesheim: Georg Olms, 1973).

Schenkeveld, Dirk Marie, *Studies in Demetrius* On Style (Amsterdam: Adolf M. Hackert, 1964).

Schevill, Rudolph, "Some Forms of the Riddle Question and the Exercise of Wits in Popular Fiction and Formal Literature," in *University of California Publications in Modern Philology*, vol. II, ed. Lucien Foulet, Charles M. Gayley, and H. K. Schilling (Berkeley: University of California Press, 1910–12), pp. 183–238.

Schnackenberg, Gjertrud, *The Throne of Labdacus* (New York: Farrar, Straus, Giroux, 2000).

Schoettgen, Christian, *Horae Hebraicae et Talmudicae* (1733).

Schönfeldt, Alfred, "Zur Analyse des Rätsels," *Zeitschrift für deutsche Philologie* 97 (1978), 60–73.

Schultz, W. [Wolfgang], "Rätsel," in Pauly, Wissowa, and Kroll, eds., *Realencyclopädie der classischen Altertumswissenschaft* IA (Munich: Alfred Druckenmüller, 1914), cols. 62–125.

Rätsel aus dem hellenischen Kulturkreise, 2 vols. in 1 (Leipzig: J. C. Hinrichs, 1909–12).

Scott, Charles T., "Some Approaches to the Study of the Riddle," in *Studies in the Language, Literature, and Culture of the Middle Ages and Later*, ed. E. Bagby Atwood and Archibald A. Hill (Austin: University of Texas Press, 1969), pp. 111–27.

Scott, W. H., "The Sibylline Riddle," *The Atlantis: A Register of Literature and Science* 2 (1859), 324–33.

Scully, Stephen, "Weisheits-Literatur," *Der Neue Pauly: Enzyklopädie der Antike*, ed. Hubert Cancik and Helmuth Schneider (Stuttgart: J. B. Metzler, 1996–), vol. XII.2, cols. 444–51, with Elisabeth Hollender (Judentum) and Christian Hünemörder (Islam).

Segal, Charles, "Oedipus Tyrannus," in his *Tragedy and Civilization: An Interpretation of Sophocles* (Cambridge, Mass.: Harvard University Press for Oberlin College, 1981), pp. 207–48.

Sewell, Elizabeth, *The Field of Nonsense* (London: Chatto & Windus, 1953).

Shakespeare, William, *The Riverside Shakespeare*, ed. G. Blakemore Evans et al. (Boston: Houghton, Mifflin, 1974).

Shaw, W. David, *The Lucid Veil: Poetic Truth in the Victorian Age* (London: Athlone, 1987).

Sherry, Richard, *A Treatise of the Figures of Grammar and Rhetoric* (London, 1550, 1555).

Shields, Carol, *Larry's Party* (Toronto: Vintage, 1997).

Shuger, Debora K., *Sacred Eloquence: The Christian Grand Style in the English Renaissance* (Princeton: Princeton University Press, 1988).

Silberman, Lou H., "The Queen of Sheba in Judaic Tradition," in Pritchard, ed., *Solomon and Sheba*, pp. 65–84.

Simpson, James, "'Et vidit Deus cogitaciones eorum': A Parallel Instance and Possible Source for Langland's Use of a Biblical Formula at *Piers Plowman* B.XV.200a, " *Notes & Queries* 33 (1986), 9–13.

Smith, John, *The Mysterie of Rhetorique Unvail'd* (1657; also repr. Menston: Scolar, 1969).

Soarez, Cyprianus, *De arte rhetorica* (Bvrdigalae, 1609).

Sonnino, Leo A., *A Hand-Book to Sixteenth-Century Rhetoric* (London: Routledge & Kegan Paul, 1968).

Sophocles, *Oedipus the King*, with *Oedipus at Colonus* and *Antigone*, trans. F. Storr (Cambridge, Mass.: Harvard University Press, Loeb, 1912).

Spitzer, Leo, "Charade," *Philological Quarterly* 23 (1944), 77–83.

Stanford, W. B., *Greek Metaphor: Studies in Theory and Practice* (Oxford: Blackwell, 1936).

Starnes, DeWitt T., and Gertrude E. Noyes, *The English Dictionary from Cawdrey to Johnson* (Chapel Hill: University of North Carolina Press, 1946).
   Renaissance Dictionaries: English–Latin and Latin–English (Austin: University of Texas Press, 1954).

Sternbach, Ludwik, *Indian Riddles: A Forgotten Chapter in the History of Sanskrit Literature* (Hoshiarpur: Vishveshvaranand Vedic Research Institute, 1975).

Sternberg, Meir, *The Poetics of Biblical Narrative: Ideological Literature and the Drama of Reading* (Bloomington: Indiana University Press, 1985).

Stevens, Wallace, *The Collected Poems* (New York: Knopf, 1954; London: Faber and Faber, 1955).
   Letters of Wallace Stevens, ed. Holly Stevens (New York: Knopf, 1966; London: Faber and Faber, 1966).
   The Necessary Angel: Essays on Reality and the Imagination (New York: Knopf, 1951; London: Faber and Faber, 1951).
   Opus Posthumous, rev. edn., ed. Milton J. Bates (New York: Knopf, 1989; London: Faber and Faber, 1989).

Stock, Brian, *Augustine the Reader: Meditation, Self-Knowledge, and the Ethics of Interpretation* (Cambridge, Mass.: Harvard University Press, 1996).

Strand, Mark, *Blizzard of One* (New York: Knopf, 1999).

Stroumsa, Guy G., "Moses' Riddles: Esoteric Trends in Patristic Hermeneutics," in *Interpretation in Religion*, ed. Shlomo Biderman and Ben-Ami Scharfstein (Leiden: E. J. Brill, 1992), pp. 229–48; also in Stroumsa,

Hidden Wisdom: Esoteric Traditions and the Roots of Christian Mysticism (Leiden: Brill, 1996), pp. 92–108.

"Myth as Enigma: Cultural Hermeneutics in Late Antiquity," in Hasan-Rokem and Shulman, eds., *Untying the Knot*, pp. 271–83; also in Stroumsa, *Hidden Wisdom*, pp. 11–26.

Strubel, Armand, "' Allegoria in factis' et 'Allegoria in verbis,'" *Poétique* 23 (1975), 342–57.

Susenbrotus, *Epitome troporum ac schematum* (London, 1540, 1562, 1621 as *Epitome troporum ac schematum et grammaticorum et rhetoricorum*).

Swift, Jonathan, *The Complete Poems*, ed. Pat Rogers (New Haven: Yale University Press, 1983).

Tabourot, Estienne, *Les Bigarrures du Seigneur des Accords* (Paris, 1572, first known edn. 1582; repr., 2 vols., Geneva: Droz, 1986, facs. of 1588 edn.).

Talon, Omer, *Audomari Talaei Rhetorica*, editio postrema (Paris: apud Andream Wechelum, 1562).

Taylor, Archer, *A Bibliography of Riddles* (Helsinki: Finnish Academy of Sciences, 1939), FF Communications, no. 126, vol. LIII 1; on folk riddles, annotated.

English Riddles from Oral Tradition (Berkeley: University of California Press, 1951).

"Folklore and the Student of Literature," in *The Study of Folklore*, ed. Alan Dundes (Englewood Cliffs: Prentice-Hall, 1965), pp. 34–42.

The Literary Riddle before 1600 (Berkeley: University of California Press, 1948).

Problems in German Literary History of the Fifteenth and Sixteenth Centuries (1939; repr. New York: Kraus, 1966).

"Problems in the Study of Riddles," *Southern Folklore Quarterly* 2 (1938), 1–9.

"The Riddle," *California Folklore Quarterly* (later *Western Folklore*) 2 (1943), 129–47.

"Riddles and Poetry," *Southern Folklore Quarterly* 11 (1947), 245–7.

"The Varieties of Riddles," in *Philologica: The Malone Anniversary Studies*, ed. Thomas A. Kirby and Henry Bosley Woolf (Baltimore: Johns Hopkins University Press, 1949), pp. 1–8.

Tennyson, Alfred, *The Poems of Tennyson*, ed. Christopher Ricks, 2nd edn., 3 vols. (Berkeley: University of California Press, 1987).

Tertullian, *Ante-Nicene Christian Library*, vol. XI, *The Writings of Tertullian* (part. 1, 1869).

Tervarent, Guy de, *Attributs et symboles dans l'art profane 1450–1600: dictionnaire d'un langage perdu* (Geneva: Droz, 1958).

Tey, Josephine, *The Daughter of Time* (1951; New York: Washington Square, 1977).

The Singing Sands (1952; Harmondsworth: Penguin, 1977).

Thomas, Keith, *Religion and the Decline of Magic: Studies in Popular Beliefs in Sixteenth- and Seventeenth-Century England* (London: Penguin, 1971).

Thomas Aquinas, *S. Thomae aquinatis Opera Omnia*, ed. Roberto Busa, 7 vols. (Stuttgart: Fromann-Holzboog, 1974–80).

Thompson, Stith, *Motif-Index of Folk-Literature: A Classification of Narrative Elements in Folktales, Ballads, Myths, Fables, Mediaeval Romances, Exempla, Fabliaux, Jest-Books and Local Legends*, rev. edn., 6 vols. (Bloomington: Indiana University Press, 1955–58), under H530–899.

Thomson, James, *The Poetical Works of James Thomson*, ed. William Michael Rossetti (London: Moxon, n.d.).

Thurber, James, *Men, Women, and Dogs*, in *The Thurber Carnival* (New York: Delta, 1945, 1964).

Tietze, Andreas, *The Koman Riddles and Turkic Folklore* (Berkeley: University of California Press, 1966).

Tizzard, Samuel, *The New Athenian Oracle, or Ladies' Companion . . . designed for the improvement of the fair sex* (London: A. Loudon, 1806).

Todorov, Tzvetan, "Analyse du discours: l'exemple des devinettes," *Journal de psychologie normale et pathologique* 60 (1973), 135–55.

    Genres in Discourse (Cambridge: Cambridge University Press, 1990), trans. Catherine Porter from *Genres du discours* (1978).

    "On Linguistic Symbolism," *New Literary History* 6 (1974), 111–32, trans. Richard Klein.

    "Recherches sur le symbolisme linguistique," *Poétique* 17 (1974), 215–45.

    "The Typology of Detective Fiction," in his *The Poetics of Prose* (Ithaca: Cornell University Press, 1977), trans. Richard Howard from *La Poétique de la prose* (1971).

Tolkien, J. R. R., *The Hobbit* (London: Unwin, 1937).

Tomasek, Tomas, *Das deutsche Rätsel im Mittelalter* (Tübingen: Max Niemeyer, 1994).

Torcszyner, Harry, "The Riddle in the Bible," *Hebrew Union College Annual* [Cincinnati] 1 (1924), 125–49.

Trypho(n), "Peri Ainigmatos" from *On Tropes*, in *Rhetores Graeci*, vol. III, pp. 193–5. M. L. West, "Tryphon *De tropis*," *Classical Quarterly* 16 (1965), 230–48.

Tupper, Frederick, *The Riddles of the Exeter Book* (Boston: Ginn, 1910).

Tuve, Rosamond, *Elizabethan and Metaphysical Imagery: Renaissance Poetic and Twentieth-Century Critics* (Chicago: University of Chicago Press, 1947).

Twain, Mark, *Life on the Mississippi* (1883; New York: Oxford University Press, 1996).

Valéry, Paul, "Lettre sur Mallarmé," in his *Œuvres*, 2 vols., ed. Jean Hytier (Paris: Gallimard, Pléiade, 1957–60), vol. I, pp. 633–43.

Vernant, J. P., "Ambiguity and Reversal: On the Enigmatic Structure of *Oedipus Rex*," *New Literary History* 10 (1978, trans. from 1970 essay), 475–501; see also Detienne.

Veyne, Paul, *Did the Greeks Believe in Their Myths: An Essay on the Constitutive Imagination* (Chicago: University of Chicago Press, 1988), trans. Paula Wissing from *Les Grecs ont-ils cru à leurs mythes?* (1983).

Vickers, Brian, ed., *English Renaissance Literary Criticism* (Oxford: Clarendon, 1999).

Virgil, *Eclogues, Georgics, Aeneid*, trans. and ed. H. Rushton Fairclough, 2 vols. (Cambridge, Mass.: Harvard University Press, Loeb, 1935).

The Eclogues of Virgil, trans. David Ferry (New York: Farrar, Straus, Giroux, 1998).

Vossius, Gerardus Joannes: for editions, see Rademaker, above.

Oratoriarum institutionum libri sex, 1606, also in later editions as *Commentariorum rhetoricorum, sive oratoriarum institutionum libri sex*, 1609, 1643 (4th edn. rev.; repr. Kronberg: Scriptor, 1974).

Etymologicon linguae Latinae (Amsterdam, 1662).

Opera (Amsterdam, 1697).

Walker, Jeffrey, *Rhetoric and Poetics in Antiquity* (New York: Oxford University Press, 2000).

Wallace, Anthony F. C., "Dreams and the Wishes of the Soul," in his *The Death and Rebirth of the Seneca* (New York: Knopf, 1970), pp. 59–75.

Weber, Eugen, *Apocalypses: Prophecies, Cults, and Millennial Beliefs through the Ages* (Cambridge, Mass.: Harvard University Press, 1999).

Welsh, Andrew, "Riddle," NPEPP, pp. 1070–2.

The Roots of Lyric: Primitive Poetry and Modern Poetics (Princeton: Princeton University Press, 1978).

Wheatley, H. B., *Of Anagrams: a monograph treating of their history* (Hertford: priv. pub., 1862).

Whitman, Jon, *Allegory: The Dynamics of an Ancient and Medieval Technique* (Oxford: Clarendon, 1987), esp. Appendix 1 on the history of the term "allegory," pp. 263–8.

Wilbur, Richard, "The Persistence of Riddles," *Yale Review* 78 (1989), 333–51.

Willard, Thomas, "The Enigma of Nicolas Barnaud: An Alchemical Riddle from Early Modern France," in *Esoterisme, gnoses et imaginaire symbolique: Mélanges offerts à Antoine Faivre*, ed. Richard Caron et al. (Leuven: Peeters, 2001).

Wind, Edgar, "Aenigma Termini," *Journal of the Warburg and Courtauld Institutes* 1 (1937–38), 66–9 (on the emblem of Erasmus).

Wood, Michael, "Consulting the Oracle," *Essays in Criticism* 43 (1993), 93–111.

Wordsworth, William, *The Poems*, 2 vols., ed. John O. Hayden (New Haven: Yale University Press, 1981).

Wright, Edmond, "Derrida, Searle, Contexts, Games, Riddles," *New Literary History* 14 (1982), 463–77.

Wünsche, August, *Die Räthselweisheit bei den Hebräern mit Hinblick auf Alte Völker* (Leipzig: Otto Schulze, 1883).

Young, Edward, *Night Thoughts or The Complaint and the Consolation*, illus. William Blake (1797; repr. New York: Dover, 1977).

Zeeman, Nicolette, "The Schools Give a License to Poets," in *Criticism and Dissent in the Middle Ages*, ed. Rita Copeland (Cambridge: Cambridge University Press, 1996), pp. 151–80.

Ziegler, K., "Gryps," *Paulys Real-Encyclopädie der classischen Altertumswissenschaft* (Stuttgart, 1912), cols. 1902–29.

Index